STUDIES FROM THE SCRIPTURES

DOCTRINES OF THE BIBLE

OUTLINES IN

SYSTEMATIC THEOLOGY

JOHN STEVENSON

Redeemer Publishing

Scripture quotations taken from the New American Standard Bible®,
Copyright © 1960, 1962, 1963, 1968, 1971, 1972, 1973,
1975, 1977 by The Lockman Foundation
Used by permission (www.Lockman.org)

To My Daughter
Sky Heather McNeill
For all the times we talked Theology,
Memorized Catechisms,
and together enjoyed the exploration of the Eternal.

Acknowledgments

The first edition of this work was penned in 1994 when my friend, mentor, and senior pastor, Dr. Paul Fowler came to me and suggested that we co-teach a Sunday evening class on the subject of Systematic Theology. I've always tended more toward Biblical and Exegetical Theology, but I agreed to the exercise. Within a month, Dr. Fowler announced that he had accepted a call to what was at that eventually going to be New Geneva Seminary in Colorado Springs and I was left on my own to teach the class. It turned out to be an excellent exercise, both for those who were in the class as well for the teacher.

I am indebted to Dr. Fowler for his contagious encouragement and enthusiasm as well as to Dr. Robert Reymond under whom I studied in the days prior to the publication of his own Systematic Theology. This work is not meant to measure up against such standards. Rather it is aimed at bringing the ideas of theology down to the street where we live.

I also wish to thank Maria Gersing who spent many hours proof reading and correcting this text. Her insights and labors were invaluable.

Finally, I wish to thank my beloved wife. Throughout my life she has been my greatest encouragement, my constant companion, my partner in ministry, my lover and my friend. She is my gift from God.

Other books by John Stevenson:

Facing the Flames: *A Fire Fighter's Meditations on the Spiritual Life*
First Corinthians: *Striving for Unity*
Galatians: *Our Freedom in Christ*
Hebrews: *The Supremacy of the Savior*
Joshua, Judges, and Ruth: *Victory, Defeat, and Hope in an Age of Heroes*
Luke: *In the Footsteps of the Savior*
Mark: *The Servant Who Came to Save*
Preaching from the Minor Prophets
Romans: *The Radical Righteousness of God*
A Survey of the Old Testament: *The Bible Jesus Used*

Table of Contents

CHURCH & LAST THINGS

Does God Fit into a Box?

The Question of Theology

Charles Schultz had some tremendous religious insights. One of his "Peanuts" cartoons pictures Lucy and Linus looking out the window at a steady downpour of rain. "Boy," says Lucy, "look at all that rain. What if it flood the whole world?"

"It will never do that," replies Linus. "In Genesis 9, God promised Noah that it would never happen again, and the sign of that promise is the rainbow."

"You've taken a great load off my mind," says Lucy with a relieved smile. Linus replies, "Sound theology has a way of doing that."

Everyone has a theology — some concept of what God and man and the universe is all about. That theology may not be systematized or even clearly stated. But it is still there. The question is not whether you hold to a theology, but rather whether that theology is sound and Biblical.

WHAT IS THEOLOGY?

The term "theology" is a compound made up from the joining of two words from the Greek language:

- Θεος (*Theos*): This is the Greek word for "God."
- Λογος (*Logos*): "Word" or "study."

1

Theology then is the study of God and those things that God has revealed. We also ought to understand what theology is NOT.

- Theology is not about man's religious experiences which God or his opinion of what God ought to be like.

- Many people like to speak about God being "real to them." This often indicates a false sense of reality in which God is real to one person but non-existent to another.

Theology is the study of God's revelation of Himself to man. This definition presupposes that God has revealed Himself to man. Were it not for the fact that God had revealed Himself, we would know nothing at all about God.

> Truth is where God has been. Revelation is where God is. -- Tenney.

Can you discover the depths of God?
Can you discover the limits of the Almighty?
They are high as the heavens, what can you do?
Deeper than Sheol, what can you know? (Job 11:7-8).

There is a "knowledge gap" between God and man. Man cannot, by his own self effort, know anything about God. It is God Himself who must bridge the gap if we are to know of Him. The good news is that God has done this, revealing Himself to man.

Today's postmodern movement tends to shy away from the study of theology. It is claimed, "I don't need theology, just give me Jesus!" But the question then arises, "Which Jesus?" It is in the subject of theology that we learn of who Jesus really is.

Those who say they love the God of the universe without knowing facts about Him are in error. You can know facts about God without knowing Him and loving Him, but it is impossible to know Him and love Him without also knowing certain facts about Him. It is like saying that you know and love your wife when you know absolutely nothing about her.

At the same time, it might be argued that it is possible to know all about God without actually knowing Him. This is true and it is one of the dangers of the study of theology. We must answer that knowing God involves more than the mere knowledge of certain basic facts about God, but also that it is not less than at least a fundamental awareness of who God is.

PROBLEMS IN THEOLOGY

Has Any End or Finishing Point (A Limit or E [handwritten]

1.   The Finite Versus the Infinite.

Endless [handwritten]
immeasurable [handwritten]
Inconceivable [handwritten]

God is infinite.   Man is finite.   We cannot grasp the concept of the infinite. We do not even have a separate word for

> It should not greatly surprise us when the infinite God of the universe does not fit in the space between two eardrums.

"infinite." Our word "infinite" is merely a negation of the positive term "finite." When we say that something is infinite, we are merely saying that it is not finite.

A finite mind cannot possibly comprehend an infinite being. This will of necessity limit our understanding of God. We are like fleas on the back of a dog trying to understand the psychological makeup of his owner. It is simply beyond our natural understanding.

2.   Holy Versus Sinful.

God is holy and righteous. His holiness and righteousness are infinite. There is no such thing as being "almost infinite." Anything less than infinite holiness and righteousness is separated from God by an infinite degree.

Man is sinful. This is not just a matter of what he does, but reflects what he is. By nature, man does not want the things of the Spirit of God.

> *But a natural man does not accept the things*
> *of the Spirit of God; for they are foolishness to him,*
> *and he cannot understand them, because they are*
> *spiritually appraised. (1 Corinthians 2:14).*

What is meant in this passage when we read of a "natural man"? The phrase in the Greek text is ψυχικος ανθρωπος (*psuchikos anthropos*)— literally, the "soulish man." He is the unbeliever. It takes the miracle of the new birth to turn a man's heart to God. This does not mean that Christians are smarter than pagans. Quite often the opposite is true. What it does mean is that God has worked faith in the heart of the one who belongs to Him so that we can hear the things of the Spirit of God and respond in belief.

3.   Reality Versus Description.

3

We must understand that there is a difference between God as He exists versus the theological descriptions that we give to God. This does not mean that those theological descriptions are inaccurate, but merely that they fall short of embracing the God who is there. C.S. Lewis describes it this way:

> *...if a man has once looked at the Atlantic from the beach, and then goes and looks at a map of the Atlantic, he also will be turning from something real to something less real: turning from real waves to a bit of coloured paper. But here comes the point. The map is admittedly only coloured paper, but there are two things you have to remember about it. In the first place, it is based on what hundreds and thousands of people have found out by sailing the real Atlantic. In that way it has behind it masses of experience just as real as the one you could have from the beach; only, while yours would be a single glimpse, the map fits all those different experiences together. In the second place, if you want to go anywhere, the map is absolutely necessary. As long as you are content with walks on the beach, your own glimpses are far more fun than looking at a map. But the map is going to be more use than walks on the beach if you want to get to America (1996:135-6).*

In a similar way, theology is our map. It tells us what God is like. That does not mean that we ought to be content with the map. The map is not an end unto itself. It is only a means to help us to understand and to appreciate the world it portrays. There is the admitted possibility that we might become so attached to the map that we fail to appreciate the world that is depicted by the map. But this would be the fault of the map and neither should it stop our utilization of maps.

Steve Brown, professor of homiletics at Reformed Theological Seminary, likens our theology to refrigerator art. When my grandchildren painted a work of art, it often ended up on our refrigerator. The quality of the artwork was not particularly adept, but we put it up there because we love them.

Our studies in theology attempt to tell us what God is like and how He works in the world. That is a good thing and we are diligent to construct an accurate system of doctrine. But we also recognize that our best efforts will be less than the sum total of what God is. At best, our efforts will be His refrigerator art. There will come a day when we will grow past that artwork to see the Lord face to face.

TYPES OF THEOLOGY

1. Natural Theology: This is the study that examines those facts concerning God and His universe that are revealed in nature. This is considered theology by our earlier definition because we are examining how God has revealed Himself in nature.

2. Exegetical Theology: This is a study of each of the individual books of the Bible, taking into account the context of each of those books, the meanings of the original Greek and Hebrew texts, and the interplay of historical, cultural and archaeological backgrounds as we seek to understand those texts. For example, we might do a study of the book of Genesis, noting the internal outline of the book and seeing how the author uses particular narratives, teachings and arguments in order to make his point.

3. Biblical Theology: This is the study that trace's God's truth about Himself and His relationship with men as that truth is developed historically in the individual books of the Bible. It was this kind of theology that Stephen presented when he preached his sermon before the Jewish Sanhedrin.
    Thus we might do a study of the book of Genesis and ask how God is revealed in that particular book, understanding that the writer and the original readers did not have the rest of the Scriptures because they had not yet been written. We would read Genesis and we would ask what was the concept of God those original readers would derive from this book.

4. Systematic Theology: This is the study that follows an analytically devised scheme to organize into a single system all of the truth that we have about God and His universe. The Apostle Paul uses this kind of systematic approach in his study of the righteousness of God in the book of Romans.

5

5.   Practical Theology: Taking all of the previous aspects of theology and putting them into practice so that my life is different than it previously was. This is the goal of all study of theology. It is so that my life will be changed so that I love God more and serve Him better.

Natural Theology	Exegetical Theology	Biblical Theology	Systematic Theology	Practical Theology
Draws its truths from a study of the universe.	Draws its study from a verse by verse study of the Bible	Draws its study from Exegetical Theology	Draws its study from Biblical Theology.	Draws its study from Systematic Theology.
Sees God revealed in nature	Sees God as He is revealed in the individual books of the Bible	Sees the revelation of God developed historically over the duration of the writing of the Bible.	Takes the revelation of God and organizes those truths into a doctrinal system.	Takes the truths from the doctrinal system and puts them into practice in our lives.

It should be understood that when we approach the organizing of a systematic theology, we are not trying to "put God in a box." This is reflected in a poem by Tennyson:

> *Our little systems have their day,*
> *They have their day and cease to be.*
> *They are but broken lights of Thee,*
> *And Thou, O Lord, are more than they.*

We must recognize that God and the Scriptures rule over our theology and not the other way around. This means that if our theology conflicts with the Bible, we need to change our theology. As such, we are to follow the example of the Bereans.

> *10 And the brethren immediately sent Paul and Silas away by night to Berea; and when they arrived, they went into the synagogue of the Jews. 11 Now these were more noble-minded than those in Thessalonica, for they received the word with great eagerness, examining the Scriptures*

*daily, to see whether these things were so. 12 Many of them
therefore believed, along with a number of prominent Greek
women and men. (Acts 17:10-12).*

Here were a group of noble-minded followers of the Lord. They
heard the message being preached by Paul and Silas and it was different from
that with which they were familiar. Their reaction was to become diligent
students of the Scriptures, examining them daily to see whether that new
message was true. It is the Scriptures that drive our understanding of
theology and not the other way around.

DANGERS IN STUDYING THEOLOGY

Though the study of theology is a good and a profitable undertaking,
there are some inherent dangers that must be faced in this endeavor.

1.   The Danger of Division: Theology divides. This should not surprise
        us. Jesus said it would divide. He said that He came to cause
        division. There are times when our theology will necessarily divide
        us from others. At the same time, there are areas of theology that
        should not necessarily become divisive to the point of bringing
        contention to the church.

                In major things we have unity.
                In minor things we have liberty.
                In all things we have love.

2.   The Danger of Pride: Paul warns in 1 Corinthians 8:1 that knowledge
        makes arrogant. It is one of the inherent dangers of knowledge. It is
        not long before we begin to become proud of the knowledge we have
        and we begin to look down on others.

3.   The Danger of Dependence on Knowledge: This is the danger where
        we are tempted to substitute relationship for theology. It is true that
        knowledge of God is necessary for relationship with God to take
        place, but knowledge alone does not equate to that relationship.

                You can learn about God's sovereignty and know all of the
        facts of His omnipotence and power, yet it is not until you are under
        the fire of suffering that you turn to that attribute and apply it to your

particular situation that you really come to depend upon the Lord.

4.   The Danger of Accepting Man's False Teachings.

> *But false prophets also arose among the people, just as there will also be false teachers among you, who will secretly introduce destructive heresies, even denying the Master who bought them, bringing swift destruction upon themselves. 2 And many will follow their sensuality, and because of them the way of the truth will be maligned; 3 and in their greed they will exploit you with false words; their judgment from long ago is not idle, and their destruction is not asleep. (2 Peter 2:1-3).*

There are false words and false teachings presented in the world today. These are brought by false teachers and some of those false teachers are to be found within the church. This means we must not blindly follow every teaching we hear. As we noted earlier, we are called to be Bereans in our searching out the Scriptures. We are to test and try the spirits to see if they really are from God (1 John 4:1).

Has God Spoken?

The Doctrine of Revelation

> *Yet we do speak wisdom among those who are mature; a wisdom, however, not of this age, nor of the rulers of this age, who are passing away; 7 but we speak God's wisdom in a mystery, the hidden wisdom, which God predestined before the ages to our glory; 8 the wisdom which none of the rulers of this age has understood; for if they had understood it, they would not have crucified the Lord of glory; 9 but just as it is written, "Things which eye has not seen and ear has not heard, And which have not entered the heart of man, All that God has prepared for those who love Him." (1 Corinthians 2:6-9).*

Men typically gain information in one of three ways: Empiricism is the means that appeals to man's senses, rationalism is the means that appeals to his logic, and faith involves the trusting in the information provided by another.

Paul tells us that there are certain things that have never been seen or heard by mortal man. Such things have not entered any realm of human observation. He goes on to say that these things have not entered the heart of man; that is, they cannot be deduced through a process of empiricism, rationalization or introspection.

What are these things that cannot be discovered through observation or rationalization or meditation? They are things in the spiritual realm. They are spiritual truths. They are the blessings that God has promised to those who are His people.

If these things cannot be perceived by the five senses and they cannot be discovered through a process of reasoning or through meditation and reflection, then how can we know about them? Paul answers this question in the next verse.

> *For to us God revealed them through the Spirit; for the Spirit searches all things, even the depths of God. (1 Corinthians 2:10).*

God has revealed to men certain things that could not otherwise be known. This process is known as revelation. Man could never know anything about God except for the act that God revealed Himself to man. This is not only because of sin, although that also has its blinding ramifications. Man cannot know God apart from revelation because there is by nature an infinite gulf between God and His creation.

God	← Infinite Gulf →	Creation

Revelation is a part of God's plan for man. Mankind was originally created to have fellowship with God. This set man apart from the rest of creation. As we read the Genesis 1 account of all of the creative works of God, we see that man was the only member of all of the created beings who mentioned in that chapter who could communicate with God. This sets mankind apart from the rest of creation. He alone could communicate with God. He could enjoy fellowship with God.

Fellowship	No Fellowship
God ↔ Man	**Rest of creation**

Man is unique in all of God's creation in that only he has a God-consciousness. You have never seen a rooster pray. A tiger does not ask a blessing for the food he is about to eat. Even the so-called praying mantis makes no intercession toward God. Only man is designed to receive and understand the revelation of God.

Man's fall into sin broke the lines of communication between God and man. Man could do nothing to repair the situation. This is important to understand. Man on his own is completely powerless to learn anything about God, both because of his finiteness as well as because of his sinfulness.

Fellowship	SIN	No Fellowship
God		Man & Rest of creation

This means it is God who must take the initiative in restoring fellowship with man. Therefore revelation is of necessity an act of God.

CHARACTERISTICS OF REVELATION

1.   Revelation is Rooted in History.

The progress of revelation is not merely God's mind relating to our mind in certain abstract thoughts. It is also God's acting in history. Christianity is much more than a philosophy or a way of living or even a set of ideas about God. It has its foundations upon the actions that God has taken both in creation and redemption.

This is not to say that God is rooted in history. God is supra-historical. He is not limited to history, but supersedes it. He transcends history. But He has also condescended to enter time and space and history and communicate to man.

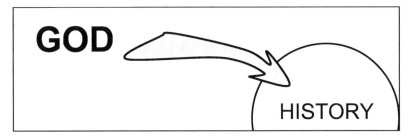

2.   Revelation has Occurred Progressively in History.

The way that God revealed Himself in the Garden of Eden to Adam and the woman does not seem to have been as detailed a revelation as that which is presented in the New Testament epistles. When Adam and Eve were given the first promise of salvation, how much revelation did they have? Only a single verse. Genesis 3:15 is very limited in scope as it speaks of how the seed of the woman would someday crush the serpent. It is only the small seed of what would be a host of future promises. God has gradually revealed greater and greater measures of His truth over a long period of time as He spoke *"at many places and in many ways"* (Hebrews 1:1).

Each aspect of revelation was based upon those which had been given prior. Thus, when Jesus stood in the Temple in Jerusalem and said, "Before Abraham was, I AM," it was presupposed that those who were listening knew that God had once told Moses, "I AM THAT I AM."

The revelation that Jesus was God in the flesh was based upon a prior revelation of who God is. This does not mean that revelation has evolved. Evolution describes the act of changing from one thing into another. Revelation does not change into that which is different from that which began. Instead the progression of revelation is a further and continuing unveiling of what unchanging truth that was previously hidden.

Evolution	Revelation
One thing changes into another	A further and more comprehensive unveiling of unchanging truth that was previously hidden.

Revelation has been likened to the raising of a theatrical curtain. There was a time when the curtain was lowered and the truth that it covered was hidden. Then the curtain was raised several inches and a small portion of the previously hidden stage was revealed. Most of the stage was still hidden, but men could see more than had been previously visible. With each new revelation, the curtain is raised a bit more.

3.   Revelation is Partial.

> *The secret things belong to the Lord our God, but the things revealed belong to us and our sons forever, that we may observe all the words of this law. (Deuteronomy 29:29).*

> *For now we see in a mirror dimly, but then face to face; now I know in part, but then I shall know fully just as I also have been fully known. (1 Corinthians 13:12).*

God has not chosen to reveal all truth to us. There are many puzzles which are not explained; many questions that are not answered. These are the secret things. They belong to the Lord. There is coming a day of complete revelation. There is coming a day when we shall know fully.

The important point is that those things which have been revealed to us belong to us. They have been given to us. And they ought to be a prized possession.

4.   Revelation is Related to God's Acts of Creation and Redemption.

Revelation does not take place in a vacuum. It is not a picture of God sitting up in heaven and sending a letter to man saying, "Hey down there! Let me explain to you the nature of the universe."

God's revelation of Himself always takes place in the context of His works of creation and redemption. He is not a disinterested bystander. He continues to hold the universe together by the word of His power.

Creator	Redeemer
God created the universe. It shows His power and His orderliness and His majesty.	God is calling out a people for Himself. This process started in the Garden of Eden with a promise of a Seed.

These two contexts also serve to point out the two types of Revelation: General versus Special Revelation.

Creator	Redeemer
General Revelation	Special Revelation
That revelation of God that is seen through the intermediate agency of that which God has created.	That revelation of God that has been given through the direct action of God or of His messengers.
Revelation through nature and through what we think of as "natural processes."	Revelation that is specific and through supernatural events and activities.

GENERAL REVELATION

1.　　Definition: When we speak of General Revelation, we speak of the way that God has revealed Himself in a general sense to men through His acts of creation and providence. It is still revelation. It is an active act of God in revealing Himself to men. But it is also general and is available for all men to see and to understand.

2.　　Scriptural Support.

> *The heavens are telling of the glory of God;*
> *And their expanse is declaring the work of His hands.*
> *Day to day pours forth speech,*
> *And night to night reveals knowledge.*
> *There is no speech, nor are there words;*
> *Their voice is not heard. (Psalm 19:1-3).*

When you go and look at the solar system and the planets and the galaxies, there is a message there for us to be seen and read. Those heavens give us a message and a declaration. They tell us something and it is something we can know if we are listening.

In Defoe's novel *Robinson Crusoe*, one footprint on the sand showed to the marooned hero that another person was on his island. In the same way, the heavens and the earth are filled with the countless footprints of the Lord.

> *...that which is known about God is evident within them; for God made it evident to them.*
> *For since the creation of the world His invisible attributes, His eternal power and divine nature, have been clearly seen, being understood through what has been made, so that they are without excuse. (Romans 1:19-20).*

Here is what we must understand about revelation. It is not merely the existence of random elements of evidence. It is deliberate. It is revelation. The signs of God's presence in the realm of nature are only visible to us because God has revealed them to us.

This is also described as "natural" revelation. This does not mean that it merely comes naturally. Rather, it means that it is revelation that takes place within the realm of nature.

14

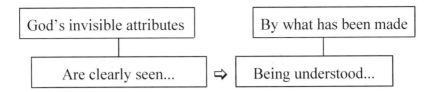

This passage states that there are two specific aspects of God's existence which are revealed in creation.

- His eternal power.
- His divine nature.

This sets forth the limitation of this general revelation. No one ever looked at a sunset and deduced the doctrine of the Trinity. You cannot look through a microscope and see the principles of justification and sanctification. General revelation is limited in what it reveals about God.

God has revealed His power and divinity through His creation. The immensity of creation shows that He is very big. The fact of creation shows God's divine nature. This revelation has broken the infinity barrier. This revelation has left men without excuse.

3.   False Views of General Revelation.

It is all we can know	Those who deny that the Bible is the word of God are left only with general revelation. But the truth is that if God has not spoken in the Bible, then God has not spoken.
It is sufficient for the unregenerate	Some have taught that the spiritual insight in the mind of a natural man can reason logically and conclude truths about God. But the truth is that there is no "spiritual insight" in the mind of the unsaved that has not been darkened by sin and blinded by Satan.
It is a natural byproduct of creation	General revelation is revelation. That is, it involves a deliberate revealing of God as the Creator of heaven and earth.

SPECIAL REVELATION

Special revelation refers to God's work of actively revealing Himself to men through various special means.

> *God, after He spoke long ago to the fathers in the prophets in many portions and in many ways,* 2 *in these last days has spoken to us in His Son (Hebrews 1:1-2a).*

In these two short verses, the writer to the Hebrews provides a summary of Special Revelation. It is the message that God spoke...

1.   In many different portions: God's revelation of Himself did not come all at once. There was a progression to its unveiling.

- He revealed Himself to Adam and Eve.
- He revealed Himself to Noah.
- He revealed Himself to Abraham.
- He revealed Himself to Moses.
- He revealed Himself to Joshua.
- He revealed Himself to Samuel.

Each of these revelations brought a little more understanding of God to man. The writer of Genesis had a certain limited amount of information. The writer of Joshua had a little more. The writer of Samuel had even more. Each writer added to the pool of knowledge about God. In each case, the Old Testament prophets came away with another glimpse into the character and person and plans of God. But the final and complete communication of God was not accomplished through any of these means.

2.   In many different ways: God's revelation of Himself over the ages took many different forms:

- He spoke to Job out of a whirlwind.
- He spoke to Joseph in dreams.
- He spoke to Moses from a burning bush.
- He spoke to Samuel in a voice in the night.
- He spoke to Elijah is a still, small voice.
- He spoke to Daniel in a vision.

Each of these various forms of revelation were different from one another. There was not one single method that stood out over all the others until the coming of Jesus.

3.   In His Son.

After God spoke through the prophets there was a great silence. For 400 years there had been no prophet to speak the word of the Lord. But now in these last days God has spoken again. This time He spoke through a new agency that had never before been used. He now has spoken to man through His Son.

This is the fullest revelation of God. It is the person of Jesus Christ. It is the person of the One who, being God, became man so that He might communicate God to us.

God has spoken...	
To the fathers...	To us...
In the prophets...	In His Son...
In many portions and in many ways	In these last days

The ultimate revelation of God took place when He clothed Himself in flesh and came to live among us (John 1:14). He said to Philip on the night of the Last Supper, *"He who has seen Me has seen the Father"* (John 14:9). None of the prophets could ever make that sort of claim. Their knowledge of God was always limited. In contrast, Jesus had an experiential knowledge of God because He is God.

Let me use an illustration. If you wanted to get to know me, you could talk to someone who knew me. They could tell you a lot about me. You might come away with a certain number of facts such as where I was born or where I went to school or where I have worked. But if you really wanted to get to know me, the best way would be to talk with me. Indeed, you would be hard-pressed to say that you really knew me if you had never had a face-to-face conversation with me. The same is true of God. The best way to learn of God is to meet Him in the flesh. You meet Him in the flesh when you meet Jesus.

4.	In the Bible.

The Bible is the written record of the revelation of God. But it is also more than that. It does not merely contain the word of God; it is the word of God.

There are some editions of the Bible that have rendered the words of Jesus in red. That is not a bad practice in that it can serve as an aid to help us differentiate between the narrative portions and the spoken words of Jesus. But we fall into error when we think that those sections in red are more a part of God's word than those that are rendered in some other color of print.

THE PLACE OF THE PROPHET IN REVELATION

God, after He spoke long ago to the father in the prophets in many portions and in many ways, in these last days has spoken to us in His Son... (Hebrews 1:1-2a).

The underlying premise of the Bible is that God has spoken. In Old Testament times, this was accomplished through His prophets. What is a prophet? The Prophets served as a mouthpiece for God. He spoke through them.

1.	Old Testament Designations for "Prophet."

Now the acts of King David, from first to last, as written in the chronicles of Samuel the SEER, in the chronicles of Nathan the PROPHET, and in the chronicles of Gad the SEER. (1 Chronicles 29:29).

a.	Prophet (Genesis 20:7 - first usage; Exodus 7:1). The term "prophet" carried the idea of one who prophesies or foretells the future, but it is not limited to that idea. More often than not, a prophet was also one who told what God is doing in the present. This is related to the next term that is used for this office.

b.	Seer (1 Samuel 9:9). A seer is one who "sees" things from a heavenly perspective. He might see the future or he might see what God is doing in the present.

    c.   Man of God (used of prophets and especially of Elisha).

2.   The Dependence of the Prophets upon the Spirit of God.

> *But know this first of all, that no prophecy of Scripture is a matter of one's own interpretation, for no prophecy was ever made by an act of human will, but men moved by the Holy Spirit spoke from God. (2 Peter 1:20-21).*

In verse 20 we have the negative aspect of revelation, what revelation is not. It is not a matter of man's own invention. In verse 21 we have the positive aspect of revelation. This is what revelation is. Revelation is that which is spoken by God. A superficial reading of this passage would seem to indicate that the author is referring to interpretation of the Scriptures. However, the issue in this context is not interpretation, but rather one of origin. Notice the statement of verse 21.

> *For no prophecy was ever made by an act of human will... (2 Peter 1:21).*

The contrast is obvious. The message of the prophets did not originate with the prophets. That message came from God.

3.   This Revelation was Multi-faceted.

> *God, after He spoke long ago to the father in the prophets in many portions and in many ways... (Hebrews 1:1).*

The Greek text of this passage places the phrase the emphasis in a different place. The verse begins, not with the subject or even with the verb, but with the preposition.

> *In many portions and in many ways, God spoke to the fathers in the prophets... (Hebrews 1:1).*

The Old Testament records many different ways in which God revealed Himself to men. Abraham saw Him as a "smoking oven and a flaming torch" (Genesis 15:17). He spoke to Joseph in dreams. He appeared to Moses in a burning bush. To Samuel he was a voice calling in the night. To Elijah he was a still, small voice.

4.   God's Revelation Coincides with His Redemptive Work.

> *Surely the Lord God does nothing unless He reveals His secret counsel to His servants the prophets. (Amos 3:7).*

God always speaks when He institutes redemptive activity. When He is not engaged in redemptive activity, there is generally no need for God to speak. This is why there was a 400-year period of silence between the Old Testament and the New Testament. It is not that God has gone on vacation, but rather that He was not engaged in any new redemptive work. In the same way, it is why there is no on-going revelation today.

5.   The Cessation of Old Testament Prophets.

The Old Testament does not make an announcement that its revelation is now at a close. However, it became generally recognized by the Jews that this was the case.

> *So there was a great affliction in Israel, the like whereof was not since the time that a prophet was not seen among them. (1 Maccabees 9:27).*

Josephus, in his work Contra Apion where he defends the trustworthiness of the Old Testament Scriptures, says that...

> *...our history has been written since Artaxerxes, very particularly, but has not been esteemed of the same authority with the former by our forefathers, because there has not been an exact succession of prophets since that time. (Contra Apion 1:8).*

6.   Jesus - the Ultimate Prophet.

Jesus fulfilled the promise of Moses that there would come one who would be a prophet of his caliber (Deuteronomy 18:15-19). He is the ultimate prophet. A prophet is one who speaks to people on behalf of God. He represents God to people and he reveals God to people.

Jesus is the ultimate revelation of God. It is for this reason that He is called "the Word" (John 1:1, 14). He is the living word of God. God has communicated Himself to us by becoming man.

THE RESULTS OF REVELATION

Now I want to ask you a question. It is the question that you should ask at the end of any Bible study. It should be asked of any teaching and after any sermon. What are the practical applications of this teaching of revelation? Or to put it in plain language: So what?

1.   We now have a higher perspective of the world in which we live. We can see it from a new point of view. The humanist seeks to do one of three things when he is confronted with the question of God.

   ♦ He denies the existence of God.
   ♦ He claims that God cannot be known.
   ♦ He tries to regulate God to a little storage cabinet among the other details of life.

   But the truth is that God has spoken. It is foolish to deny the existence of someone who is standing there talking to you. The fact that God has spoken means that you can know real truth about the world in which you live. It means you can look at this world and see it as God's handiwork.

2.   God can be known. He can be known because He has made Himself known. He has revealed Himself to us. We do not have to play guessing games to know what God is like or what He wants of us. God has spoken and told us what He wants us to know about Himself.

3.   God wants to be known. God not only can be known; He wants to be known. He is not playing a game of cosmic hide-and-seek. He is in the business of making Himself known to His people. This means

that, if we are doing the work of God, we will necessarily be making Him known to others.

4.   God has given us commands to be obeyed. Our lives dare not remain unchanged by the fact of revelation. It should make all the difference in the world. If God has revealed Himself to us, then we are called to live differently.

Who Wrote the Bible?

The Doctrine of Inspiration

At the root of the Reformation were five theological statements known as the "solas" (Latin for "alone"). These statements point to five foundational truths upon which the church stands.

Sola scripture	Scripture alone
Sola fidei	Through faith alone
Sola gratia	By grace alone
Solus Christus	By Christ alone
Soli deo gloria	To the glory of God alone

When they spoke of Sola Scriptura, they did not mean that it is wrong to read the evening paper or to do something that was not expressly commanded in Scripture. What they did mean is that the Scriptures are to be our final rule of doctrine.

By contrast, the Roman Catholic church has historically taught that the Bible carries an equal weight of authority to the church. The Roman church teaches that when the Pope speaks officially (ex cathedra— "from the seat"), his words are of an equal weight to the Bible and serve as the only possible interpretation of the Bible.

> *All Scripture is inspired by God and profitable for teaching, for reproof, for correction, for training in righteousness; that the man of God may be adequate, equipped for every good work. (2 Timothy 3:16-17).*

This is the foundational passage on the subject of the inspiration of the Bible. It says very pointedly that all Scripture is inspired by God. There are three points that need be observed.

> The doctrine of inspiration is basic to any discussion about theology. If the Bible has not been given to us by God, then we are unable to know theological truths about God.

1. The Fact of Inspiration: *All Scripture is INSPIRED by God... (2 Timothy 3:16a).*

I have heard people speak of how they were watching a beautiful golden sunset and inspired to paint a picture or to write a poem. But this is not what this verse is saying. The phrase "inspired by God" is translated from the single Greek word θεοπνευστος (*Theopneustos*). This is the only time that this word ever occurs in the New Testament. To the best of my knowledge, it is the first time this word is ever used in the Greek language. This means that

> Plutarch uses θεοπνευστος once in De Placit Philos 5:2 where it is in contrast to φυσικοι, but this is after the death of Paul.

Paul may have coined the word himself to describe the work of God in producing the Scriptures. Paul does something similar in 1 Thessalonians 4:9 when he says that *you yourselves are taught by God to love one another* — literally, you are "God-taught" (θεοδιδακτος). In both cases, Paul utilizes a compound word, made up of two commonly used Greek words which are joined together to form a new word.

* The first word is *Theos* (θεος). It is the word for God.

* The second word is *pneo* (πνεω). It is a verb meaning "to breathe" or "to blow." It is also the verbal form of the Greek word for "spirit" (πνευμα).

Therefore, we could say that "all Scripture Is God-breathed." The very breath and spirit of God has been infused into the writings of the Bible. This is why we refer to it as the Word of God.

Although the specific term that Paul coins was a new one, the concept was not. The Old Testament describes God as accomplishing the work of Creation "by the breath of His mouth" (Psalm 33:6). In the same way, the Bible is the result of the creative work of God.

2.   The Extent of Inspiration: *ALL Scripture is inspired by God...* (2 Timothy 3:16a).

All of Scripture is God-breathed. It is not just a small portion of the Bible, but every single sentence and every single word that is God-breathed. This is all-encompassing. Jesus stressed this principle when He spoke of the abiding quality of the Law in His Sermon on the Mount.

> *"For truly, I say to you, until heaven and earth pass away, not the smallest letter or stroke shall pass away from the Law, until all is accomplished."* *(Matthew 5:18).*

The Greek text is even more specific. It says, "Not one *IOTA* or one *KERAIA* shall pass from the law."

•   The *IOTA* was the smallest letter of the Greek alphabet.

•   The *KERAIA* was the little horn attached to the Hebrew letter *BETH* to distinguish it from the letter *KAPH*.

Don't miss this! Jesus says that each and every letter and dot of God's word would continue to stand. We could say that not one cross of the "T" and not one dot of the "I" will pass away. There is not one part of the Bible that is more inspired or more trustworthy than any other part. It is ALL completely God's word.

3.   The OBJECT of Inspiration: *All SCRIPTURE is inspired by God...* (2 Timothy 3:16a).

It is the Scriptures themselves that are inspired. Paul does not say that the writers of the Scriptures were inspired. He says that it is the finished content of their writings that are inspired.
If it had been merely the human authors who had received a revelation from God and then had written their own interpretation of that revelation, then we might wonder if they had not permitted error to creep in as they put this truth into their own words. However, this is not the case. It is not the writers, but the Scriptures themselves which are said to be God-breathed.
This means that God did not guarantee that everything that

Peter or Paul or any other of the human authors ever wrote were correct. No doubt, they wrote many other things that were not inspired by God and the inerrancy of those other writings is not guaranteed. Rather, it is the truthfulness of the books that make up our Bible that is guaranteed by inspiration.

At the same time, we must recognize the aspect of dual authorship. By this, I mean that there were really two authors of each book - the Holy Spirit and the human author.

There are instances where the human writers described things of which they were eye-witnesses and merely wrote of the thing that they had seen. At other times, these same writers described events that they could not possibly have known about without a supernatural revelation from God (such as those events which took place prior to the creation of man).

There were also times when they wrote and did not themselves understand the full implications of that which they wrote (Daniel writes certain things which are to be sealed up until a future time).

Therefore the principle of inspiration refers to result, not the method in which the Scriptures were written. In this way, the Bible was written both by men and yet at the same time it is the Word of God.

DEFINITION OF INSPIRATION

1.   What it is Not.

        We have all heard people speak of how they were watching a beautiful golden sunset and were inspired to paint a picture or to write a poem. This is not inspiration in the theological sense. Inspiration is not a feeling or a wonderment or an excitement or even a sense of creative energy.

2.   What it Is.

        It is the truth that God has moved certain men to write in such a way that the result of that writing, the Scriptures, are the very word of God.

3.   Contrast of Revelation versus Inspiration.

Inspiration is a narrower term than revelation. Inspiration relates to God's revelation of Himself as it is found in the pages of the Scriptures. Although all Scripture is inspired by God and all Scripture is therefore revelation from God, not all of revelation is Scripture. We have already noted how God has revealed Himself at many different times and in many different ways. The Scriptures are therefore only one of the many ways in which God has revealed Himself.

Revelation	Inspiration
God has revealed Himself	God in-breathed the Scriptures
Involves both general as well as special revelation	Confined to the Bible

FALSE THEORIES OF INSPIRATION

1.   The Mechanical Dictation Theory.

This is the theory that God told Moses to write the word, "In," and he wrote, "In." Then God said, "Write the word, 'the,'" and Moses wrote "the." Then God said, "now write, 'beginning.'"

The problem with this view is that it fails to explain how there are different styles and vocabularies used by the different human authors of the Bible. On the other hand, there were indeed times when the Lord dictated His message very explicitly to the prophets.

• *Moses wrote down all the words of the LORD* (Exodus 24:4).

• *Then the LORD said to Moses, "Write down these words, for in accordance with these words I have made a covenant with you and with Israel"* (Exodus 34:27).

• *The word which came to Jeremiah from the LORD, saying, 2 "Thus says the LORD, the God of Israel, 'Write all the words which I have spoken to you in a book.'"* (Jeremiah 30:1-2).

• *Then the LORD answered me and said, "Record the vision and inscribe it on tablets, that the one who reads it may run"*

27

(Habakkuk 2:2).

In Jeremiah 36 we have a vivid picture of God giving His message to Jeremiah and then Jeremiah dictating that same message to his servant and scribe Baruch.

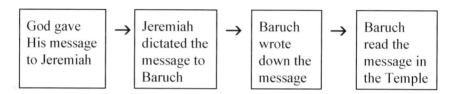

| God gave His message to Jeremiah | → | Jeremiah dictated the message to Baruch | → | Baruch wrote down the message | → | Baruch read the message in the Temple |

And it came about in the fourth year of Jehoiakim the son of Josiah, king of Judah, that this word came to Jeremiah from the LORD, saying, 2 "Take a scroll and write on it all the words which I have spoken to you concerning Israel, and concerning Judah, and concerning all the nations, from the day I first spoke to you, from the days of Josiah, even to this day. 3 "Perhaps the house of Judah will hear all the calamity which I plan to bring on them, in order that every man will turn from his evil way; then I will forgive their iniquity and their sin."

Then Jeremiah called Baruch the son of Neriah, and Baruch wrote at the dictation of Jeremiah all the words of the LORD, which He had spoken to him, on a scroll.

And Jeremiah commanded Baruch, saying, "I am restricted; I cannot go into the house of the LORD. 6 So you go and read from the scroll which you have written at my dictation the words of the LORD to the people in the LORD's house on a fast day. And also you shall read them to all the people of Judah who come from their cities. 7 Perhaps their supplication will come before the LORD, and everyone will turn from his evil way, for great is the anger and the wrath that the LORD has pronounced against this people."

And Baruch the son of Neriah did according to all that Jeremiah the prophet commanded him, reading from the book the words of the LORD in the LORD's house. (Jeremiah 36:1-8).

In this case, the message of God was given through the intermediaries of Jeremiah and Baruch, yet nothing is said to have been lost in translation.

2.   The Natural Inspiration Theory.

This view says that God had nothing to do with the Bible. It sees the authors as having been inspired in the same sense that Shakespear was inspired to write Hamlet. We have already noted that this is not a biblical picture of inspiration.

3.   The Dynamic Inspiration Theory.

This theory says that God encouraged the authors to give first-hand reports of their revelatory experiences with God. They wrote of these experiences in the best way they humanly were able.

This view likens inspiration to light passing through the stained glass of a cathedral window. The light is from heaven but it is stained and colored by the glass through which it passes. In the same way, the message of God is said to pass through the heart and mind of the original human author and come out discolored by his personality.

4.   The Limited Inerrancy Theory.

God is seen as having superintended the writing process of the Scriptures so that the redemptive truths of the Bible are without error. This view sees the Bible only authoritative on these sorts of redemptive truths and to be capable of error on issues like historical or scientific accuracy.

A BIBLICAL VIEW OF THE MECHANICS OF INSPIRATION

But know this first of all, that no prophecy of Scripture is a matter of one's own interpretation, for no prophecy was ever made by an act of human will, but men moved by the Holy Spirit spoke from God. (2 Peter 1:20-21).

Remember that Peter is writing these words in the midst of an epistle which attacks false doctrine and false prophets. There were those who were claiming to have their own revelation of God - this was the origin of Gnosticism.

Peter says that the Scripture is more authoritative because it came from a higher source and a higher will. The Scriptures are not merely a collection of private opinions. It is not even a collection of well-informed opinions. The Scriptures had their origin in God.

The writers of Scripture were able to speak from God because the were *"moved by the Holy Spirit."* The verb used here to describe this movement is φερομενοι, a present passive participle. This is the same root word used as is found in Acts 27:15 where *"the ship was caught in it, and could not face the wind, we gave way to it, and let ourselves BE DRIVEN ALONG"* (ἐφερουμεθα). Just as the driving force behind the ship was the wind, so the driving force behind the writers of Scripture was the Holy Spirit.

This is important to understand. The human writers of the Scriptures did not consider those Scriptures to be a work which was the combined viewpoints of God and man. This was God's word because it was God who had carried out the work. God was able to use...

- All of the past experiences of the human writers.
- Their vocabulary and grammar.
- Their thought process and style of writing.

...and still have the result to be the exact message which He sought to impart. How is this possible? To us it would not be. Such a work would only be possible to the Sovereign Lord of the Universe.

VERBAL PLENARY INSPIRATION

1.   Verbal Inspiration.

       This means that God in His sovereignty chose the precise words and phrases that would go into the Scriptures, at the same time using the vocabulary and grammar of the human authors.

2.   Plenary Inspiration.

       This refers to every single portion of the Bible being fully and completely inspired by God. We have already pointed to the words of Jesus in establishing this principle: *For truly I say to you, until heaven and earth pass away, not the smallest letter or stroke shall pass away from the Law, until all is accomplished (Matthew 5:18).*

Now, we must point out that it is not the many various translations of the Bible that have been inspired, but the original manuscripts as they were penned by the human authors which are "God-breathed."

The Bible has been copied and recopied. It has been translated into many languages. But none of these translations are inspired. It is only the original autographs which are inspired. Does this mean we cannot trust our various translations? No. We say instead that those various translations are dependable as they have accurately transmitted the message of those original autographs.

INFALLIBILITY AND INERRANCY

These two terms are very close to one another, but there is a slight shade of meaning between the two.

Infallible:	Incapable of error
Inerrancy:	Does not contain error

The Bible is both infallible as well as inerrant. Because of its divine origins, it contains no error and is incapable of error. However, a doctrine of inerrancy and infallibility does not demand...

1.   A strict utilization of the rules of grammar. Grammatical rules are, by their very nature, generalizations that have developed over time. The writers of the Bible sometimes used a high grammar, but more often than not, they spoke in common, everyday colloquialisms using figures of speech that were common to that day.

2.   A rigidly literalist interpretation. The Biblical writers often rounded off numbers in the same way we might speak of six million Jews dying in the German concentration camps and are not faulted because the precise number might be a few more or a few less.

3.   The technical language of modern science. Thus we can read in

Genesis 1 of the sun rising or the sun setting and we do not expect to see any mention of the rotation of the earth or its revolution around the sun. We regularly speak in a non-technical manner and the Bible speaks in the same manner.

4.   Verbal preciseness in quotations. We often have in a quote or in the relating of a narrative the general idea restated or summarized rather than the exact words that were used.

5.   A comprehensive accounting of all truth, even on any given subject. The Bible is not a sytematic theology that attempts to consolidate and state all relevant information. It is better described as a series of love letters from God to His people through the intermediary of His apostles and prophets. Inerrancy does not guarantee the exhaustive comprehensiveness of any single account or of combined accounts where those are involved.

6.   The infallibility or inerrancy of the non-inspired sources used by biblical writers. Thus Paul is able to quote the pagan Greek philosopher Epimenides where he has spoken rightly, yet does not thereby give credence to the rest of his writings.

What constitutes inerrancy? It is the teaching that the original autographs of the Scriptures were the inspired and authoritative word of God and that they were without error as to their message.

OBJECTIONS TO THE DOCTRINE OF VERBAL PLENARY INSPIRATION

The teaching of the verbal plenary inspiration of the Scriptures has come under heavy attack in recent years. There are many who would deny that each and every word of the Bible is the Word of God and without error. There have been several lines of evidence to support such a view.

1.   The Inadequacy of Language.

This objection states that human language is inadequate to the task of expressing truth about transcendent realities. Eastern religions often stress the teaching that God is inexpressible. Some actually go so far as to maintain that language is unable to express literal truth about anything. Such a view is really an attempt to limit the power of God, for it states that God is unable to draw a straight line with a crooked stick.

2.   Paul's Apparent Disclaimer of Inspiration.

In his first epistle to the Corinthians, Paul makes some statements which, at first glance, seem to deny total inspiration.

> *But to the married I give instructions, not I, but the Lord, that the wife should not leave her husband. (1 Corinthians 7:10).*

It has been suggested that Paul is showing how he is giving the commands of God rather than his own personal commands, but that in verse 12 he leaves God's instructions and moves forward with instructions that are comprised only his own personal opinion. Notice the following phrases:

> *But to the rest I say, not the Lord... (1 Corinthians 7:12).*

> *Now concerning virgins I have no command of the Lord, but I give an opinion as one who by the mercy of the Lord is trustworthy. (1 Corinthians 7:25).*

These verses might be difficult until we realize that Paul is merely contrasting the commands which have already been given by the Lord Jesus while He was on earth with the new commands that Paul is now giving. Thus, he is not denying inspiration, but rather is simply quoting the words of Christ to prove his point. In verse 25 Paul gives his opinion, but this does not mean that it is not an inspired opinion — one which "by the mercy of the Lord is trustworthy."

3.   The Problem of Imprecise Quotations.

Anyone who has read through the Bible has quickly seen that it often quotes itself. The New Testament contains hundreds of quotations from the Old Testament. A close examination of the quotations will reveal that they are not always exact. There are often variants as a word or a whole phrase is changed.

Sometimes the Septuagint (the Greek translation of the Hebrew Old Testament) is quoted, even when that translation makes a notable departure from the Hebrew text. At other times, the author gives a rather free translation. Does this mean that each and every word of the original passage is not inspired? Not at all. These quotations are often deliberately general to bring out and better illustrate the truth that is being taught.

We can view them as a divinely inspired commentary on the text which is being quoted. Indeed, much of the Old Testament Scriptures are explained and amplified in the New Testament.

4.   The Problem of Conflicting Reports.

There are a number of instances when two different writers in the Bible describe the same event. In such cases, there are sometimes major differences in the details between the two accounts. Here are just a few examples:

- The genealogy of Jesus (Matthew 1:1-17 versus Luke 3:23-38).
- The calling of the disciples (Matthew 4:18-22 with Luke 5:1-11 and John 1:40-42).
- The setting of the Sermon on the Mount (Matthew 5:1 and Luke 6:17).
- The cursing of the fig tree and the time of its actual withering (Matthew 21:18-20 versus Mark 11:12-13 and 11:20-21).
- The inscription that was placed over the cross of Jesus (Matthew 27:37; Mark 15:26; Luke 23:38 and John 19:19).
- The account of the events following Paul's conversion (Acts 9:1-31 and Galatians 1:13-17).

The following general answers can be suggested to these problems:

a.   Not all of these passages are necessarily speaking of the same event. For example, it seems that Jesus called His disciples on at least two separate occasions.

b.   Sometimes a chronological order of events is set aside and replaced with a topical order. For example, a writer of one of the gospel accounts might begin to detail the things that Jesus said during His ministry concerning a specific topic. Another writer might list those events in the order in which they took place.

    c.   Certain words and phrases are used interchangeably due to the fact that the quotations might have been made from different languages. This is seen in the case of the teaching of Jesus who probably preached in Hebrew or Aramaic while His sayings are recorded in Greek.

God has spoken. He has spoken in a way in which we can understand. He has preserved His message to us in the Scriptures. His message is true. It is complete and without error. We can believe it.

Are the Right Books in the Bible?

The Doctrine of Canonicity

> *"Heaven and earth will pass away, but My words will not pass away." (Luke 21:33).*

The Greek architects had an instrument that they used to measure various distances as they were designing and constructing a building. It was a straight rod with marks set into its side, much like our modern rulers.

- It had to be unbendable.
- It had to be dependable as to its straightness.

It was called a κανων (*kanon*). The word simply means "a ruler." From this came the idea of a body of truth or a rule of faith. The term itself is used by Paul in his epistle to the churches of Galatia.

> *And those who will walk by this RULE, peace and mercy be upon them, and upon the Israel of God." (Galatians 6:16).*

This same word came to be used by Christians to describe those books which set the rule and standard of faith. When we talk about canonizing someone, we speak of recognizing their authority. The Roman Church uses this term to confer sainthood. When the church speaks of "canon law" it refers to the infallible criteria by how things are to be measured.

THE CANON OF SCRIPTURES

When we speak of the Canon of Scripture, we are speaking of that collection of writings which constitute the authoritative and final norm or standard of faith and practice. This means that we think of the Word of God as the measuring stick for our beliefs and for our lives. We use it to check our doctrine and our daily lifestyle.

Thy word is a lamp to my feet,
And a light to my path. (Psalm 119:105).

How do we decide how we ought to live? It is by the instructions of the Word of God. Like a lamp to a darkened path, it shows the way in which we ought to walk if we are to avoid the pitfalls of life.

DEFINITION OF CANONICITY

Canonicity is the process by which the books of the Bible were gathered and collected so that they came to be regarded as the standard and norm for Christians. This means that canonicity refers to the church's recognition of the authority of the inspired writings. Don't miss this! Canonicity does not make a book into the word of God. Rather, canonicity is the process of recognizing that a book is the word of God.

The 66 books which make up our Bible are only a very small part of the many ancient documents that were written in ancient times and which have come down to us today. There are many other ancient books and possibly even books written by certain people whom we might find in the pages of the Bible.

How do we know that the books that we have are the Word of God? And how do we know that other books of antiquity are not also the Word of God? The answer is that only those books which were inspired by God — that is, which were God-breathed; only those books should be considered as canonical. This is the sole criteria for determining whether or not a book is to be considered a part of the Canon of Scriptures. However, that brings us to the next question: How do I know if a book is inspired by God?

- How are we to determine if we have the right books in the Bible?
- What about the Apocrypha?
- Are there certain books in our Bible which should not be there?

37

- Are we missing some books?
- Are there certain signs for which we can look that indicate that a book is inspired?

These are the questions that are posed in the issue of canonicity.

THE CANONICITY OF THE OLD TESTAMENT

The Old Testament was not written all at once or by a single author. In fact, there were at least 30 human authors involved in its writing and they worked over a period of more than a thousand years. After all of the books which make up our Old Testament had been written, a second collection of books began to emerge. It became known as the "Apocrypha," meaning "hidden from."

There is a considerable amount of historical testimony to show that the books which make up our Old Testament (and not the Apocrypha) are indeed to be regarded as Scripture.

1. The Testimony of the Massoretic Text: The Old Testament which we have is made up of 39 books. These were divided in the Hebrew Bible into three groups:

DIVISION	BOOKS	
TORAH Law	Genesis Exodus Leviticus	Numbers Deuteronomy
NEBI'IM The Prophets	Joshua Judges	1 & 2 Samuel 1 & 2 Kings
	Isaiah Jeremiah Ezekiel Hosea Joel Amos Obadiah Jonah	Micah Nahum Habakkuk Zephaniah Haggai Zechariah Malachi

SEPHER KAHUVIM Book of the Writings	Poetry	Psalms Job Proverbs
	Megilloth	Ruth Song of Solomon Ecclesiastes Lamentations Esther
	Histories	Daniel Ezra/Nehemiah 1 & 2 Chronicles

According to Jewish tradition, these divisions were brought about by Ezra.

2. The Testimony of Jesus: Jesus made allusion to this same division of the three groups when He spoke to His disciples after His resurrection.

> *Now He said to them, "These are My words which I spoke to you, while I was still with you, that all things which are written about Me in the Law of Moses and the Prophets and the Psalms must be fulfilled." (Luke 24:44).*

All of the Scriptures told of Christ. They all bore witness of Him. And now, we see Him bearing witness of them. Don't miss this! Jesus bears testimony of this same three-fold division of the Old Testament Scriptures (the Psalms was the largest of the third group and often used as its title). Notice that Jesus also carefully avoided speaking of the Apocrypha. In doing so, He is showing that He substantiated the books which were commonly known to make up those Scriptures. At the same time, He never suggests that any other extant books ought to be added to the Scriptures.

3. The Testimony of the Septuagint: The Septuagint was the translation of the Old Testament into Greek. During the reign of Ptolemy 2 Philadelphus (284-247 B.C.), the Library of Alexandria sponsored a translation of the Old Testament Scriptures into the Greek language

of that day.

    Tradition has it that seventy two Jewish elders were commissioned for the task. For this reason, the translation came to be called the *Septuaginta*, meaning "seventy." They translated the Law, the Prophets, and the Writings. Later on, the Apocrypha was added to the translation. Not one of the books that we presently have in our Old Testament was left out.

4.   The Testimony of the New Testament: The New Testament is full of quotations from the Old Testament Scriptures. These quotations are regularly treated as God's Word. At the same time, there is not a single reference in the New Testament when the Apocrypha is quoted and referred to in the context of being God's Word.

5.   The Testimony of Josephus: Josephus was a Jewish general who fought unsuccessfully against Rome in the days of the Jewish Revolt. He had heard of the Christians, but was not a Christian himself. He was an extensive writer, both of the history of the Jews as well as of the things he had seen at the destruction of Jerusalem in 70 A.D.

    Writing a rebuttal to anti-Jewish propaganda in the latter part of the first century, Josephus describes the Hebrew canon of scripture which was recognized by the Jews.

> *For we have not an innumerable multitude of books among us, disagreeing from and contradicting one another [as the Greeks have], but only twenty-two books, which contain the records of all the past times; which are justly believed to be divine...(Contra Apion 1:8).*

    The same 39 books that we have in our Bible were condensed into the 22 books of the Hebrew Bible. For example, they had a single book of Samuel and of Kings and of Chronicles. The Minor Prophets were grouped together into a single book called the Twelve.

    Notice that even in that day Josephus recognized that the various books of the Bible did not contradict each other. He goes on to group the books of the Scriptures into the three common divisions which we have described.

> *...and of them, five belong to Moses, which contain his laws and the traditions of the origin of*

> *mankind till his death... The prophets, who were after*
> *Moses, wrote down what was done in their times in*
> *thirteen books. The remaining four books contain*
> *hymns to God and precepts for the conduct of human*
> *life. (Contra Apion 1:8).*

Josephus puts the number of books in the Hebrew Bible at 22 and divides them into the following categories:

- Moses *(Torah)*.
- The Prophets *(Nevi'im)*.
- Hymns & Precepts *(Ketuvim)*.

The words of Josephus are important because they give us a point of view that is unbiased by Christianity. Specifically, he says that the Apocrypha did not have the same recognized authority because *"there has not been an exact succession of prophets"* since the time that the writing of the Scriptures ended.

> When you compare the end of Deuteronomy with the beginning of Joshua, you see an example of this progression. You can trace it through all of the major portions of the Old Testament.

According to Josephus, the test of authority for the Scriptures was that they were written by one who was recognized as a prophet. Who did the recognizing? The previous prophets!

But then, a day came when the last of the prophets had spoken. It was the prophet Malachi. He foretold that the Lord would come and that just prior to His coming He would be announced by Elijah. But that is not all. Notice what he has to say about the Apocrypha.

> *It is true, our history has been written since*
> *Artaxerxes, very peculiarly, but has not been*
> *esteemed of the like authority with the former by our*
> *forefathers, because there has not been an exact*
> *succession of prophets since that time. (Contra Apion*
> *1:8).*

Josephus rejects the Apocrypha because it had not been penned by a prophet and because there had been no line of prophets who spoke and who wrote the words of God.

6. The Testimony of the Apocrypha: Several books of the Apocrypha make mention of the Law and the Prophets as a separate and distinct group of extant writings.

> *Many great teachings have been given to us through the **Law** and the **Prophets** and the others that followed them, and for these we should praise Israel for instruction and wisdom. Now, those who read the scriptures must not only themselves understand them, but must also as lovers of learning be able through the spoken and written word to help the outsiders. (Sirach 1:1).*

> *Encouraging them from the **Law** and the **Prophets**, and reminding them also of the struggles they had won, he made them the more eager (2 Maccabees 15:9).*

> *While he was still with you, he taught you the **Law** and the **Prophets** (4 Maccabees 18:10).*

The books of the Old Testament never make reference to "the Law and the Prophets" in the manner that is found in either the New Testament or as in these books of the Apocrypha.

7. The Council of Jamnia: After the destruction of Jerusalem by the Romans in 70 A.D., the Jews were scattered. The remnants of the Jewish Sanhedrin, the supreme court of the Jews, moved to the ancient city of Jamnia.

    In 90 A.D. a Council was held at Jamnia under the direction of Rabbi Akiba. One of the items of discussion was the recognition of the Jewish writings which were to be reckoned as authoritative. The result of this council was that the books which make up our present Old Testament were recognized to be the Word of God. Those additional writings, such as the Apocrypha, were rejected. We must point out that this council did not establish the canonicity of these books, but rather recognized the books as being God's Word.

8. The Dead Sea Scrolls: Along with many portions of the Old

42

Testament Scriptures, the Dead Sea Scrolls also contained considerable writings of the Essene Community at Qumran. From an examination of these non-Biblical writings, it is a simple matter to determine that the Qumran Community held to essentially the same Old Testament Canon that we recognize today.

The threefold division that we saw in the Jewish tradition and in the writings of Josephus are absent in most of the Qumran literature. In its place is a twofold division of the Law and the Prophets.

The Manual of Discipline and the Zadokite Document refer to the Scriptures as "Moses and the Prophets." Does that mean they did not hold that the books making up the third portion of the Old Testament to be inspired? Not at all. They included these books in the general category of the "Prophets." Jesus did the same thing when He spoke of "the Law and the Prophets" (Matthew 5:17; 7:12; 11:13; 22:40; Luke 16:16; 16:29; 16:31; 24:27), even when He was clearly referring to a passage from the Writings.

Quotations from the Old Testament are introduced by the formula, "It is written." This formula is not used for a single quote outside of the Old Testament.

THE CANONICITY OF THE NEW TESTAMENT

The church was born with a completed canon in her hands. The earliest church already recognized the Old Testament as their Scriptures. It was not until more than 10 years after the church had begun that the first of the New Testament books began to be written. The New Testament books were written between 40-95 A.D. (it is my own personal view that it might have been completed prior to 70 A.D.). There were several different types of writing.

- Historical format (the Gospels and Acts).
- Letters to the churches and to individuals.
- The Apocalyptic format of Revelation.

---

1. Apostolic Authorship: Every book of the New Testament was either written by an apostle or by someone who had apostolic sanction.

> • Mark was given his information by Peter.
> • Luke was a disciple of Paul.

The word "apostle" come from a root meaning "to send." The Greek word ἀπόστολος (*apostolos*) is related to the inter-Testamental use of שְׁלִיחַ (*shelyach*), describing a messenger. The emphasis was not so much on the fact of sending, but rather on the authority of the person who was to perform the task. The שְׁלִיחַ fully represents the one who sent him.

> *Truly, truly, I say to you, he who receives whomever I send receives Me; and he who receives Me receives Him who sent Me. (John 13:20).*

The apostles had authority to act in the name of Jesus. Their authority was a delegated authority.

> *Therefore, holy brethren, partakers of a heavenly calling, consider Jesus, the APOSTLE and High Priest of our confession (Hebrews 3:1).*

Jesus was our Apostle. He was sent by God from heaven with authority. Thus, when people received Paul, they received him "as an angel of God, as Christ Jesus Himself" (Galatians 4:14). Ancronicus and Junias (Romans 16:7), Titus (2 Corinthians 8:23) and Epaphroditus (Philippians 2:25) are also referred to as apostles. 1 Corinthians 15:7 indicates a broader group known as the apostles that went beyond the Twelve.

The Jewish שְׁלִיחַ was a temporary status. The Christian Apostle seems to have been permanent. Thus, while there is a similarity to the שְׁלִיחַ, there was also a difference.

> There was a radical change in the apostles after Christ rose from the dead.

These apostles were authorized representatives. They had authority, identifying them fully with the One who had commissioned them. They had a "power of attorney" with Christ. The apostles themselves were given their authority by Jesus Christ, both to teach and to preach in His name. The early church fathers recognized that they themselves did not have this kind of authority.

> *The apostles received the gospel for us from the Lord Jesus Christ. Jesus Christ was sent from God, so then the apostles are sent from Christ. (Clement of Rome, 95 A.D.).*

> *I do not, as Peter and Paul, issue commandments to you. They were apostles. I am but a condemned man. (Ignatius, 117 A.D.).*

The testimony of all of the early church fathers is that the apostles were given their authority from Jesus Christ. Therefore, their writings were considered to be authoritative.

2.   Consistency: It was recognized by early Christians that all of the books of the New Testament were consistent with previous revelation. That is, when certain writings were seen to contradict prior Scriptures, it was obvious that they were not to be considered a part of the Canon.

3.   Reception by the Churches.

    a.   Books that were initially questioned.

        By 180 A.D. a total of 20 out of 27 of the New Testament documents were widely accepted as canonical. Only 7 were not. The issues were...

- Authorship.
- Content.
- Controversy.
- Circulation (if you don't have a copy of a certain epistle or book, you aren't likely to accept it as authoritative).

        The following books were accepted at this time as being on par with the Old Testament:

- Four Gospels.
- Acts.
- 13 epistles of Paul.
- 1st Peter.
- 1st John.

Irenaeus and the Muratorian Canon bear witness to this list. During the next two centuries there was debate over the remaining seven books. The Easter letter of Athenasius (written in 367) points to the accepting of all 27 books of the New Testament.

> Marcion's canon...
> • Edited version of Like.
> • 13 of Paul's epistles.
> • Tried to rid the church of Jewish influences.

b.   Factors which led to the recognition of the New Testament Canon.

   (1)   Heretics influenced the New Testament church to formalize an official canon. One thing that gave rise to a greater recognition of the canonicity of the New Testament books was the rise of certain heretics who denied that certain of these books ought to be in the Bible. For example, Marcion published his own limited canon and thereby had a catalytic effect that drove the church to account for what it already had and accepted.

   (2)   The presence of other Christian writings. Another factor that led to the recognition of a canon was the writing of many Christian books and letters. As Christianity grew and spread, believers began to write books and letters, outlining their beliefs and urging others to good works. We have letters which were written by many of the church fathers. The question arose as to whether they were to consider these new writings to be on par with the books of the New Testament.

   (3)   The coming of intense persecution. The Roman emperor Diocletian (303 A.D.) passed a law that made it illegal to possess a Bible. This brought to light the question, "For what books am I willing to die? Will I die for the Gospel According to Thomas? What about Paul's Epistle to the Romans?"

All three of these aspects -- the rise of heretics, the existence of other Christian documents, and the persecutions against Christianity -- had the result of bringing about a series of church councils that publicly recognized the New Testament Canon.

4.   Decisions of the Church Councils.

Council	Date	Result
Council of Laodicea	363	Asked that only canonical books be read from the pulpit. All our books of the New Testament listed except for Revelation.
Council of Carthage	397	Recognized our present New Testament Canon including Revelation.

5.   The Questioning of Certain Books: Why were certain books questioned as regards to their canonicity?

- James was questioned because it seemed to contradict the teaching of Justification by Faith.
- 2 Peter Hebrews were questioned because it was not known who was the human author.
- 2 John and 3 John were questioned because they seemed too short.
- Revelation was called into question because of its difficult symbolism.

6.   Criteria Used by the Early Church: The early church used the following criteria in determining the canonicity of the New Testament books.

- Apostleship or association with the Apostles.

    Not all of the writers of the New Testament were apostles, but all were written by people who were associated with the Apostles.
    - Mark
    - Luke
    - Acts
    - Hebrews
    - James

- Jude

Hebrews was only accepted after Paul was adopted as the author. However, some of the New Testament books do not have apostles as authors.

- Association with the apostles: Not all of the books of the New Testament were written by apostles. Mark and Luke had close associations with Peter and with Paul and therefore were considered to be authoritative because of those associations.

- Antiquity: Only the earliest documents of the church have been included. It was understood that God's revelatory work had ceased after that first generation had passed.

- Public reading: *I adjure you by the Lord to have this letter read to all the brethren. (1 Thessalonians 5:27).* Paul commanded that his epistle be read in the church. The problem with this is that the same instructions were given in Colossians 4:16 about a letter that Paul wrote to Laodicea - a letter which is not a part of the canon (see also 1 Corinthians 5:9).

- Acceptance by the church. Some epistles were not popular everywhere (like 2 Peter). This was especially true if the epistle had a limited audience.

Where does Scripture originate? From the Spirit of God (2 Peter 1:20-21; 2 Timothy 3:16).		In the Old Testament, the finger of God wrote on tablets of stone.

The "finger of God" was a reference to the Holy Spirit. We no longer have the word on Tablets of Stone. The Word is now written on the hearts of men.

And these words, which I am commanding you today, shall be on your heart. (Deuteronomy 6:6).

But the word is very near you, in your mouth and in your heart, that you may observe it. Deuteronomy 30:14).

I delight to do Thy will, O my God;
Thy Law is within my heart. (Psalm 40:8).

The Law of the Lord is in his heart;
His steps do not slip. (Psalm 37:31).

"But this is the covenant which I will make with the house of
Israel after those days," declares the Lord, "I will put My
law within them, and on their heart I will write it; and I will
be their God, and they shall be My people." (Jeremiah
31:33).

The apostles were to the church what a foundation is to its house. Their function took place during the period between the resurrection of Christ and His return. Our use of the Scriptures is an appeal to the teaching and the authority of the apostles and the prophets.

But there is a warning here. The origin of the Canon is not the same as its reception by the church. The church did not create the Canon. The Canon created the church. This is seen in the words of Paul when he points out the instrument that is used by God to bring about faith.

So faith comes from hearing, and hearing by the word of
Christ. (Romans 10:17).

It is the word of Christ which brings forth faith. It is this faith which is brought forth by the word which leads to the building of the church.

The Existence of the Canon	Does not equal	The Recognition of the Canon

The church did not create the canon. The canon created and still creates the church. The origin of the canon is not the same as its reception by the church.

In the 1990's, I had opportunity to visit the Grand Canyon. It is a breathtaking vista and my response was an appropriate, "Wow!" But my recognition of that vista did not create the vista. I was only recognizing that which already existed. In the same way, the church looked at the Scriptures and gave an appropriate, "Wow!" The church looked at the Scriptures and recognized that those Scriptures came from God. Their recognition did not make the Scriptures any more than my own recognition created the Grand

Canyon.

Norman Geisler provides the following chart as a study in the contrast between correct and incorrect views of the canon (2002:530).

Incorrect View of the Canon	Correct View of the Canon
Church Determines Canon	Church Discovers Canon
Church is Mother of Canon	Church is Child of Canon
Church is Magistrate of Canon	Church is Minister of Canon
Church Regulates Canon	Church Recognizes Canon
Church is Judge of Canon	Church is Witness of Canon
Church is Master of Canon	Church is Servant of Canon

Thus we conclude that the canon made the church and not the other way around. The church is not free to make the decision of which books it wishes to accept or reject. Rather, the church is called to recognize that which God has provided.

THE QUESTION OF THE APOCRYPHA

Both the Roman Catholic and the Greek Orthodox Church hold to the canonicity of the fourteen books of the Apocrypha. This is not to say that they have always held to the Apocrypha. No ecumenical council of church history ever recognized the canonicity of the Apocrypha until the Council of Trent in 1545. This was an obvious reaction to the Protestant Movement.

The word "Apocrypha" literally describes that which has been "hidden from sight." These "hidden books" were written after the time of the Maccabee Revolt (166 B.C.).

> The Roman Catholic Church prefers to use the term "Deuterocanonical" -- literally, "second canon," as they also recognize that these books were not originally accepted as were the rest of the Bible.

1.   The Makeup of the Apocrypha

The books of the Apocrypha were written during the 200 years prior to the birth of Christ. Nearly all of our copies of the Apocrypha are in Greek and most of it seems to have been originally penned in that language. They are made up of the following books:

Title	Brief Summary
Esdras	Esdras (known as 3rd Esdras in the Vulgate which entitles Ezra and Nehemiah as 1&2 Esdras) relates the history of Israel from Josiah to Ezra. There is a 4th Esdras that was rejected at the Council of Trent.
Tobit	Adventures of a Jewish family living in Assyria.
Judith	Story of Judith's rescue of the Jews from the hands of an Assyrian Army.
Additions to the book of Esther	A collection of Septuagint additions to the book of Esther.
Wisdom of Solomon	Collection of proverbs; the latter part of the book contrasts Israel versus Egypt.
Ecclesiasticus (Wisdom of Sirach)	A large collection of proverbs
Baruch	Claims to be written by the servant of Jeremiah and consists of praises, prayers and promises.
Story of Susanna	Story of Susanna who is accused of immorality but rescued by Daniel in Babylon.
Song of the Three Children	Song of Shadrach, Meshach and Abednigo on the occasion of the fiery furnace.
Bel and the Dragon	Adventures of Daniel in refusing to worship the idol of Bel or a living dragon which he kills.
Prayer of Manasseh	King Manasseh in Babylon prays a prayer of repentance.
1&2 Maccabees	Historical narratives of the Jewish War for Independence.

In addition to the Apocrypha is a much larger list of books known as the Pseudepigrapha — the "false writings." Many of these were works of fiction, supposedly written by such authors as Adam and Eve, Enoch, Abraham, Moses, and many other famous persons of antiquity. All of these books were rejected by the apostolic and church fathers.

2.   Their Internal Testimony.

Not a single one of the books of the apocrypha make a claim to having divine authority. None of them were written by a prophet or made claim to prophetic authority. Most of the books of the Apocrypha are written anonymously. There are two notable exceptions:

- Ecclesiasticus is written by Jeshua, son of Sirach of Jerusalem (Eccl 50:27). According to a prologue that is affixed to it, the book was discovered in Egypt in 132 B.C. It makes no claim at inspiration.

- Baruch claims to be written by the secretary of Jeremiah. It is filled with internal inconsistencies with the rest of the Bible (Nebuchadnezzar is said to be the king of the Assyrians).

Of the other books, 1&2 Maccabees contain some of the most accurate history, although they make no claim at all to divine authority. In describing the cleansing of the Temple under Judas Maccabeus, we read the orders of Judas in which the stones of the altar should be put aside until a prophet should arise.

> *So they tore down the altar, 46 and stored the stones in a convenient place on the temple hill until a prophet should come to tell what to do with them. (1 Maccabees 4:45-46).*

The implication is that there was no prophet in the land in those days and no one who could proclaim the word of the Lord.

3.   The Testimony of the Talmud.

The Talmud, consisting of the interpretations of the Jewish rabbis, states that *after the latter prophets Haggai, Zechariah and Malachi, the Holy Spirit departed from Israel* (Tractate Sanhedrin). The Greek Septuagint along with translations of the Hebrew Bible into Coptic, Ethiopic and later Syriac all contained at least portions of the Apocrypha. Even the original King James Version of 1611 contained the Apocrypha.

4.   The Testimony of the New Testament.

The New Testament abounds with quotations from the Old Testament Scriptures. Yet quotations from the Apocrypha are notably lacking. That is not to say that the New Testament writers were unfamiliar with the Apocrypha. They often quoted from the Septuagint and, as we have noted, the Septuagint did contain the Apocrypha. We can therefore conclude that the writers of the New Testament deliberately avoided quoting from the Apocrypha.

God has spoken. He has made His Word known to man. He has set forth His message in the writings of the Scriptures. He has seen to it that His Word has been collected and recognized by His church.

Has the Bible Been Changed?

The Science of Textual Criticism

The grass withers, the flower fades, but the word of our God stands forever." (Isaiah 40:8).

Since inspiration, by its very definition, extends only to the original manuscripts of the Bible, and since none of the original manuscripts are in existence today, how can we rely on the accuracy of our modern Hebrew and Greek Bibles? The answer to this question is found in the science of Textual Criticism.

WHAT IS TEXTUAL CRITICISM?

Textual criticism is scholarly work with available manuscripts aimed at the recovery within the limits of possibility of the original text. We do not have the original papyri that Moses used to write the Torah. We do not have the original letter of Paul to the Galatians which contains his own signature. All we have are copies. In some instances they are copies of copies of copies. Textual criticism involves carefully examining those copies to find out what is the original text.

TWO BASIC TYPES OF CRITICISM

There are two basic kinds of criticism in use among Biblical scholars today. They ought to be distinguished from the outset.

1.　　Higher Criticism: Higher Criticism looks to the outside factors of the book. It asks such questions as...
   * Who wrote the book?
   * Where was the book written?
   * When was the book written?
   * What outside factors influenced the writing of the book?
   * Why was the book written?

　　　These questions are not in themselves bad. In fact, we usually deal with these question whenever we set out to study a book of the Bible. However, many who have become involved in Higher Criticism have become geared to attacking the Bible as to its authenticity and trustworthiness.

　　　The father of this type of Higher Criticism is Julius Wellhausen (1878). He formulated and popularized a theory called the Documentary Hypothesis. Wellhausen taught that the books of the Pentateuch were not written by Moses, but rather came about through the efforts of four separate sources. This became known as the JEDP Theory, after the four supposed sources.

J -　Stands for a document written in 850 B.C. It is called this because of its extensive use of the work "Jehovah" when speaking of God.

E -　This is said to use "Elohim" for God and is said to have been written in 750 B.C.

D -　Stands for the book of Deuteronomy. It is said to be the scroll of the Law which Hilkaiah, the priest, found in the Temple during the reign of Josiah.

P -　This is said to be a Priestly Document written in 450 B.C. It is the one which contains all of the genealogies and lists, as well as the regulations concerning the sacrifices.

　　　According to Wellhausen, the Bible is not the inspired Word

of God, but rather contains mistakes and flaws all throughout. He saw the Bible as the product of natural evolutionary processes.

2.   Lower Criticism.

This is also referred to as "Textual Criticism" because it deals with the original text of the Scriptures. Its objective is to determine as closely as possible what the original text said on the basis of a study of the existing copies.

The study of Textual Criticism is not new. The early church father Origen wrote a book on the Old Testament text called the Hexapla in 250 A.D. However, discoveries of manuscripts in recent years have added a great new impetus to the science of Textual Criticism.

THE NEED FOR TEXTUAL CRITICISM

We have already noted what Textual Criticism is - the study of copies in order to determine the content of the original text. But why is Textual Criticism needed? The reason for Textual Criticism is because we do not have the original manuscripts of the Scriptures. They have long since either been lost or destroyed or crumbled to dust. All that we have left are copies that have been made.

For hundreds of years, the documents of Scriptures were copied by hand. Occasionally, a scribe might make a mistake as he was transcribing a manuscript. Years later, that mistake would be copied by another scribe who was using that manuscript as a source. Thus, certain errors might be copied in succeeding copies.

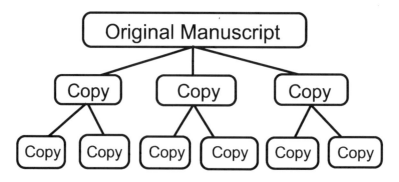

As a general rule, the older manuscripts are thought to have the fewest errors. This is because there was less of a chance for errors to creep in from the source manuscripts from which they were copied. Hence a third-generation copy might be considered to be more accurate than a sixth-generation copy.

For example, perhaps a scribe was copying from a manuscript which had been copied from the original text. The source text would then be a "second-generation" copy. As our scribe comes to Romans 8:1, he pauses for a moment to stretch his cramped fingers. Then as he begins again, his eyes slip down several lines and he begins to copy this phrase:

> *...who do not walk according to the flesh.*

Then he continues on to verse 2 and the verses which follow (keeping in mind that the verse divisions had not yet been added). Do you see what has happened? The scribe has made a mistake in copying. The source text reads:

> *There is therefore now no condemnation for those who are in Christ Jesus.*

However, the scribe's new copy now reads differently. It says:

> *There is therefore now no condemnation for those who are in Christ Jesus, who do not walk according to the flesh.*

In the years that follow, other scribes use this new manuscripts as their source text. Naturally, they will copy the same mistake that was previously made. Perhaps one of these scribes will make still another alteration so that his copy now reads (his reason might be to further clarify the text):

> *There is therefore now no condemnation for those who are in Christ Jesus, who do not walk according to the flesh, but according to the spirit.*

In the years that follow, other scribes use these new manuscripts as their source text. Naturally, they will copy the same mistake that was previously made. Further on down the line, still another scribe skips over the small Greek word μη, thus changing the text still further. Now it reads:

> *There is therefore now no condemnation for those who are in*

> *Christ Jesus, who walk according to the flesh, but according to the spirit.*

As a result of this last mistake, we now have fourth and fifth generation manuscripts which also contain this error.

Original	*There is therefore now no condemnation for those who are in Christ Jesus.*
First Error	*There is therefore now no condemnation for those who are in Christ Jesus, who do not walk according to the flesh.*
Second Error	*There is therefore now no condemnation for those who are in Christ Jesus, who do not walk according to the flesh, but according to the spirit.*
Third Error	*There is therefore now no condemnation for those who are in Christ Jesus, who walk according to the flesh, but according to the spirit.*

TYPES OF TEXTUAL ALTERATIONS

There are three general types of errors that might find its way into a text and therefore be transmitted:

1.   Unintentional Errors: These are errors which took place as a result of a mistake on the part of the scribe.

  - Errors from faulty eyesight. 1 Timothy 3:16 contains a difference in two words which look very much alike in the Greek text.
  - Errors arising from faulty hearing. Some scribes would copy from verbal dictation in which one reader would read the text aloud to a number of scribes who would write that text. There are homonyms both in English and in Greek.
  - Errors of the mind. Sometimes a tired scribe would switch words or even letters in a word by mistake.   For example, the word ἐλαβον (*"they received"*) is Mark 14:65 was changed in one

manuscript to ἔβαλον (*"they threw"*) and ἔβαλλον (*"they were throwing"*) in another.

- Additions due to personal notes. In the same way that we sometimes write a notation in the margin of our Bibles, scribes would sometimes place an interpretive notation. Since the text itself was handwritten, a later scribe might unintentionally copy down the note with the text, thinking that it was a part of the original.

2.   Intentional Changes.

In some cases, scribes made intentional changes to the manuscript which they were copying, not to hurt the text, but to either clarify or to correct what they perceived to be an error.

- Some of these are simply changes in spelling and grammar.
- Some are attempts to harmonize two like passages. This is seen in the two versions of the Lord's Prayer (Luke 11 versus Matthew 6). When Matthew 9:13 has Jesus saying, *"I came not to call the righteous, but sinners,"* some copyists could not resist adding the words "to repentance" (from Luke 5:32).
- Occasionally, an attempt was made to correct what was thought to be a historical error. Origen made such an attempt when he substituted the word *Bethabara* for *Bethany* in John 1:28, a substitution that is reflected in the KJV.
- A confluence of readings. When faced with two differing texts, a scribe would sometimes copy both readings rather than leave one out. Thus, when a scribe had two variant endings of the book of Luke, he sometimes used them both. *They were continually in the temple PRAISING God* and *They were continually in the temple BLESSING God* was combined to read *They were continually in the temple PRAISING and BLESSING God. (Luke 24:52).*
- Changes because of Doctrine. The Jehovah's Witnesses were not the first cult to attempt to rewrite the Bible. It is known that Marcion edited his own version of the Bible, cutting out those parts which were inconsistent with his own personal beliefs. In each case where an error crept into the text, it would be reproduced in any copies that were made of that text. It is for this reason that the older manuscript tends to be seen as the more trustworthy.

THE MANUSCRIPT EVIDENCE

Has the absence of the original manuscripts hurt the trustworthiness of our Bible? I do not believe so.

1.   Illustration of a Tape Measure. Dr. Laird Harris gives the following illustration:

> *Suppose we wish to measure the length of a certain pencil. With a tape measure we measure it 6 ½ inches. A more carefully made office ruler indicates 6 9/16 inches. Checking it with an engineer's scale, we find it to be slightly more than 6.58 inches. Careful measurement with a steel scale under laboratory conditions reveals it to be 6.577 inches. Not satisfied still, we send the pencil to Washington where master gauges indicate a length of 6.5774 inches. The master gauges themselves are checked against the standard United States yard marked on a platinum bar preserved in Washington. Now, suppose that we should read in the newspapers that a clever criminal had run off with the platinum bar and melted it down for the precious metal. As a matter of fact, this once happened to Britain's standard yard! What difference would this make to us? Very little. None of us has ever seen the platinum bar. Many of us perhaps never realized it existed. Yet we blithely use tape measures, rulers, scales, and similar measuring devices. These approximate measures derive their value from their being dependent on more accurate gauges. But even the approximate has tremendous value - if it has had a true standard behind it." (1971:88-89).*

Many people object that we have never seen the original manuscripts of the Bible. That is true. I have never seen a copy of the epistle to the Galatians that contained the handwritten signature of the Apostle Paul. But other people have. In 200 A.D. Tertullian said that the original writings of the apostles still existed in the churches which those apostles had started. Those original manuscripts could be examined in his day.

We have manuscripts dating back to Tertullian's day and portions which are even earlier. These copies were able to be checked against the originals.

2.   Comparison to Writings of Antiquity.

How does this compare to other writings of antiquity that have come down to us? The following chart points out the comparison between the Bible versus other ancient writings. [1]

Author	Date Written	Earliest Copy	Time between Original & Copy	Number of Copies
Pliny	61-113 A.D.	850 A.D.	750 Years	7
Plato	427-347 B.C.	900 A.D.	1200 Years	7
Demosthenes	4th Cent B.C.	1100 A.D.	800 Years	8
Herodotus	480-425 B.C.	900 A.D.	1400 Years	8
Suetonius	75-160 A.D.	950 A.D.	800 Years	8
Thucydides	460-400 B.C.	900 A.D.	1300 Years	8
Euripides	480-406 B.C.	1100 A.D.	1300 Years	9
Julius Caesar	100-44 B.C.	900 A.D.	1000 Years	10
Tacitus	100 A.D.	1100 A.D.	1000 Years	20
Aristotle	384-322 B.C.	1100 A.D.	1400 Years	49
Homer's Illiad	900 B.C.	400 B.C.	500 Years	643
New Testament	1st Century A.D.	2nd Century A.D.	Less than 100 Years	5600

None of these other writings are ever questioned, yet most of them have fewer than 50 extant manuscripts and many have less than 10. On the other hand, the Bible has literally thousands of ancient manuscripts from

---

[1] Adapted from Matt Slick: Christian Apologetics and Resource Ministry: CARM.org.

which we can conduct our investigations in our search for the true text.

In addition to this, there are thousands of quotations of the Bible from the early church fathers. Likewise, we have over 2000 lectionaries - written Bible lessons which quoted the verses which were to be read during the worship service.

This simplifies the job of the textual critic. If he reads a certain phrase in 5,994 manuscripts and finds an alternate reading in only 6 manuscripts, it becomes much easier to determine the true text. Therefore, we can conclude that the Scriptures which we have are trustworthy.

MANUSCRIPT FAMILIES

Textual Critics have divided the manuscript evidence into four major categories. These families all contains groups of texts.

1.   Old Testament Families.

> *The Masora is a fence about the Law* (Rabbi Akiba).

   a.   The Massoretic Texts.

The Massoretes were a group of Hebrew scholars who worked at preserving the Scriptures and the traditions of the Jews (the word מסורת, *masora*, means "tradition"). There were initially two groups:

   •   The Eastern Massoretes were located in Mesopotamia.
   •   The Western Massoretes began in Tiberias.

The Western Massoretes eventually gained in prominence and it is the result of their work which survives today. The Massoretes developed a system of vowel-points, but there was initial resistance to this among

> *Although verse divisions were known in the Talmudic Period, they were not numbered by chapters until the 16th Century.*

certain Jewish groups who felt that this was a sacrilegious adding to the Word of God.

   b.   The Septuagint Family.

This was the Greek translation of the Hebrew Scriptures, formed in 250 B.C. in Alexandria, Egypt. The problem with the Septuagint was that it made no attempt to be a word-for-word translation. It was, instead, a "Dynamic Equivalent," much as is the New International Version. There were also wide variations within different copies of the Septuagint.

c. The Samaritan Pentateuch.

The Samaritan Pentateuch differs from the Massoretic Text in about 6000 instances (most of these are mere differences in spelling). One interesting difference is seen in Exodus 20:17 where an eleventh commandment is inserted - to build a sanctuary upon Mount Gerazim. About 1900 of these instances the Samaritan Pentateuch agrees with the Septuagint against the Massoretic Text.

d. Dead Sea Scrolls.

The discovery of the Dead Sea scrolls had a profound impact upon Old Testament Textual Criticism. On the one hand, there was evidence that the Massoretic Scrolls were very accurate in their rendition of the Hebrew Bible. At the same time, it was discovered that there were some Hebrew manuscripts which seemed to follow the Septuagint reading. This indicates that perhaps some of the differences in the Massoretic Text versus the Septuagint are not just translational but point to differences in copiest transmission.

2. New Testament Families.

a. The Proto-Alexandrian Texts. This group is also referred to as the Neutral Text and the Hesychian Text. This family of texts is represented by some of the oldest Texts, including the Codex Sinaiticus and the Codex Vaticanus, both dating back to the 4th century. It is also represented by Papyrus 66 and Papyrus 75, both of which date to the beginning of the third century. It was originally thought that these texts do not exhibit the grammatical and stylistic polishing that were found in some of the other families. However it is now evident that these manuscripts were corrected by later scribes.

b.   The Western Text.

These texts were used in the West and particularly in North Africa. This family of texts is represented by Codex Bezae (Codex D) as well as the Old Latin and Syriac translations, some of which are as early as the 2nd century. It was used by Marcion, Irenaeus, Tertullian, and Cyprian. It was rejected by Wescott and Hort.

c.   The Byzantine Text.

Also known as the Syriac Text. It was adopted in Constantinople and was used as the common text in the Byzantine world. A great majority of late uncials and minuscules belong to this group It is from this family that Erasmus produced his Textus Receptus. Martin Luther also translated his German Bible from this family. The King James Version reflects this family of texts. Dr. Laird Harris makes the following observation about this family of texts.

> *Scrutiny of the Byzantine family reveals a multitude of small mistakes and numerous unexpected readings which seem unreasonable." (1971:92).*

It is for this reason that most of the modern translations have turned away from the Byzantine Family to use a compilation of the Western and Neutral Texts.

d.   The Alexandrian Text.

This family of texts originated in Alexandria, Egypt. It includes Codex Ephraemi (Codex C), the Coptic Versions, and certain of the Alexandrian early church fathers.

e.   The Caesarean Text.

This is thought by some to be a compilation of the Western and Alexandrian readings. It is associated with Origen and Eusebius as well as with Codex Koridethi, a manuscript containing the gospels which was discovered near the Caspian Sea and dates to the ninth century (Q).

In summary, we find that the textual evidence can be categorized into f▮ major groups. The oldest of these is the Proto-Alexandrian. The gr▮ majority of manuscripts are in the Byzantine Family.

Textual Family	Description	Dates
Proto-Alexandrian	Older Texts Sinaiticus; Vaticanus	2nd-4th Century
Alexandrian	Ephraemi	3rd-12th Century
Western	Bezae & Latin Fathers	2nd-13th Century
Caesarean	Compilation of Alexandrian & Western?	3rd-13th Century
Byzantine	Textus Receptus; KJV	5th-10th Century

Harris notes the advantages of the fact that the manuscript evidence i▮ divided into these various families. Laird Harris summarizes:

> *It thus develops that we do not have an embarrassing welter of three thousand manuscripts disagreeing in confusing ways, but that these manuscripts have been copied with considerable care from a few old and standard editions. (1971:91).*

Has God's word been lost? Not at all. When all of the texts have been examined, the total amount of differences found between the various texts is very small indeed. Furthermore, not a single doctrine is to be found to be changed in any manuscript.

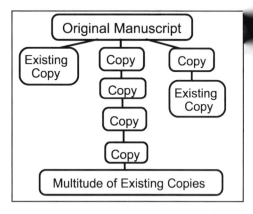

65

)DOLOGY OF TEXTUAL

ral criteria seem to be used by those engaging in the iticism:

ext is to be Preferred: The earlier the generation of the less time it would have to become corrupted by

r/Longer Text is to be Preferred: There is some debate point. It is thought by some that it is easier to ally leave out a passage than it is to add one. If this were t would be the longer text that would be preferred. This e especially true when we compare the Septuagint with the Text.

eographical Reading is to be Preferred: If a manuscript is ithin several different families of texts which originated at areas within the ancient world, then it would generally seem stworthy.

e Difficult Reading is to be Preferred: Because scribes es sought to correct what they perceived to be difficulties, which contain "problem passages" are usually thought to be trustworthy.

In Search of Ancient Manuscripts

The Tools of Textual Criticism

I am a stranger in the earth; do not hide Thy commandments from me.
My soul is crushed with longing after Thy ordinances at all times. (Psalm 119:18-19).

We have already noted the vast amount of manuscript evidence available for the textual critic, but perhaps we should also observe the extraordinary lengths to which the scribes who copied the Bible went so that errors should not creep into the text.

THE COPYING OF THE SCRIPTURES

We have none of the original autographs of the Scriptures today. That is to say that we do not have the original copy of Paul's epistle to Galatians that was signed in large letters with his own handwriting. That does not mean the Scriptures are lost to us, for they have been copied and recopied many times over, often with great care.

1.   The Ministry of the Masorites.

      a.   Their name: We have already noted that the name Masorite comes from the Hebrew word *masorah*, meaning "tradition." They were guardians of Jewish tradition.

b. Their rise: Hundreds of years after the destruction of Jerusalem by the Romans, the Masorites rose up in the Jewish community of Tiberius where work was being done in copying the Hebrew Text. This group eventually worked out a system by which they counted each letter of each page of the Scriptures. They could tell you what the first letter was on any given line of any given page of any given scroll. Nathan Ausubel gives this summary:

> *The Masorites had a passionate concern with their special statistics. They went into a bizarre counting successively of letters, words, verses, sections and chapters in each Scriptural writing and in all the twenty four books of the Bible." (1964:272).*

c. Vowel Pointing: The Masorites also worked up a system of vowel pointing for the Hebrew Text. This helped to fix the pronunciation of the Hebrew words (the Hebrew language contains no written vowels).

2. The Copying of the Old Testament.

    The Talmud contains a strict set of rules for copying the Old Testament Scriptures. An examination of these rules will show that it was very difficult for errors to creep into the codex. A synagogue scroll was to be...

    *   Written on the skin of a clean animal.
    *   Prepared by a Jew.
    *   Fastened together with strings taken from clean animals.
    *   Lined and spaced so that each page had a certain number of columns.

    The codex must meet the following requirements...

    *   The length of each volume must extend not less than 48 lines and not more than 60 lines and the breadth must consist of 30 letters.

- The whole copy must first be lined; if three words were written without first being lined, the copy must be discarded.
- The ink must be black, developed according to a special recipe.
- The transcriber could not deviate the least from the original.
- No word or letter, not even a yod, could be written from memory. The scribe must look at each word before writing.
- Between every consonant, the space of a hair or thread must intervene.
- Between every new paragraph or section, the breadth of nine consonants must intervene.
- Between every book, three lines must intervene.
- The fifth book of Moses must terminate exactly with a line.

Besides this, the copiest must...

- Sit in full Jewish dress.
- Wash his whole body.
- Not begin to write the name of God with a pen newly dipped in ink. Should a king address him while writing that name, he must take no notice of him.
- If a mistake were made in the copying, he was not allowed to erase it or cross it out, but must throw the ruined page away and start anew.

With this kind of care being taken to insure a perfect copy, it is no wonder that the scribes considered the new copy to be just as authoritative as the original.

3.   Copying of the New Testament.

What about the New Testament? Unfortunately, the scribes who copied the New Testament did not go to such great lengths to insure that errors did not creep into the text. However, through the efforts of modern archaeology, we have discovered thousands of manuscripts, some dating to within a hundred years of the writing of the original text.

At the time of the translation of the King James Version of the Bible (in 1611), the oldest Old Testament Manuscript was a Masoretic Text dating back only a few hundred years. The oldest New Testament Text was dated at about 1000 A.D. This has all changed in recent years with a number of archaeological discoveries.

CODEX ALEXANDRINUS

This manuscript contains the Old Testament Septuagint and most of the New Testament, though portions of Matthew, John and 2 Corinthians are missing. The Gospels are the very oldest example of the Byzantine Family of Texts. The rest of the New Testament follows the Alexandrian family.

1.   Its Composition: The Codex Alexandrinus, containing the Greek Bible, had been written around 450 A.D. and had eventually made its way to Constantinople.

2.   Cycil Lucar: In 1621, Cycil Lucar became the Patriarch of the Greek Orthodox Church. It is said that he was somewhat Calvinistic in his beliefs and he engaged in extensive correspondence with Christians throughout Europe.

3.   Presentation to England: He presented Codex Alexandrinus as a present to King Charles 1 of England in 1627, just 15 years after the King James Version had been completed and too late to have any impact upon that translation.

CODEX VATICANUS (CODEX B)

This manuscript dates to the middle of the 4th century and contains both Old and New Testaments along with the Apocrypha except for the books of Maccabees. The early chapters of Genesis are missing along with the last few books of the New Testament including the epistles to Timothy, Titus Philemon and Revelation.

1.   Initial Discovery: In 1809 when the French Emperor Napoleon Boneparte exiled the Pope to Avingnon, the Vatican Library was transported to France. Among the thousands of volumes was found a manuscript of the New Testament known today as Codex Vaticanus. Before any serious study could be done on the codex, Napoleon was overthrown and the Library along with Codex Vaticanus was returned to Rome.

2.   Tregelles: It was not until 1843 that Samuel P. Tregelles, a professor of New Testament Literature at Leipzig University, received

permission from the Pope to study the manuscript. He was allowed only six hours. Two years later, Tregelles was again permitted to study the manuscript, this time for three months. However, he was allowed to bring with him no writing materials and could take no notes. Guards watched him continually to make certain that he did no copying of the manuscript. During those three months, Tregelles memorized the entire manuscript, going home each day and writing down what he had memorized.

Returning to Leipzig, Tregelles published his findings. The Pope was furious at having been outwitted, but was powerless to do anything about it. Finally, Pope Pius XI allowed the manuscript to be photographed in 1859. It is now considered to have been written at about 350 A.D.

EPHRAEMI RESCRIPTUS

In 1834, a young theology student decided to write his thesis paper on the sermons of a Syrian theologian of an earlier century named Father Ephraem (1553). He went to the French National Library in Paris and found a number of volumes in the reference section. While reading, he noticed that there were indentations visible on the vellum on which the sermons had been written.

When investigated, these indentations proved to be prior writings which had been erased. Apparently an early scribe had wished to transcribe the sermons of Father Ephraem but had run short of paper, so he had taken some old vellum which he found and he had erased the writing, leaving only the indentations. Without realizing it, this unknown scribe had erased one of the oldest New Testament manuscripts (450 A.D.). Through the use of chemicals, the original manuscript has since been restored.

CODEX SINAITICUS (CODEX ALEPH)

This Codex is made up of the entire New Testament and most of the Old Testament Septuagint. It is written in uncial script.

1.   Tischendorf.

In the spring of 1844, a young German scholar named Count

Konstantin von Tischendorf was traveling through the Middle East. During his travels, he came upon an old Greek Orthodox monastery at the foot of Mount Sinai. The Russian monks who lived there invited him to spend the night.

2.   Discovery.

When the desert night became cold, the monks brought out a large waste basket of old vellum which it was their practice to burn in the fireplace. Tischendorf glanced at the vellum and then did a double take, for here was an ancient manuscript with Greek writing on it!

His face must have lit up as he asked if more of this vellum could be brought to him. Tischendorf spent several days digging through piles of old vellum and, during that time, found 129 pages of the New Testament manuscript known as Codex Sinaiticus.

From his reaction, the monks could tell that Tischendorf had discovered something important. When he asked to have the manuscript, they allowed him to take only 43 of 129 pages.

3.   Russia.

Ultimately, the text, along with other documents, was moved to Russia where Tischendorf was permitted to study it at length.

4.   England.

It was not until 1933 that the Russian Communists, having no need of old copies of the Bible, agreed to sell Codex Sinaiticus to Great Britain for 100,000 pounds. It resides today in the British Museum and has been dated at 375 A.D.

OXYRHYNCHOS PAPYRI

In 1900, Drs. Grenfell and Hunt of the Oxford University traveled up the Nile to Oxyrhynchos, a site that lies on a tributary of the Nile that flows into the Fayum Oasis. They were searching for buried treasure which they thought lay in the tombs of the pharaohs. During the course of their excavations, they came upon a great hall half filled with stuffed crocodiles. They were in the process of having their native workers move the crocodiles out of the way to see what might be beyond when one of the workers dropped a crocodile. It hit a sharp object and broke open. It was filled with papyri.

Further investigation showed that these stuffed crocodiles contained a whole library of ancient writings. These included some Biblical manuscripts from the second century as well as grammar and etymology books which led to a greater knowledge of the Koine Greek.

CHESTER BEATTY PAPYRI

On November 19, 1931, a Philadelphia millionaire named Chester Beatty was vacationing in the Middle East. When an Arab offered to sell him some Old Testament papyri in Greek, he agreed to the purchase. He turned the entire collection over to two scholars to examine, F. Kenyon and H. Saunders.

A detailed study showed that these were second and third century manuscripts containing portions of Paul's epistles and the Gospels. The manuscripts are now kept at the University of Pennsylvania.

SUMMARY OF PAPYRI

Not all of the Papyri that we have mentioned above contain all of the New Testament. Often there are only portions of a single book or collection of books that have survived. The following table summarizes some of the more significant finds:

Papyri		Contents	Date	Location
John Rylands Fragment	p52	John 18:31-33; 18:37-38	125 A.D.	John Rylands Library, England
Chester Beatty Papyrus	p46	Portions of Romans 5:17 - 15:33; Hebrews; 1&2 Corinthians; Ephesians; Galatians; Philippians; Colossians; portions of 1st Thessalonians	200 A.D.	Chester Beatty Museum, Dublin and University of Michigan Library

Bodmer Papyrus	p66	John 1:1 - 6:11; 6:35 - 14:26; 14:29 - 21:9	200 A.D.	Cologne, Geneva
p67		Matthew 3:9-15; 5:20-22; 5:25-28	200 A.D.	Barcelona

THE DEAD SEA SCROLLS

We have already noted that the Masoretes exercised great care in the transmission of the Hebrew manuscripts of the Bible. A part of that care involved the disposal of old and worn manuscripts. Because of this, the oldest Hebrew manuscripts in 1940 were only a thousand years old. This changed dramatically with a discovery by the Dead Sea.

1.　First Discovery: The first of the Dead Sea Scrolls was discovered in 1947 when an Arab shepherd boy, while looking for a stray goat, happened to throw a rock into a cave along the northwestern shore of the Dead Sea. Instead of the bleating of a goat, he heard the crash of a breaking clay pot. He investigated and found several clay jars containing old scrolls with Hebrew writing on them. The scrolls changed hands several times before finally finding their way to the authorities. When they did, they caused a stir that is still being heard today.

Caves in the cliffs overlooking Qumran where the first of the scrolls were discovered.

2.   Further Discoveries: Over the course of the next few years, archaeologists recovered 40,000 fragments of manuscripts in 11 different caves. Represented was almost the entire Old Testament, portions of which have been dated as early as 175 B.C.

3.   Significance: The significance of these finds cannot be underestimated. In a single find, the Textual Critic had jumped back 1000 years. These manuscripts provide a basis for judging the accuracy of the Hebrew Bible. How does the Masoretic Text match up to the early scrolls discovered in the Dead Sea Caves? Geisler and Nix offer the following answer:

> *Of the 166 words in Isaiah 53, there are only 17 letters in question. Ten of these letters are simply a matter of spelling, which does not affect the sense. Four more letters are minor stylistic changes, such as conjunctions. The three remaining letters comprise the word LIGHT, which is added in verse 11 and which does not affect the meaning greatly. Furthermore, this word is supported by the LXX. Thus, in one chapter of 166 words, there is only one word (three letters) in question after a thousand years of transmission - and this word does not significantly change the meaning of the passage. (1968:263).*

This is a remarkable testimony to the accuracy of the Masoretic Text upon which our Bible is based. Over a period of a thousand years, very little has change has come upon the text. We have a Bible we can trust. There is sufficient manuscript evidence to back it up.

With Men of Other Tongues

The Process of Translation

Indeed, He will speak to this people through stammering lips and a foreign tongue. (Isaiah 28:11).

The Old Testament was written in Hebrew, with small portions in Aramaic. The New Testament was written for the most part in Koine (Common) Greek. The story of how it was translated from those original languages to our present English translations is a fascinating one.

THE SEPTUAGINT (250 B.C.)

The very earliest known translation of the Bible was the Septuagint. It was a translation of the Old Testament Hebrew Bible into Greek.

1.   Ptolemy Philadelphus.

One of the great wonders of the ancient world was the Library of Alexandria in Egypt. Jewish tradition tells us that around 250 B.C. Ptolemy Philadelphus, the king of Egypt, ordered that a translation be made of the Hebrew Scriptures into the common language of that day - Greek.

Greek had become the common language ever since Alexander the Great had conquered most of the known world. Ptolemy 2nd himself was the descendant of one of Alexander's generals who had taken control of Egypt. His legacy is the completion of the great library at Alexandria.

2.   The Translators: According to tradition, this translation was the work of 72 Jewish scholars and so became known as the Septuagint (from *Septuaginta*, meaning "Seventy").

3.   Acceptance: This translation became the standard version accepted by all non-Hebrew speaking people of the ancient world. It is interesting to note that many of the quotations of the New Testament appear to have been taken from the Septuagint.

THE SYRIAN VERSIONS

Syriac or Aramaic is very close to the Hebrew language. Scholars have distinguished five different Syriac versions of all or part of the New Testament.

Old Syriac Version	Preserved in two manuscripts, both which have large gaps. They date back to the 4th and 5th centuries. They resemble the Western Textual Family of Greek manuscripts.
Peshitta (Syriac Vulgate)	Originally did not include 2 Peter, 2 & 3 John, Jude or Revelation. It attained some degree of status prior to the split of the Syrian Church in A.D. 431. More than 350 manuscripts of the Peshitta New Testament are known today, several of which date back to the 5th and 6th centuries. There are few variants among the witnesses. The Gospels seem to follow the Byzantine Family while Acts follows the Western Texts.
Philoxenian	Include the smaller General Epistles and the book of Revelation. These two families are said to have come about from 500-600 A.D.; the actual existing manuscripts are more recent.
Harclean	
Palestine Syriac	Preserved by three manuscripts dating from the 11th and 12th centuries. It seems to follow the Caesarean Family.

THE VULGATE (382 A.D.)

As time went on and the power of Rome grew, Latin began to replace Greek as the common language, especially in the West. And so, a new translation was needed.

1.   Jerome.

An Old Latin Translation appeared prior to 200 A.D. and became widely used. In 382 Pope Damascus commissioned Jerome to revise some of these already existing Latin translations which had been made of the Scriptures. Jerome had studied Greek and Latin in Rome and he also studied Hebrew in Palestine.

2.   The Translation.

His translation of the Bible into Latin became known as the *Vulgate* (Latin for "common") because it was in the common language.

EARLY ENGLISH TRANSLATIONS

1.   Caedmon (680).

As the church grew in England, Latin continued to be the language used in all of the church services, in spite of the fact that the common people spoke Anglo-Saxon. Therefore when the common people went to church, they never understood what was being said. Onto this scene came Caedmon. He was a singer and he found a monk who agreed to translate certain portions of the Bible into Anglo-Saxon.

Caedmon traveled through England singing, "In the beginning God created the heavens and the earth" in Anglo-Saxon. It was the first time that many of the people in his day had ever heard the Scriptures in their own language.

2.   Aldhelm (640-709).

Aldhelm was a bishop in southern England who was also a

Latin scholar. Caedmon's work so impressed him that he decided to translate the Psalms into Anglo-Saxon. He accomplished this work, using the Vulgate as his source text.

3.   Bede (673-735).

Bede is one of the most famous historians of the Middle Ages. His "Ecclesiastical History of the English People" has long been a major source of information about the early church in England. As a believer, he decided that the people needed a translation of one of the Gospel Accounts in their own language. He began to translate the Gospel of John. According to tradition, he finished dictating his translation to a scribe as he lay on his deathbed.

4.   Alfred the Great (849-899).

Alfred became the King of England at a time when the Danes were on the verge of overrunning England. During his reign, he repulsed the Danes and then went on to built up a military system of fortifications that would keep out invaders for the next 150 years.

Alfred was a Christian and he mandated that all of the people of England follow him in worshiping Christ. There followed a great revival of Christianity in England. He also began a tremendous program to educate his people. He was a scholar himself and under his reign, both nobles and commoners were taught to read and to write. The primer that was used was an Anglo-Saxon translation of the Bible.

In 1066 the Normans invaded England. From this time on, England was ruled by a Norman king and most of the feudal states were under Norman barons. This brought about a tremendous change in the English language so that, after a hundred years, the old translations of the Bible could no longer be understood. Also, with the Normans came a rise in Romanism so that Jerome's Latin Vulgate once again became the official Bible of the English church.

5.   John Wyclif (1329-1384).

> Wyclif is known as the "Morning Star of the Reformation."

Wyclif was a leading philosopher at Oxford University who saw the need for the English people to have a Bible in their own language. He took up the task of translating the entire

Bible into English. For this, he was branded as a heretic by the Roman Catholic Church.

Wyclif's translation was in the common speech of the day. For example, he rendered...	
Children	Brats
Father	Dad
Chariot	Cart

Here is an example of his translation:

These thingis Jesus spak; and whanne he hadde cast up hise eyen into hevene, he seide: `Fadir, the our cometh; clairfie thi sone, that thi sone clarifie thee; as thou hast yovun to hym power on ech fleische, that al thing that thou hast yovun to hym, he yyve to hem everlastynge liif.'" (John 17:1-2).

Over the next 150 years the English translation continued to change so that once again there was a need for a new translation.

6.   William Tyndale (1494-1536).

After studying at Oxford and Cambridge, Tyndale came into contact with the doctrines of the Protestant Reformation and determined that the people of England should have the Bible in their own language. However, instead of going back to the Latin Vulgate as Wyclif, Bede and Aldhelm had done, he instead used Greek and Hebrew manuscripts. In doing so, he was the first man to translate the Bible into English directly from the Greek and Hebrew.

Because of fierce persecution, Tyndale was forced to flee England. He moved to Europe where he translated the entire New Testament and part of the Old Testament. It is estimated that between 1525 and 1528 there were 18,000 copies of his translated published and spread abroad.

Tyndale was betrayed and arrested in Antwerp in 1535. He continued his work of translating while in prison until October 1536 when he was convicted of heresy and strangled and his body burned at the stake. It is reported that his last words were a prayer, "Lord, open the eyes of the King of England."

In the years that followed, a number of other English translations made their appearance.

Translation	Date	Description
The Coverdale Bible	1535	Translated from the Latin Vulgate by Miles Coverdale in 1535 (Coverdale had served as Tyndale's assistant and proofreader at Antwerp).
The Matthew Bible	1537	Published by John Rogers in 1537. He used the pen name of Thomas Matthew for this work It was a compilation of Tyndale's translation and the Coverdale Bible.
The Great Bible	1539	This second edition of the Matthew Bible was given this title because of its extreme size. When Oliver Cromwell came to power, he made the Great Bible the official Bible of England.
The Geneva Bible	1557	Geneva had become a place of refuge for Reformers such as Coverdale and John Knox. It was here that Calvin's brother-in-law, William Whittingham, produced a New Testament which had the distinction of being the first English Bible to be divided into verses. In 1560 the entire Bible was published at Geneva. It was adopted by the Puritans and is the text quoted by William Shakespear in his plays.
The Rheims-Douai Version	1582	Sponsored by English scholars who were loyal to the Roman Catholic Church. It was translated from the Latin Vulgate (the New Testament in 1582 and finally published together with the Old Testament in 1609).

THE KING JAMES VERSION (1611)

1.	The Millenary Petition.

On January 14, 1603 a delegation of Puritan Reformers came before King James of England to petition for a change in the established church services and in the various Roman Catholic rituals such as the sign of the cross.

Their petition had been signed by about 1000 Puritan leaders (hence the name, "Millenary Petition." During the debates that followed, it was suggested that there be made a new translation of the Bible from the original Greek and Hebrew text. King James agreed.

2.	The Work of Translation.

Within six months, 54 men had been chosen to do the work of translation. Each was an expert in either Greek or Hebrew. The list included both Anglicans and Puritans.

The scholars were divided into six teams and sections of the Scriptures were assigned to each team...	
Two at Oxford	Isaiah-Malachi, Gospels, Acts, Revelation
Two at Cambridge	Chronicles-Ecclesiastes, Apocrypha
Two at Westminster	Genesis-Kings, the Epistles

This explains why a word like *hagiou pneumatos* has been translated "Holy Ghost" in some portions of the Bible and "Holy Spirit" in other portions. The teams translating the Old Testament used the Masoretic Text while the teams translating the New Testament used a Beza's Greek Text - commonly known as the Textus Receptus ("the Received Text") and based upon the third edition of Erasmus which had been published by Stephanus in 1550.

3.	Erasmus.

Desiderius Erasmus had been the great enemy of Luther. In 1515 he had been commissioned by the Roman Catholic Church to

82

put together a Greek New Testament. He was able to find five Greek manuscripts, none of which contained the entire New Testament and none of which dated earlier than the 12th century.

Unfortunately, there were several chapters from the book of Revelation for which he had no manuscripts at all. This did not stop Erasmus, for he simply took the Latin Vulgate and translated it from Latin back into Greek.

To make matters worse, when he was editing his third edition, he was urged by the Roman Catholic Church to place the Vulgate's version of 1 John 5:7 into his Greek Bible. Erasmus complained that there was no Greek manuscript that contained the verse. The Catholic Church quickly complied by drafting up a Greek manuscript that contained the verse and presenting it to him. Erasmus reluctantly entered this revised verse into his 3rd edition (although he took it back out for his 4th and 5th editions). It was this same 3rd edition of Erasmus that was used by the translators of the King James Version.

4.   The Reception of the Translation.

The translation was completed in 1611. It turned out to be somewhat unpopular. The Catholics claimed that it favored the Protestants. The Arminians thought it leaned toward Calvinism while the Calvinists felt that it favored Arminianism. The Puritans objected to certain ecclesiological terms. There was only one person in all of England who did like the new translation — King James. And so, it was ratified and became the official translation for England. It has been one of the finest English translations ever produced, in spite of the poor manuscripts upon which it was based.

The Model-T was the best car of its day, and even now, it is still a fully legal car. If you ever drive one, people will smile and wave. And it sure beats walking or riding a horse. But if you ever drive one for more than a few miles, you will soon find that a car meant for dirt roads doesn't do so well on the modern highway.

The same is true with old bible versions such as the King James Version. It was the best of its day and is now just as valid as ever with still quite a large readership. But just as I prefer my new Saturn for most driving purposes over the Model-T, I prefer to use a modern English Bible over the King James Version for my regular Bible reading.

MODERN TRANSLATIONS

Since the day when the King James Version was first published, there have been literally thousands of Greek and Hebrew manuscripts discovered which are older than those used by the translators of that version. Newer translations have been able to take advantage of this increased wealth of information.

1.   The Revised Version.

A British revision committee was set up in 1870 to revise the King James Version in light of the growing manuscript evidence. They translated the Old and New Testament, completing their work in 1885. They went on to translate the Apocrypha in 1895. They made it a point to utilize Elizabethan English in this translation, changing only that language which could no longer be understood.

2.   The American Standard Version.

Working in cooperation with the British revisers, a United States committee brought out this translation in 1901. Instead of following the accepted practice of translating the tetragramatum as "LORD," they gave an anglicized version of "Jehovah."

3.   The Revised Standard Version: This translation was completed in 1952 and was a revision of the Revised Version of 1885.

> *The New Testament is quite faithful to the best Greek texts; the Old Testament often departs from Hebrew for readings in Greek, Latin, Syriac, Aramaic, or just conjecture. (Dr. William S. LaSor).*

Because it has a tendency to depart from the traditional readings of the King James Version, this translation has come under significant attack by Protestant Evangelicals.

4.   The New American Standard Version (1970).

This was the nine year effort of 58 scholars brought together by the Lockman Foundation. They worked to update the American Standard Version. Its critics argue that it is too literal.

Considerable attention has been given to translation of verb tenses with the result that it often sounds awkward and slightly pedantic. (Robert H. Mounce, Professor of Religious Studies at Western Kentucky University).

Personally, I have found that the attention to literalness of translation to be a great aid in Bible study. Admittedly, there are times when the New American Standard does not flow readily and does not show the best of English grammar, but this is only a reflection of the fact that the writers of the Bible spoke in the common language. As such, they did not worry about run-on sentences or other forms which we might take to be poor grammar. In recording this, the NAS has been most helpful.

5.   The New International Version.

This translation was the combined work of more than 100 translators and editors. In contrast to the NAS which sought a more literal rendering, the NIV set out to give a dynamic equivalence in translation.

We tried to avoid making a mechanical word for word rendition, which is the tendency of some versions that stress faithfulness to the original languages. Our translators always asked, "Knowing what the original writer was trying to communicate, how would we say the same thing today?" (Dr. Burton Goddard, interview in Eternity Magazine).

This translation has some excellent qualities. It is in modern English without resorting to slang. It is divided into paragraphs and is written in a flowing style for easy reading. It also gives the meaning behind figures of speech that might tend to be confusing if they were literally translated.

6.   The New King James Version.

For the Old Testament, the Stuttgart edition of Biblia Hebraica was used, although both the Septuagint, the Vulgate, and the Dead Sea Scrolls were consulted. The Textus Receptus was used for the New Testament, although marginal notes indicate where there is a deviation from either the Critical Text or from their Byzantine Family (referred to as the Majority Text).

7.   The New English Translation.

First published in 2004, this translation follows after the tradition of the New International Version in seeking to be a dynamic-equivalent translation, at the same time seeking to be more accurate to the Greek and Hebrew texts. Included in the translation were thousands of textual notes to further explain the translation.

COMPLETE VERSUS DYNAMIC EQUIVALENCE

One of the more recent debates has been whether a translation ought to be a complete equivalent or whether it is sufficient to be a dynamic equivalent of the original text.

- A Complete Equivalence seeks to preserve all the information in the text. This is a translation that attempts to be more literal in its rendition.

- Dynamic Equivalence commonly results in more of a paraphrase, yet it can better relate the better sense of the meaning.

The problem with Complete Equivalence is that, being overly literal, it leaves figures of speech and ambiguous customs unexplained and difficult to understand.

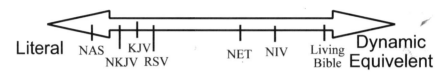

An example of this kind of literal versus paraphrase is seen in the way that various translations have rendered 1 Corinthians 13:8-11 where Paul uses the same Greek term on four consecutive occasions.

NAS	NIV	NKJV
Love never fails; but if there are gifts of prophecy, they will be done away; if there are tongues, they will cease; if there is knowledge, it will be done away. 9 For we know in part, and we prophesy in part; 10 but when the perfect comes, the partial will be done away. 11 When I was a child, I used to speak as a child, think as a child, reason as a child; when I became a man, I did away with childish things. (1 Corinthians 13:8-11).	*Love never fails. But where there are prophecies, they will cease; where there are tongues, they will be stilled; where there is knowledge, it will pass away. 9 For we know in part and we prophesy in part, 10 but when perfection comes, the imperfect disappears. 11 When I was a child, I talked like a child, I thought like a child, I reasoned like a child. When I became a man, I put childish ways behind me. (1 Corinthians 13:8-11).*	*Love never fails. But whether there are prophecies, they will fail; whether there are tongues, they will cease; whether there is knowledge, it will vanish away. 9 For we know in part and we prophesy in part. 10 But when that which is perfect has come, then that which is in part will be done away. 11 When I was a child, I spoke as a child, I understood as a child, I thought as a child; but when I became a man, I put away childish things. (1 Corinthians 13:8-11).*

There are times when such consistency of translation is neither possible or desirable, but the NAS has a much better track record for this sort of thing.

QUALITIES OF A GOOD TRANSLATION

There are so many versions of the Bible on the market today that the reader is often perplexed as to which translation he should choose. How can you choose a good translation? Are there criteria for picking a good translation of the Bible? I think that there are.

1.   It should be a True Translation.

It has become very popular to read a paraphrased edition of the Bible such as the Living Bible. It should be understood that this is not a translation from the original languages, but rather a paraphrase of the King James Version.

Other works such as the Amplified Bible or Wuest's Expanded Translation might be closer to the original language, but they still do not fit the requirement for a translation.

2.   The Theological Perspective of the Translators.

Every translation involves a certain amount of interpretation. You cannot interpret from one language into another without allowing some of your personal prejudices to influence your work. What is the perspective of the translators? Are they evangelical in their outlook? Are they trying to read into the text some particular theological viewpoint?

3.   The Readability of the Text.

There have been some translations that have either cluttered themselves with slang or are full of variant meanings to the point where they are difficult to use.

Translation	KJV	NKJV	NAS	NET	NIV
Readability	17th Century English	Old sentence structure	Formal style	Good	Excellent
Number of Translators	54	119	54	20	115
Type of Translation	Word for word			Dynamic Equivalence	
When first published	1611	1982	1971	2005	1978

What Does the Bible Say about Itself?

The Bible on The Bible

We believe the Bible to be the authoritative Word of God, not only because it was handed down to the fathers through the prophets, not only because it has preserved and copied and translated, but also because of what it says about itself.

THE CHARACTER OF THE BIBLE

1.   THE BIBLE IS THE WORD OF GOD: *Then the LORD stretched out His hand and touched my mouth, and the LORD said to me, "Behold, I have put My words in your mouth." (Jeremiah 1:9).*

The Bible is more than a book detailing men's thoughts about what God is like. It is God's communication to men. His words are transmitted to us through its pages. It is one thing to read theology books that tell about God; it is quite another to read God's love letters to you.

It is noteworthy to see the process by which this took place in the case of the book of Jeremiah.

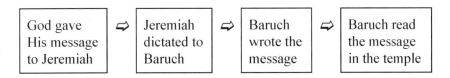

In spite of this process, it is the Word of God that is said to be

89

both the original message as well as the end of the process. This same process is seen in the New Testament in 1 Thessalonians 2:13 where Paul says, *"When you received from us the word of God"s message* [literally, "the word of hearing of God"], *you accepted it not as the word of men, but for what it really is, the word of God, which also performs its work in you who believe."*

2.   THE BIBLE IS A LIVING BOOK: *For the word of God is living and active and sharper than any two-edged sword, and piercing as far as the division of soul and spirit, of both joints and marrow, and able to judge the thoughts and intentions of the heart. (Hebrews 4:12).*

In what way is the Bible alive? It is alive in that it is the word of the Living God. It is alive in that it is active in its ministry to your heart. Like a surgeon's scalpel, it cuts through the facade to speak to the inner you. It gets down to the real heart of issues.

3.   THE BIBLE AS A PRESERVED BOOK: *The grass withers, the flower fades, but the word of our God stands forever (Isaiah 40:8).*

Voltaire was the French philosopher-scientist who, before he died in 1778, predicted that within 100 years, Christianity would be swept away from existence and pass into the obscurity of history. Within 50 years after his death, the Geneva Bible Society was using his house and printing press to produce stacks of Bibles.

4.   THE BIBLE AS A BOOK OF REALITY: *For we did not follow cleverly devised tales when we made known to you the power and coming of our Lord Jesus Christ, but we were eyewitnesses of His majesty (2 Peter 1:16).*

This Bible stands in complete distinction to the mythology of the era in which it was composed. You have only to read a little of the Greek or Roman or Egyptian or Babylonian mythologies to understand that there exists the greatest gulf between these and the Bible.

In contrast to such myths and fairy tales, Peter says, "The things about which we wrote to you are not theological speculation, but rather an eye witness account." John says the same thing when he speaks of *"what was from the beginning, what we have heard,*

90

what we have seen with our eyes, what we beheld and our hands handled, concerning the Word of Life" (1 John 1:1).

I love the testimony of Thomas regarding the resurrection. Here was a man who heard of the event and who then said, "I will not believe such news unless I am able to verify it through both visual and tactile means. I want to see and I want to touch and then I will believe."

- Moses is seen as the real author of the first five books: *Do not think that I will accuse you before the Father; the one who accuses you is Moses, in whom you have set your hope (John 5:45).*

  I think it fairly obvious that Moses did not write the very last chapter of Deuteronomy. This is the chapter that records his death. In such a case, it seems evident that the work of writing fell to the one who came after him; in this case it was likely Joshua who completed the work.

- Isaiah is a Unified Book: *That the word of Isaiah the prophet might be fulfilled, which he spoke, "LORD, who has believed our report? And to whom has the arm of the Lord been revealed?"* 39 *For this cause they could not believe, for Isaiah said again,* 40 *"He has blinded their eyes, and He hardened their heart; lest they see with their eyes, and perceive with their heart, and be converted, and I heal them."* 41 *These things Isaiah said, because he saw His glory, and he spoke of Him. (John 12:38-41).* Note that these quotes are taken from two separate sides of Isaiah that some modern critics wish to maintain are written by two separate authors.

5. THE BIBLE IS AN INERRANT BOOK: *If he called them gods, to whom the word of God came; and the Scripture cannot be broken (John 10:35).*

What does Jesus mean when He says that *the Scripture cannot be broken*? It is a reference to its continuing truth. There will never come a time when we say, "Ooops, the Bible really said the wrong thing when it came to that passage." Notice that He says this with reference to what could have been considered a problem passage to the Jews (Psalm 82:6). The point is that even such problem passages show no cracks in the trustworthiness of the Bible, but rather are only indicative of our own lack of understanding.

I've been studying and teaching the occasional class in Biblical Archaeology for over 30 years. One thing I've learned is that archaeologists change their theories about as often as I change my socks. That isn't to say that the study of archaeology is a bad thing. It is often helpful to us in our understanding of the Bible. But in all that time, the Bible has not been forced to change.

6. THE BIBLE IS A PROPOSITIONAL BOOK: *"Come now, and let us reason together," Says the LORD, "Though your sins are as scarlet, They will be as white as snow; Though they are red like crimson, They will be like wool." (Isaiah 1:18).*

God does not call us to abandon all sense of reason or thought when we come to Him. We are not to check in our brains at the door to the church and then pick them up again when we leave. He calls us to reason and to judge and to weigh out the facts of our salvation.

> *The Revelation of Jesus Christ, which God gave Him to show to His bond-servants, the things which must shortly take place; and He sent and communicated it by His angel to His bond-servant John, 2 who bore witness to the word of God and to the testimony of Jesus Christ, even to all that he saw. 3 Blessed is he who reads and those who hear the words of the prophecy, and heed the things which are written in it; for the time is near. (Revelation 1:1-3).*

Notice the propositional nature of this revelation. God says, "Here are the things that I am going to do. You read these things and hear them and heed them and you will be blessed."

7. THE BIBLE IS A NEEDFUL BOOK.

- To Direct my Life: *Thy word is a lamp to my feet, and a light to my path (Psalm 119:105).*
  Before I was afflicted I went astray, but now I keep Thy word (Psalm 119:67).

  Anyone who says that "all roads lead to Rome" has never done much traveling. I am by nature a map person. If I am traveling to an unfamiliar place, I get out a map to trace out what will be my path. The Bible is our roadmap for living. It is the light to my path.

I can still recall when one of the fire fighters from my department made the mistake of going up onto a barge without a flashlight. He couldn't see that a part of the deckplate had been removed and suffered a major injury when he stepped onto a floor that wasn't there.

- To Lift my Spirits: *I am exceedingly afflicted; Revive me, O LORD, according to Thy word (Psalm 119:107)*. While Hebrew 4:12 tells me that the Word of God is alive and powerful, here we read that this same word is able to enliven me.

- To Nourish my Soul: *And the tempter came and said to Him, "If You are the Son of God, command that these stones become bread." 4 But He answered and said, "It is written, 'Man shall not live on bread alone, but on every word that proceeds out of the mouth of God.'" (Matthew 4:3-4)*.

- To Announce His Plan of Redemption: *Surely the Lord God does nothing Unless He reveals His secret counsel To His servants the prophets (Amos 3:7)*. God always speaks when He institutes redemptive activity. And by the same token, when He does not institute new redemptive activity, there is no need for God to give new revelation.
This idea of the cessation of revelation ought not to surprise us. The revelatory process never came in an unbroken stream. It was always here a little and there a little (Isaiah 28:13). The fact that the Old Testament canon closed and that revelation ceased for a time sets up a paradigm for the closing of revelation in the New Testament.

Does that mean there will never be any new revelation? Not at all. I believe the Bible teaches that there will be such. It will take place at the return of Christ.

> *For now we see in a mirror dimly, but then face to face; now I know in part, but then I shall know fully just as I also have been fully known (1 Corinthians 13:12).*

THE ENDORSEMENT OF THE BIBLE

1.   JESUS ENDORSED THE OLD TESTAMENT: *Now He said to them, "These are My words which I spoke to you while I was still with you, that all things which are written about Me in the Law of Moses and the Prophets and the Psalms must be fulfilled." (Luke 24:44)*. Notice what is missing from this endorsement. Missing is the apocrypha -- those books known as the Deutero-canonicals. They were not considered to be a part of the Word of God.

2.   THE NEW TESTAMENT ANTICIPATED: *But when He, the Spirit of truth, comes, He will guide you into all the truth; for He will not speak on His own initiative, but whatever He hears, He will speak; and He will disclose to you what is to come. 14 He shall glorify Me; for He shall take of Mine, and shall disclose it to you. (John 16:13-14)*. With these words, Jesus promises that He would send the Holy Spirit who would direct the apostles in the communicating of God's new covenant teaching.

3.   PETER ENDORSED THE WRITINGS OF PAUL: *And regard the patience of our Lord to be salvation; just as also our beloved brother Paul, according to the wisdom given him, wrote to you, 16 as also in all his letters, speaking in them of these things, in which are some things hard to understand, which the untaught and unstable distort, as they do also the rest of the Scriptures, to their own destruction. (2 Peter 3:15-16)*.

        Notice the reference to *the rest of the Scriptures*. The KJV translates this as *the other Scripture*. When you speak of "the rest" of something or "the other" of a thing, you are implying that you have been previously speaking of that which has the same nature as that which is the rest of that thing. For example, if I speak of the members of my local church who are in attendance at a Sunday School class and then go on to speak of **the rest** of the members or the other members, I am implying that these others are also members.

        The implications are obvious. Peter speaks of Paul's writings and then goes on to speak of the rest of the Scriptures — the other Scriptures. He is placing the writings of Paul along side of the rest of the Scriptures.

94

The Bible	The 66 books of our Old and New Testament -- not including the apocrypha or other writings
Is	Not "becomes" when you read it and get a good feeling
The Word of God	2 Timothy 3:16 and 2 Peter 1:20-21 both show the source of the Scriptures as being from God
Is the Only	Not... • The Bible and the church • The Bible and Joseph Smith • The Bible and the Watchtower Society • The Bible and the Pope
Infallible	The Bible makes no mistakes; it is correct in all matters on which it comments
Rule	Obedience is not an option for the Christian
Of Faith and Practice	The Bible tells us... • What to believe • How to live

Acts 17 relates the account of Paul in Athens. While he was awaiting the rest of his company to catch up with him, he found himself in the midst of a philosophical discussion. He was brought to the Areopagus to present his views. What follows is a masterpiece of Christian apologetics. At the conclusion of his sermon, we read that *some men joined him and believed, among whom also were Dionysius the Areopagite and a woman named Damaris and others with them* (Acts 17:34).

The basis of faith for those who believed at the Areopagus was apostolic authority. They did not go and check the evidence of the resurrection or send a delegation to Jerusalem. They had the word of one apostle and it was enough. On the other hand, you have an entire New Testament. You have the written testimony of the apostles, the testimony of the church, and the witness of the Holy Spirit.

95

THE STUDY OF THE BIBLE

Why are there so many different interpretations when it comes to reading and understanding the Bible? It is not that God has been unclear in His communication; rather it is that we have problems in our reception.

This can be likened to the example of a radio and the transmitting antenna. It is entirely possible for the transmitter to be properly sending forth its signal and the radio receiver still not correctly receive the transmission.

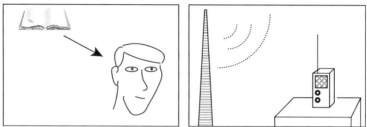

Is the problem in the transmission or the reception?

What is it that causes our "reception problems" when we come to read and study the Word of God? There are several areas:

1.   One reason is because there are so many interpreters who do not have the illumination of the Holy Spirit.

> *"But the soulish man receives not the things of the Spirit of God; for they are foolishness unto him, and he is not able to know them, because they are spiritually discerned." (I Corinthians 2:14).*

This verse points out that the unsaved man does not have the capacity or the inclination to receive the truths of Scripture. He can read through the Bible, even memorize the Bible, and still not know what it really says. To go back to our earlier example, I cannot pick up the radio waves moving through this room unless I am equipped to do so.

2.   Another reason for false interpretation is because of the interpreter's preconceived ideas.

A story is told about a captain in the U.S. Cavalry many years ago who was riding through a small town in Oklahoma. As he passed by a barn, he suddenly pulled his horse to a stop, because right there before him on the side of the barn were dozens of bull's eye circles drawn with chalk, and in the center of each one was a bullet hole.

About that time another man walked by and the captain asked him, "Do you know who is the marksman responsible for all those bull's eyes?" The passer-by nodded his head and said, "Yep, that would be Billy Hawkins. But he's a mite peculiar." The captain replied, "Well I don't care what he is like. The Cavalry can use anyone who can shoot that well."

"Yes," said the other man, "But I think you should know that Billy shoots first, then he comes over and draws those circles."

The above story is an illustration of what seems to be a common favorite pastime—making the Bible say what we want it to say. First, we shoot out a particular idea. Then we start circling verses to back up that idea. Conversely, the only legitimate approach to discovering biblical truth is to let the Bible speak for itself before we draw our conclusions. Likewise, we all would be wise to look at the many issues of our faith in their original context.

When one reads the Bible with a preconceived conclusion, then he is not subjecting himself to the guiding of the Holy Spirit which Christ has promised (John 16:13).

This is the problem with most cults and religions. They come to the Bible with a set of beliefs and then seek to find verses to prove them. We must be very careful not to do the same thing in our study habits.

There are a number of Bible Students who do not like the idea of abandoning their prejudices and beliefs when the study the Bible. "What if I come up with something that contradicts my beliefs?" If my study of the Bible leads me contrary to my beliefs, then I must throw away my beliefs. Remember, something is not true just because I believe it; or just because my teacher believes it; or just because my religion believes it. If there is no basis to my beliefs, then they are nothing but trash, and they must be discarded.

Let me also add that I do not immediately discard a doctrinal belief just because a verse at first glance seems to contradict it. As a mature believer I must be careful not to be blown about by "every wind of doctrine" (Ephesians 4:14-15).

3. We must realize that every believer has varying factors involved in his ability to interpret the Bible.

    a. Various intelligent quotas. A man who cannot read is going to have a greater problem studying and interpreting the Bible than a man who can.

b.   Various levels of Spiritual Maturity. A new believer will find that he has a much greater problem understanding Scripture than the mature believer.

c.   Time spent in Bible study. We have already seen the value of time spent in seeing what is there. A man who has been seeing what is there and looking for clues for 20 years will see much more and understand much more than a young Bible Student who has just started.

d.   Varied use of correct principles of interpretation. There are strict literary rules of interpretation that must be followed if we are to correctly understand the Scriptures.

While it is true that justification comes through faith and apart from works, the reception and understanding of the Scriptures require a diligent listening and effort of study.

Knowing God
The Ultimate Calling

> *Thus says the LORD, "Let not a wise man boast of his wisdom, and let not the mighty man boast of his might, let not a rich man boast of his riches; 24 but let him who boasts boast of this, that he understands and knows Me, that I am the LORD who exercises lovingkindness, justice, and righteousness on earth; for I delight in these things," declares the LORD. (Jeremiah 9:23-24).*

Prophets are not easy people with whom to get along. They are not politically correct. They have a way of coming in and upsetting the applecart. They are always saying things that no one wants to hear. They get under your skin.

Jeremiah was no exception to this rule. Preaching to a world that was on the brink of crisis, he spoke to a nation in need. The international superpowers of Babylon and Egypt were on a collision course that threatened to engulf the tiny kingdom of Judah that lay between them. Within Judah there were two political parties. On the one side was the pro-Egyptian party. They favored an alliance with Egypt. On the other side was the pro-Babylonian party who wanted to remain allied with Nebuchadnezzar, the king of Babylon. In the middle stood Jeremiah. He was the man who stood in the gap. He was the spokesman for God. He was the man for the crisis.

1   *Oh, that my head were waters,*
    And my eyes a fountain of tears,
    That I might weep day and night for the slain of the daughter
    of my people!
2   *O that I had in the desert a wayfarers' lodging place;*
    That I might leave my people, and go from them!

> *For all of them are adulterers, An assembly of treacherous men.*
>
> 3 *"And they bend their tongue like their bow;*
> *Lies and not truth prevail in the land; For they proceed from evil to evil,*
> *And they do not know Me," declares the LORD. (Jeremiah 9:1-3).*

Jeremiah has been called the Weeping Prophet. He wept over the sins of his people. He cried out his message to people who were on their way to destruction, pleading with them to turn back to God.

The society in which Jeremiah lived was given over to secularism and ungodliness. Religious pluralism was the order of the day. Premarital and extramarital sex was rampant. A man's word could no longer be trusted as truth and even written contracts were often dishonored. Crime was on the rise. Society was characterized by a lack of knowledge of God. Does this sound familiar? The society to which Jeremiah spoke is much like the society of today. We are a world in turmoil. One needs only to pick up the newspaper to read of wars and rumors of wars. It is enough to make any sane man want to pack up and move to a deserted island. This must be what Jeremiah had in mind when he wrote the following words:

> *O that I had in the desert a wayfarers' lodging place;*
> *That I might leave my people, and go from them! (Jeremiah 9:2a).*

Verse 3 has describes what I think was the root of the problem of the people to whom Jeremiah proclaimed his message.

> *"...and they do not know Me," declares the LORD. (Jeremiah 9:3c).*

This was a people who had a past that was rooted in a spiritual heritage. They were descended from Abraham, Isaac, and Jacob. They were the children of Israel. God had supernaturally delivered their ancestors from Egypt and preserved them as a foundling nation in the wilderness, giving them their national laws and decrees.

They had deliberately turned away from God. They had willfully determined not to recognize God as God. They had exchanged the one true God for gods of their own making. They had traded the absolute value system that God had given at Sinai for a "new morality" of their own design.

They had turned from the wisdom of God to follow after the wisdom of the world. The result was that they were about to be destroyed. They stood balanced upon the brink of chaos. If ever a passage of Scripture was relevant for us today, this is it.

This brings us to a question. What was the message that Jeremiah preached? If his situation was so much like our own, then what was his answer? What was he able to say to the nation that might have made a difference in the disastrous days that lay ahead?

> *Thus says the LORD, "Let not a wise man boast of his wisdom, and let not the mighty man boast of his might, let not a rich man boast of his riches; 24 but let him who boasts boast of this, that he understands and knows Me, that I am the LORD who exercises lovingkindness, justice, and righteousness on earth; for I delight in these things," declares the LORD. (Jeremiah 9:23-24).*

Man has dreamed up all sorts of ways to find meaning in life. Some have tried wisdom. Others have turned to power. Still others look to wealth. All of these fall short.

This is illustrated in the case of Solomon. Here was a man who had it all. He was the smartest man who ever lived. He made Einstein and Carl Barth and Stephen Hawking all look like second grade morons. He was the king in Israel when Israel was on top of the world. He had the wealth of the ancient world in his hands. He knew it all. He had done it all. He was the smartest and the most powerful and the richest and in the end it did not mean a thing. It was all empty.

There is only one way that you can remain sane in an insane world. It is the means given in verse 24. It is through the knowledge of God. There is no goal so worthy as knowing God. All other worldly endeavors pale to insignificance next to the goal of knowing God. Chuck Swindoll lists the following results of knowing God:

- It shapes our moral and ethical standards.
- It directly affects our response to pain and hardships.
- It motivates our response toward fortune, fame, power and pleasure.
- It gives us strength when we are tempted.
- It keeps us faithful and courageous when we are outnumbered.
- It enhances our worship and prompts our praise.
- It determines our lifestyle and dictates our philosophy.
- It gives meaning and significance to our worship.

- It sensitizes our conscience and creates the desire to be obedient.
- It stimulates hope to go on, regardless.
- It enables me to know what to reject and what to respect while I'm riveted to planet earth.
- It is the condition upon which everything rests (1986:93).

This brings us to the next question. If knowing God is that vital, then where do we begin? How are we to know God? It is only through reading His Word. God has revealed Himself to man. He has shown Himself in the Scriptures. Note that even in the midst of telling of the importance of knowing Himself, God reveals a part of Himself.

> *"But let him who boasts boast of this, that he understands and knows Me, that I am the LORD who exercises lovingkindness, justice, and righteousness on earth; for I delight in these things," declares the LORD. (Jeremiah 9:24).*

Notice how it is that God reveals Himself. He speaks of His character traits of *lovingkindness, justice, and righteousness*. These are not the only characteristics of the Lord, but these are traits in which He is said to delight. I believe He also delights when these traits are made evident in us.

If you have entered into God's family through the new birth, then you are now His child. It is only natural that there should be a family resemblance with your Heavenly Father.

You probably look at least a little like one or the other of your natural parents. Not only that, but it is likely that you have picked up more than a few of their mannerisms and habits. This is only natural. You grew up with them. Their personalities were imprinted on you from birth. By the same token, the more you come to know God, the more you will grow to become like Him.

Of course, our knowledge of God is limited, for we ourselves are limited. We are blinded by our sinful condition. But one day the blinders will be taken off. One day we shall see God face to face. One day we shall know God. And knowing Him, we shall become even more like Him.

> *Beloved, now we are children of God, and it has not appeared as yet what we shall be. We know that, when He appears, we shall be like Him, because we shall see Him just as He is. (1 John 3:2).*

Is Anybody Up There?

The Question of
The Existence of God

The fool has said in his heart, "There is no God..."
(Psalm 14:1a).

We had been talking at length when the subject of religion came up. As the conversation shifted and I expressed my belief in the God of the Bible, he said to me, "That is good that you have the belief you have. It is good for people to have faith. I don't believe the way you do, but it doesn't really matter as long as we believe something.

There is only one problem with that sort of relativistic thinking. The problem becomes evident if God really does exist. A little boy wrote the following letter to God:

Dear Mister God,
    What do you think about people who don't believe in you? By the way, someone else wants to know.
                                    A Friend

It is a good question. What does God think of people who don't believe in Him? The Bible does not ever attempt to present evidence for the existence of God. It does not begin in Genesis 1:1 with a five point outline on how we can know that there is a God. Instead the Scriptures assume that God does exist in the same way that any modern book naturally assumes the existence of its author.

When I began writing this article on the subject of God, I did not first

103

try to prove to you that I exist. I did not start with five points on the existence of John Stevenson. I merely assumed my own existence. After all, only a fool would read my article and conclude that I do not really exist. The same is true of the Bible. It assumes the existence of God. The handful of verses that even mention the concept of atheism deal with it in this manner.

> *The fool has said in his heart, "There is no God..." (Psalm 14:1a).*

This is not to say that such evidence for the existence of God (or of myself) is lacking. We shall look at five lines of evidence.

THE EVIDENCE OF CREATION

This line of evidence deals with the principle of first cause. In theological circles it is called the "Cosmological Argument," taken from the Greek word κοσμος (*kosmos*), meaning "world" or "universe." It is concerned with the origin of the universe. The principle is set forth in Romans 1:20.

> *For since the creation of the world His invisible attributes, His eternal power and divine nature, have been clearly seen, being understood through what has been made, so that they are without excuse. (Romans 1:20).*

The first line of evidence for God's existence is seen in the existence of the universe. You don't have to look in every corner of the world to find evidence for God. Such evidence is not hidden. It is plain for all to see. Paul says that it is *clearly seen*. The universe is an effect that demands an adequate cause.

Every cause has an effect that in turn becomes the cause of another effect. If we trace this back to the original cause, then we find a cause that has no prior cause.

Does there have to be a first cause? Is it possible that there was ever a time when there was nothing? If there was ever a time when nothing existed, then there could be nothing now.

Nothing + Nothing = Nothing

This is basic math. The fact that there is something today indicates that there has always been something. This brings us to another question. Is it possible that the universe has always been here — that matter is eternal in nature?

Interestingly enough, there have been scientists who have recognized the need for a first cause and, rather than admit the existence of God, they have suggested that the universe has always existed. The atheist Carl Sagan used to say, "The cosmos is all that is and ever was and ever will be."

If this is true, it means that the universe is infinitely old. We are not merely talking about being very old or even about being billions and billions of years old, for there is an infinite gap between anything that is very old and something that is infinitely old. If the universe is infinitely old, then everything that could possibly ever happen in the universe has already happened in the past. History has repeated itself on a planet just like this one an infinite number of times and with infinite variations. Each variation has been repeated in exactly the same way an infinite number of times. This is true of necessity if the universe is indeed infinitely old.

While such a belief staggers the imagination, it still cannot answer the problem of first cause — it only postpones it indefinitely.

The critic is quick to retort, "But who created the Creator? If there is a God, then where did He come from? Was there another God who existed earlier than God and who created Him?" The Bible provides the answer to such a question:

> "You are My witnesses," declares the LORD, "And My servant whom I have chosen, in order that you may know and believe Me, and understand that I am He. **Before me there was no God formed**, and there will be none after Me." (Isaiah 43:10).

God is eternal. He has had no beginning and He will have no end. He has always existed. There has never been a time when He did not exist. The fact that the universe is here points to the fact of His existence.

THE EVIDENCE FROM DESIGN

This line of evidence deals with the order and design of the universe. It is called the "Teleological Argument." The term "teleology" is a compound from the Greek words τελεος (*telos*, meaning "final") and λογος (*logos*, meaning "word" or "purpose"). It is the argument from design. It carries the Cosmological Argument one step further to point to the order and design of the universe.

Cosmological Argument	Teleological Argument
The fact of the existence of the universe points to a first cause: God	The presence of order and design in the universe points to an intelligent designer: God

The principle of design is illustrated in Psalm 19:1-3.

> *The heavens are telling of the glory of God;*
> *And their expanse is declaring the work of His hands.*
> *Day to day pours forth speech,*
> *And night to night reveals knowledge.*
> *There is no speech, nor are there words;*
> *Their voice is not heard. (Psalm 19:1-3).*

If one footprint in the sand convinced Robinson Crusoe that a person was on his island, then by the same logic we can be convinced that God created the world, for He left countless footprints on its surface.

The astronomer Kepler used to keep a complex model of the solar system in his office. The story is told of how an atheist once came to visit him and, upon seeing the model, inquired who had made it. He replied, "No one made it. It merely came into existence."

"You don't expect me to believe that!" retorted the atheist. "No," replied Kepler, "But you expect me to believe that our entire solar system came about by chance."

In my younger days, I used to drive a Pontiac Firebird. It was a creation. It had a purpose. Its design showed a function and an order. If I brought in a team of scientists who had never before seen an automobile; showed them all of its features, how the engine operated, how it was designed to carry people comfortably, its various features, and then if I told them that this machine had evolved merely by chance and that it had not been put together by an intelligent designer, what would be their reaction?

I can picture their faces if I were to tell them how this car just happened to come together into its present form by random amino acids joining together by chance after having been struck by a bolt of lightning. Yet there are people today who attempt to tell us that the design and order found in the universe came about by chance.

Look at the human body. Examine the functions of the eyes, the ears, the heart, the lungs and the brain. It contains a reciprocating pump, an automated cooling system, a multi-faceted sensory system and the most diverse and imaginative computer known to man. Did a design like this come about by chance?

> For every house is built by someone, but the builder
> of all things is God. (Hebrews 3:4).

I live in a house. It has doors and windows and rooms with various functions. It was obviously designed by a being with a certain degree of intelligence. It would be silly for me to believe that it merely came about by chance. So it is also with the world in which we live.

THE EVIDENCE FROM INTUITION

This is known as the Ontological Argument. It looks at the way man is. Studies in anthropology show that man is incurably God-conscious. He has an awareness within himself that God exists. The concept of God is prevalent in every human culture. It is true that this concept has often been warped by polytheism and idolatry, but the basic idea of the existence of God has been found in every culture.

> For even though they knew God, they did not honor
> Him as God, or give thanks; but they became futile in their
> speculations, and their foolish heart was darkened.
> Professing to be wise, they became fools, 23 and
> exchanged the glory of the incorruptible God for an image in
> the form of corruptible man and of birds and four-footed
> animals and crawling creatures. (Romans 1:21-23).

Notice what is said in verse 21: *They knew God.* Man has a God-consciousness. He inherently knows that God is there. But that is not all. Man has very deliberately turned away from the God who is there to go and to worship a god of his own making.

Man is unique in this area. No one has ever seen a chicken or a dog with a concept of God. No rooster ever built an altar to the Lord. No lion ever asked a blessing on the food he was about to eat. Even a praying mantis does not pray to the Lord.

God has created man in His image and has placed within him the concept of Himself. It is for this reason that men of every culture and nation have demonstrated this same God-concept.

It is also interesting to note how much effort and energy has been expended by atheists and agnostics to deny the existence of God. If there were no reason for man to believe in God, then it is unlikely that there would be so much fuss about it. Man would think about God as much as a caterpillar thinks about the Gettysburg Address.

The truth is that man has to fight the God-consciousness within himself if he is to hold to the position that God does not exist. Atheism takes real effort. This in itself is an evidence for God's existence.

THE EVIDENCE FROM MORALS

Man has a built-in sense of "ought." He feels that he ought to do what is right. He was born with this. He did not say at any time, "I think that I ought to have a sense of ought." It is not something that he has brought upon himself. It is universal to every tribe and people.

This does not mean that every man has a proper concept of right and wrong. Rather it means that every man feels that he really ought to do what is right, whatever that may entail.

In his book *Mere Christianity*, C. S. Lewis points out that people are always coming into conflict over some kind of standard of behavior that they expect the other person to observe. The quarrel might be major ("You stole my wife!") or it might be minor ("You can't sit here, these seats are saved"). In each case, one party is trying to show the other that they are wrong by appealing to this sense of right and wrong.

The remarkable thing is that the other party seldom replies that they don't care about the standard. Instead the argument usually ensues over the interpretation and application of that standard.

If there were no God to establish that there is right and wrong, then it would be illogical to speak of morals. There would be no way to say, "This is right" or "that is wrong." Left in this position, you would have to come to the place where you could talk about what is against society or what society does not like or even what you do not like, but you could no longer talk about what is right or wrong.

If there is no God and an Adolph Hitler is able to convince 51% of the population that we ought to eliminate a race of people, then who is to say that one group is right while another is wrong? If there is no God and if we are not made in the image of God, then what is the difference between killing a man and killing a cockroach? Does the size become the issue? Or is it intelligence? Does that make it right to kill a moron but wrong to shut off a computer?

All kinds of moral positions are irrational unless you realize that God exists and that He has made man in His image and has equipped him with a sense of right and wrong.

> *For when Gentiles who do not have the Law do instinctively the things of the Law, these, not having the Law, are a law to themselves, 15 in that they show the work of the Law written in their hearts, their conscience bearing witness, and their thoughts alternately accusing or else defending them (Romans 2:14-15).*

Even men who do not believe in God are troubled when they are confronted with evil and cruelty. This is the way that God has made them. They feel that to do right is better than to do wrong. They feel that good is better than evil and that truth is better than untruth. This sense that we ought to do right is still another evidence of the existence of God.

Cosmological Argument	Teleological Argument	Intuition Argument	Moral Argument
Points to the fact of existence and the need for a first cause	Points to the design of the universe requiring the need of a Designer	Points to the God-concept that is found in mankind in general	Points to man's sense of "ought"

These four lines of evidence all point to God's existence. But they are insufficient to tell us about the character of God. You cannot come to know God through nature or through looking at your own character any more than you can come to know an automobile manufacturer by driving a car that he has produced. You can only come to know God through His word -- the Bible. This is the final apologetic. It is the evidence from the Word of God.

THE EVIDENCE FROM THE WORD OF GOD

This is really the ultimate apologetic in giving evidence to the existence of God. We know that God is there because He has not been silent.

He has spoken to man. It is hard to maintain that someone does not exist when he is talking to you. Can you imagine someone saying to you, "Will you please stop talking so that I can tell people how you don't exist!"

Not only has God spoken, but He has put down what He wished to say into a book so that He could communicate to all men in all time. This is the most extraordinary book ever written. It has been translated into more languages than any other book in the world. No other book has ever come close to the Bible in its impact on human history.

1.   The Unity of the Bible.

In considering the unity of the Bible as to its message and composition, we must first note the diverse conditions under which it came about.

- The Bible was written in three different languages: Hebrew, Aramaic and Greek.
- The Bible was written by nearly 40 different human authors.
- These human authors wrote over a period of 1500 years: From about 1440 B.C. to A.D. 70.
- These human authors came from different strata of society: Kings, priests, prophets, a shepherd, fishermen, a tax collector, a physician, and a cup-bearer.
- These human authors wrote from different parts of the world: Israel, Egypt, Rome, Babylon, Ephesus, Greece, Syria, Assyria, the island of Patmos.
- These men wrote on hundreds of different topics, many of which were highly controversial and over which there might have been expressed a variety of opinions.

In spite of all of these factors, the Bible is a unified book. It contains no real contradictions in any of its teachings. That is not to say it is always easy to read, but that its teachings form a coherent whole.

If I were to take any ten people at random and ask them to write a paper on ten specific subjects, I would likely be guaranteed to have ten conflicting opinions.

When we examine the diverse backgrounds and settings of those who penned the pages of the Scriptures, we are forced to conclude that there was a single guiding force behind this writing.

2.   The Indestructibility of the Bible.

        No book in history has come under such violent and thorough
attack as the Bible. The Old Testament king Manasseh attempted to
obliterate the Bible. He succeeded in leading the people in the
worship of the false gods of the Canaanites, but he could not destroy
the Scriptures. It was after his death that a copy of the Scriptures was
found in the Temple and served as the basis for Josiah's revival.
        Antiochus Epiphanes, the Seleucid king who reigned in the
days of the Maccabees, declared it illegal to own a copy of the
Scriptures.

> *Now on the fifteenth day of Chislev, in the one*
> *hundred and forty-fifth year, they erected a desolating*
> *sacrilege upon the altar of burnt offering. They also*
> *built altars in the surrounding cities of Judah, 55 and*
> *burned incense at the doors of the houses and in the*
> *streets. 56 The books of the law which they found they*
> *tore to pieces and burned with fire. 57 Where the book*
> *of the covenant was found in the possession of any*
> *one, or if any one adhered to the law, the decree of*
> *the king condemned him to death. (1 Maccabees 1:54-*
> *57, RSV).*

        The penalty for owning a copy of the Scriptures was death.
But Antiochus failed to obliterate the Scriptures and he was
ultimately driven from Israel by the Hasmonean Revolt.
        In A.D. 303, the Roman Emperor Diocletian ordered all
Bibles to be burned. Within a few years Constantine came to the
throne and, not only legalized Christianity, but also ordered fifty
copies of the Bible to be hand-written at the expense of the state.
        The Synod of Toulouse, meeting in 1229, forbade translations
of the Bible into the common language as well as private ownership
of copies of the Bible. However Christians continued to work at
translating the Bible, even though they often paid with their lives.
        The French atheist Voltaire proclaimed that within a hundred
years from his death the Bible would be a forgotten relic and
Christianity would be a dead religion. It is reported that a hundred
years later, the printing press in his house was being used to print
Bibles.

3.   The Prophetic Accuracy of the Bible.

One of the greatest evidences that the Bible is the Word of God is in its prophetic accuracy. The Scriptures themselves refer to this type of evidence.

> *"Present your case," the LORD says. "Bring forward your strong arguments," the King of Jacob says.*
> *Let them bring forth and declare to us what is going to take place; as for the former events, declare what they were, that we may consider them, and know their outcome; or announce to us what is coming. 23 Declare the things that are going to come afterward, that we may know that you are gods; indeed, do good or evil, that we may anxiously look about us and fear together. (Isaiah 41:21-23).*

God presents this challenge to any who would claim divinity. He calls on any false gods to meet His argument. He presents predictive prophecy as proof of who He is. He will predict the future and it will come to pass with complete accuracy.

There is no other book in the world that contains the sort of prophetic substantiation that we find in the Bible. For example, consider the prophecies of the coming of the Messiah. For the sake of brevity, we will mention only a few.

- He would be born of a virgin: *Therefore the Lord Himself will give you a sign: Behold, a virgin will be with child and bear a son, and she will call His name Immanuel. (Isaiah 7:14).*
- He would be a descendant of the Royal House of King David: *"Behold, the days are coming," declares the LORD, "When I shall raise up for David a righteous Branch; and He will reign as king and act wisely and do justice and righteousness in the land." (Jeremiah 23:5).*
- He would be born in Bethlehem: *But as for you, Bethlehem Ephrathah, too little to be among the clans of Judah, from you One will go forth for Me to be ruler in Israel. His goings forth are from long ago, from the days of eternity. (Micah 5:2).*
- He would be preceded by a messenger: *A voice is calling, "Clear the way for the LORD in the wilderness; make smooth in*

the desert a highway for our God." (Isaiah 40:3).

- He would teach in Galilee: *But there will be no more gloom for her who was in anguish; in earlier times He treated the land of Zebulun and the land of Naphtali with contempt, but later on He shall make it glorious, by the way of the sea, on the other side of Jordan, Galilee of the Gentiles. 2 The people who walk in darkness will see a great light; those who live in a dark land, the light will shine on them. (Isaiah 9:1-2).*

- He would enter Jerusalem riding on a donkey: *Rejoice greatly, O daughter of Zion! Shout in triumph, O daughter of Jerusalem! Behold, your king is coming to you; He is just and endowed with salvation, humble, and mounted on a donkey, even on a colt, the foal of a donkey. (Zechariah 9:9).*

- He would be betrayed for 30 pieces of silver: *And I said to them, "If it is good in your sight, give me my wages; but if not, never mind!" So they weighed out thirty shekels of silver as my wages. 13 Then the LORD said to me, "Throw it to the potter, that magnificent price at which I was valued by them." So I took the thirty shekels of silver and threw them to the potter in the house of the LORD. (Zechariah 11:12-13).* Note that the prophecy even goes so far as to specify what would become of the money used for this betrayal.

- His hands and His feet would be pierced and lots would be cast for his clothing: *For dogs have surrounded me; A band of evildoers has encompassed me; They pierced my hands and my feet. 17 I can count all my bones. They look, they stare at me; 18 they divide my garments among them, and for my clothing they cast lots. (Psalm 22:16-18). And I will pour out on the house of David and on the inhabitants of Jerusalem, the Spirit of grace and of supplication, so that they will look on Me whom they have pierced (Zechariah 12:10a).*

- He would be buried in a rich man's tomb but would die with the wicked: *His grave was assigned with wicked men, yet He was with a rich man in His death (Isaiah 53:9a).*

- He would not remain in the grave: *For Thou wilt not abandon my soul to Sheol; neither wilt Thou allow Thy Holy One to undergo decay (Psalm 16:10).*

These are only ten prophecies out of an estimated 300 that deal with the coming of the Messiah. The chances of only these ten being fulfilled by any one man are astronomical. The conclusion with which we are left is inescapable. This is the Word of God.

4.   The Scientific Accuracy of the Bible.

This is probably one of the biggest areas of attack against the Bible today. It is often argued that the Bible does not agree with science. But I must ask the question, "Which science? Is it the science of Plato and Aristotle? How about the science of the Dark Ages? Is it the science of a hundred years ago? How about the science of twenty years ago?"

Since is always changing. Science is always finding itself in need of a n update. Its errors always stand in need of correction. A science textbook of even ten years of age is completely outdated. It needs to be rewritten.

The Bible is not like science. It has gone for nearly 2000 years without any need for corrections or revisions. It has stood the test of time. It is as accurate today as it was on the day in which it was penned.

That is not to say that men's interpretation of the Bible have always been correct. There have been erroneous interpretations of the Bible that were contradicted by proper science. When Galileo stood against the church and maintained that the earth revolves around the sun, he was contradicting the church and its interpretation of the Bible, but there was no such contradiction with the Bible itself.

It is of interest to see what the Bible does not say. The Bible does not contain any of the false cosmologies that were taught throughout the ancient world.

- The people of ancient India believed that the earth was a huge tray supported on the backs of three giant elephants who stood on the shell of a great turtle who swam in a cosmic sea.
- The Egyptians taught that the sky was a heavenly Nile along which Ra, the sun god, sailed each day.
- The Babylonians described a disk-shaped earth surrounded by a moat of sea. Beyond the sea, the inverted bowl of the sky held its borders.

In contrast to such views of the "modern science" of that day and age, what does the Bible say about the nature of the earth?

*It is He who sits above the **vault** of the earth,*

And its inhabitants are like grasshoppers,
Who stretches out the heavens like a curtain
And spreads them out like a tent to dwell in. (Isaiah
40:22).

Other translations have translated this same passage a bit more literally:

KJV	*It is he that sitteth upon the **circle** of the earth*
NIV	*He sits enthroned above the **circle** of the earth*
RSV	*It is he who sits above the **circle** of the earth*
LXX	ὁ κατέχων τὸν γῦρον τῆς γῆς

But that is not all. Not only do we see the Scriptures presenting the concept of the circularity of the earth, but Job adds an additional aspect.

He stretches out the north over empty space,
And hangs the earth on nothing. (Job 26:7).

The fact that the earth was supported in empty space was taught in the Scriptures at a time when "modern science" taught something completely different.

Thus we find that when scientists, in their endless search for the truth, climb their way up the towering heights of knowledge, they finally reach a pinnacle only to find that theologians have been patiently waiting there for hundreds of years.

5.   The Historical Accuracy of the Bible.

The Bible has come under countless attacks as to its historical accuracy. This has been especially the case among archaeologists. Yet the father of modern archaeology, Dr William Albright, although himself an unbeliever, had this to say about the Bible:

The excessive skepticism shown toward the

Bible by important historical schools of the eighteenth and nineteenth centuries, certain phases of which still appear periodically, has been progressively discredited. Discovery after discovery has established the accuracy of innumerable details, and has brought increased recognition to the value of the Bible as a source of history (1960).

The Bible has been shown to be historically accurate, even when modern historians have not. For example, the Bible describes a great nation of warriors known as the Hittites (2 Kings 7:6). For hundreds of years, the existence of the Hittites was denied by secular historians and critics of the Bible. It was not until 1906 that Professor Hugo Winckler discovered and translated certain tablets found in modern-day Turkey that historians began to recognize the existence of the great Hittite Empire that ruled Anatolia for nearly a thousand years.

A more recent example is seen in those minimalists who maintained that King David was only a mythological figure with no basis in reality. Beginning in the 1990's, archaeologists began to uncover several different inscriptions referring to בית־דוד, the "house of David."

6.   The Subjective Evidence of the Bible.

Perhaps the most convincing evidence for the Bible is the way in which it has changed the lives of men as no other book ever has. It may be argued that this sort of evidence is by its very nature subjective. But we have already seen that the Christian has an objective reality to back up and to provide the basis for his subjective experience. Josh McDowell gives this illustration:

> *A student comes into the room and says, "Guys, I have a stewed tomato in my right tennis shoe. This tomato has changed my life. It has given me peace and love and joy that I have never experienced before, not only that, but I can now run the 100 yard dash in 10 seconds flat."*
>
> *It is hard to argue with a student like that if his life backs up what he says, especially if he runs circles around you on the track* (1972:339).

Perhaps you have never experienced the work of God in your life. You can. This is the message of the Bible. It is that God sent His Son to the world to die for sins so that we could come to Him

> *For God so loved the world, that He gave His only begotten Son, that whoever believes in Him should not perish, but have eternal life (John 3:16).*

This is where Biblical Christianity departs from every major religion in the world. Instead of an outward action, God demands an inward attitude. Good works are not the issue. Church membership is not the issue. Not even sin is the issue. Jesus Christ is the issue. You are called to come to Jesus Christ today. *Truly, truly, I say to you, he who believes has eternal life* (John 6:47).

God's Calling Card
The Names of God

Glory in His holy name;
Let the heart of those who seek the LORD be glad (Psalm
105:3).

In the oriental world, a name meant much more than just a verbal designation or a vocal verbalizing of sounds. A name told something of the character of the person to whom it belonged. To know the name of a person was to have power over him. The names of the various pagan deities were used to call forth their power.

The names of God are not man-made. We read in Genesis 2 of how God created the animals and brought them to man and how it was man who named them. But this is not the case in the names of God. They are given by God Himself. This suggests that they tell us something about Him.

ELOHIM - THE STRONG ONE

For the choir director; on the Gittith. A Psalm of Asaph
Sing for joy to God our strength;
Shout joyfully to the God of Jacob. (Psalm 81:1).

On the day of the Feast of Tabernacles, the Temple Choir Director would issue this summons to call the people for this special day of worship and celebration. Their voices would echo over the city walls and out across the hills of Judah. From all over the country, the people would come to Jerusalem. The call was for the people of Israel to come and to worship Elohim.

1.   The Various Uses of Elohim.

The use of the Hebrew term Elohim is not used exclusively for the One True God, although the vast majority of times it is used in the Old Testament it does refer to the Deity.

Refers to God	Genesis 1:1. *In the beginning **God** created the heavens and the earth*
Refers to false gods	Exodus 34:17. *You shall make for yourself no molten **gods**.* Numbers 25:2. *For they invited the people to the sacrifices of their **gods**, and the people ate and bowed down to their **gods***
Moses is said to stand in the place of God to Pharaoh	Exodus 7:1. *Then the LORD said to Moses, "See, I make you as **God** to Pharaoh, and your brother Aaron shall be your prophet."* Note that the word "as" may be understood, but is not a part of the original text.
Possibly a reference to human judges	Exodus 22:7-9. *If a man gives his neighbor money or goods to keep for him, and it is stolen from the man's house, if the thief is caught, he shall pay double. 8 If the thief is not caught, then the owner of the house shall appear before the **judges**, to determine whether he laid his hands on his neighbor's property. 9 For every breach of trust, whether it is for ox, for donkey, for sheep, for clothing, or for any lost thing about which one says, 'This is it,' the case of both parties shall come before the **judges**; he whom the **judges** condemn shall pay double to his neighbor.* Psalm 82:6. *I said, "You are **gods**, and all of you are sons of the Most High."*
Used of something that is great	Jonah 3:3. *So Jonah arose and went to Nineveh according to the word of the LORD. Now Nineveh was **an exceedingly great city** (עִיר־גְּדוֹלָה לֵאלֹהִים), a three days' walk.*

In each of these instances, there is an underlying idea of strength and majesty, even when it is wrongly ascribed as in the case of the false gods.

2.   The Various Forms of Elohim.

The Hebrew language has three different forms of the word "God." Each one is correctly translated "God" in our English Bibles, yet each has a slightly different connotation.

• El (אֵל).

This is the Hebrew word for "strength" It describes one who is strong. In this way, it is often used of God. Of the 250 times it is used of God in the Old Testament, 55 are in the book of Job. Many of the other instances take place in early poetic sources: *Then she called the name of the LORD who spoke to her, "Thou art a **God** who sees"; for she said, "Have I even remained alive here after seeing Him?" (Genesis 16:13).*

• Eloha (אֱלוֹהַ).

This is a compound name made up of the joining together of *El* (אֵל), the word for "God" and *Alah* (אָלָה), "to swear or take an oath." This form is used about 57 times in the Old Testament, most often in the book of Job amidst the dialogues of Job and his three friends: *May that day be darkness; Let not **God** above care for it, Nor light shine on it. (Job 3:4).*

• Elohim (אֱלֹהִים).

This is the most commonly used of these three forms. It is found 2570 times in the Old Testament. It is the plural form of אֱלוֹהַ.

This has been generally explained as a "plural of majesty" or "plural of intensity." But all the related ancient Near Eastern cultures use the singular form *El* without a single case of *Elohim* -- there are no ancient Near Eastern parallels to support this usage. Furthermore, each time the Old Testament speaks of a **single** false god, it uses the term *El* instead of *Elohim*. On the other hand, it should be recognized that plural nouns with singular verbs may also be applied to humans: *But Jonathan answered and said to Adonijah, "No! Our **lord** (אֲדֹנֵינוּ) is the* plural form of אָדוֹן, "lord") *King David has made Solomon king." (1 Kings 1:43)*.

We should also add that when *Elohim* is used to refer to the true God, it is almost always accompanied by a singular verb and pronoun: *In the beginning God* (אֱלֹהִים) *created* (literally, "HE created") *the heavens and the earth. (Genesis 1:1)*. Another suggested translation could read: "In the beginning *Elohim* Himself created the heavens and the earth."

This means that we should probably not see the plural form of Elohim as an evidence for the Trinity. We do not believe in three gods. There is only one God. The plural use of *Elohim* seems instead to be a plural of majesty and immensity. This is indicated by the fact that it nearly always is used with a singular verb. One notable exception to this rule is found in Genesis 1:26 where we see *Elohim* used in the context of a plural pronoun:

> *Then God* (Elohim) *said, "Let **Us** make man in **Our** image, according to **Our** likeness; and let them rule over the fish of the sea and over the birds of the sky and over the cattle and over all the earth, and over every creeping thing that creeps on the earth." (Genesis 1:26)*.

It has been suggested that the plurality pictured here and again in Genesis 11:7 is that of the Trinity. This is grammatically possible from the text. On the other hand, this could also be a similar usage to the plural of majesty and immensity.

The world today has become very irreverent toward God. He is called "the man upstairs." Others wish to think of Him as an impersonal force. Philosophers have declared that God is dead or at least irrelevant. These are all false concepts of God. They miss some of the majesty of God. They do not describe the *Elohim* — the Strong One. They do not describe the Creator of heaven and earth. They do not describe the One who holds the universe together by His own strength. In the same way, our own thoughts of God are often too human. We tend to put our own attributes into our concept of God.

• Have you ever thought to yourself: "I don't know how God puts up with me"? This is a wrong concept of God. God does not put up with anyone. He is absolutely righteous and holy. He does not put up with sin. He deals with sin. He sent His Son to die for sin. He judged sin on the cross.

• Have you ever prayed: "Lord, if you are able to bring this to pass..." To whom do you think you are praying? It is the Strong One -- the God who can accomplish anything and for whom nothing is impossible.

Your concept of God is important. It will determine your response to God. It is only as you have a proper concept of God that you will be able to produce proper fruit in your life.

A shallow, plastic knowledge of God will result in shallow, plastic fruit in your Christian life. Have you ever seen plastic fruit? It looks good. It is shiny and polished. It is only when you try to bite into it that you find out that it is false. It is only an illusion of the real thing. You need to know the real God and have a real relationship with Him so that He can produce real fruit in your life. You need to recognize the God who is there. You need to get to know the Strong One.

JEHOVAH - THE COVENANT-KEEPING GOD

Though the name "Jehovah" or "Yahweh" is used in the early pages of the Bible, it is not until the book of Exodus that the meaning of the name is explained. It takes place in the context of God's revelation of Himself to Moses.

> *1 Now Moses was pasturing the flock of Jethro his father-in-law, the priest of Midian; and he led the flock to the west side of the wilderness, and came to Horeb, the mountain of God.*
>
> *2 And the angel of the LORD appeared to him in a blazing fire from the midst of a bush; and he looked, and behold, the bush was burning with fire, yet the bush was not consumed. 3 So Moses said, "I must turn aside now, and see this marvelous sight, why the bush is not burned up."*
>
> *4 When the LORD saw that he turned aside to look, God called to him from the midst of the bush, and said, "Moses, Moses!" And he said, "Here I am." 5 Then He said, "Do not come near here; remove your sandals from your feet, for the place on which you are standing is holy ground." 6 He said also, "I am the God of your father, the God of Abraham,*

*the God of Isaac, and the God of Jacob." Then Moses hid his
face, for he was afraid to look at God. (Exodus 3:1-6).*

The scene is the Sinai Desert. Into this hot, arid region comes Moses. He is a fugitive from Egypt, having escaped from the consequences of a past murder. He has found refuge in the tents of a wealthy sheik named Jethro. Over the years, he has taken a wife from among the daughters of Jethro and he has settled down to become a simple shepherd.

The years pass by until one day when Moses comes upon a strange sight. It is a bush burning on the slopes of a mountain. The strange thing is not the bush or the fact that it is burning, but that it continues to burn without burning up the bush. His curiosity aroused, Moses moves closer to investigate. As he does, God speaks to him from the midst of the bush.

God first instructs Moses to show proper reverence for the ground upon which he stands. He is to do this by removing his sandals. Forever afterward, the priests would enter the Temple of God barefoot in order to show the same reverence. Next the Lord identifies Himself to Moses:

> *He said also, "I am the God of your father, the God
> of Abraham, the God of Isaac, and the God of Jacob." Then
> Moses hid his face, for he was afraid to look at God. (Exodus
> 3:6).*

Moses had come out of Egypt. The land of Egypt was filled with gods. There was a god of the harvest and a god for the rain and a god for the sun and a god for the river and a god for the cattle. There was a god for everything in Egypt. But God identifies Himself as the God of Abraham and the God of Isaac and the God of Jacob. He is the God of Moses' ancestors.

Hundreds of years earlier, God had appeared to Abraham and had promised Him certain things. The entire history of the Israelite people had been laid out in a detailed prophecy:

> *And God said to Abram, "Know for certain that your
> descendants will be strangers in a land that is not theirs,
> where they will be enslaved and oppressed four hundred
> years. 14 But I will also judge the nation whom they will
> serve; and afterward they will come out with many
> possessions. 15 And as for you, you shall go to your fathers in
> peace; you shall be buried at a good old age. 16 Then in the
> fourth generation they shall return here, for the iniquity of the
> Amorite is not yet complete." (Genesis 15:13-16).*

Along with those promises, God had involved Himself in an elaborate covenant ritual, binding Himself to Abraham with a legal contract. This involved an ancient ceremony in which several animals were killed and their carcasses cut in two and placed in a long row. The parties involved in the covenant would then walk down the center aisle between the dead carcasses while reciting the terms of the covenant. The idea was that if either party broke the terms of the covenant, he would suffer a similar fate to those animals who had been killed and cut asunder.

This is the kind of covenant into which God had bound Himself to Abraham. He had instructed Abraham to cut the animals in two and arrange them into two groups. Then the presence of the Lord moved down the row between the pieces of the animals as He recited the terms of the covenant.

> *And it came about when the sun had set, that it was very dark, and behold, there appeared a smoking oven and a flaming torch which passed between these pieces. 18 On that day the LORD made a covenant with Abram, saying, "To your descendants I have given this land, From the river of Egypt as far as the great river, the river Euphrates: 19 the Kenite and the Kenizzite and the Kadmonite 20 and the Hittite and the Perizzite and the Rephaim 21 and the Amorite and the Canaanite and the Girgashite and the Jebusite." (Genesis 15:17-21).*

Now God tells Moses that He is the same God who made the covenant with Abraham. He is the same God who repeated the same promises to Isaac and to Jacob. He is the God of Israel, even though they have become enslaved in Egypt. He is known as the God who promises. He has not forgotten His promises. He is now going to bring them to fulfillment. Notice what He says to Moses.

> *And the LORD said, "I have surely seen the affliction of My people who are in Egypt, and have given heed to their cry because of their taskmasters, for I am aware of their sufferings. 8 So I have come down to deliver them from the power of the Egyptians, and to bring them up from that land to a good and spacious land, to a land flowing with milk and honey, to the place of the Canaanite and the Hittite and the Amorite and the Perizzite and the Hivite and the Jebusite. (Exodus 3:7-8).*

Do you see it? These are the same words that the Lord had spoken to Abraham. He now says that He is going to keep the promise that He had made to Abraham. The terms of that covenant will be fulfilled. What God had promised so many hundreds of years earlier would now come to pass.

God is going to deliver the Israelites from their bondage in Egypt. He is going to lead them through the wilderness. He is going to bring them to the land of promise.

Moses is called to return to Egypt with this message. Up to this point, Moses has been nodding his head and thinking to himself, "This is quite a good thing." But now he has an objection:

> *Then Moses said to God, "Behold, I am going to the sons of Israel, and I shall say to them, 'The God of your fathers has sent me to you.' Now they may say to me, 'What is His name?' What shall I say to them?"*
>
> *And God said to Moses, "I AM WHO I AM"; and He said, "Thus you shall say to the sons of Israel, 'I AM has sent me to you.'"*
>
> *And God, furthermore, said to Moses, "Thus you shall say to the sons of Israel, 'The LORD, the God of your fathers, the God of Abraham, the God of Isaac, and the God of Jacob, has sent me to you.' This is My name forever, and this is My memorial-name to all generations." (Exodus 3:13-15).*

This was a significant question. In the ancient world, the name of a person or a city or a deity was not without meaning. The name of a person would often describe an attribute of that person. Likewise, the name of a deity would usually indicate some specific attribute of that deity.

For example, the name "Jesus" is a Greek rendition of the Hebrew name "Joshua" and means "Yahweh saves." Thus, to believe in the name of Jesus is to believe in the saving work which His name implies (John 1:12; Acts 3:16). As Moses confronts God, he asks for a name. There are two answers given.

1.   אֶהְיֶה אֲשֶׁר אֶהְיֶה ("I AM WHO I AM").

This first answer is the repetition of the verb "I AM." This is the Qal imperfect of הָיָה ("to be"). The fact that the imperfect is used means that we could translate this as "I WILL BE WHO I WILL BE." The name indicates the attribute of continuing existence. He describes Himself as the Continuing God.

The central importance of this verse is further emphasized by the fact that it serves as the pivotal point of a chiastic parallel:

> Dr. Barton Payne suggests that this is to be taken as a paranomasia, a play on words rather than an etymology.

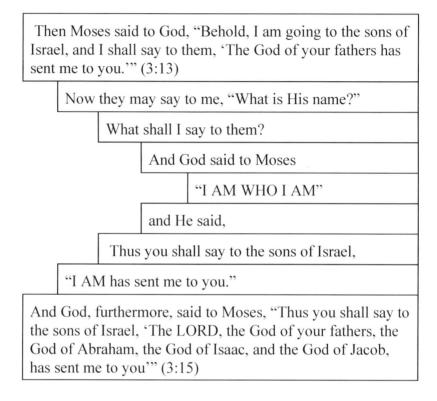

Then Moses said to God, "Behold, I am going to the sons of Israel, and I shall say to them, 'The God of your fathers has sent me to you.'" (3:13)

Now they may say to me, "What is His name?"

What shall I say to them?

And God said to Moses

"I AM WHO I AM"

and He said,

Thus you shall say to the sons of Israel,

"I AM has sent me to you."

And God, furthermore, said to Moses, "Thus you shall say to the sons of Israel, 'The LORD, the God of your fathers, the God of Abraham, the God of Isaac, and the God of Jacob, has sent me to you'" (3:15)

When you see a chiasm, you are supposed to look at the center to see if there is a pivotal statement. Everything in this paragraph is designed to focus our attention upon this central statement about God: "I am who I am."

2.	יהוה ("THE LORD" or "YAHWEH").

It appears that the י is preformative to the root word הוה, the older form and rare synonym of הוה ("to be") which would make this a 3rd masculine singular Qal imperfect ("HE WILL BE"). This would be a reference to the previous phrase "I AM WHO I AM."

A problem arises in that יהוה is said to be the God of Abraham, the God of Isaac, and the God of Jacob, even though in Exodus 6:3 the Lord says that He was not known to Abraham, Isaac and Jacob by the name יהוה.

126

*God spake further to Moses, and said to him,
"I am the LORD; 3 and I appeared to Abraham,
Isaac, and Jacob, as God Almighty, but by my name,
LORD, I did not make Myself
known to them." (Exodus 6:2-3).*

As early as Genesis 4:26 we read that "men began to call upon the name of יהוה." There also seem to be references where the name יהוה was spoken to Abraham (Genesis 18:14; 22:14). We can surmise one of two possibilities:

> Only five examples of the older form of הוה are found in the Old Testament Hebrew (Genesis 27:29; Nehemiah 6:6; Ecclesiastes 2:22; 11:3; Isaiah 16:4), although הוה is regularly used in the Aramaic portions of the Bible.

• This statement indicates that the Patriarchs had an incomplete understanding of the name and its relation to the verb יהיה which had just recently been revealed in Exodus 3:14.

• The name was not emphasized in the days of the Patriarchs. In favor of this latter premise, it is noted that, although יהוה is used often in Genesis, it usually appears in the midst of a narrative rather than in a place where one of the Patriarchs is either speaking or is being addressed. On the other hand, Laban is pictured as using the term יהוה as he enters into a covenant with Jacob (Genesis 31:49). Indeed, even the mother of Moses has a name which consists of a compound with יהוה in its abbreviated form יָד (Jokhebed).

The name יהוה is further described in Exodus 3:14-15 as the name of the Lord "forever" and as His "memorial name to all generations" (Exodus 3:15). The Hebrew text presents this as more of a parallel:

This is My name...	And	This way I am to be remembered...
Forever.		To generation after generation.

More than a thousand years after Moses, a Galilean rabbi

stood in the temple in Jerusalem and boldly proclaimed, "Before Abraham was, I AM" (John 8:58), echoing the same ἐγώ εἰμι of the Septuagint (the LXX reads ἐγώ εἰμι ὁ ὤν, adding the present participle to εἰμι to say in effect, *"I am the Existing One"*). The use of the Greek present tense accords with the Hebrew imperfect of Exodus 3:14, both indicating a continuing state of existence. The effect is to show that God is the same yesterday, today, and forever.

That means we can read of the way God acted in ages past and we can be assured that He is the same. He has not changed. He can still be trusted to care for His people.

OTHER YAHWEHIST NAMES FOR GOD

Name	Meaning	Passage
Jehovah MeKaddesh	The Lord who sanctifies	*And you shall keep My statutes and practice them; I am the LORD who sanctifies you. (Leviticus 20:8).*
Jehovah Tsidkenu	The Lord our righteousness	*"Behold, the days are coming," declares the LORD, "When I shall raise up for David a righteous Branch; And He will reign as king and act wisely And do justice and righteousness in the land. 6 In His days Judah will be saved, And Israel will dwell securely; And this is His name by which He will be called, 'The LORD our righteousness.'" (Jeremiah 23:5-6).*
Jehovah Jireh	The Lord shall Provide	*Then Abraham raised his eyes and looked, and behold, behind him a ram caught in the thicket by his horns; and Abraham went and took the ram, and offered him up for a burnt offering in the place of his son. 14 And Abraham called the name of that place The LORD Will Provide, as it is said to this day, "In the mount of the LORD it will be provided." (Genesis 22:13-14).*

128

Jehovah Rapha	The Lord Your Healer	*Then Moses led Israel from the Red Sea, and they went out into the wilderness of Shur; and they went three days in the wilderness and found no water. 23 And when they came to Marah, they could not drink the waters of Marah, for they were bitter; therefore it was named Marah. 24 So the people grumbled at Moses, saying, "What shall we drink?" Then he cried out to the LORD, and the LORD showed him a tree; and he threw it into the waters, and the waters became sweet. There He made for them a statute and regulation, and there He tested them. 26 And He said, "If you will give earnest heed to the voice of the LORD your God, and do what is right in His sight, and give ear to His commandments, and keep all His statutes, I will put none of the diseases on you which I have put on the Egyptians; for I, the LORD, am your healer." (Exodus 15:22-26).*
Jehovah Ra'ah	The Lord is my Shepherd	*The LORD is my shepherd, I shall not want (Psalm 23:1).*
Jehovah Shalom	The Lord is Peace	*When Gideon saw that he was the angel of the LORD, he said, "Alas, O Lord God! For now I have seen the angel of the LORD face to face." 23 And the LORD said to him, "Peace to you, do not fear; you shall not die." Then Gideon built an altar there to the LORD and named it The LORD is Peace. (Judges 6:22-24a).*
Jehovah Shammah	The Lord is There	*The city shall be 18,000 cubits round about; and the name of the city from that day shall be, "The LORD is there." (Ezekiel 48:35).*
Jehovah Nissi	The Lord is my Banner	*And Moses built an altar, and named it The LORD is My Banner (Exodus 17:15).*

| Jehovah Sabaoth | The Lord of Hosts | *Then David said to the Philistine, "You come to me with a sword, a spear, and a javelin, but I come to you in the name of the LORD of hosts, the God of the armies of Israel, whom you have taunted (1 Samuel 17:45).* *And David arose and went with all the people who were with him to Baale-judah, to bring up from there the ark of God which is called by the Name, the very name of the LORD of hosts who is enthroned above the cherubim (2 Samuel 6:2).* *Who is this King of glory? The LORD of hosts, He is the King of glory (Psalm 24:10).* |

ELOHISTIC NAMES FOR GOD

El Elyon	God Most High	*I will cry to God Most High, To God who accomplishes all things for me. (Psalm 57:2).* See also Genesis 14:18-22.
El Shaddai	God Almighty	*Now when Abram was ninety-nine years old, the LORD appeared to Abram and said to him, "I am God Almighty; walk before Me, and be blameless." (Genesis 17:1).*
El Olam	Everlasting God	*And Abraham planted a tamarisk tree at Beersheba, and there he called on the name of the LORD, the Everlasting God (Genesis 21:23).*

GOD AS FATHER

There is a sense in which all men can be said to be the offspring of God in that He is the Creator of all that exists (Acts 17:29). Yet in a very strict sense, it is only in the pages of the New Testament that we are presented with the specific theme of God as our Father. When Jesus was asked by His disciples as to how they ought to pray, He began with this very personal title for God: "Our Father who art in heaven..." The words of Jesus are echoed in an Old Testament promise that is cited by the Apostle Paul as he calls Christians to a life of holiness:

> *"Therefore, come out from their midst and be separate," says the Lord. "And do not touch what is unclean; And I will welcome you. 18 And I will be a father to you, And you shall be sons and daughters to Me," Says the Lord Almighty. (2 Corinthians 6:17-18).*

That which was only hinted at in the prophets today comes to us in full fruition as we are able to turn to the Lord as our Heavenly Father.

> *For all who are being led by the Spirit of God, these are sons of God. 15 For you have not received a spirit of slavery leading to fear again, but you have received a spirit of adoption as sons by which we cry out, "Abba! Father!" 16 The Spirit Himself bears witness with our spirit that we are children of God, 17 and if children, heirs also, heirs of God and fellow heirs with Christ, if indeed we suffer with Him in order that we may also be glorified with Him. (Romans 8:14-17).*

What Is God Like?

The Nature And Attributes of God

A little girl was lying on the floor with her crayons and a large drawing pad when her father came into the room and asked, "What are you drawing, honey?" Without looking up, she replied, "I'm drawing a picture of God." Her father smiled and said, "But no one knows what God looks like." Without a pause, she retorted, "They will when I am finished."

What am I? Those who know me know that I am a man, a father and a husband. In the working world I have been known by my profession. Others know me as a Christian, a Bible teacher and a servant of God. But what am I really?

The truth is that I am more than just the sum total of my attributes. I am more than a list of things. They are descriptive of what I am, but they are not me. In the same way, God is described by His attributes, but He is much more than just a list of attributes. We often make the mistake of trying to relegate God to a place in a notebook, but He is too big for that. And yet, if we are to come to know about God, we must begin with these descriptive attributes. He will be more than this list, but He will not be less than it describes.

> Our little systems have their day,
>> They have their day and cease to be.
>> They are but broken lights of Thee,
> And Thou, O Lord, art more than they. (Tennyson, In Memoriam).

The point is well taken. Even though we will be listing a number of the various attributes of God, this list is by no means exhaustive. Neither does an outlining of His attributes tell us all that there is to know about God. On the other hand, it is impossible to know God without also knowing certain facts about God. For example, I know and have a relationship with my wife, not just because I know certain facts about her, but because of our intimate communications. At the same time, I could not claim to know her if I did not know at least some facts about her.

THE NATURE OF OUR KNOWLEDGE OF GOD

Before we begin our actual examination of the attributes of God, we must ask the question of what will be the nature of our knowledge of God. Theologians have suggested three possibilities:

Equivocal Knowledge	Univocal Knowledge	Analogical Knowledge
Our understanding of truth is different from God's understanding	Our understanding of truth is the same as God's understanding	Our understanding of truth has common elements with God's understanding

1.   Equivocal Knowledge.

When you say that both a tree and a dog have a bark, you are predicating "barkness" to both of them, but you are not saying the same thing. The Equivocal theory of knowledge says that when we speak of God, we cannot comprehend Him as He truly is and that what we think of God is different from what He really is.

This position was held by Cornelius Van Til, professor of Apologetics at Westminster Theological Seminary. He said that God and man are not on the same order of being — that they are ontologically different.

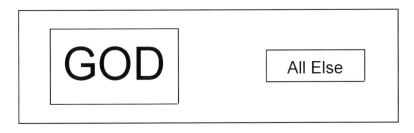

While nearly all Christians would agree with such a premise, Van Til also maintained that God's knowledge is completely different from man's knowledge.

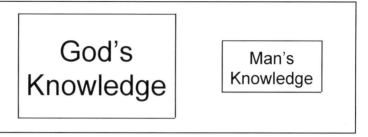

2.   Univocal Knowledge.

        When I say that Big Ben in London is a timepiece and that a sun dial is also a timepiece, I am saying the same thing with regards to what they are. That does not mean that Big Ben is the same in all respects to a sun dial, but it says that they are the same with regard to their nature as a timepiece. The Univocal position says that we understand God in the same way that He understands Himself.

        Francis Schaeffer coined the term "true truth" to describe the fact that we can truly know certain things. He sometimes signed his letters, "Yours truly, but not exhaustively."

        In the same way, the Univocal position admits that our understanding is not as comprehensive as God's understanding. When a mechanic speaks of the workings of a care, his description will be more complete than my own. And yet, we can communicate because I at least have a rudimentary knowledge of what is a radiator and a fan belt and a piston.

        In the 1940's there arose a bitter debate within the Orthodox Presbyterian Church between Cornelius Van Til versus Gordon Clark. Van Til taught that even when God is thinking about a particular thing (like a rose), His thoughts about it were never identical to man's thoughts. God thinks the thoughts of a Creator while man thinks the thoughts of a creature. Clark insisted that there is not a discrepancy between God's knowledge versus man's knowledge at every point; otherwise, man could not be said to know anything. Clark would argue that the statement "2+2=4" has the same meaning for God that it has for man.

        Van Til challenged Gordon Clark to name one truth that he could know in the same sense that God knows. Clark replied, "David slew Goliath." He was saying that his knowledge of that event, although not exhaustive as God's knowledge, was nevertheless of the same nature as God's knowledge.

3.   Analogical Knowledge.

When I say that there is an analogy between an apple and an orange, I mean that, while there may be some differences, there are at least some univocal elements; some common elements.

The problem with both the Equivocal and the Analogical views is that when I say that something is true, I do not mean that it is true in the same sense that God sees it to be true. If either the Equivocal or the Analogical view in epistemology were correct, then this entire debate would be fruitless because no matter what conclusion we came to, it would not be true in the same sense that God sees it to be true.

Jesus went against this kind of teaching when He said, *You shall know the truth* (John 8:32). If He does not mean that you could know the truth in the same sense that God knows the truth (and if we hold to the deity of Christ, then also in the same sense that He knew the truth), then what does He mean? Certainly He is not saying that you can only know something that is similar to the truth but that the truth itself cannot be known.

The arguments of the Equivocalist and the Analogicalist also fail to recognize the foundational truth (no pun intended, but they would not even recognize it as such, for it would not be truth, but only a similarity to the truth) - they fail to recognize and apply the truth that man is created by God as a being in the image of God. Certainly if this means anything, then it means that there is a basis of communication between God and man. Animals do not communicate with God, but man does.

If we say that man's knowledge is not univocal with God's knowledge, then we are forced to conclude that there are certain things that God does not know, since He does not share in the knowledge that man possesses. On the other hand, we can affirm both the continuities and the discontinuities with our thoughts versus God's thoughts:

GOD'S THOUGHTS VERSUS OUR THOUGHTS	
Discontinuities	**Continuities**
God's thoughts are uncreated and eternal	Divine and Human thoughts may have the same objects

God's thoughts decree what comes to pass	It is possible for both God's thoughts and man's thoughts to be true
God's thoughts are true because they are His	Our thoughts and God's thoughts are both validated by Him
God does not need to have anything revealed to Him.	All things are potentially knowable?
God has not chosen to reveal all things to us	
God's thoughts are all non-contradictory	

TWO TYPES OF ATTRIBUTES

The most common distinction made by theologians between the attributes of God is to view those that are incommunicable versus those that are communicable.

1.   The Incommunicable Attributes: These are the attributes of God that are not communicated to us and in which we do not share.

- Self-existence
- Infinity
- Unity
- Perfection
- Immutability
- Omnipotent
- Omnipresent
- Omniscience

2.   The Communicable Attributes: These are the attributes of God that are communicated to us and in which we do share.

- Holiness
- Love
- Grace
- Mercy

- Patience
- Goodness
- Righteousness
- Truthfulness
- Faithfulness

GOD IS SPIRIT

The Westminster Shorter Catechism gives one of the most concise definitions of God: *God is a Spirit, infinite, eternal and unchangeable in His being, wisdom, power, holiness, justice, goodness and truth.*

Non-Corporeal Being	Adjectives	Nouns
God is a Spirit	Infinite Eternal Unchangeable	Being Wisdom Power Holiness Justice Goodness Truth

The first phrase of the Catechism is taken from John 4:24 where Jesus said to the Samaritan Woman, "God is Spirit." The Greek construction of that passage is interesting. It has no verb. The verb is understood. By this construction, Jesus is not saying that God is **A** spirit, as though He were one of many spirits. Instead He is saying that the very nature of God is Spirit. The fact that God is spirit leads us to three implications.

1.   God is Personal.

        When the Bible speaks of spirit, it describes that which is alive, self-conscious and self-determining. The fact that God is spirit points to the truth of a personal God.

2.   God is Non-Corporeal.

        When Jesus appeared before the disciples in His resurrection body, He invited them to touch Him to be certain that He had truly risen from the dead because *a spirit does not have flesh and bones* (Luke 24:39).

This means that when we read of Jesus sitting at the right hand of God or when we read of the arm of the Lord being flexed, we should not understand these terms literally as though God has a hand or an arm. We refer to these as anthropomorphism -- attributing human qualities to the Lord to describe His actions.

This also means that we should not take the statement of Genesis 1:26-27 with regard to man being created in the image and likeness of God to refer to some outward physical characteristic.

3.   The Second Commandment prohibited the making of graven images.

> *You shall not make for yourself an idol, or any likeness of what is in heaven above or on the earth beneath or in the water under the earth (Exodus 20:4).*

What is wrong with making an image or a likeness of God? Such an image is a denial of the truth that God is spirit. This is explained in Deuteronomy.

> *Then the LORD spoke to you from the midst of the fire; you heard the sound of words, but you saw no form-- only a voice. 13 So He declared to you His covenant which He commanded you to perform, that is, the Ten Commandments; and He wrote them on two tablets of stone. 14 And the LORD commanded me at that time to teach you statutes and judgments, that you might perform them in the land where you are going over to possess it.*
>
> *So watch yourselves carefully, since you did not see any form on the day the LORD spoke to you at Horeb from the midst of the fire, 16 lest you act corruptly and make a graven image for yourselves in the form of any figure, the likeness of male or female, 17 the likeness of any animal that is on the earth, the likeness of any winged bird that flies in the sky, 18 the likeness of anything that creeps on the ground, the likeness of any fish that is in the water below the earth. 19 And beware, lest you lift up your eyes to*

heaven and see the sun and the moon and the stars, all the host of heaven, and be drawn away and worship them and serve them, those which the LORD your God has allotted to all the peoples under the whole heaven. (Deuteronomy 4:12-19).

So watch yourselves, lest you forget the covenant of the LORD your God, which He made with you, and make for yourselves a graven image in the form of anything against which the LORD your God has commanded you. (Deuteronomy 4:23).

Do you see the point that is made? It is that God has no outward, physical image. He is the invisible God.

Now to the King eternal, immortal, invisible, the only God, be honor and glory forever and ever. Amen. (1 Timothy 1:17).

...He who is the blessed and only Sovereign, the King of kings and Lord of lords; 16 who alone possesses immortality and dwells in unapproachable light; whom no man has seen or can see. To Him be honor and eternal dominion! Amen (1 Timothy 6:15b-16).

THE INFINITE AND ETERNAL GOD

"I am the Alpha and the Omega," says the Lord God, "who is and who was and who is to come, the Almighty." (Revelation 1:8).

God calls Himself the Alpha and Omega. These are the first and last letters of the Greek alphabet. We would say that He is the A and the Z. The encyclopedia of human history begins and ends with Him. In the beginning there was God. In the end there will be God. He is and He was and He is to come.

This verse deals with God's infinity in relation to time. He transcends the beginning of all things. He has no beginning or ending. He has always existed and will always continue to exist. This quality is graphically portrayed in a Psalm attributed to Moses.

> *A Prayer of Moses the man of God.*
> *Lord, Thou hast been our dwelling place in all generations.*
> *Before the mountains were born,*
> *Or Thou didst give birth to the earth and the world,*
> *Even from everlasting to everlasting, Thou art God. (Psalm 90:1-2).*

There is nothing that seems so permanent as a mountain. Nothing in our realm of existence is so immovable. Yet God says that He existed and that He was God before the birth of the mountains. The same God to whom we pray is the same God who was God before the earth existed.

We tend to view existence through a very limited perspective. All things in our realm of experience have a beginning and an end. Such is not the case with God. He exists independently of time. He transcends time. This is why He calls himself Yahweh -- "I am."

I recall once standing on the top floor of the Landmark Building in Fort Lauderdale and watching a trail go by. From my vantage point of thirty stories, I could see the entire length of the train in a single glance, even though it stretched almost a mile across the city. I think that might illustrate the way God sees the progression of time. God sees all of history in one glance. We, on the other hand, have a lower perspective. We stand on the street corner of time and watch the events go rolling by us.

The eternity of God speaks directly to His self-existence. He is the uncaused Cause. Nothing ever happened to bring Him about. He transcends the entire chain of cause and effect relationships. There never was a time when He was anything less than He is now. He has not grown any older. He has not become any smarter. He is the eternal God.

THE UNCHANGING GOD

> *For I, the LORD, do not change; therefore you, O sons of Jacob, are not consumed. (Malachi 3:6).*

We believe that the Bible is the Word of God -- that it is the written communication of the Creator of the universe to mankind. As such, there is little doubt that it is the most important book ever written. Yet as we pick it up and read it in our quest to know God, we often find ourselves overwhelmed by a myriad of events of ancient history. The people described therein seem very long ago and far away. They are of other cultures and of other lands and their problems and struggles do not seem relevant to the modern world of today. It may be of interest to historians and stuffy professors, but how can the common man relate to the teachings of a book that was written thousands of years ago?

Bible teachers have pointed out that the Biblical characters shared many of the same problems that we deal with today, but there is still a sense of remoteness as we read of their various situations.

- God never spoke to me from a burning bush.
- I have never been a king of Israel or a king of anything.
- I was not thrown into a fiery furnace.
- I have never tried to walk on water.
- No angels have ever addressed me.

No matter how hard I try, I find that there is still a sense of remoteness between the issues and problems that I face on a day to day basis and those characters of the Bible. So what is the answer? How can I see the Bible as relevant in the 21st century? The answer is seen in the truth that we have an unchanging GOD.

> *For I, the LORD, do not change; therefore you, O sons of Jacob, are not consumed. (Malachi 3:6).*

God does not change. He has not learned anything new in the last 4000 years. His outlook on life has not grown with age. Neither have His absolute standards of righteousness undergone any revision.

This is hard to comprehend because we change all the time. I am not the same person I used to be. I am constantly growing and changing. I continue to learn new things that change my old outlook on life.

God hasn't changed. He is the same as when He created the heavens and the earth. He is the ancient of days. That does not mean that He is getting old. He is not "getting" anything. He is the same yesterday, today and forever (Hebrews 13:8). His knowledge is always fresh and up to date.

We look at people who haven't changed with the times and think of them as "old-fashioned." But God doesn't have to change with the times. He is fully aware how times change. He made them that way. He is the one constant in an ever-changing universe.

25 *Of old Thou didst found the earth;*
And the heavens are the work of Thy hands.

141

26 Even they will perish, but Thou dost endure;
    And all of them will wear out like a garment;
    Like clothing Thou wilt change them, and they will be changed.
27 But Thou art the same,
    And Thy years will not come to an end. (Psalm 102:25-27).

When the universe has come and gone there will only be One who has not changed -- the Unchanging God. This brings up an interesting question. What do we do with certain passages like Genesis 6:6 or Jonah 3:10 that tell us God repented? If this repentance is to be understood as a change in attitude, then is this not an example of God changing?

In answering, we must first ask whether these passages reflect a real change in the character and purposes of God. For example, when Jonah says that God repented in His plan to destroy Nineveh, it is not that God's attitude toward the people of Nineveh had changed, but rather the Ninevites themselves who had changed. This in turn brought about a change in God's actions toward them. Thus, it did not involve a change in the character or the purposes of God.

The sun is not showing a change in character just because it melts ice but hardens clay. The change is not in the sun, but in the objects on which it shines. Neither do I change in my character because I punish my child for disobedience but praise that same child for doing what is right.

Here is the principle. God's character never changes. But His dealings with men do change as men themselves change in their attitudes toward Him.

Now I want to ask you a question. Is this principle relevant for today? Does the fact that God does not change make a difference in the way I live? I believe that it does. When I am faced with the remoteness of the Biblical records, I am able to balance that remoteness with a reminder that God has not changed. The same God who spoke to Moses from a burning bush is listening to my prayers right now. The same God who protected the young men who were cast into the fiery furnace can protect me as I drive on the highway. The same God who provided manna in the wilderness can make sure that I have a hamburger to eat for lunch. The same God who raised Jesus from the dead is going to raise me as well. The same God who sent the flood upon the earth has promised that He will come again.

Circumstances have changed. Problems have changed. Society had changed and is still changing. But God never changed.

THE IMMENSITY OF GOD

Many years ago, I had the opportunity to return to the Junior High School that I had attended as a youth. The first thing that I noticed is that it had shrunk in size. The halls that were once so wide and spacious were now rather narrow. The ceiling was now so low that I could reach up and touch it. What had happened? Had the building really shrunk? No. It is that I had grown. That is the way it is with almost everything. The older and the bigger and the smarter you get, the less things impress you. It is that way with everything except God. With Him it is the complete opposite. The older you get in the Lord and the more you come to know Him, the bigger He becomes.

In his Chronicles of Narnia, C. S. Lewis tells us of a meeting between Lucy and Aslan, the Christ figure of his story. "Aslan," said Lucy, "you're bigger. "That is because you are older, little one," answered he. "Not because you are?" "I am not. But every year you grow, you will find me bigger."

12   *Who has measured the waters in the hollow of His hand,*
      And marked off the heavens by the span,
      And calculated the dust of the earth by the measure,
      And weighed the mountains in a balance,
      And the hills in a pair of scales?
13   *Who has directed the Spirit of the LORD,*
      Or as His counselor has informed Him?
14   *With whom did He consult and who gave Him understanding?*
      And who taught Him in the path of justice and taught Him
      knowledge,
      And informed Him of the way of understanding?
15   *Behold, the nations are like a drop from a bucket,*
      And are regarded as a speck of dust on the scales;
      Behold, He lifts up the islands like fine dust. (Isaiah 40:12-
      15).

21   *Do you not know? Have you not heard?*
      Has it not been declared to you from the beginning?
      Have you not understood from the foundations of the earth?
22   *It is He who sits above the vault of the earth,*
      And its inhabitants are like grasshoppers,
      Who stretches out the heavens like a curtain
      And spreads them out like a tent to dwell in. (Isaiah 40:21-22).

Isaiah was a man who was in tune with the majesty and the holiness and the immensity of God. This was not due to any lack of growth on his part. He did not consider God to be great and awesome because he was only a primitive and inexperienced man. To the contrary, the Hebrew of Isaiah is of the highest literary quality.

Isaiah was in awe of the majesty of God because he had been an eyewitness of that majesty. At the outset of his ministry, Isaiah had partaken in an experience to which few can lay claim.

> *In the year of King Uzziah's death, I saw the Lord sitting on a throne, lofty and exalted, with the train of His robe filling the temple. 2 Seraphim stood above Him, each having six wings; with two he covered his face, and with two he covered his feet, and with two he flew. 3 And one called out to another and said, "Holy, Holy, Holy, is the LORD of hosts, The whole earth is full of His glory." 4 And the foundations of the thresholds trembled at the voice of him who called out, while the temple was filling with smoke. (Isaiah 6:1-4).*

Can you imagine anything more profound than to be in the presence of the Creator of the universe? Isaiah was filled with a holy terror. Yet it was not a terror that drove him away, but only one that attracted him to the throne. The Apostle John had a similar experience. John also saw a vision with the Lord seated upon His throne and attended by angels.

> *And the four living creatures, each one of them having six wings, are full of eyes around and within; and day and night they do not cease to say, "Holy, holy, holy, is the LORD God, the Almighty, who was and who is and who is to come." (Revelation 4:8).*

Do you see it? The song has not changed. John hears the same song that Isaiah heard seven hundred years earlier. The reason for this is that God has not changed. He is the same God *who was and who is and who is to come*. He is the same today.

THE ALL-KNOWING GOD

1   *For the choir director. A Psalm of David.*
       O Lord, Thou hast searched me and known me.
2   *Thou dost know when I sit down and when I rise up;*

> *Thou dost understand my thought from afar.*
> 3 *Thou dost scrutinize my path and my lying down,*
> *And art intimately acquainted with all my ways.*
> 4 *Even before there is a word on my tongue,*
> *Behold, O LORD, Thou dost know it all.*
> 5 *Thou hast enclosed me behind and before,*
> *And laid Thy hand upon me.*
> 6 *Such knowledge is too wonderful for me;*
> *It is too high, I cannot attain to it. (Psalm 139:1-6).*

This is a Psalm of David. He lived in a day when the world had been turned upside down. He came to the throne of Israel at a time when the tiny kingdom was about to collapse. Surrounded by enemies both within and without, David was under constant attack.

The Philistines of David's day had the ultimate military weapon -- the secret of smelting iron. This meant that their weapons were more advanced in every way. Not only did David have to deal with those surrounding nations who were enemies of Israel, but there were also those who had supported his old archenemy Saul, the previous king. These saw David as a usurper to the throne. To make matters worse, members of David's own household eventually rose up against him, seeking to take his throne away.

What was David's point of stability in the midst of such unstable situations? How did he handle such stress without going off the deep end? How did he cope? I believe the answer is to be found in this Psalm.

This is a song of praise to Yahweh, the God of Israel. It begins with a statement concerning the knowledge of God.

> 1 *O Lord, Thou hast searched me and known me.*
> 2 *Thou dost know when I sit down and when I rise up;*
> *Thou dost understand my thought from afar.*
> 3 *Thou dost scrutinize my path and my lying down,*
> *And art intimately acquainted with all my ways. (Psalm 139:1-3).*

Notice how David pictures God. He could have spoken about how God knows all historical events. He could say that God knows all things, both past, present and future. He could say that nothing is hidden from the knowledge of God. But instead, David makes this very personal. He says to God, "You know me."

David didn't want to give you a lesson in systematic theology. He didn't want to give you a seven point outline that you could place into your notebook and forget. He wants to bring you face to face with the living God.

I've got news for you. If the all-knowing God knew David, then He also knows you. He has searched you and knows you. He knows when you sit down and when you rise up. He understands your thoughts from afar. He scrutinizes your path and your lying down. He is intimately acquainted with all your ways.

That puts things into a slightly different light. God knows me! He knows you. He understands what you are going through. He knows your own unique situation. You aren't merely a number on a heavenly database. You aren't lost amidst the millions. The God of the universe is personally aware of your day-to-day problems.

This puts a whole new emphasis upon personal prayer. God doesn't have an angelic staff who goes through all of His prayer mail and who only forward the really important correspondence. God personally hears your prayers. He hears your prayers before you even pray them.

> *Even before there is a word on my tongue,*
> *Behold, O LORD, Thou dost know it all. (Psalm 139:4).*

God knows your thoughts. He knows your mind better than you do. He knows what you think and He knows all your needs and desires. Have you ever come to a point where you wanted to pray to the Lord, but just could not find the words to say? Don't worry, for at such a time the Holy Spirit is interceding on your behalf.

> *Thou hast enclosed me behind and before,*
> *And laid Thy hand upon me. (Psalm 139:5).*

What does this mean? It is couched in military terms. David was a military man. He knew the value of strong fortifications. He went on to build a whole series of fortifications to link up the tribes of Israel.

Here is the best kind of fortification. It is the fortification that God provides. David recognizes that God has set up defenses both behind him and in front of him. Nothing can come into his realm of existence without God knowing about it and taking an active part in it. The same is true for you. Nothing comes into your life that has not first come through a nail-scarred hand.

You might be thinking, "This is a bit much to take in." Many people have a limited view of God because they cannot imagine anyone with such knowledge and such power. Do you feel that way? If so, you are not alone. Look at the next verse:

Such knowledge is too wonderful for me;
It is too high, I cannot attain to it. (Psalm 139:6).

David is blown away by this kind of knowledge. He admits that he cannot grasp it. He cannot imagine that God could have such knowledge. And yet, he believes. This is his point of stability. He believes in a God that is beyond belief. That is because his concept of God is not dependent upon himself. David didn't dream up this kind of God. This is the God who revealed Himself. This is the God who is there.

What else does the Bible say about the knowledge of God? How far does His knowledge go? What is the extent of His knowledge? Here are a few verses that give us some insight into the knowledge of God.

> Nash makes this observation: *Divine omniscience means that God holds no false beliefs. Not only are all of God's beliefs true, the range of His knowledge is total; He knows all true*

1.   There is Nothing Hidden from God.

> *Why do you say, O Jacob, and assert, O Israel, "My way is hidden from the LORD, And the justice due me escapes the notice of my God"?*
> *Do you not know? Have you not heard? The Everlasting God, the LORD, the Creator of the ends of the earth Does not become weary or tired. His understanding is inscrutable. (Isaiah 40:27-28).*

God knows all things. He doesn't get bogged down in details so that He misses some. His mind never gets overloaded. He is not like last year's computer that runs short on memory and needs an upgrade. He understands all things with an infinite understanding.

2.   God's Knowledge Spans Every Event in the Universe.

> *He counts the number of the stars;*
> *He gives names to all of them.*
> *Great is our Lord, and abundant in strength;*
> *His understanding is infinite. (Psalm 147:4-5).*

God's knowledge is not confined to planet earth. He is the supreme expert in all matters of astronomy and science. He created the universe and holds it together. At the same time, He is concerned and aware of the most insignificant of events.

> *Are not two sparrows sold for a cent? And yet not one of them will fall to the ground apart from your Father. 30 But the very hairs of your head are all numbered. 31 Therefore do not fear; you are of more value than many sparrows. (Matthew 10:29-31).*

God knows about the tiniest details of His creation. He knows how many hairs you have on your head at any given moment. He is aware of all things. This is a message of comfort. If God is aware of sparrows and their daily problems, then He is also aware of you. He accounts you to be of much more value than a whole swarm of sparrows. He is concerned for you and is watching over you.

3.   The Unchangeableness of God's Knowledge.

> *And who is like Me? Let him proclaim and declare it;*
> *Yes, let him recount it to Me in order,*
> *From the time that I established the ancient nation.*
> *And let them declare to them the things that are coming*
> *And the events that are going to take place. (Isaiah 44:7).*

God issues a challenge to those who would compare His infinite knowledge with their own finite and limited knowledge. His knowledge extends to the past, to the present and to the future.

If God knows that there will be an accident at a certain intersection on a specific time and date, then that accident will take place. Nothing can happen (not even man's "free will") that will be apart from God's foreknowledge.

At the same time, God's foreknowledge is not a black box placed within your soul that moves you in a particular way despite your own intellect and will. You have a freedom of spontaneity that normally allows you to choose and act in accordance with your own choices.

4.   God's Knowledge Includes All Possibilities.

Jesus alluded to this kind of knowledge when He compared the cities of Capernaum to the other cities that had not heard His preaching.

> *Then He began to reproach the cities in which most of His miracles were done, because they did not repent. 21 "Woe to you, Chorazin! Woe to you, Bethsaida! For if the miracles had occurred in Tyre and Sidon which occurred in you, they would have repented long ago in sackcloth and ashes. 22 Nevertheless I say to you, it shall be more tolerable for Tyre and Sidon in the day of judgment, than for you. 23 And you, Capernaum, will not be exalted to heaven, will you? You shall descend to Hades; for if the miracles had occurred in Sodom which occurred in you, it would have remained to this day. (Matthew 10:20-23).*

Jesus claims knowledge of what would have happened in a different situation. He says that the cities of Tyre and Sidon would have reacted in a certain way if they had witnessed the miracles of Jesus.

A lesson that we can draw from such a statement is that God knows all of the possibilities. He knows what could have happened if things had been different.

At this point, we ought to consider the relevance of such a teaching. What difference does it make in my life to know that God is omniscient? Is this merely an academic thesis on a subject that has little or no value for day to day living? It is unfortunate that this is exactly the way in which this subject is often presented.

Is this relevant? It certainly is! If you are a normal human being, then you have certain problems in your life. They might be big problems or they might be little problems that only look like big problems. I have news for you. God knew about your problems long before the creation of the universe. Not only did He know about them, but He also made provision for them.

> *He has built the answer to our prayers into the very structure of the universe* (Dr. James Buswell, Jr).

149

God designed the universe with you in mind. It has been custom-built to your specifications. He knew everything about you before you were even born. And He has not forgotten. He is not senile. His knowledge is still fresh. He is the all-knowing God.

THE OMNIPOTENT GOD

> *Ah Lord God! Behold, Thou hast made the heavens and the earth by Thy great power and by Thine outstretched arm! Nothing is too difficult for Thee, 18 who showest lovingkindness to thousands, but repayest the iniquity of fathers into the bosom of their children after them, O great and mighty God. The LORD of hosts is His name; 19 great in counsel and mighty in deed, whose eyes are open to all the ways of the sons of men, giving to everyone according to his ways and according to the fruit of his deeds; 20 who hast set signs and wonders in the land of Egypt, and even to this day both in Israel and among mankind; and Thou hast made a name for Thyself, as at this day. (Jeremiah 32:17-20).*

These words were not written in a seminary library. They were written by Jeremiah in a day of imminent danger. They were written by a man who was witnessing the fall of Jerusalem and who was surrounded by enemies both within and without.

These times were especially dark for Jeremiah. The tide of public opinion had turned against him. The king did not care for his preaching and had thrown him into prison. From the depths of his prison, Jeremiah could still realize the truth that God was in control of all of these events.

God is all-powerful. There is nothing that He is not able to do. He made everything that exists from His power. When earth's mightiest telescopes continue to explore the furthest reaches of the countless galaxies, they are bringing testimony to God's handiwork. There is nothing that is stronger than God because there is nothing that was not made by God. This is a great source of comfort for the believer. You need to be aware of this basic truth when you are facing trouble.

- God is big enough to help. There is no situation that He cannot handle.
- God is smart enough to help. He knows what to do about your problems.

- God is concerned enough to help. He demonstrated His love for you when He sent His Son to die upon the cross.

There is no situation that can ever come into your life that is too difficult or too complex for God to handle.

28 *Do you not know? Have you not heard?*
The Everlasting God, the LORD, the Creator of the ends of
the earth does not become weary or tired.
His understanding is inscrutable.
29 *He gives strength to the weary,*
And to him who lacks might He increases power.
30 *Though youths grow weary and tired,*
And vigorous young men stumble badly,
31 *Yet those who wait for the LORD will gain new strength;*
They will mount up with wings like eagles,
They will run and not get tired,
They will walk and not become weary. (Isaiah 40:28-31).

The principle is clear. Nothing will ever be able to exhaust the infinite resources of the Almighty God. Because He is almighty, He is able to give strength to us in our weakness. At the same time, we must point out that there are things for which it is impossible for God to do.

1. God cannot do the Irrational: God does not do pseudo-tasks like making a stone that is too heavy for Him to lift or making a four-cornered triangle. God is rational and He has created a rational universe that operates accordingly.

2. God cannot do that which is Contrary to His Character: The Scriptures tell us that God cannot lie (Titus 1:2) or break His promise (2 Corinthians 1:20) and that He cannot change (Numbers 23:19). His actions will always be in accordance with who and what He is.

3. God cannot Exhaust His Power: The Lord does not tire. When God created all things in the space of six days, it did not tire Him and it was not a "rushed job." He rested only because He had finished His work. This means He will never find our prayer requests too difficult to handle.

In the midst of his discourse with his three friends, Job gives a graphic description of the creative works of God.

6   *Naked is Sheol before Him*
       And Abaddon has no covering.
7   *He stretches out the north over empty space,*
       And hangs the earth on nothing.
8   *He wraps up the waters in His clouds;*
       And the cloud does not burst under them.
9   *He obscures the face of the full moon,*
       And spreads His cloud over it.
10   *He has inscribed a circle on the surface of the waters,*
       At the boundary of light and darkness.
11   *The pillars of heaven tremble,*
       And are amazed at His rebuke.
12   *He quieted the sea with His power,*
       And by His understanding He shattered Rahab.
13   *By His breath the heavens are cleared;*
       His hand has pierced the fleeing serpent.
14   *Behold, these are the fringes of His ways;*
       And how faint a word we hear of Him!
       But His mighty thunder, who
       can understand? (Job 26:6-
       14).

> The little boy listened in silence as his father told him about how God is able to see him at all time. Finally he commented, "God must have big eyes."
>
> *The eyes of the LORD are in every place,*
> *Watching the evil and the good. (Proverbs 10:3).*
>
> *"Lo, I am with you always..."* (Matthew 28:28b).

Notice how Job sums up his description in verse 14. When we look at all the wonderful works of God and consider what He has accomplished, we are only seeing *the fringes of His ways* and the *faint word* of His might. We must always recognize that our knowledge of God is necessarily limited.

THE OMNIPRESENT GOD

7   *Where can I go from Thy Spirit?*
       Or where can I flee from Thy presence?
8   *If I ascend to heaven, Thou art there;*
       If I make my bed in Sheol, behold, Thou art there.
9   *If I take the wings of the dawn,*

> *If I dwell in the remotest part of the sea,*
> 10   *Even there Thy hand will lead me,*
>   *And Thy right hand will lay hold of me.*
> 11   *If I say, "Surely the darkness will overwhelm me,*
>   *And the light around me will be night,"*
> 12   *Even the darkness is not dark to Thee,*
>   *And the night is as bright as the day.*
>   *Darkness and light are alike to Thee. (Psalm 139:7-12).*

We have already seen the first portion of this Psalm of David that looks at the omniscience of God. He has shown that God knows all things. Now David moves to a new subject. It is the subject of the omnipresence of God. David begins with a question. It is really a rhetorical question. It is a question with an obvious answer because it obviously has no answer:

> *Where can I go from Thy Spirit?*
> *Or where can I flee from Thy presence? (Psalm 139:7).*

It is not that David is actually seeking to escape God's presence. He asks these two questions to drive home a point. He wants to point out the truth that it is impossible to escape the presence of God. No matter where you go or what happens to you, God is still there.

> 8   *If I ascend to heaven, Thou art there;*
>   *If I make my bed in Sheol, behold, Thou art there.*
> 9   *If I take the wings of the dawn,*
>   *If I dwell in the remotest part of the sea,*
> 10   *Even there Thy hand will lead me,*
>   *And Thy right hand will lay hold of me. (Psalm 139:8-10).*

I am reminded of the prophet Jonah. Here is a man who is told by God to go to Nineveh, the capital city of the Assyrian Empire. Jonah is commissioned to take the message of God to the Assyrian people.

Jonah doesn't want to go. It isn't that he doesn't believe; it is that he has absolutely no use for the Assyrian people. Jonah is a bigot. He decides to go as far from the Assyrians as possible. He wants nothing to do with the Assyrians. He knows that there is one place where no Assyrian has ever gone. No Assyrian ever traveled by water. They had no navy. They were a mountain people. So what does Jonah do? He gets on a boat headed in the opposite direction. In so doing, he escapes the presence of the Assyrians; but he cannot escape the presence of God.

153

Imagine the scene. The boat is well on its way and Jonah has gone below decks to catch up on his sleep. Dark clouds appear on the horizon and soon spread over the entire sky. The wind begins to blow and the waves soon reach monstrous proportions. The ship is in danger of sinking. The sailors frantically seek to lighten the ship. When that does not work, they come down to where Jonah is sleeping and awaken him. Perhaps if he prays to his God, the storm will abate.

Jonah hears and he knows why the storm has come. He knows that it is directed against his own willful disobedience. He instructs the sailors to throw him overboard as a means of escaping the judgment of God. At their wits end and having tried every possible alternative, the sailors take Jonah that throw him into the depths of the Mediterranean Sea.

If this were not enough, Jonah is swallowed by a great fish. You would think that this would be the end of the story. But even in the depths of the sea and in the belly of a fish, Jonah has not escaped the presence of God. You cannot escape the presence of God. This can be a great comfort to the believer in the area of prayer.

God is always there when you pray. Imagine what it would be like if this were not so. You might start to pray and suddenly a voice would come down from heaven saying, "Good afternoon, this is the Lord. I'm so glad you called. I'm away from my desk, but if you will just leave your name and number I will get back with you..."

God doesn't use mail-messaging. He doesn't use a pager. He isn't even hard of hearing. He is always available. He is not just the God who is there -- He is also the God who is here. The truth of God's omnipresence is also a warning to those who would be disobedient to His commands.

> *The eyes of the Lord are in every place,*
> *Watching the evil and the good (Proverbs 15:3).*

Have you ever been in a situation where you thought that it did not matter what you did because no one was looking? There are no secret things. God is there. He is watching the good that you do and He is also watching the bad that you do. That should be a warning to you when you are tempted to sin. At the same time, the omnipresence of God is a comfort as it means you are never so far that He cannot help in time of need. The omnipresence of God is at the same time both a warning and a comfort. This is seen in the following chart:

The Omnipresence of God is a Warning	The Omnipresence of God is a Comfort
For the word of God is living and active and sharper than any two-edged sword, and piercing as far as the division of soul and spirit, of both joints and marrow, and able to judge the thoughts and intentions of the heart. 13 And there is no creature hidden from His sight, but all things are open and laid bare to the eyes of Him with whom we have to do. (Hebrews 4:12-13).	*Let your character be free from the love of money, being content with what you have; for He Himself has said, "I will never desert you, nor will I ever forsake you," 6 so that we confidently say, "The Lord is my helper, I will not be afraid. What shall man do to me?" (Hebrews 13:5-6).*

THE HOLINESS OF GOD

> *In the year of King Uzziah's death, I saw the Lord sitting on a throne, lofty and exalted, with the train of His robe filling the temple.*
> *Seraphim stood above Him, each having six wings; with two he covered his face, and with two he covered his feet, and with two he flew. 3 And one called out to another and said, "Holy, Holy, Holy, is the LORD of hosts, The whole earth is full of His glory." (Isaiah 6:1-3).*

This is a glorious vision. It is a vision that takes us into heaven and into the very throne room of God. Isaiah begins with a brief but historical footnote. His account begins by rooting the event in time and space. What Isaiah is about to describe takes place in real history. It is not a "once upon a time" fairy tale. God really did speak. He did so...

In the year of King Uzziah's Death...

The reign of Uzziah is described in 2 Chronicles 26. He began his reign by doing right in the sight of the Lord. And because of this, the Lord blessed him and made the kingdom of Judah to be prosperous. But Uzziah became proud. And in his pride, he took it upon himself to enter into the Temple and to offer incense upon the altar of incense. This was something that only a priest was permitted to do.

As a result, God smote Uzziah with leprosy. Because he was a leper, he was no longer to even approach the Temple. He was ceremonially unclean and he remained in this state for the rest of his life. Indeed, he could not even continue to rule his kingdom. Although he held to the title of king, his son Jotham served as regent and defacto ruler in his place.

Now the king had died. And in that same year, Isaiah was given a vision. It was a vision of the Temple. Not the Temple which Solomon built, but of heaven itself.

In contrast to the sullied career of court and king, the vision of Isaiah is one of wonder and majesty. It is a vision of the presence of the Lord. He is accompanied by Seraphim -- the Hebrew word *sereph* describes "fire" -- these are "fiery ones." They comprise a royal honor guard around the throne. They are there with a message to proclaim. Their message is a declaration of the character of their Creator:

> *And one called out to another and said, "Holy, Holy, Holy, is the LORD of hosts, The whole earth is full of His glory." (Isaiah 6:3).*

The first question that we must ask in approaching this passage concerns the definition of this quality known as holiness. What does it mean to be holy?

Being holy has often thought to be the same as being spiritual or being good, but this is not necessarily the case. The Hebrew word קָדוֹשׁ (*qadosh*) describes that which has been set apart and made special.

- It is used of places such as the ground where God showed Himself to Moses (Exodus 3:5).

- It is used to refer to the Sabbath Day that had been set apart as a day of rest and remembrance of God (Genesis 2:3; Exodus 20:8).

- It is used to speak of people such as the priests of God who were set apart from the rest of the nation (Exodus 28:41).

One synonym that can be used to express this quality of holiness is "otherness." Each of these things is said to be set apart and other than the rest of those things that surround them.

This brings us to a question: In what way is God holy? He is set apart from the rest of His creation. There is nothing else in the universe that is like

Him. He is other than the rest of creation.

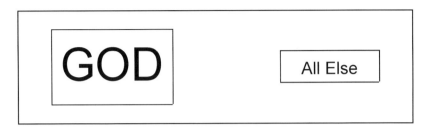

The message of these Seraphim points to the holiness of God. They say it repeatedly: *"Holy, Holy, Holy, is the LORD of hosts, The whole earth is full of His glory."* Hebrew has no punctuation marks. When you wish to make something emphatic in Hebrew, you do so by repeating it again and again and again.

For example, when Jesus is speaking with Nicodemus and He wants to make a point, He doesn't just say, "I am telling you the truth when I say you must be born again." He says, "Truly, truly." He repeats it. This emphasizes and underlines what He is saying. When Peter is given the vision of the clean and unclean animals coming down from heaven, the vision is given three times.

These seraphim repeat this three times. They say, "Holy, holy, holy." There are not many things that are repeated three times in the Bible. This should cause us to rise up and take notice. God is holy.

When Isaiah looked into heaven and saw this picture of the holiness of God, what exactly did he see? He saw the glory. He saw the seraphim. But that is not all. This incident is quoted in John 12:39-41.

> *For this cause they could not believe, for Isaiah said again,* 40 *"He has blinded their eyes, and He hardened their heart; lest they see with their eyes, and perceive with their heart, and be converted, and I heal them."* 41 *These things Isaiah said, because he saw His glory, and he spoke of Him. (John 12:39-41).*

The portion of Isaiah that is quoted is from the same chapter in which we were reading. It is from Isaiah 6:10. It is from the same context as Isaiah's vision. Here is the point. When Isaiah saw the glory of God, he was not seeing God because God is unseeable. He was seeing Jesus. That is what John tells us in verse 41 -- *he spoke of Him.*

THE WRATH OF GOD

> *For the wrath of God is revealed from heaven against*
> *all ungodliness and unrighteousness of men, who suppress*
> *the truth in unrighteousness (Romans 1:18).*

The subject of the wrath of God is perhaps one of the most neglected topics in the church today. It has become something of a taboo for preachers to speak about God being angry with sin. It is almost with embarrassment that some Christians admit that God is a God of wrath. Yet it is a subject found throughout the Scriptures.

1.   God's Wrath and God's Goodness.

Is God's wrath consistent with His goodness? Can I still love a God who is a God of wrath? Can He love me? Will a study of the wrath of God be edifying to me? The answer to all of these questions is a resounding "Yes!"

> *"See now that I, I am He, And there is no god*
> *besides Me; it is I who put to death and give life. I*
> *have wounded, and it is I who heal; and there is no*
> *one who can deliver from My hand. 40 Indeed, I lift up*
> *My hand to heaven, and say, as I live forever, 41 if I*
> *sharpen My flashing sword, and My hand takes hold*
> *on justice, I will render vengeance on My adversaries,*
> *and I will repay those who hate Me. 42 I will make*
> *My arrows drunk with blood, and My sword shall*
> *devour flesh, with the blood of the slain and the*
> *captives, from the long-haired leaders of the enemy."*
> *Rejoice, O nations, with His people; for He*
> *will avenge the blood of His servants, and will render*
> *vengeance on His adversaries, and will atone for His*
> *land and His people. (Deuteronomy 32:39-43).*

The God of the Bible is a God of anger and of judgment. But notice against whom the judgment is directed. It is against those who hate Him and who have rejected Him. Rather than a cause of sorrow, verse 43 says that this is a cause of rejoicing. The Lord will win in the end and so will all who have believed in Him.

At the same time, God has given a measure of His love to all mankind. This "common grace" is alluded when Jesus speaks of how the Father sends rain upon the righteous and the unrighteous (Matthew 5:45). It is on the basis of this example of God's common grace that we are called to love our enemies (Matthew 5:44).

2.   The Object of God's Wrath.

There are more passages in the Bible that deal with the wrath and anger and judgments of God than there are those that deal with His love and grace and mercy. Why is this? It is because God hates sin. Sin is at enmity with the righteousness of God.

The wrath of God is always directed against sin. If this were not so, if God did not become angry over sin, then He would be condoning sin and He would be sinful Himself. If God were not angry over sin, then he would be imperfect and He would not be God.

This means that you can never understand grace apart from the wrath of God. You can never see what it took to send Jesus to the cross until you realize how much God hates sin. This is why Paul begins his epistle to the Romans with the wrath of God.

Can you rejoice in the wrath of God? Can you see this as a doctrine of comfort and of joy? You can if you have a proper concept of God.

God hates sin. He condemns and judges sin. But God loved you enough to send His Son to the earth to be identified with the sins of the world and to be judged for those sins so that you could be made free from that sin. Thus recognizing the wrath of God against sin makes the love of God more loving and the grace of God more gracious.

3.   The Patience of God.

God is patient. He is patient with His own people and He is also patient with those who deny Him. The same God who holds the universe together by His power daily holds together the life of the unbeliever who hates Him.

> *The Lord is not slow about His promise, as some count slowness, but is patient toward you, not wishing for any to perish but for all to come to repentance (2 Peter 3:9).*

When you sin, God does not send down a great bolt of lightning and blast you into oblivion. He is patient. He is waiting for a time of future judgment. Why? It is because He does not want any of His people to perish. He is waiting for all those who will become His people to come to Him.

What would have happened if God had grown impatient and decided to punish sin four days before you came to know Christ? You would have been judged and condemned and cast into hell. The reason that you are saved today is because God was patiently withholding His judgment against sin until you had come to Him in faith.

Don't miss this! The reason you are saved today and not roasting in hell is because God has been patient toward you. He is not willing that you should perish. He waited for you to come to repentance.

He is still waiting. He is waiting for others to come to Him in faith, trusting the provision that He has made for them. He is waiting for others to believe in Jesus Christ and be saved. But He will not wait forever. There is coming a day when judgment will come. There is coming a day when the waiting will be at an end and when the Lord will return to judge those who have rejected His salvation. There is coming a day when the heavens will pass away and the earth with all of its wickedness will be destroyed.

> *But the day of the Lord will come like a thief, in which the heavens will pass away with a roar and the elements will be destroyed with intense heat, and the earth and its works will be burned up. (2 Peter 3:10).*

What is to be our response to this terrible vision? What effect does this teaching about the wrath of God have in our lives? This is an important question. This prophecy was not given to satisfy our curiosity about future events. Prophecy is never given for that reason. Why was it given? It was given to bring about a change in our lives.

> *Therefore, beloved, since you look for these things, be diligent to be found by Him in peace, spotless and blameless, 15 and regard the patience of our Lord to be salvation; just as also our beloved*

160

brother Paul, according to the wisdom given him,
wrote to you (2 Peter 3:14-15).

The response to this teaching about the wrath of God is to be twofold. These two responses are the reason for the teaching. The first response is to be inward. It concerns your personal life. Once you have seen what is God's attitude concerning sin, it should have an effect in your life. You are to be at peace. You are to be spotless and blameless. You are to be free from sin. This teaching of the wrath of God is to be a motivation to personal godliness.

The second response is to be upward. It concerns your view of the patience of God. When you see sin going unpunished and wrong and evil-doing flourishing, you should not be disheartened. Rather you need to see this as a sign of the patience of God that has brought about your salvation.

Let me put this on a personal level. Have you suffered a wrong that has not been righted? Have you been stepped on by others? Does it seem to you that you have gotten the short end of the stick? You are seeing the patience of God at work. That same patience was necessary for your salvation. It is a sign of your salvation. Because of that, you can rejoice even in the difficult times.

THE LOVE OF GOD

For God so loved the world, that He gave His only
begotten Son, that whoever believes in Him should not perish,
but have eternal life. (John 3:16).

This has been called the greatest verse in the Bible. It is the gospel in brief. It is a striking acclamation of the love of God. This is the first time that the Bible ever says that God loved the world. The Jews knew that God loved Israel. He had chosen Abraham to make a covenant with him and with his descendants. The people of Israel were God's chosen people. They were aware that God loved His people. But they never dreamed that this love would be extended to the Gentiles. This was a unique teaching to them. It was a revolutionary concept. God loved the world.

The word that is translated "love" in this verse is the Greek word ἀγαπεω. It was a common word in the Greek language. It had a variety of uses.

- It could be used of the love of a man for his wife.
- It could be used of the love of a mother for her children.
- It was even used of more general things like the love that a man might have for money or possessions.

However it was never used in secular Greek of the love that one had for an enemy. Such a concept would have been totally foreign to the pagan Greeks. It was unthinkable that you might show love toward an enemy. That is exactly what God did toward us. God directed His love toward us when we were His enemies.

> *For one will hardly die for a righteous man; though*
> *perhaps for the good man someone would dare even to die. 8*
> *But God demonstrates His own love toward us, in that while*
> *we were yet sinners, Christ died for us. (Romans 5:7-8).*

The love of God produced an effect. The effect was that He gave His Son. God loved the world so much that He gave. This is what true love is all about. True love always produces a corresponding action.

John 3:16 teaches that *God... gave His only begotten Son.* God's gift is unique. It was the gift of His only begotten Son. This is a title for the Son of God. He is the only begotten Son. This title emphasizes two unique aspects of the person of Jesus. First, it emphasizes the unique birth of Jesus. His birth was completely different from any other birth in history. He was born of a virgin and He was born without sin. Secondly, His title emphasizes the unique position of Jesus. He is the unique Son of God in a sense in which no other man or angel can claim. His position is unique.

The first part of this verse says that God sent His Son. The second part of this verse tells us why God sent His Son:

> *...that whoever believes in Him should not perish, but*
> *have eternal life. (John 3:16).*

God sent His Son so that whoever believes in Him should have eternal life. That was the purpose for the incarnation. It was the reason for Christmas. This brings us to a question: What does it mean to believe in Christ?

The idea of belief or faith always describes an attitude held by the one who believes. This word "belief" is never used of an outward action, even though it will result in an outward action. When directed toward a person, belief can have one of two possible characteristics.

- The first is confidence in a person's character or motives.
- The second is confidence in that person's ability to perform a certain function.

Both of these characteristics are in view when we believe in Jesus. We place our confidence in His character that He will keep His word. We believe that He **wants** to save us. We also consider Him able to perform our salvation. We believe that He has the **ability** to save us. The result of such faith is that the believing one has eternal life.

> *...that whoever believes in Him should not perish, but have eternal life. (John 3:16).*

The destiny of those who believe in Christ is brought out in both a negative and a positive statement.

Negative Statement	BUT	Positive Statement
Should not Perish		*Have eternal life*

The Greek construction of this passage is noteworthy. The phrase translated *"should not perish"* is in the Greek aorist tense. This tense views the action in a point in time. It looks to a point in the future when the unbeliever will perish. It points to a time of coming judgment in the future.

However the phrase *"but have eternal life"* is in the present tense. This is the tense of continuing action. Rather than looking to something that is coming in the future, it looks to a present, ongoing event. Here is the point. If you are a believer in Jesus Christ, then you have eternal life right now. You won't only have it in the future. It is your present possession. You may not be able to see it. You can't smell it. You may not feel like you have it. But it is yours. You have eternal life.

THE GOD OF TRUTH

> *Paul, a bond-servant of God, and an apostle of Jesus Christ, for the faith of those chosen of God and the knowledge of the truth which is according to godliness, 2 in the hope of eternal life, which God, who cannot lie, promised long ages ago, 3 but at the proper time manifested, even His word, in*

the proclamation with which I was entrusted according to the commandment of God our Savior (Titus 1:1-3).

In his introduction to the epistle to Titus, Paul refers to *"God who cannot lie."* This is a unique and often overlooked title for God. He is the God who cannot lie.

The actual Greek phrase that Paul uses is ἀψυδης Θεος (*apseudes Theos*) The Greek word ψυδης (*pseudes*) is the word for a liar, one who never tells the truth. It is used by Paul in verse 12 to describe the Cretans who "are always liars." When a Greek word has the letter α prefixed to it, the effect is that it negates the word, something like our English prefix "non" in words such as nonsense, non-working or non-lying.

Here in Titus 1:2 we can literally translate the words of Paul to speak of "the Non-lying God." This is a title for God. It describes who and what He is. He is the Non-lying God.

The false gods that populated the Greek and Minoan mythologies are well known to us today. The ancients had a god for every conceivable characteristic. There was a god for war and a god for wine and a god for love and a god for death. But here we see a title for God that stands in opposition to all of those false gods. Never in all of the Greek or Minoan pantheon was there ever a Non-lying God.

All of the Greek and Minoan gods had characteristics much like their human worshipers. They possessed all of the human failings of the men who created them. But the Non-lying God is seen in contrast to the gods of the Greek and of the Cretans. He is seen in contrast to the Cretans who are "always liars" (Titus 1:12). He is the Non-lying God.

But that is not all. There is more here than merely an interesting lesson in theology. There is more here than just another title for God. There is a vital reason why Paul uses this title here. The reason that this title is so important is because the Non-lying God has spoken. He has given promises to us.

...in the hope of eternal life, which God, who cannot lie, promised long ages ago (Titus 1:2).

Notice what it is that God has promised. It is the eternal life for which we hope. God has promised eternal life. The only reason that we can look forward to eternal life is because it has been promised to us by the Non-lying God.

A promise is no stronger than the character of the one who has made the promise. When a man makes a promise, we look to the character and the ability of the man who made the promise when we determine whether it will be fulfilled. If a man's character is questionable, then we have reason to suspect that the promise might prove false.

God has a perfect character. This is seen dramatically in God's dealing with Abraham when God entered into a covenant with Him. God used a legally binding treaty ritual to bind Himself to Abraham. God did not have to do this. He could have just promised Abraham the things that He was going to do and left it at that. But He wanted Abraham to understand that the promise would be kept, so He used a legal oath.

> *For when God made the promise to Abraham, since He could swear by no one greater, He swore by Himself, 14 saying, "I will surely bless you, and I will surely multiply you." (Hebrews 6:13-14).*

It was the custom in the ancient world for a man to swear by the power of something else. He might swear by his own head. Or he might swear on the head of his son. Or he might swear by his king or by his country. The idea was that the higher the object of the oath, the more solid was considered to be the promise that was given by it. The underlying idea was that, if the oath failed to be carried out, then the thing upon which the oath was made was to be cursed and destroyed.

Now we begin to see the true significance of God's oath to Abraham. God is saying in effect, "Abraham, if I do not keep My promise to you, then may I cease to exist."

> *And thus, having patiently waited, he obtained the promise. 16 For men swear by one greater than themselves, and with them an oath given as confirmation is an end of every dispute.*
>
> *In the same way God, desiring even more to show to the heirs of the promise the unchangeableness of His purpose, interposed with an oath, 18 in order that by two unchangeable things, in which it is impossible for God to lie, we may have strong encouragement, we who have fled for refuge in laying hold of the hope set before us. (Hebrews 6:15-18).*

Do you see it? When God wanted to prove to believers that His plan on our behalf would never falter or be changed, He guaranteed it with an oath. Our salvation is as secure as the very life and existence of God. If God were to fail to keep His promise to you, then God would cease to be God.

165

Has God ever broken His word? Has He ever spoken and it did not come to pass? Has history borne witness to the truth of His title? Is He truly the non-lying God?

> *Ask the wastes of Nineveh,*
> *Ask the mounds of Babylon,*
> *Ask the coasts of Tyre and Sidon*
> *If God is truthful to His word.*
> *They will all answer that God cannot lie.* (Dr. S. Lewis Johnson).

Confess Before Prayer Always

Is There One God or Three?

The Triune God

Doctrine is important, not just to theologians and seminary professors, but to all Christians. Jesus thought that this was the case. When He was tempted by Satan, He responded with doctrinal answers. He told Satan that...

- The study of doctrine is important: *"It is written, 'Man shall not live on bread alone, but on every word that proceeds out of the mouth of God'"* (Matthew 4:4).
- The holiness of God is to be trusted: *"It is written, 'You shall not put the Lord your God to the test.'"* (Matthew 4:7).
- The worship of God is to be unique: *"For it is written, 'You shall worship the Lord your God, and serve Him only'"* (Matthew 4:10).

In this chapter, we want to examine another vital doctrine of Christianity - the Trinity. In coming to terms with the Christian doctrine of the Trinity, it is first necessary to confront the unity of God. There is a reason for this. If we can demonstrate that...

(1) There is only one God.
(2) The Father, the Son and the Holy Spirit are all God.
(3) The Father, the Son and the Holy Spirit are each separate persons,

Then we have made a case for the doctrine of the Trinity. It is for this reason

167

that we begin our study of this section with the fact of the unity of God.

THE UNITY OF GOD

1.   God is One.

> *Hear O Israel: The Lord is our God, the Lord is one. (Deuteronomy 6:4).*

This is known among the Jews as the *Shammah* - "that which is to be heard." It is one of the foundational truths of the Old Testament. It is a proclamation of the unity of God. It says that God is one. If we were to examine this verse in the Hebrew language in which it was originally written, it would read like this:

> *Hear O Israel: JEHOVAH is our Elohim, JEHOVAH is one. (Deuteronomy 6:4).*

This is interesting. It is interesting because the word *Elohim* ("God") is found in the plural. But even though Elohim is plural, it does not mean that we are to think of God in the plural. This instead is a literary use known as the "plural of majesty." It was a way of ascribing greatness to a person or thing.

> The Mormons hold to a multiplicity of gods. They teach that Adam became Elohim and joined with a "mother god" in order to produce two sons - Lucifer and Jesus.

This principle of the unity of God is not merely an Old Testament teaching. The God of the New Testament is not different from the God of the Old Testament. This same truth was taught by Paul.

> *For there is one God, and one mediator also between God and men, the man Christ Jesus. (1 Timothy 2:5).*

The unified teaching of the Bible is that there is only one God. This means that the Christian doctrine of the Trinity can never be used to indicate a multiplicity of Gods.

2.   God is Unique.

> *To you it was shown that you might know that*
> *the LORD, He is God; there is no other besides Him*
> *(Deuteronomy 4:35).*

The question is sometimes brought up as to whether there could be another god over God. Was God created by a Being that was superior to Himself? The answer is given in the book of Isaiah.

> *"You are My witnesses," declares the Lord,*
> *"And My servant whom I have chosen, in order that*
> *you may know and believe in Me, and understand that*
> *I am He. Before me there was no god formed, and*
> *there will be none after Me." (Isaiah 43:10).*

God is unique. He is one of a kind. In all of the universe, there is not another who is like Him. He is the only God. If this is true, then we would not expect anyone else beside God to be called God. It is then striking that Jesus is described in terms of deity.

THE PLURALITY WITHIN THE GODHEAD

While holding firmly to the unity of God, we must also note that there is also a plurality within God. In theological terms, this plurality is known as the Trinity. Although this term is not found in the Bible, its truth is seen many times.

1.   The Name Elohim.

The Hebrew word for God (*Elohim*) is found most often in the plural form, indicating three or more. Hebrew has separate forms for singular, dual and plural. This has often been used by Christians to suggest the possibility of a trinity within God. However this is more probably to be understood as a "plural of majesty," especially as the same form is also used of the individual false gods.

2.   The Use of the Plural Pronoun.

In the Creation, Fall, and Babel Accounts (Genesis 1, 3 and

11), we see an interesting use of the plural pronoun as God is speaking.

> *Then God said, "Let US make man in OUR image, according to OUR likeness..." (Genesis 1:26).*

> *Then the Lord God said, "Behold, the man has become like one of US, knowing good and evil..." (Genesis 3:22).*

> *And the Lord said, "Behold, they are one people and they all have the same language. And this is what they begin to do, and now nothing which they purpose to do will be impossible for them.*
> *"Come, let US go down and there confuse their language, that they may not understand one another's speech." (Genesis 11:6-7).*

Still another example is seen in Isaiah 6:8 where the Lord asks: *"Whom shall I send, and who will go for Us?"* How are we to understand these uses of "us" and "our"? It has been argued that perhaps God was merely speaking with the angels. However, in each case, the context indicates that it is God who accomplished the planned action. For example, after the stated intention to create man, we read...

> *And GOD created man in His own image, in the image of God He created Him; male and female He created them. (Genesis 1:27).*

It does not say that man was created in the image of God and the angels. Neither do we ever read that the angels had any part in that creative work. Man is said to have been created by God and in the image of God.

It has been argued that this is also an example of the Hebrew plural of majesty. However, it is conversely argued that there is no other ancient example of such a plural of majesty being used in the form of a pronoun of anyone other than God. It may be that the early church fathers were correct in seeing this use of the plural pronoun as being a very early suggestion of the tri-unity of God.

3.   The Deity of Jesus Christ: The gospel of John opens with a striking affirmation of the deity of Jesus Christ.

> *In the beginning was the Word, and the Word*
> *was with God, and the Word was God. (John 1:1).*

The use of the imperfect tense in the three verbs of this passage is striking. The imperfect tense in the Greek describes the continuation of action in the past time. It does not look to a point in time, but rather to an ongoing process.   Thus, we might be permitted to translate this passage like this:

> The anti-Trinitarian cults like to take this passage and insert the indefinite article, making this to read that "the word was a god." In addition to being polytheistic in their outlook, such a stance does not conform to rules of Greek grammar.

> *In the beginning already was the Word, and*
> *the Word already was with God, and the Word*
> *already was God. (John 1:1).*

Don't miss this! The Word did not become God at Creation. We are told that when everything else began, the Word already was God. This is significant when we realize the identity of this One known as "the Word."

> *And the Word became flesh, and dwelt among*
> *us, and we beheld His glory, glory as of the only*
> *begotten from the Father, full of grace and truth.*
> *(John 1:14).*

The Word was not originally a Jewish carpenter named Jesus. But at a point in time, the Word became flesh and thus became the One whom we know as Jesus. This is an important distinction and it is necessary that we not get it backwards. This is contrasted in the following chart:

We DO believe	The Word became flesh. One who was in the beginning and who was with God and who was Himself God took on humanity, becoming a man so that He was now both God and man in one person
We do NOT believe	The flesh became the Word It would be wrong to conclude that the man Jesus somehow became deity during his life

He is called the Word because He was sent to communicate the truth of God to men. In this, He did more than the prophets. They proclaimed God in words. He was the Word. He was the very essence of God in the flesh. He communicated the character of God by who He was. This is the purpose for Christ coming to earth - to reveal God to man and to break down the barriers between God and men.

> *No man has seen God at any time; the only begotten God, who is in the bosom of the Father, He has explained Him. (John 1:18).*

Notice the identity of the two persons who are here mentioned. First there is God who has never been seen by man. He is also called the Father. But there is also "the only begotten God." This is God who was born in human flesh. This is Jesus.

Do you see the implications? Both the Father and the Son are described as God. This is an indication of the plurality which exists within the One God.

4.   A Triune Baptismal Formula.

Matthew records some of the last words of Jesus before He was caught up into heaven. As He spoke to His disciples on the slopes of the Mount of Olives, He gave still another indication of the plurality which exists within God. It is found in the words of the Great Commission.

> *"Go therefore and make disciples of all the nations, baptizing them in the name of the Father and the Son and the Holy Spirit." (Matthew 28:19).*

Notice that the disciples were not told to baptize in the names of the Father and the Son and the Holy Spirit. Rather, it is in the name of these three persons. Do you see what has happened? We have one name, but three persons. A similar formula is to be found in the apostolic benediction in Paul's second epistle to the Corinthians.

> *The grace of the Lord Jesus Christ, and the love of God, and the fellowship of the Holy Spirit, be with you all. (2 Corinthians 13:14).*

When the term "God" is used in the New Testament, it is generally a reference to the Father. This threefold formula is suggestive of the Christian doctrine of the Trinity. It could be argued that such a benediction would be inappropriate without the Trinitarian understanding.

5.   God deals with God: There are several passage of the Bible which relate God having dealings with God.

> *Thy throne, O God, is forever and ever;*
> *A scepter of righteousness is the scepter of Thy kingdom.*
> *Thou hast loved righteousness and hated wickedness;*
> *Therefore God, Thy God, has anointed Thee. (Psalm 45:6-7).*

This is a case where God is seen anointing God. This is not mere reflexive language. It is not a case of God anointing Himself. It is one member of the Triune Godhead anointing another member. Less there be any mistake on this, the writer to the Hebrews quotes this passage and informs us that the Father is speaking of Jesus (Hebrews 1:8).

This same type of language is used in Psalm 110. It is a Psalm of David. King David is the speaker in this Psalm.

> *The Lord says to my Lord:*
> *"Sit at My right hand,*
> *Until I make Thine enemies a footstool for Thy feet."*
> *(Psalm 110:1).*

Once again, the Hebrew text helps us to more fully understand the flow of thought in this passage.

> *JEHOVAH says to my ADONAI:*
> *"Sit at My right hand,*
> *Until I make Thine enemies a footstool for Thy feet."*

Remember that it is David speaking. He is the King of Israel. He is the highest human authority in the land. There is no other person in the land whom he can address as "lord." He is the lord of the land. And yet, he does have a lord. His Master is God. He pictures a heavenly conversation when he pictures Jehovah speaking to His Lord.

Jesus once quoted this passage to the Jewish teachings in the Temple. The subject of their conversation was the identity of the Messiah. He first asked them who the Messiah was supposed to be. They replied that the Messiah would be the son of David. This was a correct answer. But it raised a problem. The problem was that Psalm 110 has David calling the Messiah by the term *ADONAI* - "Lord." A father does not refer to his son as "lord." It is the other way around. In what way is Jesus both the son of David and the Lord of David? He is both humanly descended from David, but He is also the Son of God. He is the God-man.

6.   Common Designations: Jesus is said to do things which can only be done by God.

- He creates all things: *All things came into being by Him, and apart from Him nothing came into being that has come into being (John 1:3); In the beginning God created the heavens and the earth (Genesis 1:1); Thus says the LORD, your Redeemer, and the one who formed you from the womb, "I, the LORD, am the maker of all things, stretching out the heavens by Myself, and spreading out the earth all alone" (Isaiah 44:24).*
- He forgives sin (compare Mark 2:5-11 with Isaiah 43:25). In Mark 2:9 Jesus asks the question, *"Which is easier, to say to the paralytic, 'Your sins are forgiven'; or to say, 'Arise, and take up your pallet and walk'?"* The truth is that neither are easy to say truthfully, for only God can do these things. But Jesus nevertheless continues: *"But in order that you may know that the Son of Man has authority on earth to forgive sins" -- He said to*

the paralytic-- 11 *"I say to you, rise, take up your pallet and go home" (Mark 2:10-11).*

Over against this are the words of the Lord in Isaiah 43:25. *"I, even I, am the one who wipes out your transgressions for My own sake; and I will not remember your sins."*

- He is called God (Isaiah 9:6; Hebrews 1:8; Titus 2:13-14; Hebrews 1:8).

> *For a child will be born to us, a son will be given to us; And the government will rest on His shoulders; And His name will be called Wonderful Counselor, Mighty God, Eternal Father, Prince of Peace (Isaiah 9:6).*
>
> *...looking for the blessed hope and the appearing of the glory of our great God and Savior, Christ Jesus (Titus 2:13).*
>
> *But of the Son He says, "Thy throne, O God, is forever and ever, And the righteous scepter is the scepter of His kingdom." (Hebrews 1:8).*

- He is the Alpha and Omega, the beginning and the end, the first and the last (Revelation 1:8 with Revelation 1:17-18).

> *"I am the Alpha and the Omega," says the Lord God, "who is and who was and who is to come, the Almighty." (Revelation 1:8).*

> *And when I saw Him, I fell at His feet as a dead man. And He laid His right hand upon me, saying, "Do not be afraid; I am the first and the last, 18 and the living One; and I was dead, and behold, I am alive forevermore, and I have the keys of death and of Hades." (Revelation 1:17-18).*

Jesus is described as *the image of the invisible God, the first-born of all creation (Colossians 1:15)* and we read that it is *in Him all the fulness of Deity dwells in bodily form (Colossians 2:9).*

7. The Personality of the Holy Spirit.

When we deal with the question of the Trinity, it is immediately obvious to most people that the Father is God. The issue of the Son is whether He is also God. The issue of the Holy Spirit it whether or not He is a separate person. [2]

a.   Personal properties are ascribed to Him.

- He has understanding and wisdom: *For to us God revealed them through the Spirit; for the Spirit searches all things, even the depths of God. (1 Corinthians 2:10).*
- He has a will: *But one and the same Spirit works all these things, distributing to each one individually just as He wills (1 Corinthians 12:11).*
- He has power: *Now may the God of hope fill you with all joy and peace in believing, that you may abound in hope by the power of the Holy Spirit. (Romans 15:13).*

b.   Personal activities are ascribed to Him.

(1) He speaks: *And while they were ministering to the Lord and fasting, the Holy Spirit said, "Set apart for Me Barnabas and Saul for the work to which I have called them"(Acts 13:2); but say whatever is given you in that hour; for it is not you who speak, but it is the Holy Spirit. (Mark 13:11b).*

(2) He teaches: *And it had been revealed to him by the Holy Spirit that he would not see death before he had seen the Lord's Christ. (Luke 2:26). But the Helper, the Holy Spirit, whom the Father will send in My name, He will teach you all things, and bring to your remembrance all that I said to you. (John 14:26).*

(3) He warns: *But the Spirit explicitly says that in later times some will fall away from the faith, paying attention to deceitful spirits and doctrines of demons (1 Timothy 4:1).*

---

[2] It has been argued by some that personal pronouns are used of the Holy Spirit — that the Holy Spirit is a "he" and not an "it." The problem with this assertion is that the neuter pronoun is sometimes used to refer to the Holy Spirit. This is not surprising since the Greek word for "Spirit" (πνευμα) is neuter and thus would demand a neuter pronoun. One exception to this is in John 15:26 where the masculine pronoun refers back to the "Helper" (παρακλητος).

(4) He helps: *And I will ask the Father, and He will give you another Helper, that He may be with you forever (John 14:16).*

(5) He can be grieved: *And do not grieve the Holy Spirit of God, by whom you were sealed for the day of redemption (Ephesians 4:30).*

THE EXTENT OF THE PLURALITY WITHIN GOD

Now that we have established the fact of a plurality within God, we must ask a crucial question. How far does this plurality extend? Is it merely a matter of different functions? Or does it also involve different manifestations? Or does it even entail different persons?

1.   Different Functions.

It is immediately obvious from the Scriptures that there are different functions within God. For example, we see different functions within God as He brings about salvation.

- God the Father planned salvation: For God so loved the world, that He gave His only begotten Son, that whoever believes in Him should not perish, but have eternal life (John 3:16).

   Blessed be the God and Father of our Lord Jesus Christ, who has blessed us with every spiritual blessing in the heavenly places in Christ, 4 just as He chose us in Him before the foundation of the world, that we should be holy and blameless before Him. In love 5 He predestined us to adoption as sons through Jesus Christ to Himself, according to the kind intention of His will, 6 to the praise of the glory of His grace, which He freely bestowed on us in the Beloved. (Ephesians 1:3-6).

- God the Son executed this plan: *For while we were still helpless, at the right time Christ died for the ungodly (Romans 5:6).*

- God the Holy Spirit reveals this plan to men: *I have many more things to say to you, but you cannot bear them now. 13 But when He, the Spirit of truth, comes, He will guide you into all the truth; for He will not speak on His own initiative, but whatever He hears, He will speak; and He will disclose to you what is to come. 14 He shall glorify Me; for He shall take of Mine, and shall disclose it to you. (John 16:12-14).*

There are different functions within the Godhead even as there are different functions within my own life. I am a father and a husband and an employee and a teacher, yet I am one. This brings us to a question. Can we explain the plurality within God only in terms of function? Or is there more?

2.   Different Manifestations.

The Scriptures also indicate that God has manifested Himself to man in a variety of forms. He appeared to Moses in a burning bush. To Elijah He was a still, small voice. In the form of Jesus, He was manifested in the flesh.

> *And by common confession great is the mystery of godliness:*
> *He who was revealed in the flesh,*
> *Was vindicated in the Spirit,*
> *Beheld by angels,*
> *Proclaimed among the nations,*
> *Believed on in the world,*
> *Taken up in glory. (1 Timothy 3:16).*

A great many of the Greek manuscripts show a textual variation in the personal pronoun. Instead of, *"HE who was revealed in the flesh,"* they read, *"GOD was revealed in the flesh."* In either case, the context refers to God and teaches that God was revealed in the flesh.

The use of the aorist tense indicates a point in time when this came about. It means that there was a time when God was not flesh and then He became flesh. We have already seen this same truth expressed in John's Gospel.

> *And the Word became flesh, and dwelt among us, and we beheld His glory, glory as of the only*

begotten from the Father, full of grace and truth. (John 1:14).

Could this be the extent of the plurality of God? Is it merely that the One God has been revealed in different ways to me? Or is there even more? I think that there is.

3.   Different Persons.

The primary aspect which indicates that the plurality within the Godhead is made up of different persons is the Bible's description of the interaction which takes place between those persons. For example, when we examine the prayer of Jesus in John 17, we find Jesus interacting with the Father.

> *"And now, glorify Thou Me with Thyself, Father, with the glory which I had with Thee before the world was." (John 17:5).*

Don't miss this! Here we have the Son speaking to the Father about the personal relationship which they enjoyed before the creation of the world. In verse 24 there is even more.

> *"...for Thou didst love Me before the foundation of the world." (John 17:24b).*

This is the language of relationship. And a relationship implies two distinct persons. One does not have this kind of relationship with himself. The implication is that the Father and the Son were loving each other long before the Son was manifested in the flesh. They existed as separate persons long before God was revealed to man in any form. They existed as separate persons before man was even created. They have always existed as separate persons.

The different actions of God can be explained by a difference in function. The mention of different members of the Godhead can be explained by a difference in manifestations. But the various interactions which take place among the members of the Godhead can only be satisfied by the existence of different persons within that Godhead.

Christians have struggled in all sorts of ways to describe this doctrine of the Trinity. They have come up with a variety of illustrations, all of which fall flat. C.S. Lewis makes this observation:

> *We must remind ourselves that Christian theology does not believe God to be a person. It believes Him to be such that in Him a trinity of persons is consistent with a unity of Deity. In that sense it believes Him to be something very different from a person, just as a cube, in which six squares are consistent with unity of the body, is different from a square. (Flatlanders, attempting to imagine a cube, would either imagine the six squares coinciding, and thus destroy their distinctness, or else imagine them set out side by side, and thus destroy the unity. Our difficulties about the Trinity are of much the same kind.)* — C.S. Lewis.

It is commonplace today to find those who agree to the existence of a deity, but who want to reject the idea of a personal God. Lewis agrees that God is not merely a person, but that He is supra-personal. He is not less than a personal God; He is more than a mere personal God. He is multi-personal.

THE SIGNIFICANCE OF THE TRI-UNITY OF GOD

Now I want to ask you a question. It is the question you should ask whenever you approach a doctrine of the Bible. What is the importance of this teaching? What is the significance to me in knowing that God is triune? Is it just so much spare doctrinal baggage? Not at all.

The Godhead is a family. It is One God with three distinct persons. It is the most tightly knit family in the universe. It is the eternal family. Here is the point. If you have placed your faith in Christ, then you have become a member of that family. You have been adopted into that family and become a child of God. You have become a recipient of that love with which the Father loved the Son before the foundation of the world.

> Jesus said, "If anyone loves Me, he will keep My word; and My Father will love him, and We will come to him, and make our abode with him" (John 14:23). When you become a Christian, the entire Trinity comes and lives within you.

When we come together to worship, it is a family reunion. The God of the universe has united Himself with us. With such a rich heritage, we can scarcely be attracted by the foolishness of the life that the world offers.

> *Let us draw near with a sincere heart in full assurance of faith, having out hearts sprinkled clean from an evil conscience and our bodies washed with pure water.*
>
> *Let us hold fast the confession of our hope without wavering, for He who promised is faithful; 24 and let us consider how to stimulate one another to good deeds, 25 not forsaking our own assembling together, as is the habit of some, but encouraging one another; and all the more, as you see the day drawing near. (Hebrews 10:22-25).*

God's Sovereign Plan

God's Work of Predestination and Providence Over Creation

> *This is the plan devised against the whole earth; and this is the hand that is stretched out against all the nations. 27 For the Lord of hosts has planned, and who can frustrate it? And as for His stretched-out hand, who can turn it back? (Isaiah 14:26-27).*

The Scriptures abound with statements describing God's plan and purpose for creation, for man and for history. These statements will go far beyond the normal question of predestination of certain men to salvation. They look to the entire scope of God's having predestined all events in all of history.

THE EXTENT OF THE PLAN OF GOD

The fact of creation via an omniscient Creator presupposes that God has a plan and an order for the universe the He has created. This plan was made by God Himself before the act of creation took place.

1.   God's Plan was formed before the Creation.

During his Olivet Discourse, Jesus described the kingdom as having been prepared for believers *"from the foundation of the world"* (Matthew 25:34). The implication is that the kingdom over which Christ reigns was already planned and designed when God created mankind. The earth was made with this end in view, that there should be a kingdom. In the same way, God ordained those who would be His people before the foundation of the world.

> *Just as He chose us in Him before the foundation of the world, that we should be holy and blameless before Him. (Ephesians 1:4).*

> *Who has saved us, and called us with a holy calling, not according to our works, but according to His own purpose and grace which was granted to us in Christ from all eternity. (2 Timothy 1:9).*

These verses indicate that God's plan for His people goes back to the time before the creation of the universe - indeed, to "all eternity." Thus when we speak of God decreeing or determining, we do not mean that there was a time in the past when His plan was not yet formed or that it came into being at a certain time. His plan is from all eternity.

2.   God's Plan is Everlasting.

In the 33rd Psalm, the temporal plans of mankind are contrasted with the eternal plans of the Lord. The Psalmist says, *"The Lord nullifies the counsel of the nations; He frustrates the plans of the peoples. The counsel of the Lord stands forever, the plans of His heart from generation to generation."* (Psalm 33:10-11).
Notice the contrast between the plans of men and the plans of God. Men's plans often fail. God's plan never does. It will continue on its course throughout all eternity.

3.   God's Plan is Unchangeable.

The plan of God is unchangeable, even though it sometimes appears to change from man's point of view. We refer to this characteristic as "immutability."

> *Every good thing bestowed and every perfect gift is from above, coming down from the Father of lights, with whom there is no variation, or shifting*

shadow. (James 1:17).

> *God is not a man, that He should lie, nor a son of man, the He should repent; has He said, and will He not do it? Or has He spoken, and will He not make it good? (Numbers 23:19).*

When the Scriptures speak of the Lord repenting, this does not mean that His sovereign decree has been scrapped and that He has to go back to the drawing board and start over again. Rather it is a reflection that there has been a change in His actions as revealed to us. Such a revelational change should not be confused with an actual change in the person or plan of God.

Thus when God gave Isaiah a prophecy concerning the coming destruction of Assyria, He guaranteed its fulfillment by pointing to the unchangeable character of His plan.

> *This is the plan devised against the whole earth; and this is the hand that is stretched out against all the nations. For the Lord of hosts has planned, and who can frustrate it? And as for His stretched-out hand, who can turn it back? (Isaiah 14:26-27).*

We can conclude from this that God's plan was both determined before the creation, that it is unchangeable, and that it will continue to stand forever in this unchangeable state.

GOD'S PLAN INCLUDES ALL EVENTS IN HISTORY

People often tend to think of predestination only in terms of who will be saved and who will be lost. The Bible presents the scope of predestination in a far wider range. All events have been ordained by God.

1.   God's Plan includes "all things."

> *In Him also we have obtained an inheritance, having been predestined according to His purpose*

who works all things after the counsel of His will.
(Ephesians 1:11).

To what do these "all things" refer? Paul does not define or limit what we are to understand as the "all things" that God works. I would therefore suggest that we understand it as similar to the "all things" in Romans 8:28 where we read that *God causes all things to work together for good to those who love God, to those who are called according to His purpose.* We do not limit the "all things" of this passage only to those things that come into our life via our own volition. We instead take the statement to refer to all things that come into our life, no matter what their apparent source.

The reason that Romans 8:28 is true is because Ephesians 1:11 is true. The reason that *God causes all things to work together for good to those who love God* is because that same God *works all things after the counsel of His will.*

The same implications are given here by Paul. He says that God has predestined us to enjoy certain blessings. The reason that we know that He is able to predestine us to those blessings is because He works all things in accordance to His divine plan.

2. God's Plan includes where and when men live.

> *"And He made from one, every nation of mankind to live on all the face of the earth, having determined their appointed times, and the boundaries of their habitation." (Acts 17:26).*

The phrase "having determined" is translated from the aorist active participle of the Greek verb ὁριζω (*"horizo"*). It is a general rule of Greek grammar that the action of an aorist participle precedes the action described by the main verb which governs it. In this case, the main verb is found in the phrase, "He made from one" and refers to the creation of man. This means that God has predetermined when and where on earth all men would live.

> *Thine eyes have seen my unformed substance;*
> *And in Thy book they were all written,*
> *The days that were ordained for me,*
> *When as yet there was not one of them. (Psalm 139:16).*

185

This passage says that our days have been ordained and that this ordaining took place befour we had any days. Who did this ordaining? It is obvious from the context of this chapter that it is God who has ordained our days.

3. God's Plan includes all of the Acts of Men.

This is stated as a general principle in the book of Proverbs where we read: *"The mind of man plans his way, but the Lord directs his steps."* (Proverbs 16:9).

This is illustrated many times and in many ways throughout the Scriptures. It is seen in the decision of Absalom. Prince Absalom, the rebellious son of David, sought advice from his counselors on how he might bring about the defeat of his father. After hearing the advice from two key counselors,

Robert Reymond makes the following observation: *Reformed theology does not deny that men have wills (that is, choosing minds) or that men exercise their wills countless times a day. To the contrary, Reformed theology happily affirms both of these propositions. What Reformed theology denies is that a man's will is ever free from God's decree, his own intellection, limitations, parental training, habits, and (in this life) the power of sin. In sum, there is no such thing as the liberty of indifference; that is, no one's will is an island unto itself, undetermined or unaffected by anything* (1998:373).

he made a decision to follow the plan of Hushai. This was the poorer of the two plans and would ultimately lead to Absalom's defeat and death.

> *Then Absalom and all of the men of Israel said, "The counsel of Hushai the Archite is better than the counsel of Ahithophel." For the Lord had ordained to thwart the good counsel of Ahithophel, in order that the Lord might bring calamity on Absalom. (2 Samuel 17:14).*

We are told that the reason Absalom decided to listen to Hushai instead of Ahithophel was because the Lord had ordained it. God had set Himself to the task over defeating Absalom and to this end, He was involved in the decision-making process.

There is a significant parallel between the human action and the divine plan of that action. On the one hand, Absalom made the decision as to whose advice he would adopt. On the other hand, God had determined that he would make that decision and, according to the Biblical narrative, this was the overriding factor that caused the wrong decision to be made.

Human Action	Divine Plan
Absalom determined via his "free will" to adopt the advice of Hushai	God determined that Absalom would make this decision

The same principle is further illustrated in the decree of Cyrus the Great. Cyrus came to power in the 6th century B.C. and within the space of a few short years, merged Babylon, Persia and Media into a single great empire. His actions were prophesied in the book of Isaiah.

> *It is I who says of Cyrus, "He is My shepherd!*
> *And he will perform all My desire." And he declares*
> *of Jerusalem, "She will be built," and of the temple,*
> *"Your foundation will be laid." (Isaiah 44:28).*

Over a hundred years before the coming of Cyrus, God declared through the prophet Isaiah that this same Cyrus would perform His will by ordering the rebuilding of Jerusalem. Cyrus had not even been born when this was written.

> *For the sake of Jacob My servant, and Israel,*
> *My chosen one, I have also called you by your name;*
> *I have given you a title of honor though you have not*
> *known Me. (Isaiah 45:40).*

The Lord states that He chose Cyrus to perform certain things even though Cyrus himself was an unbeliever who did not know the Lord. God is not restricted to using believers to carry out His plan.

Cyrus	The Lord
Cyrus had his own agenda	God had His own plan and purpose

Cyrus did not know the Lord	God proclaimed His purpose for Cyrus a hundred years before the birth of that king
Cyrus was an independent king with his own "free will"	God proclaims that Cyrus will *perform all My desire*

In the same way that He used Cyrus, so also the Lord used the pharaoh of the Exodus.

> *For the Scripture says to Pharaoh, "For this very purpose I raised you up, to demonstrate My power in you, and that My name might be proclaimed throughout the whole earth." (Romans 9:17).*

It was the Lord who raised up the unbelieving pharaoh of the Exodus to his position of leadership over Egypt. He did this so that, by bringing him to defeat through the plagues and through the incident at the Red Sea, the name of the Lord might be proclaimed throughout the whole earth.

Are we to take these instances of Cyrus and the pharaoh of Egypt as being the exceptions rather than the rule? Does God's plan only extend to the great and the powerful while ignoring the humble and the weak? Not at all! If there were anyone who was said to have "free will," it was the king. He could point to someone and say, "Off with his head" and that head would topple. Thus, when the book of Proverbs states the principle of God's sovereignty over rulers as a general principle, the implication is that God is sovereign over all men.

> *The king's heart is like channels of water in the hand of the Lord; He turns it wherever He wishes. (Proverbs 21:1).*

It has been said that man's free will flows in the channels which have been dug by the sovereignty of God. Such a concept is presented here. It is the Lord who directs men's will. Paul takes this principle a step further to teach that the rulers themselves are placed in their positions of authority by the Lord.

> *Let every person be in subjection to the*

governing authorities. For there is no authority except from God, and those which exist are established by God. (Romans 13:1).

Paul was not speaking in the context of a Christian king or governor. It was during the reigns of the Roman Emperors that he penned these words. He did not say that only those authorities which are obedient to divine laws are established by God, but all authorities.

This means that, whether a leader has taken a throne by force of arms or through inheritance or even through a national election by the vote of the "free will" of the populace, it is ultimately the Lord who places in office those whom He has chosen.

While it is true that the Lord ordains the lives of kings and princes, it is also true that He ordains the lives of peasants and peons. Job sums up the truth that the whole of a man's life has been determined by God.

Man, who is born of woman, is short-lived and full of turmoil. (Job 14:1).

Since his days are determined, the number of his months is with Thee, and his limit Thou hast set so that he cannot pass. (Job 14:5).

The very length of a man's life is determined. It has been set by the Lord Himself. There is a sense in which it is impossible for you to "die before your time." And it is equally impossible for you to live beyond the time that God has ordered.

> It has been said that if you try to explain the doctrine of election and you may lose your mind. Try to explain it away and you may lose your soul.

4.   God's Plan includes the Sinful Acts of Men.

God's plan includes the acts of men which are sinful and evil in nature. This principles is illustrated in the sin of the sons of Jacob in selling their brother Joseph into slavery.

But Joseph said to them, "Do not be afraid, for am I in God's place? And as for you, you meant evil against me, but God meant it for good in order to bring about this present result, to preserve many people alive." (Genesis 50:19-20).

Joseph's brothers had exercised their own "free wills" in deciding to sell him into slavery. The slave traders had exercised their own wills in purchasing him, in taking him to Egypt and in selling him to Potiphar. Potiphar's wife had exercised her "free will" in trying to seduce Joseph and then in influencing her husband to throw him into prison. Yet in spite of the evil intentions of Joseph's brothers, the slave traders, and Potiphar's wife, God had planned these decisions for the ultimate good of His people.

In the same way, the Lord later brought about a prejudice in the hearts of the Egyptians toward the Israelites who were sojourning in their land prior to the Exodus.

> *Israel also came into Egypt; thus Jacob sojourned in the land of Him. And He caused His people to be very fruitful, and made them stronger than their adversaries. He turned their heart to hate His people, to deal craftily with His servant. (Psalm 105:23-25).*

The reason that Egyptian public opinion turned against the Israelites who were living in the land is said to have been because God developed this hatred in their hearts. It was He who turned their hearts in this direction.

The ultimate example of the Lord incorporating the evil actions of men in His own plan and purpose is seen at the crucifixion of Christ. This is described by Peter in the most exacting terms:

> *"For truly in this city there were gathered together against Thy holy servant Jesus, whom Thou didst anoint, both Herod and Pontius Pilate, along with the Gentiles and the peoples of Israel, to do whatever Thy hand and Thy purpose predestined to occur." (Acts 4:27-28).*

The word "predestined" used here is translated from the Greek word προοριζω (*pro-orizo*). It is a compound word. We have already seen όριζω used in a way that describes something which has been "determined." The use of the prefix προ tells us that this is something which was PRE-determined. It was decided beforehand.

Don't miss the implications of this! Both Herod Antipas and Pontius Pilate, as well as a host of other Jews and Gentiles, found themselves in Jerusalem doing the very things that God had predestined for them to do. We should not take this to mean that they did this against their will. They were not saying, "I don't really want to put Jesus to death, but God is countermanding my own free will and so I am being forced to crucify Him." They are described as being responsible for their actions. But this responsibility in no way takes away from the fact that it took place in accordance with the predetermined plan and foreknowledge of God.

> *"Men of Israel, listen to these words: Jesus the Nazarene, a man attested to you by God with miracles and wonders and signs which God performed through Him in your midst, just as you yourselves know - this man, delivered up by the predetermined plan and foreknowledge of God, you nailed to a cross by the hands of godless men and put Him to death." (Acts 2:22-23).*

Here is a single passage we see God predestinating certain events to occur and, at the same time, sinful men are held responsible for their actions, being described as "godless men." Though they had no intention of doing so, Pilate and Herod were fulfilling the will of God. They were acting according to God's plan and purpose. But they are nevertheless judged for their unrighteous intentions because they were willing participants in the death of Christ.

5.   God's Plan includes "Chance Happenings."

The plan of God includes those events which appear to be merely "chance happenings" - those events which seem to come about just by chance. The principle is stated in Proverbs.

> *The lot is cast into the lap, but its every decision is from the Lord. (Proverbs 16:33).*

Every cast of the dice and every flip of the coin is known and has been planned by God. The human mind hears this and screams,

"Impossible!" But there is nothing that is impossible for God to accomplish. Nothing is too difficult for Him.

This means that those events which seem to us to be happening randomly were carefully planned and purposed by God. When the brothers of Joseph threw him into a pit and then sat down to plan his death, it was not by chance that a caravan just happened along. When Moses happened to come upon an Egyptian taskmaster beating an Israelite slave, it was not just a chance meeting. Neither was it just by chance that a Moabite girl named Ruth happened to find herself gleaning grain in the field of a wealthy Jew named Boaz. Just because we do not live in those days does not mean that God has changed the way He operates the universe. His world has never run haphazardly.

This teaching has some very practical consequences. It means that when something unexpected comes into your life, it is a divine interruption and you have every right to look for God's handiwork in it. All things that have every happened or that ever will happen have been ordained by God.

Chosen for Salvation

God's Work of Predestination in Salvation

"O, Arminian, Arminian, thou that distortest the prophets and misinterpretest them that are sent unto thee; how often have I told you your children the plain truth... and ye would not let them understand." — Gordon Clark.

Once it has been established that all of the events of history have been planned and ordained by God, it is a simple step to understand that this plan includes the destiny of those who shall be saved and those who shall be lost.

At this point, many Christians will object that such a thing just could not be true. After all, doesn't the Bible teach that anyone can believe in Jesus Christ and be saved? How could anyone claim that God has chosen certain people to be cast into an eternal death in hell? However valid these questions may seem to be, we cannot hide behind them to ignore the multitude of passages found in the Bible which teach the doctrine of predestination and election. Our first question must not be whether or not I like this teaching, but what does the Bible say?

JESUS TEACHES ELECTION

The sixth chapter of John relates a discourse which Jesus gave at Capernaum by the shore of the Sea of Galilee. He speaks to those who have seen His miracles. There are many who are now listening who had been present when He fed the five thousand (compare John 6:5-11 with John

193

6:26). They had seen an obvious miracle. They had tasted the bread and eaten the fish which He miraculously produced. And yet, they had not recognized that this One is the Son of God. They have been following Him merely for the sake of benefitting from His miracles. They have seen, but they still have not believed. There has been no commitment on their part. It is in this context that Jesus now introduces His teaching on election.

> *Jesus said to them, "I am the bread of life; he who comes to Me shall not hunger, and he who believes in Me shall never thirst. But I said to you, that you have seen Me, and yet do not believe." (John 6:35-36).*

Jesus begins with the simple declaration that He is the "Bread of life." This is seen in contrast to the bread that He had recently produced to feed the multitude. They sought only to satisfy their physical hunger and thirst. Jesus offers much more. In verse 36, Jesus points out the root of their problem. They have seen the miracles, heard the teachings, but they still have not believed. Why had they not believed? The answer is given in the following verses.

> *"All that the Father gives Me shall come to Me, and the one who comes to Me I will certainly not cast out. For I have come down from heaven, not to do My own will, but the will of Him who sent Me. And this is the will of Him who sent Me, that of all that He has given Me I lose nothing, but raise it up on the last day." (John 6:37-39).*

Jesus says that certain people have been given to Him by the Father. All of those who have been given to Him will come to Him. He does not say that all men have been given to Him. This would be universalism and Jesus never taught that. He does say that those which the Father had given to Him would eventually come to Him. This means that there are not any who have been given to Him by the Father who will not come. Now this is not speaking of some higher level of spirituality. The issue is not the super-spiritual. The issue concerns the converted versus the non-converted. This is speaking of salvation. Jesus is speaking to the unbelieving multitude. Many of them shall not come to Him. Why? From their point of view, it is because they refuse to commit themselves to Him. But there is a deeper, more underlying reason. The deeper reason that they will not come to Him will be because they are not among those whom the Father has given to the Son. On the other hand, those who do come will never be cast out. No man ever need worry that he might come to Jesus and then find that he has not been chosen. All who come to Him in faith will be saved.

At first this seems to be contradictory. On the one hand, those who have been chosen to be given to the Son are the ones who come to Him. On the other hand, anyone who comes to Him will not be cast out. Does this mean that there will be others who come to Him who were not chosen to be given to the Son? Not at all. The truth is that no man will come to the Son unless the Father draws him. This will be pointed out by Jesus in verse 44.

You might be reading this and beginning to seethe. How dare that I suggest that such a thing is so! You are in some interesting company. As Jesus said these things, the Jews who are listening to Him also began to seethe and to grumble. They were ready to believe that Jesus is a miracle-worker. But they could not believe that He is the Son of God who came down from heaven. They will come to Him to eat the food as He feeds the five thousand, but they will not come to Him to receive the bread of life. Why won't they come? Jesus answers in verses 43-44. It is because there is a sense in which they are unable to come.

> *Jesus answered and said to them, "Do not grumble among yourselves. No one can come to Me, unless the Father who sent Me draws Him; and I will raise him up on the last day." (John 6:43-44).*

Jesus said that the only people who are able to come to Him are those whom the Father draws to Him. Unless a man has been drawn by God, he simply will not come. Why? Why is it that men cannot come to God on their own initiative? Why will they not come unless they are first drawn by God? It is because man is inherently sinful and rebellious against God. Man's will has been corrupted by sin.

> *As it is written, "There is none righteous, not even one; there is none who understands, there is none who seeks for God." (Romans 3:10-11).*

It has been said that the man who chokes on the doctrine of election has not yet swallowed the truth of his own depravity. As a sinner, man is totally helpless to turn to God for help. It is God who first turns him toward Himself so that he will even begin to seek a cure. Therefore it is only when a man is drawn by God that he will come to Jesus and be saved.

This is not a new teaching that Jesus was giving to the multitude on that day. It was a teaching that went all the way back to the Old Testament

Scriptures. Jesus Himself quotes from the prophet Isaiah to show that it is God who initiates His work in the hearts of men so that they come to Him.

> *"It is written in the prophets, 'And they shall all be taught of God.' Everyone who has heard and learned from the Father, comes to Me." (John 6:45).*

Jesus is not talking about the entrance of Christians into some higher level of Christian service. He says these things to unbelieving Jews. The implications are obvious. The reason that they have not come to Him in faith is because they have not been drawn by God.

If you are having problems with these sayings of Jesus, then I want you to know that you are not alone. There were many of the disciples of Jesus who also found these teachings to be difficult. The reason that they were difficult was not because of their lack of exposure to the truth. Rather it was because they had not really believed.

At this point, you might be saying, "Ah, I knew that in the end it would be a matter of whether you believe or not!" Before you get too excited, look at what Jesus said to His disciples.

> *"But there are some of you who do not believe." For Jesus knew from the beginning who they were who did not believe, and who it was that would betray Him. And He was saying, "For this reason I have said to you, that **no one can come** to Me, **unless it has been granted Him** from the Father." (John 6:64-65).*

The words of Jesus could not be more clear. The reason that these pseudo-disciples did not believe was because it had not been granted to them from the Father to believe.

In conclusion we see that salvation is a free gift which is offered to all men. Any man who comes to Jesus Christ in faith shall be saved. No man who places his faith in Christ shall ever find that he has been cast out because he was not one of the elect. However it is also true that none but those who have been chosen and drawn by the Father is able to come to Jesus. It is only when God intervenes in a man's will and accomplishes His work in a man's heart that such a man will come and believe in Christ.

I have often heard it argued that Jesus claimed that He would draw all men to Himself - that He draws all men and only those who believe in Him out of their own free will actually come. The passage which is used to prove this teaching is John 12:32 where Jesus says:

> *"And I, if I be lifted up from the earth, will draw all men to Myself." (John 12:32).*

How are we to understand this verse? Does it teach a universal drawing of all men to Christ? If it does, then it teaches too much, since Jesus has already used this very same term to describe the drawing of certain men in John 6:44 and, within that context, He has explained that all who are drawn to Him will be raised up on the last day (John 6:44), will be taught of God (John 6:45), and will certainly not be cast out (John 6:37). Unless one is willing to adopt the doctrine of universalism - that all men everywhere will be saved and that none will ever be condemned - then one cannot take this reference in John 12:32 to describe a universal drawing of the same sense described in chapter 6.

How are we to understand this drawing of "all men"? Once again, it is the context that explains the passage. When Jesus speaks of "drawing all men" to Himself, He does so in a situation in which some Greeks had just been brought to Him. He responds by speaking of His impending crucifixion, the result of which will be to draw all men. Up to this point, the ministry of Jesus had been almost exclusively directed toward the Jews. But this will now change. Once Christ has gone to the cross, He will gather into one body both Jews and Gentiles. There will be no distinction between races or sexes or social strata. He will draw all types and races and people.

THE HIDDEN GOSPEL

One of the most remarkable prayers of Jesus is the one which He delivered after pronouncing His condemnation upon the Galilean cities of Chorazin, Bethsaida and Capernaum.

> *At that time Jesus answered and said, "I praise Thee, O Father, Lord of heaven and earth, that Thou didst hide these things from the wise and intelligent and didst reveal them to babes. Yes, Father, for thus it was well-pleasing in Thy sight." (Matthew 11:25-26).*

We dare not divorce what Jesus says in these verses from the previous paragraph. Jesus has just denounced Chorazin, Bethsaida and Capernaum for their unbelief. He has compared their unrepentant state to Sodom, Tyre and Sidon, three of the most infamous cities in Israel's history. Now He turns to the Father and thanks Him that things are still going according to plan. He thanks the Father for hiding the truth of the gospel from these cities.

Sometimes we get the idea that, when people hear the gospel and do not accept it, God's plan has somehow failed. This is not the case. It was the Lord's will to hide His message of salvation from these certain cities.

Now I want to ask you a question. What is the deciding factor in whether the gospel is hidden from someone or revealed to that person? Is it his faith? Or is it his willingness to believe? No, it is ultimately the willingness of the Son to reveal the gospel to him.

> *"All things have been handed over to Me by My Father; and no one knows the Son, except the Father; nor does anyone know the Father, except the Son, and anyone to whom the Son wills to reveal Him." (Matthew 11:27).*

The only people who come to know the Father are those whom the Son determines will have the Father revealed to them. It is in this context that the familiar invitation is made for all who are weary and heavy-laden to come and to find rest.

THE GOAL OF PREDESTINATION

In his first epistle to the Corinthians, Paul makes the point that men do not come to God on the basis of their intellectual reasonings. It is not the intelligent who are chosen by God. It is often just the opposite.

- Not the wise, but the foolish.
- Not the mighty, but the weak.
- Not the noble, but the base and the despised.

I can imagine Paul sitting back for a moment to reflect over the status of the membership of the church at Corinth. He asks the Corinthians to do the same.

> *For consider your calling, brethren, that there were not many wise according to the flesh, not many mighty, not many noble (1 Corinthians 1:26).*

Paul is speaking to believers. He exhorts them to consider their calling. They have been called to become followers of Jesus. To put it in the terms that Jesus used, they are among those whom the Father has drawn.

There were very few among the Corinthians believers who were rich or powerful or famous or influential. To be sure, Paul does not say that there were not any wise or mighty or noble. But he does indicate that the majority of the church did not fit this description. Why is this? Why do most Christians come from the ranks of the foolish and the weak and the base and the despised? Karl Marx suggested that it was because the oppressed classes and the weak turned to religion as a crutch to hold them up and to stabilize them. But this is not a Biblical answer. Paul says that the reason Christianity is filled with the foolish and the weak and the base and the despised is because God has chosen these kings of people to be in His kingdom. Notice the emphasis that Paul places upon the elective activity of God. Three times in this passage Paul repeats that it is God who has chosen:

> *For consider your calling, brethren, that there were not many wise according to the flesh, not many mighty, not many noble; 27 but **God has chosen** the foolish things of the world to shame the wise, and **God has chosen** the weak things of the world to shame the things which are strong, 28 and the base things of the world and the despised, **God has chosen**, the things that are not, that He might nullify the things that are, 29 that no man should boast before God. 30 But by His doing you are in Christ Jesus, who became to us wisdom from God, and righteousness and sanctification, and redemption, 31 that, just as it is written, "Let him who boasts, boast in the Lord." (1 Corinthians 1:26-31).*

The phrase "God has chosen" is repeated three times in this passage. It emphasizes the fact that our calling and our salvation is God's choice. God has not chosen to leave these things up to blind chance. Paul's entire point is that it is *by His doing you are in Christ Jesus* (1:30).

The point is made that God has not chosen the wise or the strong or the noble. Why not? Why have the wise and the strong and the noble been rejected? It is so *that no man should boast before God* (1:29). No man can ever say, "I found God as a result of my clever intellect or as a result of my strength of will or because of my noble birth." You will never be able to boast that you gained eternal life by choosing God, for the truth is that He chose you.

The result of understanding this truth is that God is glorified. If a man were saved on the basis of his own decision, then he might boast that he at least had the good sense to come to Christ and to place his faith in Christ. But Paul removes any such ground for boasting by showing us that we have been chosen apart from any reason within us. The result? *"Let him who boasts, boast in the Lord."*

THE AUTHOR OF PREDESTINATION

In setting forth the infinite and eternal blessings that God has bestowed upon the believer, Paul begins with the doctrine of predestination.

> *Blessed be the God and Father of our Lord Jesus Christ, who has blessed us with every spiritual blessing in the heavenly places in Christ, 4 just as He chose us in Him before the foundation of the world, that we should be holy and blameless before Him. In love 5 He predestined us to adoption as sons through Jesus Christ to Himself, according to the kind intention of His will, 6 to the praise of the glory of His grace, which He freely bestowed on us in the Beloved. (Ephesians 1:3-6).*

One cannot help but to notice the complete lack of any mention of man's involvement in the process of salvation. God is the One who is seen accomplishing salvation; man is seen only as the receiver of such blessings.

In the same way in which God has blessed us with every spiritual blessing, so also in that same way He chose us. Just as He is the source of our every blessing, so also He is the source of our election. As we did not bring the blessing upon ourselves through our action, so also we did not bring our election upon ourselves. It was God who chose us.

Furthermore, God is said to have chosen us long before we ever chose Him. He chose us before the foundation of the world. When God placed Adam and Eve into the Garden of Eden, He had already determined those who would be in Christ. This was a determination made in the eternal mind of God.

This is more than a mere knowledge of future events. This is more than an election and predestination of the plan of salvation as if God merely predestined the plan of salvation but not who would be a part of that plan. This is personal. Paul says that God chose us. God predestined us.

Why? For what reason did God predestine us? It was certainly not because of any merit on our part. Paul says that it was *according to the kind intention of His will* (1:5). God is the reason that God chose us. This is amplified when we come to verses 11-12.

> *In Him 11 also we have obtained an inheritance,*
> *having been predestined according to His purpose who works*
> *all things after the counsel of His will (Ephesians 1:11).*

The Arminian would prefer to read that we have been "predestined according to our faith by the One who works all things after the way His foreknowledge sees that we shall believe." Instead we see that predestination is according to His purpose and is accomplished after the counsel of His will.

PREDESTINATION AND THE SAVING WORK OF CHRIST

It is sometimes argued that, if God has predestined only certain people to be saved, then it is inconsequential whether Christ has died for their sins, since the elect will be saved regardless. In answering this objection, we must point out that a proper understanding of predestination will greatly enhance the value of the saving work of our Lord. Paul explains the relationship between predestination and the saving work of Christ.

> *Therefore do not be ashamed of the testimony of our*
> *Lord, or of me His prisoner; but join with me in suffering for*
> *the gospel according to the power of God, 9 who has saved*
> *us, and called us with a holy calling, not according to our*
> *works, but according to His own purpose and grace which*
> *was granted us in Christ Jesus from all eternity, 10 but now*
> *has been revealed by the appearing of our Savior Christ*
> *Jesus, who abolished death, and brought life and immortality*
> *to light through the gospel (2 Timothy 1:8-10).*

In the midst of exhorting Timothy to join him in suffering for the sake of the gospel, Paul describes the salvation to which that gospel proclaims. There are five parts to that description:

1. This salvation, as well as its accompanying call, is *not according to our works* (1:9). This is contrary to the heart of man. Man naturally wants to approach God on his own terms. He thinks that he can do something that will satisfy God. But salvation is not on the basis of anything that man does. It is provided on the basis of what Christ did on man's behalf and quite apart from anything that we might try to

add to it.

2.   This salvation has been provided *according to* God's *own purpose and grace which was granted us in Christ Jesus from all eternity* (1:9). We have already seen from Ephesians 1:4 that God chose us to be in Him before the foundation of the world. From all eternity, it has been determined that you would be in Christ Jesus. Who made this determination? It was not you, for you did not yet exist. Nothing existed except for God and so no plan could have yet existed except for His eternal counsel.

3.   This plan was selective. It did not merely call anyone who happened perchance to believe. It did not draw a circle in the sand and say that anyone who steps within that circle would be saved. Paul is very careful to say that we were called *not according to our works*, that is to say, not by anything that we did, *but according to His own purpose and grace* (1:9).

4.   It is not only the salvation, but also the calling that is according to the purpose and plan of God. This means God did not only plan the fact that you would be saved, but He also ordained the means and the method by which that salvation would be brought to you. The substitutionary death of Jesus Christ on the cross has always been a part of the plan and purpose of God. This does not render it insignificant. To the contrary, it means that the death of Christ is the most significant event in all of time and eternity.

5.   At the appointed time this salvation was *revealed by the appearing of our Savior Christ Jesus* (1:10). It was at this time that the central factor of God's plan of predestination and election came to pass. This is the central point of all of history. All of the events of human history have focused and will forever focus upon this one moment in time when God became flesh and died for sins.

ELECTION AND THE PROCESS OF CONVERSION

If we are to understand that man's salvation is predetermined by God, then is it necessary for man to hear the message of the gospel and to respond to it in faith and repentance? Shall men not be saved solely on the basis of whether they have been predestined and quite apart from their faith and repentance? What if a man who has been elected by God dies before he hears the gospel and believes?

The answer to all of these questions is quickly understood when we realize that God's predetermined plan is not limited to the area and scope of who shall be saved. It also involves the means and the manner in which that salvation is to be brought to each individual.

In the last chapter, we established that all events in history have been ordained by God. The fall of every sparrow and the plucking of each grey hair has been carefully planned by the Lord of the universe. Every decision, every discovery and every chance happening has been foreordained by Him.

What does all of this have to do with salvation? It means that God has determined and planned all of the events that work together in a man's life to bring him to the point where he repents and believes the gospel. God's plan included who would be the one to tell you of the sacrifice that was made for your sins. It included the Holy Spirit's regenerating work in your heart as you heard the message of the gospel. It included the decision that you made to believe that message and trust in Jesus Christ to save you.

God's plan included all of these things. This is visibly illustrated in the book of Acts when we read of the salvation of the Gentile believers in Antioch.

> *And when the Gentiles heard this, they began rejoicing and glorifying the word of the Lord; and as many as had been appointed to eternal life believed. (Acts 13:48).*

These Gentiles heard the message of the gospel and a number of them believed the message and were saved. Luke describes this number as *those who had been appointed to eternal life*. Notice who is described as doing the action in each of these clauses:

The Gentiles did this action...	The Gentiles are passive...
They heard... They began rejoicing and glorifying... They believed...	They had been appointed to eternal life

Who appointed these Gentiles to eternal life? One might try to suggest that they appointed themselves, but that would be an improper use of the passive voice. Furthermore, the Greek verb is a perfect passive participle (τεταγμένοι). The action of the perfect tense precedes the action of the main verb. This means the appointment of these Gentiles to eternal life took place before they believed.

Since it is in the passive voice, the action was been done TO them - they were not the ones doing the appointing, but rather someone else had already done that. The same form of the same word is used in Acts 22:10 where Paul is told to *"arise and go on into Damascus, and there you will be told of all that HAS BEEN APPOINTED for you to do."* Paul did not appoint himself to be an apostle and these Gentile believers did not appoint themselves to eternal life.

At the same time, we see that these Gentiles were not saved apart from the hearing of the message or apart from the believing of that message. Paul and Barnabas preached to them the good news of the gospel. They heard the message and considered it. The Holy Spirit worked in their hearts to bring them to an understanding and an acceptance of that message. As a result, they believed. And yet, we are made to understand that those who now believed had been previously appointed to eternal life. Who appointed them? The answer is obvious. It was the Lord who appointed them.

God had previously ordained that these Gentiles would have eternal life. But that is not all that God had ordained. He had also ordained that they should happen to be at Antioch on that particular day and that they would hear the preaching of Paul and Barnabas and that they would believe. Truly they were saved by the One who works ALL things after the counsel of His will (Ephesians 1:11).

PREDESTINATION AND EVANGELISM

It is often argued that a belief in the Biblical doctrine of predestination will lead to a falling away in the area of evangelism. If the salvation of men has been predetermined, then why should I witness? If I teach that men's destinies have been determined by God, then will it not stop believers from their motivation to spread the gospel?

An examination of Church History shows that this has not been the case. Men such as Calvin, Luther, Whitefield and Spurgeon give ample evidence from the past that an understanding of this teaching need not be a deterrent to evangelism. A modern-day example is seen in the president of Evangelism Explosion International, Dr. D. James Kennedy.

The fact that God's sovereignty is not a deterrent to evangelism is understood when we realize that God has not merely predestined the end result of man's salvation, but also the means from which that end was obtained. God has predestined the evangelistic process just as He determines those who will respond to that process. Rather than being a hindrance, this can serve as a great impetus to evangelism.

Paul sets forth this principle in his last epistle to Timothy. He writes this epistle from a prison in Rome. He has been arrested and is awaiting trial before the Emperor Nero. He knows that he will soon be put to death. He has suffered great hardships for the cause of the gospel. In the midst of this situation, he writes of his motivation in enduring these sufferings:

> *Remember Jesus Christ, risen from the dead, descendant of David, according to my gospel, for which I suffer hardship even to imprisonment as a criminal; but the word of God is not imprisoned. For this reason I endure all things **for the sake of those who are chosen**, that they may obtain the salvation which is in Christ Jesus and with it eternal glory. (2 Timothy 2:8-10).*

Paul endured all of these things *for the sake of those* whom God had chosen. He saw himself as an instrument which God was using to bring those chosen ones to salvation. Thus we see that in the very context of his teaching on election, Paul proclaims his own responsibility in bringing men to Christ. But this is not all. Paul also realized that the message of the gospel would not be imprisoned just because he was now in a Roman dungeon.

Paul knew that God's plan would not fall apart just because Paul was not there to oversee it. He knew that God would not fail. He knew that God had planned for Paul's imprisonment and that, by enduring that imprisonment, the cause of the gospel would be furthered.

If it is true that God has predestined men to be saved and, if it is also true that God has ordained the means through which they will come to Christ (ie., the hearing of the gospel), then predestination is a guarantee that my faithfulness in the preaching of the gospel will bear fruit. The reason that the Lord can say that His word shall accomplish what He desires (Isaiah 55:11) is because He has determined the fruitfulness of the presentation of His gospel.

This has a very practical application. It means that whenever I share the gospel, God has ordained both the fact of my being there to do that service, as well as the result which the gospel will have on those who hear. If I have a correct view of election, then I will realize that I have the guarantee of success in my presentation of the gospel. There is nothing that is more motivating to an evangelist than a guarantee from the God of the universe that his evangelistic effort will be successful.

THE QUESTION OF FOREKNOWLEDGE

All Christians believe in predestination. They cannot help but to do so, for the Bible very clearly says on a number of occasions that God predestines and chosen.

- *He **predestined** us to adoption as sons through Jesus Christ to Himself, according to the kind intention of His will (Ephesians 1:5).*

- *...we have obtained an inheritance, having been **predestined** according to His purpose who works all things after the counsel of His will (Ephesians 1:11).*

- *But we should always give thanks to God for you, brethren beloved by the Lord, because God has **chosen** you from the beginning for salvation through sanctification by the Spirit and faith in the truth (2 Thessalonians 2:13).*

All Christians hold these verses to be a part of the Bible and an accurate reflection of God's actions. Where theologians part company is over the question: Did God predestine men according to His own will and purpose, or has God merely chosen certain men on the basis of what He foreknew their decision would be? Stated differently, we ask, "Does our salvation depend upon God who has chosen us, or does it depend upon our own free decision?" One popular view is the one stated by Dr. Thiessen, the former chairman of the Faculty of the Wheaton Graduate School.

> *By election we mean that sovereign act of God in grace whereby He chose in Christ Jesus for salvation all whom he foreknew would accept Him* (1949:344).

Over against such an interpretation are an abundance of passage that clearly state that it is God who has chosen us according to His will (Ephesians 1:5) and that it does not depend upon the man who wills or the man who runs (Romans 9:16).

However we ought not to neglect those passages that mention the relationship of foreknowledge with predestination. There are two primary passages that deal with this subject. They are Romans 8:29-30 and 1 Peter 1:1-2.

1.   Whom He Foreknew, He also Predestined.

> *For whom He foreknew, He also predestined to become conformed to the image of His Son, that He might be the first-born among many brethren; 30 and whom He predestined, these He also called; and whom He called, these He also justified; and whom He justified, these He also glorified. (Romans 8:29-30).*

How are we to understand this foreknowledge? The Arminian states that this means God foreknew what each believer's decision would be and then predestined him on that basis. Thus God is said to have "looked down the corridors of time" to see that John Stevenson would believe in Christ and He said, "Since I can see that John is going to believe the gospel, I shall elect him to be one of My chosen people."

The problem is that this verse does not state this to be the case. Paul does not say that God knew something about certain individuals. He says that He knew them.

This is important. We know that God foreknows all things and all people, both saved and unsaved. There is nothing that God does not know and there is nothing that God does not know beforehand. Yet we read here that it is those people who have been foreknown that have been predestined and justified and glorified. The Arminian wishes to make the passage appear as such:

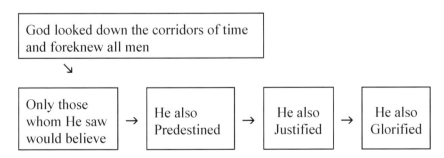

If we say that this passage merely refers to God's knowledge of of all men, then it must refer to both believers as well as to unbelievers, since God's awareness is not just limited to that of believers. If His foreknowledge is of all men equally, then this passage not only says that God foreknows all men, but also that He predestines and justifies and glorifies all men. Unless one is prepared to hold to a doctrine of universal salvation in which every man under the sun is to be eventually saved, we much conclude that the foreknowledge described in this verse refers to more than a mere general knowledge about all men.

Paul's statement does not fit Arminian Theology. He says that all those whom were foreknown were also predestined and justified and glorified.

What kind of knowledge is this describing? It is the knowledge of relationship, similar to that which is described in Genesis 4 where we read that "Adam knew his wife." This is an idiom for the closest possible relationship. In the same way, there are a number of passages that demonstrate the use of the term "knowledge" to describe that special relationship that God has with His people.

- *God has not rejected His people whom He **foreknew** (Romans 11:2).*

- *But if anyone loves God, he is **known** by Him (1 Corinthians 8:3).*

- *But now that you have come to know God, or rather to be **known** by God, how is it that you turn back again to the weak and worthless elemental things, to which you desire to be enslaved all over again? (Galatians 4:9).*

It is obvious that each of these examples uses the term "knowledge" to refer to that which is much deeper than merely an understanding of all of the fact. In each case, the term is used to describe a love relationship.

> *"Many will say to Me on that day, 'Lord, Lord, did we not prophesy in Your name, and in Your name cast out demons, and in Your name perform*

many miracles?' 23 *And then I will declare to them, 'I never **knew** you; depart from Me, you who practice lawlessness.'" (Matthew 7:22-23).*

Whether or not a person is known by the Lord is seen as the determining factor in one's eternal destiny. When Jesus says to certain men, "I never knew you," He does not mean that He did not know anything about them. Rather He means that they shared no relationship.

Is Predestination Morally Right?

The Justice of Election

The difficulty that most people have with the doctrines of election and predestination is not the lack of Biblical passages dealing with the subject. The Old and New Testaments are replete with statements that God had chosen and elected and predestined.

The problem that most have with this doctrine is how we deal with all of the implications which this doctrine raises. Chief among these difficulties is the question of the justice of divine election. How is God to be considered as just and righteous if He arbitrarily sends some people to hell and allows others into heaven. The theological term for this question is *Theodicy*. It comes from a joining of two Greek words.

- Θεος (*theos*) is the word for "God."
- Δικη (*dike*) is the word for "righteous."

THE QUESTION PRESENTED

> *What shall we say then? There is no injustice with God, is there? May it never be! (Romans 9:14).*

Notice the question. Is there any injustice with God? It is the justice and the righteousness of God which is being questioned here. This question arises from the previous verses. Is God just in choosing Isaac and not

Ishmael? Is God just in choosing to love Jacob and hate Esau? Is God just in choosing Israel to be His chosen people and in not choosing another of the nations of the world? Is God just in choosing some to be saved and not choosing others? A similar question will be raised in verse 19 when Paul asks the question, "If God has determined our actions, then how can He find fault in us and judge us?"

Before we look at the answer to these questions, I want you to notice something. These two objections which Paul brings up would never have arisen if we were not meant to understand that the choice of election rests with God. If Paul had been teaching that God merely looks down the corridors of time to see what men will choose and then elects them on the basis of their own decision, then there would be no basis for the question of whether God is just in choosing certain men.

The very fact that God's justice in election is questioned in this passage points to the fact that election originates and is based only in God. Paul's doctrine of election raises this objection. I would suggest that any view concerning election which does not give rise to this question is an improper view of election. If we come to a proper view of election, then this objection concerning God's justice will always arise.

How do we answer the question? Is God unjust? Paul retorts, "May it never be! Absolutely not!" But if God is absolutely just and righteous, then why is He able to choose some and not choose others? Why isn't this unrighteous? The answer is found in the following verses.

THE SOVEREIGN MERCY OF GOD

> *For He says to Moses, "I will have mercy on whom I have mercy, and I will have compassion on whom I have compassion." (Romans 9:15).*

The answer is seen in the sovereign mercy of God. It is because God is God. He is absolutely free to act according to the attributes of His own character. Paul illustrates this principle with a quote from the Old Testament.

He takes us back to the Sinai Desert. Moses has been on Mount Sinai for forty days. While he is on the mountain, the people of Israel turn away from God to worship a golden calf. As a result, God judges the Israelites and decrees that they shall not be permitted to enter into the Promised Land. It is in this context that God proclaims the principle of His sovereign mercy.

> *And He said, "I Myself will make all My goodness*

pass before you, and will proclaim the name of the Lord before you; and I will be gracious to whom I will be gracious, and will show compassion on whom I will show compassion." (Exodus 33:19).

Moses has been pleading for the forgiveness of the people. God responds by declaring that He is free to decide toward whom He shall be merciful. There is a principle here. It is that the doctrine of election is based upon the mercy of God. For God to choose some to salvation is for Him to show mercy toward those individuals.

God showed that kind of mercy toward Israel. Israel was not given mercy because of her faith. She was not given mercy because she was more righteous than the surrounding nations. Israel's mercy did not come from any quality that Israel possessed. It was the mercy of God.

God is not under any obligation to show mercy to anyone. Prayer does not even obligate God to show mercy. Nothing can dictate to God toward whom He must show mercy. There is no injustice in this. Neither is there any injustice in God's withholding mercy from those whom He has not chosen.

If ten people owed me money and I chose to forgive the debt of three of them, but still required the other seven to pay their debt, I would not be unjust. In the same way, there is no injustice in God being merciful to some and not being merciful to others. You might protest that this is unfair. To do so, you would be implying that God is under some obligation to treat all men equally. This is not true. God is not obligated to treat all men equally and He does not treat all men equally.

Some men have IQ's of 130 while others are lower in intelligence. Some are born into wealthy homes while some are poor by birth. Some have very long life spans while some die very young in life. Some have great athletic ability while some are 97 pound weaklings. It has been said that if all men are created equal, then some are more equal than others. We are not treated equally by God. God is not obligated to treat anyone equally and there is no injustice in this.

THE BASIS OF ELECTION

In verse 16, Paul draws a conclusion from the fact that God is sovereign in the bestowal of His mercy. The conclusion is introduced by the words "so then." The conclusion concerns the basis of God's election.

> *So then it does not depend on the man who wills or the*
> *man who runs, but on God who has mercy. (Romans 9:16).*

God's election is not based upon the will of man. God did not look down the corridors of time to see what man will choose and then grant mercy on the basis of what man's decision would be. Election is not based upon what man wills.

Election does NOT depend upon...	
The Man who Wills	The Man who Runs
Emphasis upon the decision of man	Emphasis upon the actions of man

Neither is election based upon what man does. It is not based upon any of his good works, his morality, his ethics, or anything else that he does. It is not even based upon man's faith. God is completely free to show mercy on whomever He chooses to show mercy. Paul now goes on to illustrate this point in the story of Pharaoh, the king of Egypt who was judged by God at the exodus.

> *For the Scripture says to Pharaoh, "For this very*
> *purpose I raised you up, to demonstrate My power in you,*
> *and that My name might be proclaimed throughout the whole*
> *earth." (Romans 9:17).*

You remember the story. Pharaoh was the king of Egypt. He was the sovereign of the mightiest kingdom on the face of the earth. His armies had marched all the way to the Euphrates River. But the Lord says that He is the one who raised up Pharaoh. He is the one who placed Pharaoh on the throne of Egypt.

This is astounding when we realize that Pharaoh's program was the subjugation of the people of God. He resorted to infanticide to bring this about. He had Hebrew male children put to death (mandatory post_birth abortions). He was directly opposed to God. And yet, it was God who had chosen Pharaoh and who had placed him on the throne of Egypt. God chose to raise up Pharaoh, to harden his heart, and then to bring him to ruin so that God might be glorified.

Here is Paul's point. It is not Pharaoh who wills or Pharaoh who runs, but God! This brings us to a new conclusion. It is presented in verse 18.

So then He has mercy on whom He desires, and He hardens whom He desires. (Romans 9:18).

Paul's new conclusion is again introduced by the phrase "so then." It is a conclusion based upon the two previous illustrations of Israel and of Pharaoh.

1.   God has mercy on whom He desires: We have already seen this principle in the case of Israel. Paul quoted Exodus 33:19 to show that God is not obligated to show mercy to anyone. He is free to bestow His mercy on whom He desires.

2.   God hardens whom He desires: This conclusion is based upon the case of Pharaoh to which Paul has just referred. It is often argued that Pharaoh hardened his own heart and that God was not the initiator of this hardening process. William Evans attempts to make an appeal to such an argument when he says:

> *"Pharaoh was responsible for the hardening*
> *of his heart even though that hardening process was*
> *foreknown and foretold by God"* (1981:31).

We can turn to passages in Exodus which say both that God hardened Pharaoh's heart and also that Pharaoh hardened his own heart. It is frequently maintained that God did not harden Pharaoh's heart until he had first hardened his own heart. Thus the hardening of Pharaoh's heart is not seen to be God's initial doing, but Pharaoh's.

This passage teaches just the opposite. Paul makes it very clear that Pharaoh's decision to harden his own heart ultimately came from God. The whole point that Paul is making is that God works and chooses and hardens and has mercy according to His own will. He is the instigator of His plan. This is confirmed in the Old Testament account when the Lord revealed His plan to Moses.

> *And the Lord said to Moses, "When you go back to*
> *Egypt, see that you perform before Pharaoh all the wonders*
> *which I have put in your power; but **I will harden his heart***
> *so that he will not let the people go." (Exodus 4:21).*

God told Moses that He would harden Pharaoh's heart. For us to maintain that God was only a secondary source of this hardening process would be to attribute the actions of God to Pharaoh. The fact that it was God who was the initiator of this hardening process is evidenced by the objection that Paul raises concerning God's righteous judgment of Pharaoh.

THE QUESTION OF GOD'S RIGHTEOUS JUDGMENT

You will say to me then, "Why does He still find fault?
For who resists His will?" (Romans 9:19).

There is a difference between the question which is asked in verse 14 and the question which is asked here. The contrast between the two questions is seen in the following chart:

Verse 14	Verse 19
"What shall we say, then?"	"You will say to me then..."
First Person ("we"): This is a question raised by Christians	Second Person ("you"): This is a question of unbelief
There is no injustice with God, is there?	Why does He still find fault? For who resists His will?
This question is answered from the Old Testament.	The questioner is rebuked from the Old Testament.

Here is the question which Paul raises. How can God hold men responsible for their disobedience when it is God who hardens their hearts? How can God judge Pharaoh for sinning when Pharaoh is acting according to God's divine plan? If God is responsible for hardening Pharaoh's heart, and if it is impossible for Pharaoh to resist the will of God, then how can God judge him for what he has done? Why does God still find fault with Pharaoh?

This is a very relevant question. We could ask, "If it is God who has chosen certain men to believe and to be saved, and if he has hardened other men against the gospel, then how can He direct his wrath and anger and condemnation against those who are hardened?"

The usual response of a Christian when he is presented with this objection is to back off and explain that God has merely chosen men on the basis of what He knew they would believe. By doing so, the well_meaning Christian is seeking to "take God off the hook" so that He will not be seen to be responsible for sin. However, to do so is to take God down off His throne and to treat Him as a creature instead of recognizing Him as the sovereign Creator. Paul takes a very different approach to this question. We can describe his approach both in the negative as well as in the positive.

1.   Paul does not back off of what he has taught. He does not try to soften his teaching nor does he feel the need to clarify or defend what he has previously taught with regard to election. The question is only valid if the premise is valid. The premise of the question is that God is sovereign, and that He does choose to save some but not others. If the premise was wrong, then Paul would have corrected it here and now. But he does not correct the premise. This further confirms that Paul is teaching the doctrine of individual election.

2.   Paul indicts the questioner for talking back to God. The question and the questioner are out of order. It is a question which man has no right to ask. The creature has no right to question his Creator. Modern man wants to elevate himself to the position of judge over the actions of God, but that is not our option.

3.   Paul answers the charge of injustice with an Old Testament illustration. The illustration is of a potter and his clay.

THE ILLUSTRATION OF THE POTTER AND THE CLAY

>   *On the contrary, who are you, O man, who answers back to God? The thing molded will not say to the molder, "Why did you make me like this," will it? 21 Or does not the potter have a right over the clay, to make from the same lump one vessel for honorable use and another for common use? (Romans 9:20-21).*

The charge was that God could not find fault with sinners if it is He who has mercy and if it He who hardens. Paul does not argue the charge. He does not try to defend God. God needs no defense. God is not on trial. It is man who is on trial. And it is the height of human arrogance for a man to try to pass judgment upon the righteousness of God.

Paul does not answer the charge. Instead he repels the charge. He

216

proclaims that the objection is out of order. He states that it is not a valid objection. He proclaims that man has no right to make a charge against God. For a man to try to judge God is for him to claim that his standard of justice is higher than God's standard.

Paul illustrates this by using a familiar Old Testament example. It is the example of a potter and his clay. The same illustration is used several times by the prophets.

> *You turn things around! Shall the potter be considered as equal with the clay, that what is made should say to its maker, "He did not make me"; or what is formed say to him who formed it, "He had no understanding"? (Isaiah 29:16).*

> *Woe to the one who quarrels with his Maker - an earthenware vessel among the vessels of earth! Will the clay say to the potter, "What are you doing?" Or the thing you are making say, "He has no hands"? 10 Woe to him who says to a father, "What are you begetting?" Or to a woman, "To what are you giving birth?" (Isaiah 45:9-10).*

> *But now, O Lord, Thou art our Father, we are the clay, and Thou our potter; and all of us are the work of Thy hand. (Isaiah 64:8).*

> *Then I went down to the potter's house, and there he was, making something on the wheel. 4 But the vessel that he was making of clay was spoiled in the hand of the potter; so he remade it into another vessel, as it pleased the potter to make. 5 Then the word of the Lord came to me saying, 6 "Can I not, O house of Israel, deal with you as this potter does?" declares the Lord. "Behold, like the clay in the potter's hand, so are you in My hand, O house of Israel." (Jeremiah 18:3-6).*

The illustration is of a potter sitting at his wheel. He takes a portion of clay from his pile and he fashions a beautiful vase to be sold at the market for a vast sum. Then from that same lump of clay, he might take another portion of clay and mold a basin to be used by a farmer for feeding his pigs.

No one would ever think of charging the potter with injustice because he had not given equal treatment to both lumps of clay. No one can question the potter's right to do with the lump of clay as he will. The principle is the same here. As the sovereign Creator, God can do anything with His creation that He desires. He is free to act as He chooses.

Now we admit that man is not the same as clay. Man has emotions and feelings and he is an intelligent creature. But he is still a creature. He was created. Thus God is free to make from that lump a Moses who will lead the Israelites out of Egypt. God is also free to make from that same lump a Pharaoh who will be used in spite of himself to glorify his Creator.

VESSELS OF MERCY AND VESSELS OF WRATH

Paul has just given us the illustration of the potter. In that illustration, he suggested that there are two kinds of pots -- one for honorable use and one for dishonorable use. Now he takes that illustration one step further.

1.   Vessels of Wrath.

> *What if God, although willing to demonstrate His wrath and to make His power known, endured with much patience vessels of wrath prepared for destruction? (Romans 9:22).*

This verse opens with a conditional clause. It is a first class condition. It assumes the truth of the statement which it proceeds. We could translate it "since." This is not merely a possible hypothesis, but an established fact.

From the lump of humanity there are some who have been designed as "vessels of wrath." These vessels of wrath have been prepared for the purpose of destruction. We call this the doctrine of reprobation. Their destiny is destruction.

At the same time, Paul does not specifically say that God created them to be vessels of wrath, but only that he endured those vessels. The point is that, although God's plan has included the sinful acts of men, we should not take this to mean that God has actively caused men to sin. To take such a position would be to make God the author of sin, a position against which the Bible is clearly opposed.

2.   Vessels of Mercy.

> *What if God, although willing to demonstrate*
> *His wrath and to make His power known, endured*
> *with much patience vessels of wrath prepared for*
> *destruction? 23 And He did so to make known the*
> *riches of His glory upon vessels of mercy, which He*
> *prepared beforehand for glory, 24 even us, whom He*
> *also called, not from among Jews only, but also from*
> *among Gentiles. (Romans 9:22-24).*

Why would God allow vessels of wrath? Verse 23 tells us the reason. This verse tells us why the sinner continually goes through this life without divine judgment being poured out on him. It tells us why God allows sin to continue in the world. It is so that God might make known the riches of His glory upon the vessels of mercy which He also created.

It is for our benefit. It is so that He might save us from the very worst and then freely give to us the very best so that, in the end, He might be glorified. Peter says it this way:

> *The Lord is not slow about his promise, as*
> *some count slowness, but is patient toward you, not*
> *wishing for any to perish, but for all to come to*
> *repentance. (2 Peter 3:9).*

This verse says that God wishes for all to come to repentance. Notice to whom the "all" refers. It is to the same group toward whom God is patient. It refers to "you." Peter is speaking to believers. He is speaking to those who are among the elect. He is speaking to those who have been chosen by God. This election has been manifested by the fact that these have come to faith in Jesus Christ. In effect, Peter is saying that God is being patient toward those whom He has chosen because He is not willing that any of them should perish.

Peter concludes that he wants believers to *regard the patience of our Lord to be salvation* (2 Peter 3:15). When we look at the patience of the Lord and realize that He is withholding His judgment of sin, we are not to think that God does not care about sin. Rather, the continuance of sin and suffering in the world is for our benefit and our salvation. If God had stopped all sin and all suffering 100 years ago, we would not have been saved. The fact that He has not done so is a sign of our salvation.

Paul says the same thing here in Romans. He says that God is enduring "with much patience vessels of wrath" (9:22). This is why Christ has not yet returned. He is withholding His judgment until all whom He has chosen are saved so that none should perish, but that all should come to repentance. There will be no objects of mercy who will be lost. God knows those who are His even before they know Him. And He has promised not to lose any.

THE TESTIMONY OF THE PROPHETS

If it is true that there are none of God's chosen people who will be lost, then how do we explain the case of Israel? After all, Israel is God's chosen people. Yet there are many of the Jews who rejected Jesus as the Messiah.

Paul has already given a partial answer in verse 6 when he said that "they are not all Israel who are descended from Israel." Now he goes on to show that this was in accordance with the promises of the Old Testament.

1.   The Promise of the Salvation of the Gentiles.

> *As He says also in Hosea, "I will call those who were not My people, 'My people,' and her who was not beloved, 'Beloved.'" 26 And it shall be that in the place where it was said to them, 'You are not my people,' there they shall be called sons of the living God." (Roman 9:25-26).*

Paul quotes from two separate passages in the book of Hosea (Hosea 2:23 and 1:10). His purpose is to show that God promised in the Old Testament to make those who were "not God's people" to become "God's people."

Unbelieving Gentiles	Believing Gentiles
Those who were not My people	My People
Her who was not beloved	Beloved

You are not my people	Sons of the Living God

Hosea wrote in a day of apostasy. The 10 tribes of the northern kingdom of Israel had rebelled against God. Because of their rebellion, the Lord said that He would reject them. Those who had been considered to be His people would no longer be His people. But with this message of judgment also came a message of grace. There was hope for the future. Although Israel would be taken away into captivity and scattered among the Gentile nations, God would gather from among those same Gentile nations a people for Himself. Those who were "not God's people" would become "His people." Though they had sinned and had become "non-Israelites," they could repent and return and become the people of God.

2.   The Promise of the Preservation of the Jews.

> *Isaiah cries out concerning Israel, "Though the number of the sons of Israel be like the sand of the sea, it is the remnant that will be saved; 28 for the Lord will execute His word on the earth, thoroughly and quickly."*
> *And just as Isaiah foretold, "Unless the Lord of Sabaoth had left to us a posterity, we would have become like Sodom, and would have resembled Gomorrah." (Romans 9:27-29).*

Paul now turns to Isaiah. This passage promises that there shall always be a remnant. This is a promise of hope. It is a promise that, even though not all Israel is Israel and even though those who are not God's people are going to become God's people, there shall continue to be a remnant of Israel who shall be Israel. Apart from the grace of God, Israel would have degenerated to the moral depravity of Sodom and Gomorrah.

Do you see the principle? Man without God always degenerates. It is only by God's gracious election that some men are saved. Apart from God's gracious choice, none would ever be saved.

3.   The Promise of Israel's Failure leading to Gentile Victory.

> *What shall we say then? That Gentiles, who*

did not pursue righteousness, attained righteousness, even the righteousness which is by faith; 31 but Israel, pursuing a law of righteousness, did not arrive at that law.

Why? Because they did not pursue it by faith, but as though it were by works. They stumbled over the stumbling stone, 33 just as it is written, "Behold, I lay in Zion a stone of stumbling and a rock of offense, and he who believes in Him will not be disappointed." (Romans 9:30-33).

Paul now presents a general contrast between Jews and Gentiles as they relate to the righteousness of God. That contrast is set forth in the following chart:

Gentiles	Jews
Did not pursue righteousness	Pursued a law of righteousness
Attained the righteousness which is by faith	Did not arrive at that law because they did not pursue it by faith

The righteousness which the Gentiles attained is the one which Paul set forth in Romans 3 -- the righteousness which is imputed through faith in Christ. The irony is that the Gentiles were not all that concerned with righteousness in the first place. It was the Jews whose very culture consisted of a search for righteousness. The problem is that they could never manage to attain that for which they sought. It seems a bit unfair. The Gentiles stumble onto righteousness with no effort at all. Where did the Jews go wrong? The answer is seen in verse 32. They stumbled. The cause of their stumbling was a stone.

Paul combines Isaiah 8:14 with Isaiah 28:16, both of which speak of a "stone of stumbling." Those who trust in Jesus as the Messiah find Him to be their rock of salvation. But to those who reject Him, He is a stone of stumbling. What kind of a "stone" is Jesus to you? Is He the rock of your salvation, or is He a stone of offense? Is Jesus the basis of your stumbling or the source of your salvation?

My Assignment

Angels

The Messengers of God

The Bible is not primarily a book about angels or demons. It does mention them, to be sure, but even when it does, it is usually to make a bigger point. This means that a study of angels and demons will be a study of that which is on the periphery of a Biblical focus. There is nothing wrong with such a study, but it should be recognized that a study of such a side issue is exactly that.

Angels are seen from Genesis to Revelation. They are mention over a hundred times in the Old Testament and some 165 times in the New Testament. One might even say that, while they are not the focus of the Biblical message, that they form a backdrop against which that message is given.

THE ORIGIN OF THE ANGELS

1 Praise the LORD!
Praise the LORD from the heavens;
Praise Him in the heights!
2 Praise Him, all His angels;
Praise Him, all His hosts!
3 Praise Him, sun and moon;
Praise Him, all stars of light!
4 Praise Him, highest heavens,
And the waters that are above the heavens!
5 Let them praise the name of the LORD,

For He commanded and they were created. (Psalm 148:1-5).

From the infinite solitude of eternity, God spoke and the universe sprang into existence. In a single moment of time, the heavens were woven together in a glorious tapestry as newborn stars blazed forth their light, moving out to form spinning galaxies. No man was present at that moment. No human eye was there to gaze upon the wonders of creation. No mortal was present to appreciate the handiwork of the Creator.

There were others who were there. There were supernatural beings who witnessed the hand of the Architect of the universe at work. These special servants of God gazed upon the grand design of the cosmos and they sang forth the praises of the God of creation.

> *4 Where were you when I laid the foundation of the earth?*
> *Tell Me, if you have understanding,*
> *5 Who set its measurements, since you know?*
> *Or who stretched the line on it?*
> *6 On what were its bases sunk?*
> *Or who laid its cornerstone,*
> *7 When the morning stars sang together,*
> *And all the sons of God shouted for joy? (Job 38:4-7).*

These special servants of the Lord who sang His praises at the creation are described by Job as "the sons of God." We know them as angels. They are God's created beings, glorious and mysterious and supernatural creatures.

How do we know that angels were created by God and that they did not come about in some other manner? Because the Scriptures are specific to tell us about creation.

> *For by Him all things were created, both in the heavens and on earth, visible and invisible, whether thrones or dominions or rulers or authorities-- all things have been created by Him and for Him. (Colossians 1:16).*

Notice that it is not merely things or the earth of things that are visible that have been created by the Lord. This is a universal statement of creation that deliberately takes in those invisible, heavenly beings we know as angels.

THE MINISTRY OF THE ANGELS

What is an angel? Both the Hebrew as well as the Greek word for angel have the same meaning. In both languages, the term refers to a messenger. As such, it can refer to an earthly messenger or it can refer to a heavenly messenger. It is the context that helps us to determine which is in view.

(1)   Our English word "angel" is a transliteration from the Greek word ἀγγελος, the word for a messenger.

(2)   The Hebrew word for "angel" is מַלְאָךְ (*malach*) and also means "messenger."

We see a number of instances throughout the Bible where supernatural creatures bear God's message to mortal men.

- Two angels accompanied the Lord when He came and spoke to Abraham.
- Two angels met Lot in the city of Sodom and warned him of the coming judgment.
- An angel wrestled with Jacob in the night and blessed him and changed his name to Israel.
- An angel spoke to Joshua and gave him instructions on how to take the city of Jericho.
- An angel spoke to Gideon and commissioned him to drive the enemies of Israel from the land.
- An angel shut the mouths of the lions when Daniel was cast into the den of lions.
- A certain angel came to Mary and told her that she would give birth to the Messiah.
- Angels appeared to the shepherds and announced the birth of Christ.

One of the most significant ministries of angels in the Old Testament was the transmission of the Mosaic Law. This is attested a number of times in the Scriptures.

> *This is the one who was in the congregation in the wilderness together with the angel who was speaking to him on Mount Sinai, and who was with our fathers; and he received living oracles to pass on to you. (Acts 7:38).*

225

> *...you who received the law as ordained by angels, and yet did not keep it. (Acts 7:53).*

> *Why the Law then? It was added because of transgressions, having been ordained through angels by the agency of a mediator... (Galatians 3:19a).*

Angels were somehow involved in the transmission of the law to Moses at Mount Sinai. Their involvement in this process is described to underscore the monumental importance of the law.

JEWISH VIEWS ON ANGELS

The Jews had a very high regard for angels. They considered that if a message was given by an angel, it carried a much greater weight than if it had been spoken by a mere man. The Jewish writings taught that angels served as mediators between God and men. This was correct as far as it went, but they also taught that angels were involved in God's decision making processes. They thought that God always consulted His angels before making up His mind on what course of action He was going to take. They pointed to Genesis 1:26 as a proof text for this belief.

> *Then God said, "Let US make man in Our image, according to Our likeness; and let them rule over the fish of the sea and over the birds of the sky and over the cattle and over all the earth, and over every creeping thing that creeps on the earth." (Genesis 1:26).*

This verse was interpreted by the Jewish rabbis to picture God talking to His angels, asking their advice concerning the creation of man. The Jews also believe that the angels were responsible for keeping the stars in place, for holding back the sea, for the control of the weather and for the keeping of time. They also believed there to be angels who served as prison wardens in hell and who tortured the people who were sent there.

By the New Testament times, there is evidence in the apocryphal writings that the Jews had entertained all sorts of extra-biblical ideas regarding angels. Books such as Enoch and Tobit and 4th Esdras speaks of specific angels such as Uriel, Raphael, Peniel, Metatron. The book of Enoch suggests that Enoch was elevated to the status of an angel when he walked with God. It is possibly the result of such influences that leads to Paul's cryptic warning in Colossians 2:18 against the worship of the angels.

JESUS AND ANGELS

The epistle to the Hebrews spends an entire chapter dealing with people who had been raised to believe many of the rabbinical concepts of angels. As a result, they assumed that there could be nothing that was greater than the angels. There were some who had even gone to the extreme of worshiping angels (Colossians 2:18). Eventually, a teaching known as Gnosticism would arise that would teach Jesus was an angel.

The message of the book of Hebrews is that Jesus is better. The covenant He brought is better than the first covenant that was brought by angels. His covenant is a better covenant because He is better than the angels.

1. Sons of God: *Having become as much better than the angels, as He has inherited a more excellent name than they. 5 For to which of the angels did He ever say, "Thou art My Son, Today I have begotten Thee"? And again, "I will be a Father to Him And He shall be a Son to Me"? (Hebrews 1:4-5).* Even though the term "sons of God" is used in the Old Testament in a context that seems to refer to angels (Job 1:6; 2:1; 38:7), that does not mean that angels are the sons of God in the same way that Jesus is the Son of God. They are sons of God in the sense that they have been created by God. By contrast, Jesus is the Son of God in a totally unique sense.

2. Angels and Worship: *And when He again brings the first-born into the world, He says, "And let all the angels of God worship Him." (Hebrews 1:6).*

    The next reason Jesus is better than the angels is because He is to be worshiped by the angels. This passage is another quotation from the Old Testament. It is a prophecy found in the book of Psalms.

    > *Let all those be ashamed who serve graven images,*
    > *Who boast themselves of idols;*
    > *Worship Him, all you gods. (Psalm 97:7).*

    This raises a question. The psalm that is cited by the author to the Hebrews does not specifically mention angels. It is only in the

Greek Septuagint that the word translated "gods" (*Elohim*) is translated with the Greek ἀγγελοι (angels). The writer to the Hebrews is evidently citing the Septuagint and indicates this verse as containing a prophecy of Jesus that was fulfilled when the angels worshiped Him.

Do you recall the story of the angelic announcement at the birth of Jesus? The scene was the rolling hills outside the village of Bethlehem. A group of shepherds were gathered together in the cool of the night. Suddenly the stillness of the night was broken.

> *And an angel of the Lord suddenly stood before them, and the glory of the Lord shone around them; and they were terribly frightened. (Luke 2:9).*

The reaction to this angelic visitor was the reaction of which we normally read in the Bible when it describes people being confronted with angels. It is the reaction of fear. The shepherds were not merely frightened. They were terribly frightened. They were frightened with great fright. As a result, the angel says to the shepherd the same thing that angels always say to people when they appear. They tell them not to be afraid.

> *And the angel said to them, "Do not be afraid; for behold, I bring you good news of a great joy which shall be for all the people; 11 for today in the city of David there has been born for you a Savior, who is Christ the Lord. 12 And this will be a sign for you: you will find a baby wrapped in cloths, and lying in a manger." (Luke 2:10-12).*

The angelic messenger had come with a very specific message. It was to tell these shepherds of the birth of Jesus. It was to give them the sign so they would be able to identify Him.

As great a sight as this angel was to the shepherds, his presence was to serve a still greater purpose. He had come to bear witness of One that was greater than himself. He was sent to announce the one who is Christ the Lord. The fact that the lesser is bearing witness to the greater is seen in what takes place in the next two verses.

> *And suddenly there appeared with the angel a*

> *multitude of the heavenly host praising God, and saying, 14 "Glory to God in the highest, And on earth peace among men with whom He is pleased." (Luke 2:13-14).*

The single angel gave way to a host of angels -- an entire army of angels. These same angels who sang for joy at the creation of the cosmos are now pictured praising the Lord at the announcement of the birth of the One who created the cosmos.

3.   The Role of Angels: *And of the angels He says, "Who makes His angels winds, And His ministers a flame of fire." (Hebrews 1:7).*

The angels are seen in contrast to Jesus as regards their separate roles. The angels are described as spirits and ministers. The quotation is taken from the Psalms. Psalm 104 is a song of praise. It describes God as the One who controls all of creation.

> *He makes the winds His messengers,*
> *Flaming fire His ministers. (Psalm 104:4).*

This is a picture of the sovereign God. He controls the universe. The wind and the rain and the lightning all do His bidding. Notice that the Hebrews passage substitutes the word "angel" for "messenger." This is because they are the same word in both the Greek and the Hebrew. In the context of the Psalms, the writer is speaking of the physical world and of God's control of the winds. But here in the epistle to the Hebrews, a higher truth is in view. Here we see that God is in control of the spiritual world as well as the physical world.

This brings us to another question. Why are angels identified as "winds?" The Greek word translated "winds" is πνευματα, the plural of πνευμα. It can be translated "wind." The same Greek word can also be translated "spirit." It is the latter meaning that is used by the writer to the Hebrews.

Angels are spirit beings. They are spirit oriented. They can see spiritual events in the same way that we can see physical events. The spiritual world is just as real and as experiential to them as the physical world is real and experiential to us.

I believe in the spiritual world, but I cannot see the spiritual world. I cannot see my prayers ascending to heaven. I cannot see my sins being forgiven. I cannot see the spiritual conflict going on around me. These things are intangible to me. But I am not so certain that they are intangible to the angels. This is because angels are made differently than we are. They possess a different set of senses. They have a different kind of body.

4.   Ministering Spirits: *But to which of the angels has He ever said, "Sit at My right hand, Until I make Thine enemies A footstool for Thy feet"? 14 Are they not all ministering spirits, sent out to render service for the sake of those who will inherit salvation? (Hebrews 1:13-14).*

The next point of contrast between Jesus Christ and the angels is that God has made Jesus the sovereign ruler over all things: *Sit at My right hand, until I make Thine enemies a footstool for Thy feet (1:13).* This was never said to angels. They were never invited to sit in the seat of honor at the right hand of God. On the contrary, angels have the role of servanthood. They are ministering spirits. They have a ministry. Their ministry is one of rendering service. They have been assigned the task of rendering service to those who will inherit salvation.

Now let me ask you a question. Who are the heirs of salvation? We are! When a person believes in Jesus Christ and trusts in Him as Savior and Lord, he becomes an heir of God's salvation.

Here is a fantastic truth. These supernatural beings have been assigned the task of ministering to you. You are not aware of all the dangers that face you through the day. But God is aware. And He has assigned His holy angels to protect you. They keep harm from coming your way. They allow nothing to touch you that has not been approved by the Lord. And, when the day finally comes that you are called home, they will act as your royal escort to heaven (Luke 16:22).

THE ELECT ANGELS

There are two basic categories of angels described in the Bible, just as there are two basic kinds of people. There are those who love the Lord and who seek to follow Him and there are those who do not.

1.   Designations of Angels.

There are several different designations that are used to describe those angels who are aligned with the Lord and in His service.

Holy Angels	Jesus described the Son of Man coming in His glory with the holy angels (Mark 8:38; Luke 9:26)
Angels of God	Jacob's vision of a ladder stretching to heaven was populated with the angels of God (Genesis 28:12; John 1:51).
Angels of heaven	Jesus speaks in Matthew 24:36 of how not even the angels of heaven know the timetable of His coming.
Chosen Angels	Paul speaks of the witness of the chosen angels in 1 Timothy 5:21). This suggests that the destiny of the angels rest ultimately in the hands of the one who chose them.

2.   Characteristics of Angels.

They cannot die	*...those who are considered worthy to attain to that age and the resurrection from the dead, neither marry, nor are given in marriage; 36 for neither can they die anymore, for they are like angels (Luke 20:35-36).*
They are mighty	*...the Lord Jesus shall be revealed from heaven with His mighty angels in flaming fire (2 Thessalonians 1:7).*
They are subordinate to Christ	*...Jesus Christ, 22 who is at the right hand of God, having gone into heaven, after angels and authorities and powers had been subjected to Him. (1 Peter 3:22).*
They cannot tell what we are thinking	This is suggested in the prayer of Solomon as he speaks to the Lord, saying: *Thou alone dost know the hearts of all the sons of men (1 Kings 8:39).*

Perhaps it is only happenstance that angels are always described in the masculine gender. They occasionally appear in the form of men, but we never read of them appearing in feminine form. This is not to suggest that such a thing is impossible.

3.   The Role of the Angels.

- They shall gather the elect at the second coming of Christ (Matthew 24:31).
- They carry the saved to heaven (Luke 16:22).
- They served as messengers to bring the law (Acts 7:53; Galatians 3:19).
- They are ministers to the elect (Hebrews 1:14).

TYPES OF ANGELS

1.   The Angel of the Lord: The reference to that angel of the Lord is often used in a way that suggests it to be a manifestation of God Himself. For example, in Genesis 31:11-13, the angel of the Lord appears to Jacob in a dream and identifies Himself as "the god of Bethel." Similarly, in Exodus 3:2 the angel of the Lord appears to Moses in the burning bush and identifies Himself in verse 6 as the God of Abraham, Isaac and Jacob.

2.   Cherubim: This is the plural form of the singular "cherub." Modern English conjures up an image of a winged baby with fat little cheeks, but the Hebrew carries no such idea. The Hebrew כְּרוּב seems to be related to the Akkadian verb, "to bless." [3]

3.   Seraphim: The seraphim are mentioned only in Isaiah 6. The Hebrew term שָׂרַף (*saraph*) means "to burn." These are therefore the "burning ones." This is in keeping with the description of Hebrews 1:7 where the Lord is seen as the one *who makes His angels winds, and His ministers a flame of fire.*

---

[3] Laird Harris, Theological Wordbook of the Old Testament. Moody Press, 1980. Page 454.

SPECIFIC ANGELS

There are only two angels in the Bible that are specifically named and designated. They are Michael and Gabriel.

1.   Michael the Archangel.

Michael is mentioned by name as "one of the chief princes" in the angelic community in Daniel 10:13 where he comes to the aid of another angelic messenger. He is mentioned again in Daniel 12:1 as *the great prince who stands guard over the sons of your people*. This guardianship is alluded to in Jude 1:9 when we read of Michael disputing with Satan over the body of Moses.

In Revelation 12:7-9, we are treated to a vision in which Michael leads the holy angels into a war against Satan and his forces. The end comes when Michael and his hosts cast out Satan and his followers.

2.   Gabriel.

The angel Gabriel is known for his announcements to Daniel (Daniel 8:16; 9:21), to Zacharias (Luke 1:11-20) and to Mary (Luke 1:26-37). He describes himself as the one who *stands in the presence of God* (Luke 1:19).

THE PERSON AND CAREER OF SATAN

1.   Names and Designations.

Our English name "Satan" is a transliteration of the Hebrew שָׂטָן, which means "enemy." The verbal form שָׂטַן means "to oppose." It is interesting to note that the first Biblical use of this word describes the angel of the Lord:

> *But God was angry because he was going, and the angel of the LORD took his stand in the way as an* **adversary** *against him. Now he was riding on his donkey and his two servants were with him. (Numbers 22:22).*

Another example of where שָׂטָן refers to someone other than Satan is in the account of those who rose up in opposition to the reign of Solomon.

> *Then the LORD raised up an adversary to Solomon, Hadad the Edomite; he was of the royal line in Edom. (1 Kings 11:14).*

There are several other designations and titles for Satan. He is called most often in the New Testament ὁ διάβολος (*ho diabolos*), "the slanderer" or "the schemer." This term was often used in the Septuagint to translate שָׂטָן, not only when it referred to the supernatural enemy of God, but even when it spoke of a normal adversary. Other titles for Satan include:

- The tempter (Matthew 4:3).
- Beelzebul (Matthew 12:24).
- The evil one (Matthew 13:19).
- The father of lies (John 8:44).
- The ruler of this world (John 12:31).
- Belial (2 Corinthians 6:15).
- The prince of the power of the air (Ephesians 2:2).
- The adversary (1 Peter 5:8).
- Abaddon and Apollyon, both of which mean "destroyer" (Revelation 9:11).
- Deceiver of the whole world (Revelation 12:9).
- The Great Dragon (Revelation 12:9).
- Accuser of the brethren (Revelation 12:10).

2.   The Fall of Satan.

The prophet Ezekiel gives a series of lamentations over the ancient city of Tyre and against its leadership. In the midst of one of these lamentations, he begins to speak of the "king of Tyre" in a way that seems to go beyond the identity of a mere mortal.

> *12 Son of man, take up a lamentation over the king of Tyre, and say to him, "Thus says the Lord God,*
> *'You had the seal of perfection,*
> *Full of wisdom and perfect in beauty.*

13 You were in Eden, the garden of God;
Every precious stone was your covering:
The ruby, the topaz, and the diamond;
The beryl, the onyx, and the jasper;
The lapis lazuli, the turquoise, and the emerald;
And the gold, the workmanship of your settings and sockets,
Was in you.
On the day that you were created
They were prepared.
14 You were the anointed cherub who covers,
And I placed you there.
You were on the holy mountain of God;
You walked in the midst of the stones of fire.
15 You were blameless in your ways
From the day you were created,
Until unrighteousness was found in you.
16 By the abundance of your trade
You were internally filled with violence,
And you sinned;
Therefore I have cast you as profane
From the mountain of God.
And I have destroyed you, O covering cherub,
From the midst of the stones of fire.
17 Your heart was lifted up because of your beauty;
You corrupted your wisdom by reason of your splendor.
I cast you to the ground; I put you before kings,
That they may see you.
18 By the multitude of your iniquities,
In the unrighteousness of your trade,
You profaned your sanctuaries.
Therefore I have brought fire from the midst of you;
It has consumed you,
And I have turned you to ashes on the earth In the
eyes of all who see you.
19 All who know you among the peoples
Are appalled at you;
You have become terrified,
And you will be no more." (Ezekiel 28:12-19).

This is part of a larger oracle against the city of Tyre. The earlier part of this chapter speaks out against the "Prince of Tyre."

Now the address changes. These verses are directed against the "King" of Tyre. He is the real power behind the throne. There are some things said of this person that lead some Bible scholars to believe that this is a reference to Satan.

- He was in Eden, the garden of God (28:13).
- He was created (28:13).
- He was the anointed cherub (28:14).
- He was on the holy mountain of God (28:14).

This description seems to go beyond the realm of mortal man. Though some scholars would see this description as mere Semitic poetry describing an exalted monarch, it seems to me that there is meant to be a greater understanding and that the one in view is Satan himself.

3.   Satan in Eden.

Satan is not mentioned by name in the Pentateuch. However, we can see him behind the scenes in the early chapters of Genesis. We read of the temptation by the serpent in Genesis 3 and we can note that one of the titles given to Satan is *that old serpent, called the Devil, and Satan* (Revelation 12:9).

Rabbinic legend has it that the serpent originally walked erect and that it was not until God's curse on this animal in Genesis 3:14 that it was reduced to moving upon its belly as it does today. The unusual aspect about the serpent was that it manifested the ability to speak to the woman. This brings us to a dilemma. Snakes cannot talk. The most likely resolve to this issue is to view Satan himself as the speaking power behind the serpent. Such a phenomenon is not unknown to the Scriptures. Satan is regularly seen working through intermediate agencies. He uses his demons and he uses human agents, either through possession or through indirect manipulation. The use of animals is seen in Matthew 8:28-32 where Jesus casts demons out of two men and permits them to enter into a herd of pigs.

4.   The Satanic Conflict.

Genesis 3 introduces a cosmic conflict between the followers of Satan and One who is described as the Seed of the woman.

14 And the LORD God said to the serpent,
"Because you have done this,
Cursed are you more than all cattle,
And more than every beast of the field;
On your belly shall you go,
And dust shall you eat
All the days of your life;
15 And I will put enmity
Between you and the woman,
And between your seed and her seed;
He shall bruise you on the head,
And you shall bruise him on the heel." (Genesis 3:14-15).

This conflict is ordained between the seed of the serpent and the Seed of the woman. Just as the woman had been involved in the transgression, so also now she would be involved in the redemption. As through her came sin, so also through her would come the Savior.

> *But when the fulness of the time came, God sent forth His Son, born of a woman, born under the Law (Galatians 4:4).*

The "seed of the woman" anticipates the coming of One who would be born, not of the seed of a man, but exclusively through a woman. This promise finds its eventual fulfillment in the One who was born of a virgin and apart from the seed of a man. At the same time, Jesus was a man of flesh and blood so that He could live and die as a man and pay in His own body the penalty for the sins of men.

> *Since then the children share in flesh and blood, He Himself likewise also partook of the same, that through death He might render powerless him who had the power of death, that is, the devil (Hebrews 2:14).*

The defeat of Satan is accomplished in two parts. First, Christ defeated Satan when He died for sins upon the cross and then rose in victory from the grave.

> *...having canceled out the certificate of debt consisting of decrees against us and which was*

hostile to us; and He has taken it out of the way, having nailed it to the cross. 15 When He had disarmed the rulers and authorities, He made a public display of them, having triumphed over them through Him. (Colossians 2:14-15).

The rulers and authorities that Jesus disarmed through His death were not the Roman or Jewish officials. This is speaking of spiritual rulers and authorities. Satan's defeat came through the death of Christ. What appeared to be a defeat for the Seed of the woman was instead the way to victory over the serpent and his seed.

Seed of the Serpent	Seed of the Woman
Satan	Jesus Christ
Fatally bruised for all eternity	Temporarily bruised upon the cross
Pictured by a bruise to the head	Pictured by a bruise to the heel

The picture is of a man who stomps upon the head of a snake, being bitten on his foot in the process. He wins the conflict over the serpent, but only at the cost of great pain. This was fulfilled upon the cross when Jesus defeated Satan by undoing that which he had accomplished in the garden.

At the same time, the ultimate and final defeat of Satan is still in the future. Paul tells us that *the God of peace will soon crush Satan under your feet* (Romans 16:20). Just as the snake is destroyed by striking him on the head, that most vulnerable part of his body, so Jesus Christ will neutralize Satan.

5.   The Continuing Conflict: *Be of sober spirit, be on the alert. Your adversary, the devil, prowls about like a roaring lion, seeking someone to devour.* (1 Peter 5:8).

Though Satan was defeated upon the cross, there is an element of the conflict that still continues today. Like a lion that has been mortally wounded, he is still able to cause great damage. The good news is that he can be resisted.

> *But resist him, firm in your faith, knowing that the same experiences of suffering are being accomplished by your brethren who are in the world. (1 Peter 5:9).*

> *Submit therefore to God. Resist the devil and he will flee from you. (James 4:7).*

The devil is pictured as a hungry, roaring lion in search of a meal. The good news is that we worship the God who is able to close the mouths of hungry, roaring lions.

One of the lessons we learn from the book of Job is that Satan can do nothing unless he receives permission from the throne of heaven. God is sovereign over all creation and even Satan cannot ultimately resist His will.

> *You are from God, little children, and have overcome them; because greater is He who is in you than he who is in the world. (1 John 4:4).*

Our victory is found in the person of Christ. Because He has won the victory in His victorious resurrection, so we enjoy the status of victors in the Satanic conflict. At the same time, there continues a spiritual struggle.

> *For our struggle is not against flesh and blood, but against the rulers, against the powers, against the world forces of this darkness, against the spiritual forces of wickedness in the heavenly places. (Ephesians 6:12).*

Our battle in this ongoing conflict is of a spiritual nature. When it degenerates into flesh and blood, it is because we have lost sight of the true nature of the conflict. The real battle is found in a spiritual realm for spiritual goals -- the very souls of men. Just as the conflict is of a spiritual nature, so also the weapons of our warfare are of a spiritual nature.

- Your loins girded with truth (6:14).
- The breastplate of righteousness (6:14).
- Your feet shod with the preparation of the gospel of peace

(6:15).
- The shield of faith with which you will be able to extinguish all the flaming missiles of the evil one (6:16).
- The helmet of salvation (7:17).
- The sword of the Spirit, which is the word of God (7:17).

Of course, we also need to be aware of the Satanic strategy. Satan does not show up with a pitchfork and a red union suit. He tries to pass himself off as a counterfeit of the truth.

> *For such men are false apostles, deceitful workers, disguising themselves as apostles of Christ. 14 And no wonder, for even Satan disguises himself as an angel of light. 15 Therefore it is not surprising if his servants also disguise themselves as servants of righteousness; whose end shall be according to their deeds. (2 Corinthians 11:13-15).*

Much of what passes under the guise of human religion today has the prince of darkness at its center.

EVIL ANGELS

The evil angels are given several designations in the Bible. They are known under a variety of labels.

1. Demons: Our English word "demon" comes from the Greek δαιμονιον (*daimonion*). Both in secular Greek as well as in the Septuagint, it referred to a spiritual influence, either good or bad. Such a secular usage is seen in Acts 17:18 where some of the Greeks viewed Paul as *a proclaimer of strange deities*, literally, a "proclaimer of strange demons." Most other references to demons in the New Testament refer to the demonic fallen angels who follow after Satan.

2. The Devil's Angels: Jesus spoke of *the eternal fire which has been prepared for the devil and his angels* (Matthew 25:41).

3. Fallen Angels: Jude speaks *of the angels who did not keep their own domain, but abandoned their proper abode* (Jude 1:6). They are said

to be kept under bonds as they await their judgment. These seem to be a reference to angels who were cast into hell and *committed to pits of darkness, reserved for judgment* (2 Peter 2:4).

4.   Spirits: These are seen alternately as unclean spirits (Matthew 10:1; Mark 1:27; 3:11; 5:13; 6:7), evil spirits (Acts 19:12-13), seducing spirits (1 Timothy 4:1) and spirits of devils (Revelation 16:13-14).

Based upon some of these passages, we can conclude that there are two types of fallen angels.

Those who are Free	Those who are Bound
When Jesus confronted the man with the legion of demons who were possessing him, they begged not to be thrown into the abyss. Jesus allowed them instead to enter a herd of swine (Luke 8:26-33).	*God did not spare angels when they sinned, but cast them into hell and committed them to pits of darkness, reserved for judgment* (2 Peter 2:4). *Angels who did not keep their own domain, but abandoned their proper abode, He has kept in eternal bonds under darkness for the judgment of the great day.* (Jude 1:6).
If the demons at Gardassa did not want to be bound, then the implication is that there are some demons who have been bound.	

- Demons believe in God: *You believe that God is one. You do well; the demons also believe, and shudder (James 2:19).*

- Demons were able to recognize Jesus: *And there was a man in the synagogue possessed by the spirit of an unclean demon, and he cried out with a loud voice, 34 "Ha! What do we have to do with You, Jesus of Nazareth? Have You come to destroy us? I know who You are-- the Holy One of God!" (Luke 4:33-34).*

- Demons have their own teachings: *But the Spirit explicitly says that in later times some will fall away from the faith, paying attention to deceitful spirits and doctrines of demons (1 Timothy 4:1).*

- The disciples were given power and authority over the demons: *And He called the twelve together, and gave them power and authority over all the demons, and to heal diseases. (Luke 9:1).*

- Even unbelievers have on occasion been able to cast out demons: *Many will say to Me on that day, "Lord, Lord, did we not prophesy in Your name, and in Your name cast out demons, and in Your name perform many miracles?" 23 And then I will declare to them, "I never knew you; depart from Me, you who practice lawlessness." (Matthew 7:22-23).*

Anthropology
The Study of Man

4 What is man, that Thou dost take thought of him?
And the son of man, that Thou dost care for him?
5 Yet Thou hast made him a little lower than God,
And dost crown him with glory and majesty!
6 Thou dost make him to rule over the works of Thy hands;
Thou hast put all things under his feet,
7 All sheep and oxen,
And also the beasts of the field,
8 The birds of the heavens, and the fish of the sea,
Whatever passes through the paths of the seas. (Psalm 8:4-8).

What is man? The Psalmist asks this as a rhetorical question. It expects no actual answer. What is man? Is he worthy of God's consideration? No. The only reason that God considers man is because of God's own mercy and grace.

We can imagine that David wrote this Psalm one evening as he looked out into the silver starlight over Jerusalem. He sees the splendor of the heavens and he bursts forth in song. As David looks at the awesome works of the Lord, he asks why would such a God ever bother with mankind.

Go out and look at an anthill. Those ants are so much smaller and so much more insignificant than you are. The gap between God and man is infinitely greater than that which is between you and those ants. And yet, God has not only bothered with man, but He has crowned him with glory and honor and has appointed him over the creation and has put all things in subjection under his feet.

Mankind today is going through an identity crisis. He is seeking to find out who and what he is. He is looking for meaning to his life. He is searching for some basis of self-worth. He has not been able to find the answer to this quest in modern science. Modern science told him that he is merely a chance happening, a random collection of genetic mistakes. This left him without any basis for self worth.

Postmodernism came along and rejected the conclusions of modernism, but has nothing with which to replace it. Man has been left to try to re-invent himself, knowing that such re-invention is too shallow a foundation upon which to find his needed self worth.

The only real answer to man's identity crisis is found in the Word of God. By looking into the Scriptures, I can learn who I am and what I am. It is here that I can find that I have worth. God has declared that I have infinite worth, since He paid an infinite price for me when He sent His Son to die in my place.

It is a common phenomena that the way we think about ourselves is not based upon how we see ourselves, but upon how we think that others think of us. The Christian is to have a different perspective. He is to see himself based upon how God thinks of him. God has said that you are valuable. He has placed infinite value upon you. You were made in His image and after His likeness. You can know who you are and what you are.

Man has been given an exalted in creation. That position will one day be exalted even higher. The writer to the Hebrews says that man is only a little lower than the angels (Hebrews 2:7). That is quite high. That is higher than anything else in creation. But this lower status is not permanent. It is only for a "little while." There is coming a day when man will be equal to the angels. Jesus said that those who attain to the resurrection of the dead will be like the angels (Luke 20:34-36).

THE ORIGIN OF MAN

> 26 Then God said, "Let Us make man in Our image, according to Our likeness; and let them rule over the fish of the sea and over the birds of the sky and over the cattle and over all the earth, and over every creeping thing that creeps on the earth." 27 And God created man in His own image, in the image of God He created him; male and female He created them. (Genesis 1:26-27).

The creation of man was the crowning of God's creation. It serves as the climax of the creation account. That account describes the origins of light, of dry land, of birds and fish and animals. Each of those creative acts were introduced with similar language:

Let there be light...
Let there be an expanse in the midst of the waters...
Let the earth sprout vegetation...
Let the earth bring forth living creatures...

Now we find something different. It is a new formula. It breaks the mold of the previous descriptions of God's workings and brings our attention to a new endeavor.

Let Us make man in Our image, according to Our likeness...

There is a special care and concern taken in the creation of man. It is seen in the use of the plural: *Let US make man.* Some have seen this as an early indication of the Trinity. Others see it as a use of the plural of majesty. In either case, it reflects a special care and concern in God's deliberations as God prepares to create that which is special.

1.   In the Image and Likeness of God.

There is, on the one hand, a sense in which man is like the rest of creation. He is a creature along with all the rest of the creatures. He was created along with the rest of creation.

God
Man
Animals
Birds and Fish
Vegetation
Heavens and Earth

There is a barrier between God and the rest of His creation. God is set apart from His creation in the sense that He is "other" than His creation. He is unique. He alone had no beginning. He alone is infinite. At the same time, there is another sense in which man is joined to God and set apart from the rest of creation.

God
Man
Animals
Birds and Fish
Vegetation
Heavens and Earth

Man has been created in the image of God. That fact sets him apart from the rest of creation. He is not just an advanced animal. He is distinct in sharing the image and the likeness of his Creator.

2.   Ramifications of Man's Image and Likeness.

When we speak of man being in the "image and likeness" of God, this presents a problem. God is invisible. He has no outward image or likeness. How then can man be said to be made in the image and likeness of God? Theologians have suggested a number of ways.

> Wayne Grudem points out that "when the Creator of the universe wanted to create something 'in His image,' something *more like himself* than all the rest of creation, He made us. This realization will give us a profound sense of dignity and significance as we reflect on the excellence of all the rest of God's creation: the starry universe, the abundant earth, the world of plants and animals, and the angelic kingdoms are remarkable, even magnificent. But we are more like our Creator than any of those things" (1994:449).

a.   Dominion.

This is suggested in the context of Genesis 1. Following the mention of man being made in the image and likeness of God, the writer goes on to speak in the very next verse of the dominion that man is to have over the rest of creation.

And God blessed them; and God said to them, "Be fruitful and multiply, and fill the earth, and subdue it; and rule over the fish of the sea and over the birds of the sky, and over every living thing that moves on the earth."

(Genesis 1:28).

Man is in God's place, the place of rulership, with respect to the rest of life on this planet. He is the divine representative on planet earth. He has been given the position of federal headship over the earth. It is because of this that man's fall was able to impact all of the rest of creation. When man fell into sin, the rest of creation followed suit because it was under man's dominion.

b.   Self consciousness: Man is aware of his own existence and is able to think and to meditate upon who and what he is.

c.   Moral reason: Man feels that he ought to do what is right. He has been given a conscience that urges him to do what is right and to refrain from doing that which is wrong. That does not mean the conscience always gives the correct answer to what is right or wrong. The Bible tells us that the conscience can be seared (1 Timothy 4:2). It can be so hardened that it becomes insensitive to that to which it was once sensitive.

d.   Intellect and Creativity: Man has a much greater mental and intellectual capacity than is found in animals. Though animals often have keener eyesight, greater strength, faster reflexes, and a hardier stamina, it is at the point of his intellect and creativity that man is seen to be superior.

e.   Free volition: Man has volitional capabilities and is able to make decisions. That does not mean he is able to exercise that volition apart from his nature, but he does make decisions within the realm allowed by the bounds of his nature. Such a statement does not discount or diminish the sovereignty of God. Man's free will operates within the framework of God's plan and purposes. Man's will flows through the channels laid by the sovereignty of God. *The king's heart is like channels of water in the hand of the LORD; He turns it wherever He wishes. (Proverbs 21:1).*

f.   Spiritual capacity: It has been said that man is the only religious animal. This is one of the things that sets man apart from the rest of creation. No animal has ever been seen building an altar or praying to God. It is true that this spiritual capacity to communicate with God has often been distorted by sin. Men have turned away from the one true God to worship idols of wood and stone. Yet even in this, man demonstrates his spiritual capacity, for there is within the unbeliever a God-shaped vacuum that he tries to fill with various religious systems and idolatries. Man is a worshiping creature. He always worships something.

Man continues to be in the image of God today, although that image has been tarnished and diminished by sin.

At Creation	Man made in the image and likeness of God
At the Fall	God's image in man distorted, but not lost
At Regeneration	Man enters into a progressive recovering of more and more of God's image
At Christ's Return	Redeemed man will be completely restored to God's image.

It is due to our understanding of man being in the image of God that we have a basis for seeing others with worth and dignity. Because we are in the image of God, we can say that...

- Racism is wrong because we are all descended from the same parents who were made in the image of God.
- Abortion and euthanasia involve taking the life of that which is in the image of God.
- Civil rights are based on the idea that all men are created in the same image. Genesis 9:6 is specific to link the reason that murder is wrong is because murder involves the slaying of one who is made in the image of God.

The evolutionist has no basis for seeing racism as wrong since a particular race or people might be seen as having a higher position up the evolutionary scale. He has no basis for seeing value in the unborn or in the aged because he holds instead to the survival of the fittest and they do not qualify. He has no basis for supporting civil rights for all people because not all people are equal.

3. The Man's Body and Soul: *Then the LORD God formed man of dust from the ground, and breathed into his nostrils the breath of life; and man became a living being. (Genesis 2:7).*

Man's body was formed of dust from the ground. This is a play on words. הָאָדָם (*Ha-Adam*) was formed of dust from הָאֲדָמָה (*Ha-Adamah*). Man's very name is taken from the source from which his body is created. Yet the creation of man's physical frame was not the sum of his existence. He is more than a biological entity. There is something special about His substance, for the Lord Himself is seen inbreathing life into him.

There is a sense in which we were all once like Adam before he received this breath of life. We were all once spiritually lifeless. We were

> The Hebrew actually speaks of God breathing into his nostrils the "breath of lives." But we should not read too much into this plural usage. It is a Hebrew colloquialism to speak of life in the plural.
>
> Some have tried to take from this plurality that man was made as a trichotomy: a body, a soul and a spirit. But a careful study of these terms shows that the Scriptures do not always make a distinction between soul and spirit.

spiritually dead in our trespasses and sins (Ephesians 2:1). We could do nothing to make ourselves alive. It took a creative act of God to bring spiritual life into us.

The fact that the body was created by God underscores the fact that the body is intrinsically good. This stands in contrast to Greek thought that said the spirit is good while the body is bad. Yet the creation of man's physical frame was not the sum of his existence. He is more than a biological entity. The Lord then *breathed into his nostrils the breath of life; and man became a living being*, literally, "He became a SOUL" (נֶפֶשׁ). The soul speaks of that inner part of a man. It is your life force. It is who you are apart from your physical body.

James tells us that *the body without the spirit is dead* (James 2:26). Likewise the Preacher speaks of how a man dies and *then the dust will return to the earth as it was, and the spirit will return to God who gave it* (Ecclesiastes 12:7). Speaking from the vantage of one who looks at life "under the sun," he elsewhere says that *the fate of the sons of men and the fate of beasts is the same. As one dies so dies the other; indeed, they all have the same breath and there is no advantage for man over beast, for all is vanity. 20 All go to the same place. All came from the dust and all return to the dust* (Ecclesiastes 3:19-20). Thus for physical life to be present, it seems evident that there must be both soul and spirit.

In view of all that the Bible says concerning the spiritual life, one is tempted to maintain that the spirit is somehow created and/or enlivened by the process of regeneration. However both James 2:26 and Ecclesiastes 12:7 describe the human spirit as being a functioning part of mankind in general and not merely on behalf of the regenerate man. When Moses wished to speak of all of the human life that died in the flood, he described it as *all in whose nostrils was the breath of the spirit of life* (Genesis 7:22).

4.   Man's Rulership: *And God blessed them; and God said to them, "Be fruitful and multiply, and fill the earth, and subdue it; and rule over the fish of the sea and over the birds of the sky, and over every living thing that moves on the earth." (Genesis 1:28).*

We have already noted that man was given dominion and rulership over the world. This was a delegated position as he was called to rule the earth on behalf of God by virtue of the fact that he was made in the image and likeness of God.

That likeness was distorted by man's fall into sin. When man sinned, he gave up his right to rule over creation. The created was cursed on his behalf. Animals became wild and would threaten him. Thorns and thistles rose up against him. The plant kingdom would no longer serve him and he must labor over crops in order to eat their produce. To this day, the creation groans and travails over the effects of the curse.

> *For we know that the whole creation groans*
> *and suffers the pains of childbirth together until now.*
> *(Romans 8:22).*

But there is hope. The same Christ who died for us to redeem us from sin will also one day redeem the world from the effects of the curse.

> 19 *For the anxious longing of the creation waits eagerly for the revealing of the sons of God.* 20 *For the creation was subjected to futility, not of its own will, but because of Him who subjected it, in hope* 21 *that the creation itself also will be set free from its slavery to corruption into the freedom of the glory of the children of God. (Romans 8:19-21).*

Just as man was enslaved to sin, so also the entire creation today suffers under the effects of sin. In the same way that we have been delivered from the bondage of sin, so also the creation looks forward to a coming deliverance.

5. Man's Sexuality: *And God created man in His own image, in the image of God He created him; male and female He created them (Genesis 1:27).*

Genesis 1 describes the creation of both the male and the female. The term "man" in this passage is therefore to be treated as gender neutral. Man was both male and female. The details of the forming of separate genders is set forth in the second chapter of Genesis.

> *Then the LORD God said, "It is not good for the man to be alone; I will make him a helper suitable for him." (Genesis 2:18).*

The woman is designed to be a "helper suitable." Of special interest to us is this term "helper." *'Izer* (עֵזֶר) is the noun form of the Hebrew verb *'Azar* (עָזַר), "to help." The noun is used most often in the Old Testament, not to describe the role of the woman, but rather to describe God Himself in His helping us (Exodus 18:4; Deuteronomy 33:7; 33:26; 33:29).

This helps us to understand that woman was not created to be a mere underling (we would never think of defining God that way), but rather as one who standing beside and works together with him. It was not until later, as a result of the fall, that sin brought about a change which has been reflected all throughout history.

It should be remembered that there was not a separate word in the Hebrew (or in the Koine Greek) for husband and wife. Normally when you see the word "husband" in the Hebrew, it is either *ISH* ("man") or *BA'AL* ("lord" is the same term used of the false god of the Canaanites). By the same token, when you see the word "wife" in the Old Testament, it is nearly always the Hebrew word *ISHA* (female of *ISH*) and can be translated simply as "woman." The context makes it clear that all women are not designed to be helpers standing with all men, but rather that this is descriptive of a special husband and wife relationship. The foundation for this relationship is described in this chapter.

> *For this cause a man shall leave his father*
> *and his mother, and shall cleave to his wife; and they*
> *shall become one flesh (Genesis 2:24).*

There are three verbs used in this verse. They describe the action involved in the making of a marriage.

- Leave.

  There is to be the breaking off from the old family as the two people come together to begin their new family.

- Cleave.

  The couple is now to be glued together. There is a releasing from the first relationship so that there can be holding to this new relationship. This is the ordinance of marriage.

  Every once in a while, I come across someone who has the idea that marriage is what takes place in sex. Nothing could be further from the truth. Marriage involves a commitment. It involves the joining of two people so that they become a single entity.

• Become one flesh.

The joining together of a husband and wife is physically manifested in their sexual union. This was designed to bring them into a physical intimacy that is to mirror their emotional and spiritual intimacy. Both marriage and sex were instituted by God before sin entered the world. The perfect environment of the Garden of Eden included sex and marriage.

Reproduction is not mentioned in this chapter. Genesis 1 relates the command to multiply and fill the earth, but no such injunction is repeated here. This implication is that the sexual union is to be more than a mere means of procreation. It was designed to consummate and to bond a marriage.

Marriage involves a separation from the previous son/daughter relationships and a binding together of the two marriage partners in a new relationship. This is a commitment. It involves a joining of two people so that they become a single entity. This is physically illustrated in the sexual union, but it does not end there. It extends to every area of life. You are no longer two separate people. You are now a single entity.

This is not an easy process. When two people who have totally diverse backgrounds get together and try to become one, there is going to be friction. It will be like two porcupines who try to snuggle up together to keep warm. There will invariably be sticking points. This takes place because you each have been brought up with a different set of customs, a different set of values, and a different set of ideas.

I've heard couples comment, "Those things won't matter because we are so much in love." Then, three weeks into the marriage, that loving wife tells you to take out the garbage and you answer, "I'm not supposed to take out the garbage. After all, my father never took out the garbage."

Do you see the problem? It is that you were each raised under a different set of house rules. Many of those house rules were unspoken. They were simply understood. But that new marriage partner is unfamiliar to the new mate's house rules. It takes some time for a new couple to adjust and to redevelop their own house rules.

That is why in-laws can be such a problem. When a young couple go to visit the parents, the child of those parents knows and understands all of the unspoken house rules. But the partner of that child is in unfamiliar territory. It is like trying to graft a lemon onto an apple tree. There is friction and that friction can turn into trouble.

The joining of two people into one is meant to be permanent. It is "till death do you part." I believe marriage in the church today would be transformed if each couple going into marriage accepted the presupposition that there is no way out. If there is no way out, then you will have to solve any relational problems that arise. The moment you consider divorce as a fire escape, it will not be long before you are moving in that direction.

MAN'S FALL INTO SIN

When you look at man today, he is abnormal. He is abnormal because he is not the way he was created to be. On the one hand, there is a nobility about him. He sometimes reflects the greatness of the image and likeness of God. On the other hand, there is a cruel part of man. This part of man did not belong to man from the beginning. There is a part of man that is evil and which fills him with guilt and shame.

The Biblical account of man's transition from righteousness to sin is found in Genesis 3. Genesis 2 closes with the man and the woman in the garden. At the beginning of chapter 3, we are introduced to a new character. It is the serpent.

1.   The Temptation.

> *Now the serpent was more crafty than any east of the field which the Lord God had made. And he said to the woman, "Indeed, has God said, 'You shall not eat from any tree of the garden'?"*
>
> *And the woman said to the serpent, "From the fruit of the trees of the garden we may eat; 3 but from the fruit of the tree which is in the midst of the garden, God has said, 'You shall not eat from it or touch it, lest you die.'"*

> *And the serpent said to the woman, "You*
> *surely shall not die! 5 For God knows that in the day*
> *you eat from it your eyes will be opened, and you will*
> *be like God, knowing good and evil." (Genesis 3:1-5).*

Rabbinic legend has it that the serpent originally walked erect and that it was not until God's curse on this animal in Genesis 3:14 that it was reduced to moving upon its belly. There is nothing in the Bible to specifically state such a position and therefore such an interpretation is reduced to mere speculation. The significant actor here is not the snake, but the true power behind the snake—that old serpent, the devil.

Satan often works through intermediate agencies. He uses fallen angels. We refer to them as demons. He also uses human agents, either through possession or merely through indirect manipulation. In this case, it seems logical to assume that he utilized an animal. Such an example of the manipulation of animals was seen in Matthew 8:28-32 when Jesus can demons out of two men and permitted them to enter into a herd of pigs.

In this case, Satan was careful to appear in a form that would not arouse terror or revulsion in the woman. He came in the guise of a beast of the field. There is a lesson here. It is that Satan does not go around with a red suit and a pitchfork. He is a counterfeiter and a deceiver. He dresses in the clothes of the clergy and he speaks religious words, making his lies attractive.

His tactics, as demonstrated in this passage, involved suggesting what seemed to be a harmless gratification of a natural desire. He does not present himself as an enemy of God, but only as a neutral bystander who is somehow surprised by what he presents as God's unreasonable demand. He works to place God on trial in the mind of the woman. She will be asked to pass judgment upon the actions of God.

People do the same thing today when they ask, "How could a loving God pass judgment upon people?" When they ask such a question, they are following in the footsteps of Satan as he denies God's promise of judgment. The idea that there is no future judgment comes from Satan himself.

2. The Sin.

> *When the woman saw that the tree was good*

for food, and that it was a delight to the eyes, and that the tree was desirable to make one wise, she took from its fruit and ate, and she gave also to her husband with her, and he ate. (Genesis 3:6).

The Lord had given some very specific instructions regarding their behavior in the Garden. There was a great deal of liberty regarding their actions with only a single prohibition given.

And the Lord God commanded the man, saying, "from any tree of the garden you may eat freely; 17 but from the tree of the knowledge of good and evil you shall not eat, for in the day that you eat from it you shall surely die." (Genesis 2:16-17).

This condition gave man the freedom to choose for God or against God. He could obey and live or he could disobey and die. There are several things which we ought to note from this temptation.

a.   First of all, notice that the temptation came from an outside source. There was nothing within them to tempt themselves. Allow me to let you in on a secret. I don't need an outside source to tempt me to sin. And neither do you. I have something within me that likes sin—that finds sin fun. It isn't that the "devil made me do it." It is that I wanted to do it.

We call this a sin nature. It is an orientation to sin. But Adam and Eve were not created in this way. They had no orientation to sin. They had the ability to choose not to sin. And so, their choice to sin was all the more despicable.

b.   The temptation began by questioning and misdirection: *And he said to the woman, "Indeed, has God said, 'You shall not eat from any tree of the garden'?"*

> The serpent plays the role of a neutral bystander who is shocked by the limitation God has placed upon His creatures. He is placing God on trial. The same argument is used when the unbeliever asks, "How could a loving God pass judgment upon His people?"

The serpent did not begin the conversation with an immediate denial of what God had said. Instead, he merely posed the question of what God had said. He did this by means of a deliberate misquote of the words of God. He asked, "Is it true that God will not let you eat from any of the trees of the garden?" The question is designed to make the woman focus upon that particular tree that was forbidden.

Satan's tactics have not changed. He continues to draw your attention to that which is forbidden. In so doing, he draws your attention away from that which God has given you.

c.   The temptation proceeded with a misunderstanding of the danger: *And the woman said to the serpent, "From the fruit of the trees of the garden we may eat; 3 but from the fruit of the tree which is in the midst of the garden, God has said, 'You shall not eat from it or touch it, lest you die.'" (3:3-4).*

In repeating the prohibition, the woman says that they are not permitted either to eat or even to touch the forbidden fruit. Yet when the prohibition is initially given in Generis 2:16-17, there is no mention of a prohibition against touching the fruit. It is only eating the fruit that is forbidden.

This may reflect a misunderstanding on the part of the woman. She may have thought there was something physically poisonous about the fruit. This created a conflict in her mind when she looked at the tree and it looked good.

d.   The woman looked at the tree and it looked good -- she *saw that the tree was good for food, and that it was a delight to the eyes, and that the tree was desirable to make one wise (3:6).*

If you let your life be driven by what looks good, you will doom your life to an existence of sin and misery. We are never called to follow that which looks good. We are called to follow that which is good.

There are three areas of impact that are mentioned in light of this temptation. These three areas correspond to three types of temptation outline in 1 John 2:16. *For all that is in the world, the lust of the flesh and the lust of the eyes and the boastful pride of life, is not from the Father, but is from the world. (1 John 2:16).*

The tree was...	Good...	Delight...	Desirable...
	for food	to the eyes	to make one wise
	The lust of the flesh	The lust of the eyes	The boastful pride of life

Temptation is like that. It does not just manifest itself in one form. Its attractions are often multifaceted.

It is almost as though it were an afterthought that the text adds that *she gave also to her husband with her, and he ate.* We are not given any further details as to his involvement in the temptation, though it is striking that her husband was *with her* and that this may have also been true throughout the temptations. Some have speculated that Adam's sin was deliberate while Eve's was the result of her temptation. The words of Paul are used to give evidence to such an idea.

> *And it was not Adam who was deceived, but the woman being quite deceived, fell into transgression. (1 Timothy 2:14).*

Paul's words are evidently citing the temptation and fall. When he points out that it was not Adam who was deceived, he is citing the woman as the object of the original temptation. It is an unwarranted assumption to conclude that Adam's involvement in the transgression was beyond that of a passive participant in following the example of his wife.

THE RESULTS OF SIN

A surface reading of the passage seems to indicate that the Serpent initially told the truth. Their eyes WERE opened. They DID come to and experiential understanding of good and evil. And most importantly, they didn't die! Or did they?

If we may read between the lines, then let me suggest that a death did take place on that day. It was a spiritual death. Their ability to freely communicate with God was disrupted. This is seen in their reaction to the presence of God.

> *And they heard the sound of the Lord God walking in*
> *the garden in the cool of the day, and the man and his wife*
> *hid themselves from the presence of the Lord God among the*
> *trees of the garden. (Genesis 3:8).*

Have you ever walked into a room and turned on the lights and seen a big cockroach? What does it do? It scurries out of the light. It hates the light. It tries to hide from the light. Adam and Eve tried to do the same thing.

> *And this is judgment, that the light is come into the*
> *world, and men loved the darkness rather than the light, for*
> *their deeds were evil.*
> *For everyone who does evil hates the light, and does*
> *not come to the light, lest his deeds should be exposed. (John*
> *3:19-20).*

It's easy to be dirty in the dark. It doesn't show. But put a bright light on dirt and everyone can see it. So it is with sin. Sin doesn't look so bad when you get away from the presence of the Lord. But when HE comes, sin looks awful. That is why pagans don't like to be around Christians. It makes them feel strangely uncomfortable.

Furthermore, there was also the beginnings of a physical death that would eventually come upon the human race as a result of Adam's sin. They did not die immediately, but their eventual death and decay was no less certain.

Finally, the human race would stand in danger of eternal death. Hell was not created for man. It was prepared for the devil and his angels (Matthew 25:41). But when man became a follower of Satan in his rebellion against God, hell became man's ultimate destination.

We therefore can conclude that a number of things happened to Adam and Eve upon the eating of the forbidden fruit. Three deaths took place.

1. Spiritual Death.

> In describing the pre-regeneration experiences of the Ephesians, Paul says, *You were dead in your trespasses and sins* (Ephesians 2:1). He goes on to say that there came a time when *God, being rich in mercy, because of His great love with which He loved us, 5 even when we were dead in our transgressions, made us alive together with Christ* (Ephesians 2:4-5). Colossians 2:13 speaks

similarly of *when you were dead in your transgressions and the uncircumcision of your flesh, He made you alive together with Him, having forgiven us all our transgressions*. This is why a new birth is necessary. Sin brings about a spiritual death and the solution is a spiritual rebirth.

2.   Physical Death.

The bodies of Adam and Eve began a process that would one day culminate in physical death. They did not die immediately, but their eventual physical death was now a certainty. This same curse of death was passed on to all of creation. *It is appointed for men to die once and after this comes judgment* (Hebrews 9:27). This is evidently a reference to physical death.

3.   Eternal Death.

Adam and Eve and all of their descendants became subject to the final judgment and to the resulting eternal death. Matthew 25:41 speaks of this eternal death as having been created for the devil and his angels. As mankind has become a follower of Satan in his rebellion against God, so Satan's destiny has become man's destiny.

On four separate occasions the book of Revelation speaks of the "Second Death." This is defined in 21:8 as that time when all sinners are placed into the Lake of Fire. The righteous, on the other hand, are said to be unaffected by the second death (2:11; 20:6).

4.   The Federal Effects of Sin: *Therefore, just as through one man sin entered into the world, and death through sin, and so death spread to all men, because all sinned (Romans 5:12)*.

Having followed his wife into sin, Adam now became a sinful being, different than the way in which he had been created. Following God's natural laws, Adam's offspring would be "after his kind," having a sinful nature and spiritually dead from birth.

When Adam sinned, there was a sense in which all men are said to have sinned. He was acting as the official representative of the human race. Adam's sin was credited to all of his descendants. It did not matter that you had not yet been born. It did not matter that you had not yet been given to opportunity to sin. Adam sinned in your place.

When Congress declared war on Japan in December 1941, most Americans did not have any say in the matter. They had taken no active part in that decision. This made no difference. The United States and all of its citizens were now at war with Japan. By the same token, when Adam sinned, he acted as the representative of the entire human race and officially declared war against God.

Notice that sin did not come by "one woman." The woman was not the head of the human race. Man was responsible, even though it was the woman who first sinned. Why? Because man was the woman's head. The fact that he stood back and took a passive role in her temptation does not change his headship. What does Paul mean when he says that *"all sinned"*? He does not mean that all sinned individually. He means that all sinned in Adam.

> *For until the Law sin was in the world, but sin is not imputed where there is no law. (Romans 5:13).*

Paul has already demonstrated that sin and death always go together (Romans 3:23). Wherever you see one, you will also see the other. Satan always tries to divide them. "You shall not surely die." And the world has always believed this lie. You cannot sin with impunity. If you sin, you will soon smell the odor of death.

Here he brings up another point. It is that sin existed without law even though, by strict definition, there is no sin without law. The syllogism goes like this:

Major Premise	Sin is imputed to the one who breaks God's Law.
Minor Premise	There was a time when sin was in the world but when the Law had not been given.
Conclusion	Sin was imputed some other way besides the breaking of God's Law - i.e., through the sin of Adam.

It is impossible to sin when there are no commands to sin against. It is impossible to break the speed limit when there is no speed limit. Yet prior to the law, *"sin was in the world."* How do we know that sin was in the world? Because death reigned. Those long genealogies in Genesis over which we normally skip contain a continuing refrain with each name mentioned: "And he died."

Adam sinned and death entered. The result was that "all sinned."	Death reigned ⟹	The Law was given to Moses at Mount Sinai.

Sin is not imputed where there is no law (Romans 5:13c). You cannot disobey God's law unless He has given a law. Anyone living after Adam but before Moses could not break any of God's laws because God had not given any laws. On the other hand, people continued to die during the period between Adam and Moses.

> Verses 13-14 prove the doctrine of imputation of sin presented in verse 12.

However, the penalty of death was not inflicted upon men because of their transgression of the Law. Therefore, the reason that death reigned from Adam to Moses was because of Adam's sin.

> *Nevertheless death reigned from Adam until Moses, even over those who had not sinned in the likeness of the offense of Adam, who is a type of Him who was to come. (Romans 5:14).*

If sin always is accompanied by death, then how could death reign in the period from Adam to Moses if sin had not been legally imputed? It is because Adam's sin was imputed. We often ask, "What about the man in Africa who has never heard of God's law?" Paul goes one better by asking, "What about the man who lived before the Law where noone had heard of God's law?" The answer is found in the imputation of Adam's sin. Adam's sin was imputed to all of his descendants, even though they had not sinned in the same way that Adam had sinned.

In this way. Adam was a type of Christ (*"a type of Him who was to come"* - 5:14). Adam was a type of Christ in this respect - that he served as a federal head of many. He sinned. His actions were imputed to others.

Christ also served as the federal head of many. He performed a single act - dying upon the cross. Like Adam, the actions of Christ actions were imputed to others. Just as all are said to have sinned in Adam, in the eyes of the law, all who were identified with Christ were crucified with Him.

UNREGENERATE MAN

Since the fall, unregenerate man has been characterized by a quality of sinfulness. The Westminster Confession defines sin as "any want of conformity unto or transgression of the law of God." This definition is taken from the pages of John's first epistle.

> *Everyone who practices sin also practices lawlessness; and sin is lawlessness. (1 John 3:4).*

> *All unrighteousness is sin... (1 John 5:17a).*

In addressing those who had rejected Him, Jesus spoke of the nature of the one who follows in the footsteps of Satan.

> *You are of your father the devil, and you want to do the desires of your father. He was a murderer from the beginning, and does not stand in the truth, because there is no truth in him. Whenever he speaks a lie, he speaks from his own nature; for he is a liar, and the father of lies. (John 8:44).*

The word "nature" is supplied by the translators, yet the idea is present as it tells us that the devil speaks from what he is. He is a liar and a liar tells lies. That is what makes him a liar. In much the same way, we can say that sinners sin because they are sinners. It is who they are. It is a part of their nature to sin.

1.   Sin is a continuing choice.

Though this sin has been both imputed and inherited, it is also the result of man's continuing choice. Man continues to be in a state of ongoing rebellion against God.

> *For the wrath of God is revealed from heaven against all ungodliness and unrighteousness of men, who suppress the truth in unrighteousness (Romans 1:18).*

Paul's language is set in the most general terms. He takes us to a vantage point from which we can look at unregenerate man as a whole. It is not that unregenerate man has no knowledge of what is true. God has revealed truth to him. It is that he makes a decision to suppress that truth and to replace it with a lie of his own making.

This brings up an interesting point. It is that no one can stop believing. There is something within you that demands you believe in something. You cannot help yourself. You are a believing creature. If you do not believe in God, then you will necessarily turn to believe in something else.

> *21 For even though they knew God, they did not honor Him as God, or give thanks; but they became futile in their speculations, and their foolish heart was darkened. 22 Professing to be wise, they became fools, 23 and exchanged the glory of the incorruptible God for an image in the form of corruptible man and of birds and four-footed animals and crawling creatures. (Romans 1:21-23).*

When unregenerate man worships, he does not do it to get to the true God, but to move away from Him. Marx said that religion is the opium of the people, but the truth is that religion is an attempt to escape from God by constructing a substitute. Unregenerate man wants to worship a god of his own making.

2. Sin has an absolute character.

There is no neutral condition between good and evil, although there are degrees of both. You cannot remain neutral either to God or to sin. You are always on one side or the other.

> *He who is not with Me is against Me; and he who does not gather with Me scatters. (Matthew 12:30).*

You are never in neutral. You are either moving toward the Lord or you are moving away from Him. You are either on His side or you are against Him. The myth of philosophic neutrality says that man is able to look at God objectively and is able to make a decision about God merely by weighing the evidence for or against his existence. The truth is that no one is neutral when it comes to God. You are either for Him or you are against Him. Jesus said this in very straightforward terms.

> *He who is not with Me is against Me, and he who does not gather with Me scatters. (Matthew 12:30).*

The corollary to this principle is that its opposite is also true. Jesus went on to say on another instance, *"He who is not against us is for us" (Mark 9:40).* The point is that it is impossible to be neutral to the Lord. You are either on His side or you are against Him. You are either unregenerate or you are regenerate. You are either born again or you are still in your sins.

3.   Sin is not limited to overt acts.

The Pharisees seem to have adopted the idea that sin only involved overt and outward actions.

> *You have heard that it was said, "You shall not commit adultery"; 28 but I say to you, that everyone who looks on a woman to lust for her has committed adultery with her already in his heart. (Matthew 5:27-28).*

The law of God forbids men and women to engage in sexual relations outside the bonds of marriage. Jesus teaches us that this law does far more than to merely forbid outward actions. It also teaches an inward attitude.

The Pharisees taught that you should not commit adultery, but it was assumed that anything short of adultery was permissible. Such a stance ignores the commandment which says, "You shall not covet your neighbor's wife" (Exodus 20:17). The law against coveting speaks against the corresponding inner attitudes pertaining to all of the other commandments.

The standard given by Jesus goes far beyond that which was held by the scribes and the Pharisees. They were concerned with outward appearances. They said, "Look, but don't touch." Jesus said, "Don't even look." He is saying that God is not only concerned with what you do but also with what you think. This is not a new teaching.

> *If I regard wickedness in my heart,*
> *The Lord will not hear (Psalm 66:18).*

Does this mean if you see a pretty girl and find her attractive, that you have sinned? Does it mean that if you find yourself suddenly tempted with an impure thought that you are in sin? I do not think so. Rather, it is when you take that impure thought and begin to entertain it that you move from natural desires to sin.

4.   The Transmission of Sin.

Man was created in the image and likeness of God (Genesis 1:26-27). We have defined that in the context of Genesis to speak of his rulership over the creation, though these are likely many other points of similarity. When Adam fell into sin, that image was tarnished and infected with the disease of sin. Adam's descendants were not born in the image of God, but in Adam's fallen image.

> *When Adam had lived one hundred and thirty*
> *years, he became the father of a son in his own*
> *likeness, according to his image, and named him Seth.*
> *(Genesis 5:3).*

Adam's sinful state was passed on to all of his descendants so that all men find themselves in a sinful state. Man continues to be in the image of God (1 Corinthians 11:7; James 3:9), but that is today a tarnished image in that God is without sin while man is a sinner.

5.   The Universality of Sin.

The Scriptures uniformly teach that all of mankind is in a state of sin. All have sinned and all continue to sin.

> *2 The LORD has looked down from heaven upon the sons of*

men,
To see if there are any who understand,
Who seek after God.
3 They have all turned aside; together they have become corrupt;
There is no one who does good, not even one. (Psalm 14:2-3).

Who can say, "I have cleansed my heart,
I am pure from my sin "? (Proverbs 20:9).

Indeed, there is not a righteous man on earth who continually does good and who never sins. (Ecclesiastes 7:20).

For all have sinned and fall short of the glory of God (Romans 3:23).

The parallel passages in 1 John 1:8 and 10 are particularly compelling as they speak both to our present condition as well as our past condition.

1 John 1:8	1 John 1:10
If we say that we have no sin...	*If we say that we have not sinned...*
...we are deceiving ourselves, and the truth is not in us.	*...we make Him a liar, and His word is not in us.*

Each of these passages bears testimony of man's fallen condition. We have all sinned and fallen short of that which is commanded us by our Creator. We are sinners both because we sin and also because it is our nature to sin.

And you were dead in your trespasses and sins, 2 in which you formerly walked according to the course of this world, according to the prince of the power of the air, of the spirit that is now working in the sons of disobedience. 3 Among them we too all formerly lived in the lusts of our flesh, indulging the desires of the flesh and of the mind, and were by nature children of wrath, even as the rest. (Ephesians 2:1-3).

Notice the part of this description that describes the state of the unbeliever as being "by nature" a child of wrath. The story is told of a man living in India who was trapped by a flood. He made his way to some high ground and found that a tiger had also come to this small refuge. The tiger was completely docile in the face of the flood, yet the man took his gun and shot the tiger. Why? Because he knew that after a day or so the tiger would become hungry and that he would become a threat. The tiger is a hunter and a meat-eater. It is a part of his nature. So it is with the unregenerate man. He is by nature a child of wrath and a sinner.

6.   The Extent of Sin.

It has become customary to speak in theological circles of "total depravity." What does this term imply?

It does NOT mean...	It DOES mean...
• That every man is as bad as he can be. • That the sinner has no knowledge of God. • That the sinner has no conscience that can discriminate between good and evil. • That man is no longer in the image of God.	• That every part of man has been affected and infected by sin. • That the sinner has no spiritual good within himself that makes him deserving of God's mercy.

Total depravity means that you are a total sinner, but it does not mean that you sin totally. When we speak of total depravity, we should also speak of man's total inability. By this, we mean that man in his own strength is unable to fulfill the demands of God's law. Indeed, he is unable even to appropriate the things of the Lord.

But a natural man does not accept the things of the Spirit of God; for they are foolishness to him, and he cannot understand them, because they are spiritually appraised. (1 Corinthians 2:14).

Apart from the work of the Holy Spirit in his heart, the unbeliever does not accept the things of the Spirit of God. He looks at the things of the Spirit of God and wants no part of them because he deems them to be foolishness. It is only when the Spirit has come and done a regenerating work within him that he will begin to accept the things of the Spirit of God. Paul describes the unregenerate man when he speaks to the Ephesians about their former lifestyle prior to coming to Christ.

> *And you were dead in your trespasses and sins, 2 in which you formerly walked according to the course of this world, according to the prince of the power of the air, of the spirit that is now working in the sons of disobedience. 3 Among them we too all formerly lived in the lusts of our flesh, indulging the desires of the flesh and of the mind, and were by nature children of wrath, even as the rest. (Ephesians 2:1-3).*

Notice the elements of this description. It speaks to your former condition, your former manner of life, and your former family connection.

- Spiritually dead: *You were dead in your trespasses and sins (2:1).*

- Walking in sin: *You formerly walked according to the course of this world (2:2).*

- By nature children of wrath: *We... were by nature children of wrath (2:3).*

A pig acts like a pig because he is a pig by nature. It is a part of his makeup and nature to act in such a way. You can dress him up and give him sheep lessons, but the pig nature will eventually emerge.

This is why humanistic efforts at reformation so often meet with dismal failure. They are operating under the wrong assumption that mankind is not all that bad. More often than not, the education of a criminal results, not in an honest citizen, but in an educated criminal. It is because there is no change from the inside out. Man is, at his heart, a sinner. He sins because it is a part of his very nature to sin. When he sins, he is acting in accordance to who and what he is.

How does this impact man's free will? Augustine taught that man continues to have a free will, but he is not morally free because of his sinful nature. His free will, such as it is, is only free to operate within the confines of his sinful nature. We can illustrate Augustine's fourfold view of man like this:

Pre-Fall Man	Post-Fall Man	Reborn Man	Glorified Man
Able to sin	Able to sin	Able to sin	Able not to sin
Able not to sin	Unable not to sin	Able not to sin	Unable to sin

7.   Benefits of Understanding Total Depravity.

There are good and sufficient reasons why the doctrine of total depravity is presented in the Bible and why we ought to be aware of this teaching.

- It will stop you from unjustly judging others. We are warned against judging until we have first judged ourselves (Matthew 7:5). That does not mean you cannot discern the sin in someone else and it does not disallow church discipline to take place, but it means that we enter into such activities with a sense of our own failings.
- It will clear up any false teachings regarding your own works for salvation. We are saved by works; but it is not our own works of righteousness, but those done by Jesus Christ and imputed to us through faith.

> A wrong view of the disease will always bring with it a wrong view of the remedy.

- It will help you to understand yourself. God, in His grace, only lets you see the tip of the iceberg of the sin in your own heart. As you grow in Christ, He sometimes allows you to see just a little more. Such self revelations are designed to drive you to the cross.

THE REGENERATE MAN

The Scriptures portray two kinds of men. There are those who are saved and those who are unsaved. There are those who are spiritually alive and those who are spiritually dead. All of mankind was plunged into spiritual death through the fall of Adam. If man is to have life, it must be through the process of regeneration.

> What is Regeneration? It is that process whereby God, operating through His Holy Spirit, makes the believer alive and renewed unto Himself.

This process of regeneration is described in a number of different ways throughout the Scripture. At its very core, it is a movement from death to life.

1.   From Death to Life.

> *And you were dead in your trespasses and sins, 2 in which you formerly walked according to the course of this world, according to the prince of the power of the air, of the spirit that is now working in the sons of disobedience.*
> *Among them we too all formerly lived in the lusts of our flesh, indulging the desires of the flesh and of the mind, and were by nature children of wrath, even as the rest. (Ephesians 2:1-3).*

This passage begins with our past condition. It was one of death. There was a time when we were all spiritually dead. The sphere of our death was in our trespasses and sins. No matter what our nationality, our religious or cultural background, we all share in this common heritage. We were all dead in our sins. We were helpless. A dead person cannot help himself. A dead person can do nothing for himself. There is no question of a dead person being able to help himself. All the preaching in the world will not save him or move him to action. He is dead.

When was the last time you saw a revival meeting in a graveyard? A corpse cannot respond to injunctions to change his life. He cannot do anything. He is dead. If you are going to do anything at all with a dead person, you must raise him from the dead. He needs a new life. He needs a resurrection. The turning point of this hopeless situation comes in verse 4 with the words, "But God..."

> *But God, being rich in mercy, because of His great love with which He loved us, 5 even when we were dead in our transgressions, made us alive together with Christ (by grace you have been saved), 6 and raised us up with Him, and seated us with Him in the heavenly places in Christ Jesus (Ephesians 2:4-6).*

This section is introduced with the conjunction, "but." We were dead, but God made us alive. We were disobedient in following after the world and the devil, but God raised us out of the world and out of the domain of the devil. We were depraved, but God seated us with Christ and gave us a new nature. We were doomed, but God showed us the surpassing riches of His grace.

The contrast shows how we were apart from Christ versus what God did to bring us to life in Christ. You have seen those "before" and "after" advertisements that are shown on television. This is a similar showing. It portrays a "before" and "after" we came to Christ. This will be seen in the following chart that contrasts the way we were versus what God has accomplished on our behalf:

	The Way We Were		What God Did
Y O U	Were dead in your trespasses and sins	B U T	Made us alive together with Christ
	Walked... according to the course of this world according to the prince / the spirit	G O D	Raised us up with Him
	Formerly lived in the lust of our flesh		Seated us with Him

With this simple conjunction (δε), we are transported from death to life - from the darkness of the grave to the light of everlasting life.

a.   He made us alive: *Even when we were dead in our transgressions, made us alive together with Christ (Ephesians 2:5a).*

We have been reborn into God's family. Just as a baby is unable to give birth to itself, so we had nothing to do with causing our own birth. It was given to us, not by our own will, but in accordance with the will of God.

> 12 *But as many as received Him, to them He gave the right to become children of God, even to those who believe in His name,* 13 *who were born not of blood, nor of the will of the flesh, nor of the will of man, but of God. (John 1:12-13).*

We have been born into a new life. We have a new relationship with God and a new position in Christ. There is a wonderful newness in the life of the Christian.

b.   He raised us up with Him: *And raised us up with Him... (Ephesians 2:6).*

We have already been resurrected in the mind of God. Just as Jesus rose from the dead, we are also considered and reckoned to have risen from the dead. We have been identified with Christ and that means we share all that belongs to Him. We are reckoned to have been raised up with Him.

c.   He seated us with Him: *And raised us up with Him, and seated us with Him in the heavenly places in Christ Jesus (Ephesians 2:6).*

What does it mean to be seated? It means that the work is finished. That the victory is complete. When a priest went into the temple, the one thing that he never did was to sit down. He was always standing in the presence of God. Even when the animal sacrifice had been offered, he still stood.

Because the next day there would have to be another sacrifice offered. And another. And another. It was never-ending. But Jesus was the final sacrifice. When He died upon the cross, He said, "It is finished!"

When Jesus ascended into heaven, He sat down at the right hand of the Father. He sits at the side of God. It is a position of honor and authority. We hold the same position. We are reckoned to be seated in heaven with Jesus. We are co-heirs with Christ.

The utter magnitude of God's gift to us beings us to an obvious question. Why? Why has God acted like this? Why has God so richly gifted us? The answer is seen in verse 7:

> *So that in the ages to come He might show the surpassing riches of His grace in kindness toward us in Christ Jesus. (Ephesians 2:7).*

The purpose of your salvation is everlasting. It is so that throughout eternity you might be a trophy of God's grace and His kindness in Christ. You will be the display of what God has done to deliver a human life from the bondage of sin.

In the second year of the War Between the States, an informer in the prison camp at Palmyra disappeared. The Commander in charge ordered that 10 men would be shot in reprisal. One of those men was William T. Humphrey, a husband and father of a number of children. Hearing that Humphrey was under the sentence of death, a young man named Hiram Smith came forward, explaining that he was unmarried and without a family. He asked permission to take the place of Humphrey, stating that perhaps it would be better for a single man to die than a man with a family. I am told that if you go to the cemetery of the Mount Pleasant Church in what used to be the town of Mount Salem, you will find a stone that has been erected with the following inscription:

> *"This monument is dedicated to the memory of Hiram Smith. The hero who sleeps beneath the sod here was shot in Palmyra, October 17, 1862 as a substitute for William T. Humphrey, my father."*

That is what Christ has done for us. He has become our

substitute. And as a result, we have become an eternal monument to the riches of His mercy and to the overabundance of His grace.

2.   The Death of the Old Man.

> *3 Or do you not know that all of us who have been baptized into Christ Jesus have been baptized into His death? 4 Therefore we have been buried with Him through baptism into death, in order that as Christ was raised from the dead through the glory of the Father, so we too might walk in newness of life. (Romans 6:3-4).*

The same identification truth is seen in this passage. When we were baptized into Christianity, we were being identified with Jesus Christ and specifically with His death on the cross. Because He died on the cross, you are declared to

> The major significance in baptism is identification. When you are baptized, you are being identified with the movement or church or religion or system of beliefs held by those into whom you are being baptized.

have died with Him. You were condemned to death because of your sins and the sentence of death was carried out against Christ.

You might be inclined to think it might have been better if the sentence of death had merely been forgotten. But God does not forget. He is righteous. His righteous nature demands that the sentence of death be carried out. It was carried out in Christ. He died in your place. When you believed in Him, you were identified with that death.

3.   The Birth of the New Man.

> *22 Since you have in obedience to the truth purified your souls for a sincere love of the brethren, fervently love one another from the heart, 23 for you have been born again not of seed which is perishable but imperishable, that is, through the living and abiding word of God. (1 Peter 1:22-23).*

I have a friend, Bill Iverson, who used to pose the following riddle: "Born once, die twice. Born twice, die once." The answer to the riddle is that the believer has been born twice. His first birth was a physical birth. His second birth is a spiritual birth. The first birth brings a life that will eventually perish. The second birth brings a life that will never die.

Just as the first birth gives certain characteristics and attributes to the newborn baby, so also the new birth brings certain characteristics and attributes.

a. The new man is your identity. Many Christians have been taught that the new man is merely a force or a "new nature" that has come into them and which helps to guide them to do good. But this is too shallow a view compared to the richness of what the Bible teaches. The new man is not something that has come into you. It is what you have become.

> *Therefore if any man is in Christ, he is a new creature; the old things passed away; behold, new things have come. (2 Corinthians 5:17).*

The believer is not just one who is indwelt by a new creature. He has actually become a new creature. We became a creature by the fact that we had a Creator. We become a new creature in the same way. There is One who performed a new creation and made new creatures of us. When you trusted in Jesus Christ as your Lord and Savior, you were born again into the family of God. You might not have felt any physical change. Perhaps you experienced no great emotional release. Maybe you did not feel any different. But you became a new person.

b. The new man is growing. When you were born physically, you were a complete person. You probably had all of the usual number of arms and legs, fingers and toes, eyes and ears. However, this did not mean you were fully grown. The same is true of the new man. You have been born again. You have become a child of God. You are a new person, complete in your new identity. But you still need to grow.

> *Therefore we do not lose heart, but though our outer man is decaying, yet our*

inner man is being renewed day by day. (2 Corinthians 4:16).

Scientists tell us that from the day you were born, your physical body began to die. It continues this process until it finally goes to the grave. Your eyesight will dim, your hearing will fade, and your strength will wither. But you need not lose heart. The person that you have become is being renewed day by day.

...but speaking the truth in love, we are to grow up in all aspects into Him, who is the head, even Christ (Ephesians 4:15).

We are becoming like Jesus Christ. When we first believed, we became like Him in the same way that a baby is like the old man he will one day become. Our goal is to grow within the realm of those communicable attributes.

c.   This brings a new responsibility. Privilege always brings with it responsibility. If you have been declared by God to be righteous, then you are also to live in a righteous way. If you are deemed holy by God, then you are to be holy. If you are a son of God, then your manner of life should be such as befits a son of God.

22 ...that, in reference to your former manner of life, you lay aside the old self, which is being corrupted in accordance with the lusts of deceit, 23 and that you be renewed in the spirit of your mind, 24 and put on the new self, which in the likeness of God has been created in righteousness and holiness of the truth. (Ephesians 4:22-24).

You are no longer the old creature. He has passed away. He is dead and buried. You are a new creation and that calls for a new way of living. The problem is that many Christians continue to wear the rags of their former manner of life. They continue to indulge in the sinful habits of their old life. Those things need to be laid aside. They no longer have a legitimate part of your life. They do not fit you any longer. You should not be wearing them. They are like wearing someone else's clothes. You have a whole new set of clothes. This new set of clothes matches your new mind and your new self. This is not talking about physical clothes. It does not mean you have to run around wearing a t-shirt that says, "Holy Spirit" printed on it. This is not physical clothing. It speaks of your manner of life. You need to clothe yourself in a manner of life that is in keeping with the new man that you have now become.

This brings us to a crucial question. What about the presence of continuing sin in my life? If I have become a new creature, then why do I continue to sin? The answer is found in the problem of the flesh.

4.   The Problem of the Flesh.

> *But I say, walk by the Spirit, and you will not carry out the desire of the flesh. 17 For the flesh sets its desire against the Spirit, and the Spirit against the flesh; for these are in opposition to one another, so that you may not do the things that you please. (Galatians 5:16-17).*

There is an opposition between that which is "of the flesh" as opposed to the Spirit. They are by nature in opposition in the same way that the two poles of a magnet are opposed to one another. The practical result of this in the Christian's life is that *you may not do the things that you please*.

> *For we know that the Law is spiritual; but I am of flesh, sold into bondage to sin. 15 For that which I am doing, I do not understand; for I am not practicing what I would like to do, but I am doing the very thing I hate. 16 But if I do the very thing I do not wish to do, I agree with the Law, confessing that it is good. 17 So now, no longer am I the one doing it, but sin which indwells me. 18 For I know that nothing good dwells in me, that is, in my flesh; for the wishing is present in me, but the doing of the good is not. 19*

For the good that I wish, I do not do; but I practice
the very evil that I do not wish. (Romans 7:14-19).

Paul says the problem of the believer is that he is still "of flesh." It is this flesh—this presence of sin within the believer—that remains in bondage to sin. When the old man died, his corpse remained. Paul is not talking about your physical body, for that would be Greek dualism that says the soul is good and the body is bad. Instead, Paul is speaking of the presence of sin that continues to make itself known within you. This sin is like a foreign invader—a cancer. Because of this invader, you find yourself doing the very things you know are inconsistent with your new life. The result is a battle.

20 But if I am doing the very thing I do not
wish, I am no longer the one doing it, but sin which
dwells in me. 21 I find then the principle that evil is
present in me, the one who wishes to do good.
(Romans 7:20-21).

Paul uses his own experience as a Christian to describe the ongoing struggle that is experienced by the Christian as he seeks to follow Christ. He finds that he now has a new desire in his new relationship with Christ, but that there is still a continuing struggle with sin.

22 For I joyfully concur with the law of God in
the inner man, 23 but I see a different law in the
members of my body, waging war against the law of
my mind, and making me a prisoner of the law of sin
which is in my members. (Romans 7:22-23).

You are involved in a battle. The battleground is within you. The enemy is that continuing presence of sin. Many Christians have become virtual prisoners of war. But there is still hope, both for the present and for the future.

For by these He has granted to us His
precious and magnificent promises, in order that by
them you might become partakers of the divine
nature, having escaped the corruption that is in the

world by lust. (2 Peter 1:4).

This is not to say that the Christian is a schizophrenic. We are not two separate people. We are a new person. We have a new identity and that identity is rooted in Christ. The Christian is one who has been made a partaker of the divine nature. This new nature provides both the motivation and the strength for a new way of living.

> *9 Do not lie to one another, since you laid aside the old self with its evil practices, 10 and have put on the new self who is being renewed to a true knowledge according to the image of the One who created him. (Colossians 3:9-10).*

Paul says the reason you are not to lie to one another is because you have a new identity. You have laid aside the old identity and have put on the new identity. Furthermore, this new identity is constantly being renewed into the original image of the Creator.

5.   Provisions for the Battle.

We are not left without the necessary provisions and supplies for our battle. The Lord has provided four sources of strength.

- The Word of God. Psalm 119:11 says, *Thy word I have treasured in my heart, that I may not sin against Thee."* When Jesus was tempted by the devil in the wilderness, He utilized the word of God to defeat those temptations.

- The interceding Christ. Hebrews 7:25 says that Jesus *lives to make intercession* for us. Hebrews 8:34 speaks of Christ *who is at the right hand of God, who also intercedes for us.*

- The indwelling Spirit. John 16:13 says that one of the ministries of the Spirit is to guide us into all truth. He is our Guide and our Helper. Galatians 5:16 says, *"Walk in the Spirit, and you will not carry out the desire of the flesh."* Romans teaches us that *the Spirit also helps our weaknesses* with regard to prayer.

- The encouraging Church. Hebrews 10:25 warns us against

forsaking our own assembling together, as is the habit of some. By contrast, that verse goes on to charge us with the ministry of *encouraging one another.*

6.   Victory in the Battle.

We are not left in doubt as to the outcome of this spiritual battle. The message of the Scriptures is that Jesus wins.

- The victory of the cross: *And when you were dead in your transgressions and the uncircumcision of your flesh, He made you alive together with Him, having forgiven us all our transgressions, 14 having canceled out the certificate of debt consisting of decrees against us and which was hostile to us; and He has taken it out of the way, having nailed it to the cross. 15 When He had disarmed the rulers and authorities, He made a public display of them, having triumphed over them through Him (Colossians 2:13-15).*

    When Jesus died upon the cross, it looked for all the world as though the powers of Satan had won. The Son of God nailed spread-eagle on wooden crossbeams. The enemies of Christ rejoicing and mocking Him. Thieves on either side of him joining in the taunting. Even the governor's taunting inscription nailed to the cross, as if to say, "Here is what I think of the concept of a Jewish king!"

    Do you remember the inscription? It read, "Jesus of Nazareth, King of the Jews." The Jewish leaders didn't like that and they petitioned Pilate to have it changed, but he would not. And so, it remained. It was the custom of that day to post the crimes for which a criminal was being executed on the cross where he hung. This would serve as a warning to other would-be criminals. What was the crime of Jesus? His crime was in being the King.

    This passage tells us there was another inscription posted on the cross that day. It was an inscription unseen by human eyes. It was the inscription *"consisting of decrees against us and which was hostile to us."* It was the inscription of our sins. Don't miss this! Your sins were nailed to His cross. This indicates that He died for you.

- Christ died, that's history.

- Christ died for you, that's salvation.

  A student was taking a test in college and he wrote on his exam, "Only God could pass this test." When he got it back, the professor had written on it, "God gets an *A* and you get an *F*." Christ took the test and nailed it to His cross. He passed the test for you. And then He said, "No More Tests!"

- The present victory of faith. 1 John 5:4 tells us that *whatever is born of God overcomes the world; and this is the victory that has overcome the world—our faith.*

- A continuing assurance of victory. Philippians 1:6 says that *He who began a good work in you will perfect it until the day of Christ Jesus.*

- The ultimate victory. 1 Corinthians 15:54 says that *when this perishable will have put on the imperishable, and this mortal will have put on immortality, then will come about the saying that is written, "Death is swallowed up in victory.*

THE ESSENTIAL NATURE OF MAN

There are three differing views that are held by scholars as to the essential nature of man.

1. Trichotomy.

    This view states that man is composed of a body, soul, and spirit. It sees a triune makeup in the being of man. The soul is seen as the life force of man while the spirit is that part of man that communes with God.

Soul	Spirit
The realm of man's relationship with other men	The realm of man's relationship with God

- Hebrews 4:12 speaks of how the word of God is sharp enough to be able to pierce *as far as the division of soul and spirit.*

- In 1 Thessalonians 5:23, Paul gives a closing benediction and says, "May your spirit and soul and body be preserved complete, without blame at the coming of our Lord Jesus Christ."

2.   Dichotomy.

This view sees man as primarily existing in two parts: the material body and the immaterial part that is unseen and unmeasured. This is not a denial of the soul versus the spirit, but sees these two as aspects of the immaterial part of man.

- The Scriptures to not clearly delineate between the soul and the spirit of man. For example, we can read of one's soul being troubled (Genesis 41:8; Psalm 42:6) as well as of one being troubled in spirit (John 13:21).
- The terms for both spirit and soul are used of animals: *Who knows that the breath of man ascends upward and the breath of the beast descends downward to the earth? (Ecclesiastes 3:21).*
- At the time of death, the Bible speaks of both the departure of the soul (Genesis 35:18; 1 Kings 17:21) as well as the departure of the spirit (Ecclesiastes 12:7; John 19:30).
- The Bible speaks of both the salvation of the soul (1 Peter 1:9) and also of the saving of the spirit (1 Corinthians 5:5).
- We regularly read of God's Spirit, but both the Old and New Testament also make mention of God's soul. In the Hebrew of Amos 6:8, God swears "by His soul." Isaiah 42:1 describes the delight of God's soul. In Jeremiah 9:9 God says His soul will be avenged. Hebrews 10:38 points out that God's soul has no pleasure in those who do not believe.

3.   Monism.

This is the secular view that states man is a collective whole with no separate soul or spirit and nothing beyond his physical body. By contrast to this view, the Scriptures speak of an immaterial part of man that exists apart from his body.

The observation of John Murray, the late professor of Systematic Theology at Westminster Seminary, might be helpful.

The evidence does not support the tripartite construction. We need not suppose, however, that soul and spirit are always synonymous and are interchangeable. The entity denoted by soul and by spirit is to be viewed from different aspects. When one aspect is in view, the term 'spirit' is the appropriate designation, and when another aspect is in view the term 'soul' (1984b:31-32).

The term "soul" generally looks at man as having life that is resident within a body while the term "spirit" generally focuses upon that life as having originated from God.

THE ORIGIN OF THE SOUL AND SPIRIT

The Bible tells us that Adam became a living soul at the time God breathed into his nostrils the breath of life. This explains the origin of Adam's soul, but it leaves the question of from where do our souls come? There are two common answers to this question:

1.   Creationism.

This view states that all souls are created by God and thus produced from nothing and without pre-existing materials.

- Ecclesiastes 12:7 describes physical death as that time when *then the dust will return to the earth as it was, and the spirit will return to God who gave it.*
- When Adam sees the woman, he says, "This is bone of my bone and flesh of my flesh," but he does not say, "This is soul of my soul."
- In Isaiah 57:16, the Lord speaks of *"the breath of those I have made."*
- Zechariah 12:1 introduces the Lord *who stretches out the heavens, lays the foundation of the earth, and forms the spirit of man within him,*
- Hebrews 12:9 refers to God as *the Father of our spirits* and contrasts Him with the *"fathers of our flesh."*

One branch of Creationism states that God created the souls of all men in the beginning. Those who hold to this view would therefore maintain the pre-existence of all souls since the creation of Adam.

2.   Traducianism.

This view is taken from the Latin and speaks of the propagation (Latin: *traducem*) of the soul. This view sees those verses that speak of God giving and forming the spirit of man as being descriptive of God as the Creator through Adam and not necessarily creating each individual soul. For example, the Scriptures teach that God sends the rain upon the just and the unjust, but most would agree that God does this through secondary causes and would not deny the reality of clouds and weather patterns and evaporation and water vapor and the part they play in the bringing of rain.

- Just as all animals reproduced after their own kind, so also man is said in the Scriptures to reproduce after his kind. In Genesis 5:3, Adam bore a son who was in his own image and likeness.
- God has rested from His work of creation and is not actively creating either bodies or souls.
- The Hebrew of Genesis 46:26 speaks of "all the souls that came with Jacob into Egypt, who came from his loins" (see the KJV which gives a more literal translation).
- Hebrews 7:9-10 speaks of how Levi was in the loins of Abraham and thus was involved in giving the tithe to Melchizedek.

Indeed, the Scriptures describe not only God's creating and forming of our souls, but also the creating and forming of our bodies.

13 For Thou didst form my inward parts;
Thou didst weave me in my mother's womb.
14 I will give thanks to Thee, for I am fearfully and wonderfully made;
Wonderful are Thy works, And my soul knows it very well.
(Psalm 139:13-14).

Before I formed you in the womb I knew you,
And before you were born I consecrated you;
I have appointed you a prophet to the nations. (Jeremiah 1:5).

Jesus the Messiah

Prophecies of the Christ

He was born in an obscure village.
He worked in a carpenter shop until He was thirty.
He then became an itinerant preacher.
He never held an office.
He never had a family or owned a house.
He never went to college.
He had no credentials but Himself.
He was only thirty-three when the public turned against Him.
He was turned over to His enemies.
He was deserted by his friends.
He went through the mockery of a trial.
He was nailed to a cross between two thieves.
While He was dying, His executioners gambled for His clothing, the
only property He had on earth.
He was laid in a borrowed grave.

Twenty Centuries have come and gone, and today
He is still the central figure of the human race.
All the Armies that ever marched,
all the Navies that ever sailed,
all the Parliaments that ever sat,
and all the Kings that ever reigned
have not affected the life of man on this earth
as much as that ONE SOLITARY LIFE. (From a 1926 sermon by
James A. Francis).

What do you think of Jesus Christ? Who was he? I have asked that same question to many people over the years. The responses to that question are varied.

- He was a good man.
- He was a teacher.
- He was a rebel.
- He was crazy.
- He was a prophet.

In asking people their opinion of Jesus, I have often been given the reply, "I don't like to discuss religion." Yet that same person is often willing to discuss Buddha or Confucius or Islam of Charles Darwin. What is it about Jesus that engenders such a response?

Perhaps it is because of the fantastic claims Jesus made about Himself. He said things about Himself that went far beyond those made by any other religious leader of history. He said that God was His Father. He claimed to be the unique Son of God. He said that his death would pay for the sins of the world. He promised eternal life to those who believe in Him.

Who is Jesus? Who is this man that so drastically changed the face of the world? On the afternoon following His resurrection, Jesus appeared to two of His disciples as they walked along the road to Emmaus. They did not recognize Him and when Jesus asked about their conversation, they related the events of the past week and how their hopes had been dashed by the turn of those events. At this, Jesus rebuked them for their lack of understanding of the Old Testament.

> *25 And He said to them, "O foolish men and slow of heart to believe in all that the prophets have spoken! 26 Was it not necessary for the Christ to suffer these things and to enter into His glory?" 27 And beginning with Moses and with all the prophets, He explained to them the things concerning Himself in all the Scriptures. (Luke 24:25-27).*

Notice the repetition of the word "all." Jesus used both the writings of Moses and all the prophets to show that He was revealed by all the prophets in all the Scriptures. This suggests that a proper understanding of the Old Testament will not really be a proper understanding unless it includes a portrait of Jesus.

THE PROMISE OF A SEED

> *And I will put enmity Between you and the woman, And between your seed and her seed; He shall bruise you on the head, And you shall bruise him on the heel. (Genesis 3:15).*

This prophecy was given in the Garden of Eden. The words are spoken to the serpent. We can understand from our perspective that Satan had used the serpent to lead the first man and woman into sin. God comes on the scene and pronounces judgment upon everyone involved. An intense hatred is pronounced between the serpent and the woman and between their offspring -- their seed.

The first seed was to be the seed of the serpent. It was the seed of rebellion. It was the seed of sin. It was made up of all who walked in the way of Adam in turning against God.

There is also a second seed promised. It is the seed of the woman. This second seed is set over against the first seed. The two seeds are at war with one another. And God has decreed that the second seed shall ultimately win.

From our vantage point, we know that this second seed is ultimately fulfilled in Jesus Christ - the One who was bruised for our iniquities as He crushed underfoot the Serpent's Head.

> *Since then the children share in flesh and blood, He Himself likewise also partook of the same, that through death He might render powerless him who had the power of death, that is, the devil; 15 and might deliver those who through fear of death were subject to slavery all their lives. (Hebrews 2:14-15).*

The defeat and destruction of Satan is accomplished in two parts. First, Christ defeated Satan when He died for sins upon the cross and then rose in victory from the grave (Colossians 2:14-15). The ultimate conquest will be completed at the second coming of Christ -- Paul speaks in Romans 16:20 of how *the God of peace will soon crush Satan under your feet.* Just as the serpent is destroyed by striking him on his head, the most vulnerable part of his body, so Jesus Christ will destroy and neutralize Satan.

The Old Testament is a history of the Satanic attacks on the seed of the woman and the royal line of Christ. Satan may have considered either Cain or Abel to be the seed of the woman, and so he tempted one into murdering the other. It would not be too far a stretch to imagine that the sinfulness that brought about the flood in the days of Noah was due in part to the temptations wrought by Satan. Later attacks can be seen against Abraham and his descendants, against the nation of Israel and against the Davidic line.

When Jesus was born, there came a great intensification of these attacks. Herod tried to have the child assassinated. The Pharisees and the Sadducees plotted with the priesthood to put Him to death. Even Satan himself came and tried to entice Jesus to sin. In the end, it was Jesus who conquered. That conquest took place upon the cross. In the very process of striking a death blow tot he head of the serpent, Jesus Christ suffered and died upon the cross.

> *But He was pierced through for our transgressions,*
> *He was crushed for our iniquities;*
> *The chastening for our well-being fell upon Him,*
> *And by His scourging we are healed. (Isaiah 53:5).*

The crushing of Satan's head is not the only crushing that takes place in this prophecy. In His crushing of Satan, Jesus was also crushed.

The Seed of the Serpent	The Seed of the Woman
Points to Satan	Points to Jesus Christ
He receives a wound to the head -- this is a fatal wound.	He receives a wound to the heel -- painful but not lasting.
He was fatally bruised for all eternity.	He was temporarily bruised while on the cross.

The picture is of a man stomping upon the head of a serpent in order to kill it, but being bitten on his heel in the process. The one suffers that which is painful, the other suffers a crushing and fatal wound.

THE PROMISE TO ABRAHAM

When the Lord revealed Himself to Abram, He gave to him certain promises that were to form the foundation of a covenant relationship.

> *Now the Lord said to Abram,*
> *"Go forth from your country,*
> *And from your relatives*
> *And from your father's house,*
> *To the land which I will show you;*
> *And I will make you a great nation,*
> *And I will bless you,*
> *And make your name great;*
> *So you shall be a blessing;*
> *And I will bless those who bless you,*
> *And the one who curses you I will curse.*
> *And in you all the families of the earth shall be blessed."*
> *(Genesis 12:1-3).*

There are three major promises in this passage that are later confirmed and developed in greater detail.

1. The promise of a land (Genesis 12:1, 7; 13:14-17; 15:7-8; 17:8). The Lord promised that He would give to Abram and to his descendants all of the land of Canaan for an eternal inheritance. This promise was fulfilled when Joshua led the Israelites into Canaan.

2. The promise of a multiplied seed (Genesis 12:2; 13:;16; 15:2-5; 17:4-6; 22:15-17). God promised that He would make a great nation from the descendants of Abram. This was fulfilled in part when Moses led an entire nation out of Egypt. Both the nations of Israel, Edom and Arabia descend from the loins of Abraham. But that is not all. The ultimate fulfillment of this promise is the church, the spiritual seed of Abraham that is made up of every nation, tribe and people.

3. The families of the earth are to be blessed by Abram (Genesis 12:3). Paul alluded to this promise as being fulfilled in the person of Jesus Christ.

> *And the Scripture, foreseeing that God would justify the Gentiles by faith, preached the gospel beforehand to Abraham, saying, "All the nations shall be blessed in you." 9 So then those who are of faith are blessed with Abraham, the believer. (Galatians*

3:8-9).

Paul sites this promise as a forerunner of the truth that God would justify the Gentiles by faith. By giving this promise to Abraham, God was preaching the gospel to him. This means that the Abrahamic Covenant not only contins the seeds of the gospel, but also that it forms the basis of the New Covenant into which we enter when we believe the gospel.

We have been promised a new country. It is not a country of this world, but a new heavens and a new earth in which righteousness dwells. We have been given a commission to spread the seed of the gospel, a seed that brings blessings to all who experience its harvest.

A SCEPTER FROM JUDAH

As he lay on his deathbed, Jacob called his sons together and blessed them. When He came to Judah, his third son, he had a special promise.

> *8 Judah, your brothers shall praise you;*
> *Your hand shall be on the neck of your enemies;*
> *Your father's sons shall bow down to you.*
> *9 Judah is a lion's whelp;*
> *From the prey, my son, you have gone up.*
> *He couches, he lies down as a lion,*
> *And as a lion, who dares rouse him up?*
> *10 The SCEPTER shall not depart from Judah,*
> *Nor the RULER'S STAFF from between his feet,*
> *Until SHILOH comes,*
> *And to him shall be the obedience of the peoples. (Genesis 49:8-10)*.

Judah is pictured as a lion's cub. It is no mistake that Jesus would be given the title of :Lion from the tribe of Judah" in Revelation 5:5. We are left in no doubt as to what this image means. It indicates kingship. This is evidenced by the mention of the scepter and the ruler's staff. It was from Judah that King David and his descendants would come.

This promise says that the rightful kingship of Israel would pass down through the descendants of Judah until the coming of "Shiloh." The word *shiloh* (שִׁילֹה) is related to the more familiar *shalom*. It speaks of being at rest, of well-being and of peace.

- Jesus is the prince of peace (Isaiah 9:6).
- His message is the gospel of peace (Romans 10:15; Ephesians 6:15).
- He is our peace (Ephesians 2:14).

This prophecy began to be fulfilled when David ascended to the throne. He was from the tribe of Judah. Even when the kingdom was divided, a descendant of Judah sat upon the throne of the Southern Kingdom of Judah. The line of David continued to rule in Jerusalem until the Babylonian Captivity. At that time, the descendants of David were given a prophecy from the hand of Ezekiel.

> *Thus says the Lord God, "Remove the turban, and take off the crown; this will be no more the same. Exalt that which is low, and abase that which is high. 27 A ruin, a ruin, a ruin, I shall make it. This also will be no more, until He comes whose right it is; and I shall give it to Him." (Ezekiel 21:26-27).*

Because of their sins, the descendants of David were removed from the throne. They were told there would be no one to wear the crown of Israel until the coming of the One *whose right it is*.

This prophecy was graphically fulfilled. No descendant of David ever took the title of king after the Babylonian Captivity. There were some who ruled as governor such as Zerubbabel. There were also some from the tribe of Levi who eventually took the crown during the period between the Old and New Testaments. There were even some, like the Herods, who were awarded the crown by the hands of the Roman Empire. But only one descendant of David ever emerged after the Babylonian Captivity to take for Himself the title of king. It was Jesus.

A STAR AND A PROPHECY

When the prophet Balaam was hired by Balak, king of Moab, to come and to prophesy against the Israelites, he instead foretold the future greatness of Israel. In the midst of this prophecy, he gave this cryptic description:

I see him, but not now;
I behold him, but not near;
A star shall come forth from Jacob,
And a scepter shall rise from Israel,
And shall crush through the forehead of Moab,
And tear down all the sons of Sheth. (Numbers 24:17).

Whereas Jacob had promised that the scepter would not depart from Judah, Balaam says that the scepter shall arise from Israel. They are actually saying the same thing, but with a different emphasis.

Jacob	Balaam
Genesis 49:19	Numbers 27:17
Emphasizes that, once the scepter has come, it will not leave the house of Judah.	Emphasizes that the scepter will come to Israel.

To what does this star refer? Is there a star connected to the coming of Messiah? Yes, there is. It might be significant that the only Messianic prophecy in the Old Testament tells of the single sign that was used to bring the foreign Magi to Israel to greet the newborn King of the Jews.

> *Now after Jesus was born in Bethlehem of Judea in the days of Herod the king, behold, magi from the east arrived in Jerusalem, saying, 2 "Where is He who has been born King of the Jews? For we saw His star in the east, and have come to worship Him." (Matthew 2:1-2).*

What was it that drew the Magi to Israel in search of the newborn king? It was the star. It was the fact that they *saw His star in the east*. They did not know of the prophecy of the Bible that the Messiah would be born in Bethlehem, so they naturally came to Jerusalem, the capital of Israel. They made no mention of any other prophecy of the Scriptures, but they somehow knew that the star signified the birth of One who was destined to be the King of the Jews. It may be that there had been passed down to them the prophecy of Balaam and that it was for this reason they saw the star and noted its significance.

A PROPHET LIKE MOSES

Near the end of the life of Moses, the Lord promised that another prophet would come who would be like Moses.

> *The LORD your God will raise up for you a prophet like me from among you, from your countrymen, you shall listen to him. (Deuteronomy 18:15).*

This prophet would speak with the words of power that were equal to those spoken by Moses. The New Testament apostles recognized that the fulfillment of this prophecy was seen in Jesus (Acts 3:19-22). The prophecy goes on to describe in exactly what way the future prophet would be like Moses.

> *I will raise up a prophet from among their countrymen like you, and I will put My words in his mouth, and he shall speak to them all that I command him. 19 And it shall come about that whoever will not listen to My words which he shall speak in My name, I Myself will require it of him. (Deuteronomy 18:18-19).*

What made Moses so special that he should be compared with the Messiah? It was that he had the words of the Lord. But that is not all. All of the prophets that followed had the word of the Lord. There was something even more special about Moses. It is that he saw God. No man before or since ever saw God. Moses caught a mere glimpse of God's "afterglow" (Exodus 33:18-23). Only Jesus has seen God in His fulness.

> *No man has seen God at any time; the only begotten God, who is in the bosom of the Father, He has explained Him. (John 1:18).*

Notice also the tenses that are used. Jesus is described, not as the One who was in the bosom of the Father, but as the One who is in the bosom of the Father. This verse takes us full circuit from the beginning to the incarnation and then to the ascension of Christ. When we come to meet Him, we come to meet One who is in the very bosom of the Father.

A SON OF DAVID

The following promise was given to King David and regards his son and successor.

> *"When your days are complete and you lie down with your fathers, I will raise up your descendant* [seed] *after you, who will come forth from you, and I will establish his kingdom.*
>
> *"He shall build a house for My name, and I will establish his kingdom forever.*
>
> *"I will be a father to him and he will be a son to Me; when he commits iniquity, I will correct him with the rod of men and the strokes of the sons of men,* 15 *but my lovingkindness shall not depart from him, as I took it away from Saul, whom I removed from before you.*
>
> *"And your house and your kingdom shall endure before Me forever; your throne shall be established forever."* (2 Samuel 7:12-16).

The promise to David revolves around the establishment of a seed. This takes us all the way back to the promise we saw back in Genesis 3:15. It was there that the Lord had promised Adam and Eve that there would come One who would be of the seed of the woman. This Seed would crush the serpent's head. He would be the destroyer of the works of Satan.

> Dead Sea Scroll 4Q Florilegium, a midrash scroll, shows that the Qumran scribes took the "son" in verse 14 to be a reference to Messiah.

This promise is fulfilled in two parts. The immediate fulfillment will be in the person of Solomon. He will be the seed who will build a house in the name of the Lord. It will be Solomon who constructs the temple of God in Jerusalem. Solomon will found the Davidic dynasty. But the ultimate fulfillment of this prophecy is seen in Jesus.

Solomon	Jesus
Son of David.	Ultimate son of David.
Established the united monarchy of Israel.	Established the kingdom of God upon earth.

295

Built the temple.	He WAS the temple.
Established a kingdom that would continue until 586 B.C.	Established an eternal kingdom that will never end.
Chastened because of his iniquity.	Took upon Himself the sins of the world.

The first part of verse 14 (*"I will be a father to him and he will be a son to Me"*) is quoted twice in the New Testament.

- Hebrews 1:5 quotes it in a context that speaks of Jesus as the Son of God.
- 2 Corinthians 6:18 gives a partial quote as the Lord tells US that *"I will be a father to you, and you shall be sons and daughters to Me."*

THE LORD'S MESSIAH

Psalm 2 was traditionally sung at the coronation of the kings of Israel. It gives a threefold description of the Chosen One of God. He is Messiah, King and Son of God.

> *₁ Why are the nations in an uproar,*
> *And the peoples devising a vain thing?*
> *₂ The kings of the earth take their stand,*
> *And the rulers take counsel together*
> *Against the LORD and against His Anointed (Psalm 2:1-2).*

The nation of Israel was a Theocratic Kingdom. God was the true king of Israel. The One who sits upon the throne is God's Anointed One. He is the Messiah. He is the true king of Israel. He is the One to whom the Lord says, *Thou art My Son, today I have begotten Thee* (Psalm 2:7). He is Jesus Christ.

This Psalm begins with the nations in an uproar. They are in an uproar because the people have devised a vain thing. What is the answer to such an uproar? It is the gospel. Jesus has called us to make disciples of the nations by teaching them the good news.

THE PROMISE OF A RESURRECTION

In the midst of a Psalm of David in which he calls out for refuge in the midst of trouble, there is a verse that has Messianic implications.

For Thou wilt not abandon my soul to Sheol;
Neither wilt Thou allow Thy Holy One to undergo decay.
(Psalm 16:10).

How do we know this to be a Messianic Psalm? It is explained in Paul's interpretation of it in Acts 13:35. Paul pointed to this Psalm as an Old Testament prophecy of the resurrection of Jesus. He pointed out how David had lived and had died and was buried and remained in his tomb, but, by contrast, Jesus was raised from the dead so that His body did not undergo decay.

THE SUFFERING AND DEATH OF THE MESSIAH

Psalm 22 is another song of David that reflect both the experiences of that king as well as the sufferings and death of the greater Son of David.

1.   The cry from the cross.

My God, my God, why hast Thou forsaken me?
Far from my deliverance are the words of my
groaning. (Psalm 22:1).

These words were echoed by Jesus upon the cross. They point to the mysterious separation that took place there. They hint that, for a brief instant of time, the Son was separated from the Father as He bore our guilt upon the tree.

2.   The mockery of the onlookers: *All who see me sneer at me; they separate with the lip, they wag the head, saying, 8 "Commit yourself to the LORD; let Him deliver him; let Him rescue him, because He delights in him." (Psalm 22:7-8).* Those who mock King David in his troubles are a mere shadow of the men who would one day mock the Messiah.

297

3.   The physical sufferings.

> *14 I am poured out like water,*
> *And all my bones are out of joint;*
> *My heart is like wax; It is melted within me.*
> *15 My strength is dried up like a potsherd,*
> *And my tongue cleaves to my jaws;*
> *And Thou dost lay me in the dust of death.*
> *16 For dogs have surrounded me;*
> *A band of evildoers has encompassed me;*
> *They pierced my hands and my feet.*
> *17 I can count all my bones.*
> *They look, they stare at me (Psalm 22:14-17).*

The spiritual and emotional suffering of the Messiah was accompanied by real physical suffering. Crucifixion was an agonizing death that often included dislocation and muscle cramps that added to the pain of piercing hands and feet.

4.   The divided garments: *They divide my garments among them, and for my clothing they cast lots. (Psalm 22:18).*

All four of the gospel accounts make mention of the dividing of the clothes of Jesus among the soldiers (Matthew 27:35; Mark 15:24; Luke 23:34; John 19:24).

THE PRIEST KING

Psalm 110 is the most quoted in the New Testament. It is the Psalm that Jesus used to challenge the religious leaders of Jerusalem. It is the Psalm of the Priest-King. The superscription ascribes it to David.

> *A Psalm of David.*
> *The LORD says to my Lord:*
> *"Sit at My right hand,*
> *Until I make Thine enemies a footstool for Thy feet." (Psalm 110:1).*

As we approach this Psalm, we see at the outset that there are three people mentioned. This cast of characters is seen in the first verse.

1. King David: The superscription calls this a Psalm of David. He is the king of Israel. Yet David seems to be overshadowed by the other two characters in the Psalm. This is unique. Kings are normally the most important people around. Kings are not used to taking second place to anyone. David does not even rank second in the Psalm. He ranks a distant third.

2. The Lord: This is God. He is the God of Abraham, Isaac and Jacob. He is called here by His divine name - Yahweh. He is the God who led His people through the Red Sea. He is the covenant keeping God.

3. David's lord: This is the third character of this first verse. He is really the main character of this Psalm. The entire Psalm is addressed to Him. He is seen here as David's lord and He is seek in verse four as a Priest after the order of Melchizedek. He is Jesus Christ.

The Lord (Yahweh)	David's Lord	David the King
Yahweh said...	To my lord...	
"Sit at My right hand, *Until I make Thine enemies a footstool for Thy feet."*		

To be seated at one's right hand was to be in the place of honor. Thus when Joseph brought his sons to be blessed by Jacob, he was careful to place the older son at that Patriarch's right hand and was displeased when his father crossed his hands to put the hand of blessing upon the head of the younger son.

David was the beloved of the Lord, but David was not called to sit at the right hand of God. That special place was reserved for another. This is the place of highest honor. It can only be held by the One who deserves all honor and glory. It is held by the Son of God.

David is only a bystander in this drama. He listens to the conversation of two that are greater than he. The conversation involves sitting in the place of honor. This is especially significant when we consider that the One who sits is described in verse 4 as a priest. One thing that a priest did not do when he came into the temple is to sit down. Jesus is the priest who sat down. He sat down because His work upon the cross was completed.

Notice the patience of God. The Father is pictured as speaking to the Son: "Sit here until..." We are in the between times today. We are awaiting a final consummation. The consummation takes place when the enemies of David's Lord serve as a footstool for His feet. When we think of a footstool, we think of a comfortable piece of furniture on which you set your feet when you kick back to watch the afternoon football game. But this is not the image that is in view in this verse. This reflects the ancient practice of a king bowing in complete submission to a master conqueror.

This same passage was the object of discussion in one of the key confrontations of Jesus and the religious leaders. It is recorded in all three of the Synoptic Gospels. The setting was Jerusalem. It was just prior to the Passover and the city was packed with Jewish pilgrims from all over the world. The crowds were gathered in the temple as they came to hear the teaching of a Galilean rabbi. For several days, he had been preaching in the temple. The Jewish leaders have challenged Him repeatedly and He has answered all of their objections. Now it is His turn to ask a question.

> *41 Now while the Pharisees were gathered together, Jesus asked them a question, 42 saying, "What do you think about the Christ, whose son is He?" They said to Him, "The son of David." (Matthew 22:41-42).*

The question that Jesus asks concerns the identity of the Christ -- the identity of the Messiah promised from the Old Testament. Whose son will he be? What will be his lineage? From what family will he come? The Pharisees know the answer. The Messiah is to come from the house of David. He will be the son of David. This brings up a second question.

> *43 He said to them, "Then how does David in the Spirit call Him 'Lord,' saying, 44 'The Lord said to my LORD, "Sit at My right hand, Until I put Thine enemies beneath Thy feet"? 45 If David then calls Him 'Lord,' how is He his son?"*
>
> *46 And no one was able to answer Him a word, nor did anyone dare from that day on to ask Him another question. (Matthew 22:43-46).*

Jesus refers to Psalm 110. It was recognized by the Jews to be a Psalm of David and a Psalm that spoke of the Messiah who was to come. The Jews recognized that there were three characters in this Psalm.

David	He is the one who writes Psalm 110

| The Lord | The Hebrew of Psalm 110 uses the term Yahweh to describe the Lord |
| My (David's) Lord | This unidentified one is told to sit at the right hand of Yahweh. The only other clue to his identity is that he is David's lord (*adoni*) |

The question revolves around the true identity of the one whom David describes as "my lord." He is shown to be a different person from Yahweh, for it is Yahweh who says to Him, "Sit here."

Here is the point of the question. A son is not by nature greater than his father. Fathers do not bow down before their sons. Fathers do not look to their sons for leadership. If this is the sake, then how can the Messiah be both...

- David's Son
- David's lord

The Scriptures make it quite clear that the Messiah is both David's son as well as David's lord. How can this be? It can only be the case if the Messiah's existence predated his birth. It can only be the case if the Messiah had a pre-incarnate existence. The Messiah is to be both the Son of Man and the Son of God.

THE BRANCH OF THE LORD

> In that day the Branch of the LORD will be beautiful and glorious, and the fruit of the earth will be the pride and the adornment of the survivors of Israel. 3 And it will come about that he who is left in Zion and remains in Jerusalem will be called holy -- everyone who is recorded for life in Jerusalem. (Isaiah 4:2-3).

This is the first time in the Bible that the Messiah is described in terms of a Branch. It seems to look back to the Lampstand which stood in the Tabernacle. This Lampstand had seven branches. It also had flowers and fruit built into its design. It was a representation of the Tree of Life.

The Tree of Life had stood in the Garden of Eden. It symbolized continued relationship with God. When that fellowship had been broken, mankind had been cast out of the Garden and had been banned from the Tree of Life. That fellowship had been restored. It had been restored through a new promise and a new covenant. It was the promise of a Redeemer - a Life-Bringer.

That redemption was found within the nation of Israel. It was to Israel that the Tabernacle was entrusted. It was in Israel that the Temple was constructed. It was Israel who fathered the prophets and it was Israel to whom were given the oracles of God.

Psalm 80:8-9 describes Israel as a vine which was transplanted from Egypt and replanted within the land of Canaan. But Israel in itself was unable to provide redemption. Israel was itself in need of redemption. The faithful city had become like a harlot (Isaiah 1:21). Jerusalem had become a spiritual Sodom and Gomorrah (1:9-10; 3:9).

The good news is that there is the promise of a Branch. It is described as the "fruit of the earth" (the Hebrew can read "the fruit of the land"). This can be understood in one of two ways:

- It can refer to the fact that Messiah is to come from the land of Israel - an indication of His birthplace.
- It could be a veiled reference to the One who was crucified, dead and buried - and who then came forth from the earth.

From this time onward and through the rest of the Old Testament prophets, there continues to be a promise of One who will be known as the Branch.

> *1 Then a shoot will spring from the stem of Jesse,*
> *And a BRANCH from his roots will bear fruit.*
> *2 And the Spirit of the LORD will rest on Him,*
> *The spirit of wisdom and understanding,*
> *The spirit of counsel and strength,*
> *The spirit of knowledge and the fear of the LORD. (Isaiah 11:1-2).*

> *5 "Behold, the days are coming," declares the LORD,*
> *"When I shall raise up for David a righteous Branch;*
> *And He will reign as king and act wisely*
> *And do justice and righteousness in the land.*
> *6 "In His days Judah will be saved,*
> *And Israel will dwell securely;*
> *And this is His name by which He will be called,*
> *'The LORD our righteousness.'" (Jeremiah 23:5-6).*

15 In those days and at that time I will cause a righteous Branch of David to spring forth; and He shall execute justice and righteousness on the earth. 16 In those days Judah shall be saved, and Jerusalem shall dwell in safety; and this is the name by which she shall be called: the LORD is our righteousness. (Jeremiah 33:15-16).

The image that is seen in these verses is of a tree that is grown by the Lord and which has a stem that is Jesse from which comes a shoot. This small shoot grows into a branch that bears great fruit.

Then say to him, "Thus says the LORD of hosts, 'Behold, a man whose name is Branch, for He will branch out from where He is; and He will build the temple of the LORD.'" (Zechariah 6:12).

Zechariah ties the idea of the Branch to the promise that He would *branch out from where He is.* It is significant that Jesus described Himself as the "True Vine" (John 15:1). He went on to say that any branch that is unfruitful or that is not a part of the vine is thrown aside and cast into the fire.

IMMANUEL

Therefore the Lord Himself will give you a sign: Behold, a virgin will be with child and bear a son, and she will call His name Immanuel. (Isaiah 7:14).

The passage begins with a series of historical events. This prophecy did not take place in a historical vacuum. This is true of all of the prophecies of the Bible, but in this case we are given detailed information of the very real need and the situation in which it arose. From the context that is given, we learn that the promises contained in this prophecy do not speak only to issues within the four walls of the church. The message is placed in a context that was relevant to the world affairs of that day. The implication is that it will also be a message that will be relevant to all of mankind today.

1.   The Historical Context of the Prophecy.

Now it came about in the days of Ahaz, the son of Jotham, the son of Uzziah, king of Judah, that Rezin

> *the king of Aram and Pekah the son of Remaliah, king*
> *of Israel, went up to Jerusalem to wage war against*
> *it, but could not conquer it.*
>
> *When it was reported to the house of David,*
> *saying, "The Arameans have camped in Ephraim,"*
> *his heart and the hearts of his people shook as the*
> *trees of the forest shake with the wind. (Isaiah 7:1-2).*

Isaiah prophesied at a time when the Assyrian Empire was at its zenith and the fierce Assyrian warriors had spread their reign of terror throughout most of the known world, plundering and burning wherever they went. The small kingdoms that lay along the shores of the Mediterranean were no match for these hoards and they decided that the only way they could resist the onslaught was to band together into a single alliance. Accordingly, Egypt, Aram (Syria) and the Northern Kingdom of Israel formed an alliance and asked Judah to join with them. Ahaz, the king of Judah, refused.

Tensions mounted as the confederation threatened to invade Judah and install a puppet king of their own choosing. Ahaz found himself surrounded by enemies on all sides. It was into this scene that Isaiah came with a message from the Lord. The message was one of hope in the midst of what had all the appearances of an eventual collision of forces.

It was into this scene that Isaiah came. He was a man with a message. The message was from God. The message was that the enemies of God would fail.

2.   A Promise in Time of Trouble.

> *Then the LORD said to Isaiah, "Go out now to*
> *meet Ahaz, you and your son Shear-jashub, at the end*
> *of the conduit of the upper pool, on the highway to the*
> *fuller's field, 4 and say to him, 'Take care, and be*
> *calm, have no fear and do not be fainthearted because*
> *of these two stubs of smoldering firebrands, on*
> *account of the fierce anger of Rezin and Aram, and*
> *the son of Remaliah. 5 because Aram, with Ephraim*
> *and the son of Remaliah, has planned evil against*
> *you, saying, 6 "Let us go up against Judah and*
> *terrorize it, and make for ourselves a breach in its*
> *walls, and set up the son of Tabeel as king in the*

midst of it," 7 thus says the Lord God, "It shall not stand nor shall it come to pass. 8 For the head of Aram is Damascus and the head of Damascus is Rezin (now within another 65 years Ephraim will be shattered, so that it is no longer a people), 9 and the head of Ephraim is Samaria and the head of Samaria is the son of Remaliah. If you will not believe, you surely shall not last." '" (Isaiah 7:3-9).

God gives a prophecy to Ahaz. He tells Ahaz what will take place in the future. The collision of armies is not the end of the story. There is salvation at hand and it will not come by anything that Ahaz can do. The only part that he must play is to believe.

3.   The Offer of a Sign.

Then the LORD spoke again to Ahaz, saying, 11 "Ask a sign for yourself from the LORD your God; make it deep as Sheol or high as heaven." 12 But Ahaz said, "I will not ask, nor will I test the LORD!" (Isaiah 7:10-12).

The Lord does not call for a "blind faith." Faith is required, but it is a faith that is accompanied by a sign. God offers to put His signature to the promise that He has given. In the case of Ahaz, God even permits Ahaz to choose what the sign shall be. He says, "Ask anything you want. Make it as great a sign as you desire. Make is something whereby the greatness of My strength will be seen." But Ahaz refuses to ask for such a sign. *But Ahaz said, "I will not ask, nor will I test the LORD!"* (Isaiah 7:12).

At first glance, Ahaz seems to be doing a very noble and pious thing. He gives the excuse that he does not want to test the Lord. But that is not a correct response. It is like the man who says, "I do not pray because I do not want to bother God with my problems." Such a stance is the result of a heart of unbelief.

The good news is that the story does not end here. God turns from this unbelieving king and gives a promise to those who will believe. Here is the sign. A virgin will conceive and shall be with child. She will have a son. He will be called Immanuel. It is a name that means "God is with us."

305

4.   The Sign of Immanuel.

> *Then he said, "Listen now, O house of David! Is it too slight a thing for you to try the patience of men, that you will try the patience of my God as well? 14 Therefore the Lord Himself will give you a sign: Behold, a virgin will be with child and bear a son, and she will call His name Immanuel. 15 He will eat curds and honey at the time He knows enough to refuse evil and choose good. 16 For before the boy will know enough to refuse evil and choose good, the land whose two kings you dread will be forsaken. (Isaiah 7:13-14).*

There is a "child motif" that runs through this section of Israel from chapter 7 to chapter 9 and include the mention of five different children.

- Shear-jashub (Isaiah 7:3).
- Immanu-el (Isaiah 7:14; 8:8).
- Maher-shalal-hash-baz (Isaiah 8:3).
- Isaiah's children (Isaiah 8:18).
- The Royal Child (Isaiah 9:6-7).

Immanu-el stands out in contrast to the other children in that there is no father mentioned. Even the mother is not named except to refer to her as "the virgin." In this regard, Immanu-el and the Royal Child of chapter 9 are seen to be similar. This same "child motif" is seen in the book of Hosea. This is notable because Hosea is commonly thought to have been a contemporary of Isaiah.

The sign is that a young maiden shall be with child. She shall have a son. He will be called Immanuel. But the prophecy does not end here. It goes on to tell what the sign will signify. The sign has been given for a specific localized reason.

> *He will eat curds and honey at the time He knows enough to refuse evil and choose good. 16 For before the boy will know enough to refuse evil and choose good, the land whose two kings you dread will be forsaken. (Isaiah 7:15-16).*

The sign was not to end with the birth of Immanuel. It was only to begin there. The rest of the sign was that the child would grow and develop into a young boy. Before that boy had reached the age of being able to tell the difference between right and wrong, the kings of both Aram and Israel would die.

I believe that the sign of Immanuel was given as a partial fulfillment in the days of Ahaz. This is seen in the following chapter where Immanuel himself is addressed (Isaiah 8:8). But that is not the end of the story. Even though his name was Immanuel and expressed the truth that God was working in the lives of His people, there remained a further and more complete fulfillment.

That fulfillment is seen in the person of Jesus. Matthew 1:22-23 presents to us the truth that Jesus is the ultimate fulfillment of the Immanuel. He is God with us.

It is no mistake that Isaiah used the specific word that he did. The Hebrew word *Almah* (translated "virgin") technically means a "young maiden." Every time it is used in the Old Testament, it describes a young unmarried damsel. Unmarried young girls are assumed to be virgins, though that is not the specific meaning of the word that is used. What is it about the virgin birth of Christ that is so important?

- Because sin is passed down from the father?
- Because of the supernatural origin of Jesus?
- Because Jesus is God?

None of these are taught in the Scriptures or in this specific passage. Instead, the significance of the virgin birth is that this was the promised sign. This sign points to the fulfillment of the promise that God would be with us.

THE LIGHT OF GALILEE

1 But there will be no more gloom for her who was in anguish; in earlier times He treated the land of Zebulun and the land of Naphtali with contempt, but later on He shall make it glorious, by the way of the sea, on the other side of Jordan, Galilee of the Gentiles.
2 The people who walk in darkness
Will see a great light;

Those who live in a dark land,
The light will shine on them. (Isaiah 9:1-2).

Isaiah did not have a popular message. It was a message of gloom and doom. The previous verses at the end of chapter 8 reflect this. But in the midst of this gloom and doom, there breaks through those dark clouds a shining ray of hope. Note the emotional content of this description.

> In anguish
> Contempt
> Walk in Darkness
> Live in a Dark Land
> No more gloom
> Glorious
> See a great Light
> The Light will Shine on them

Israel was at war and facing the onslaught of the full weight of the Assyrian military machine. Within a short time Israel would fall and the Southern Kingdom of Judah would also be besieged. In the midst of this sober threat, God promises peace.

Zebulun and Naphtali were beautiful lands with a major problem. The problem is that they were the buffer zone between Israel and the hostile forces to the north. Every time the Assyrians came down, the first place through which they would come were Zebulun and Naphtali.

By the days of Jesus, this region had come to have a high Gentile population. It would be known as "Galilee of the Gentiles." This would give rise to a proverb: "Can anything good come out of Galilee?"

This is the place where God chose to send His Son. Not Jerusalem. Not the Temple. Not Rome, the capital of the Empire. But Galilee. Jesus was not sent to those who already had the light. He was sent to those in darkness. He came to heal the sick, not the healthy. We live in a world that is in darkness. There are bad times ahead. But there is good news. A light has come. The light has come.

THE PROMISE OF A SON

6 For a child will be born to us, a son will be given to us;
And the government will rest on His shoulders;
And His name will be called Wonderful Counselor, Mighty God, Eternal Father, Prince of Peace.
7 There will be no end to the increase of His government or of peace,

On the throne of David and over his kingdom,
To establish it and to uphold it with justice and righteousness
From then on and forevermore.
The zeal of the LORD of hosts will accomplish this. (Isaiah 9:6-7).

For the past three chapter we have seen a "son motif" running through the pages of Isaiah. It began in Isaiah 7 with the virgin-born son named Immanuel. Throughout chapter 8 we read of Isaiah giving names to his children that had prophetic significance. Now we come the final promise of a Son. Isaiah opens this section with a bit of typical Hebrew parallelism:

> *For a child will be born to us,*
> *A son will be given to us.*

There are many celebrations that we observe throughout the year during which we have developed a tradition of giving gifts. There is Mothers Day and Fathers Day and there are birthdays. Of all of these, there is only one in which everyone is given gifts. It is Christmas. Though it has become commercialized, perhaps it is appropriate that this is a time of giving gifts because it commemorates the time when the Son was given. The great truth of the gospel is that God so loved the world that He gave His only begotten Son.

1. His Profession: *And the government will rest on His shoulders.*

The Hebrew word here for "the government" (הַמִּשְׂרָה) is used only here and in verse 7. It is derived from the Hebrew שָׂרָה (*sarah*) describing a prince or ruler. To which government does this refer? Verse 6 does not say. But verse 7 indicates that it is His government. It is the government of the Throne of David.

The problem with this is that, from a physical perspective, the throne of David is long gone. There is a nation of Israel today, but no one identifies modern Israel with the throne of David. And yet, the promise says that this will be a reign of righteousness which shall last forever. And that of this government there shall be no end.

What is this government? I would suggest that this "government" refers to the Kingdom of Heaven. It is the government which has gone out to make disciples of all the nations (Matthew 28:18). It is the government which shall survive when all other rule and authority and power has been abolished (1 Corinthians 15:24). It is the government of God's people. Today we call it the church.

2.   His Personality: *Wonderful Counselor*.

When we think of a counselor, it brings to mind one who has the answers to our problems. Jesus has the answer because He is the answer. He is the way, the truth and the life (John 14:6).

3.   His Power: *Mighty God*.

The phrase "mighty God" is not all that common in the Old Testament, but when it is used, it points to God (Isaiah 10:21 and Jeremiah 32:18). In this case, it points to the deity of the Son.

4.   His Permanence: *Eternal Father*.

The Hebrew of Isaiah 9:6 speaks of the Messiah being the "eternal Father." It uses the single word אֲבִיעַד. What does this mean? Some have taught that this is an indication of Modalism — that Jesus is the Father and that they are both one person in the same way that I am a son and I am also a father.

The Hebrew phrase is a compound word. This seems to be a Hebraism. There are a number of examples of this:

- Abiethon (2 Sam. 23:31), "father of strength," means "strong."
- Abiaseph (Ex.6:24), "father of gathering," means "gatherer."
- Abigail (1 Chron.2:16), "father of exultation," is a woman's name meaning "exulting."

If this is the same sort of Hebraism, then the term "father of eternity" in Isaiah 9:6 means simply that the promised Son would be eternal.

5.   His Peace: *Prince of Peace*.

The ministry of the Son was to bring the most important peace of all; the peace that is between God and man. He is our peace (Ephesians 2:14) and He has not only made peace between God and men, but also He has broken down every wall that divides men.

THE SERVANT OF THE LORD

In the same way that a child motif runs through the early chapters of Israel, so also there is a "servant motif" that runs through the latter part of the book. Of all the ways in which the Messiah is presented, this is the most striking. We would expect the God of the universe to appear as a king, a conqueror, a wise teacher, but a servant?

1.   The Voice in the Wilderness.

> *3 A voice is calling,*
> *"Clear the way for the LORD in the wilderness;*
> *Make smooth in the desert a highway for our God.*
> *4 Let every valley be lifted up,*
> *And every mountain and hill be made low;*
> *And let the rough ground become a plain,*
> *And the rugged terrain a broad valley;*
> *5 Then the glory of the LORD will be revealed,*
> *And all flesh will see it together;*
> *For the mouth of the LORD has spoken." (Isaiah 40:3-5).*

When we first read these words, we might have a tendency to try to take them literally. We might imagine mountain-moving bulldozers that raise valleys and level mountains and pave highways. To do so would be to try to impose a 21st century interpretation on an ancient writing. It would be missing the entire point. The Scriptures themselves explain to us the meaning of this passage when it is quoted in the New Testament.

> *As it is written in Isaiah the prophet, "Behold, I send My messenger before Your face, who will prepare Your way; 3 the voice of one crying in the wilderness, 'Make ready the way of the Lord, make His paths straight.'" (Mark 1:2-3).*

Mark says that this is "written in Isaiah, the prophet" (1:2). Actually, the quote is taken from two separate passages of the Old Testament.

> *"Behold, I am going to send My messenger, and he will clear the way before Me,,," (Malachi*

311

3:1a).

> *A voice is calling, "Clear the way for the Lord in the wilderness; make smooth in the desert a highway for our God." (Isaiah 40:3).*

Mark tells us that both of these passages have reference to the same thing. They both point to John the Baptist who was the messenger and the voice calling for the way to be prepared in the wilderness.

> *3 A voice is calling,*
> *"Clear the way for the LORD in the wilderness;*
> *Make smooth in the desert a highway for our God.*
> *4 Let every valley be lifted up,*
> *And every mountain and hill be made low;*
> *And let the rough ground become a plain,*
> *And the rugged terrain a broad valley;*
> *5 Then the glory of the LORD will be revealed,*
> *And all flesh will see it together;*
> *For the mouth of the LORD has spoken." (Isaiah 40:3-5).*

John was the voice calling in the wilderness who came to prepare the way for the coming of the Lord's Messiah. He built a highway upon which the ministry of Jesus entered history. John prepared the way. But notice for whom it was that he prepared the way. It is seen in verse 5. He prepared the way for the glory of Yahweh.

> *Then the glory of the LORD will be revealed,*
> *And all flesh will see it together;*
> *For the mouth of the LORD has spoken." (Isaiah 40:3-5).*

I cannot read these words without thinking of the incident of Moses in the wilderness. Moses had seen some great things. He had seen the plagues of Egypt. He had seen the parting of the Red Sea and the destruction of the armies of Pharaoh. He had seen the cloud by day and the pillar of fire by night. He had seen the Lord's daily provision of the manna in the wilderness.

Was there anything more for which a man could ask? Only one thing remained. Moses asked that he might be permitted to see the glory of God. Moses asks, "Show me your glory!" And the Lord replies, "You cannot do that and live; but I will permit you to catch a glimpse of My afterglow." The Lord places Moses into a cleft in the rock and covers it and then His goodness passes by and Moses is allowed to see the afterglow of God's glory.

But here is a promise that *the glory of the LORD will be revealed.* That for which Moses could only long is given to men. How can such a thing be?

> *And the Word became flesh, and dwelt among us, and we beheld His glory, glory as of the only begotten from the Father, full of grace and truth. (John 1:14).*

In the person of Jesus men were able to see the glory of the Lord. On the night of Jesus' arrest, his disciples asked Him about this.

> *Philip said to Him, "Lord, show us the Father, and it is enough for us." 9 Jesus said to him, "Have I been so long with you, and yet you have not come to know Me, Philip? He who has seen Me has seen the Father" (John 14:8-9).*

2.   The Servant as the Embodiment of Israel: In Isaiah 41:8-9, the Lord describes Israel as the servant of the Lord.

> *8 But you, Israel, My servant,*
> *Jacob whom I have chosen,*
> *Descendant of Abraham My friend,*
> *9 You whom I have taken from the ends of the earth,*
> *And called from its remotest parts,*
> *And said to you,*
> *'You are My servant,*
> *I have chosen you and not rejected you. (Isaiah 41:8-9).*

However, as we continue reading the prophecies of Isaiah, we come to the power where the servant is pictured, not as the entire nation, but as being embodied in a single individual. This faithful servant is contrasted to Israel, the unfaithful servant.

313

1 "Behold, My Servant, whom I uphold;
My chosen one in whom My soul delights.
I have put My Spirit upon Him;
He will bring forth justice to the nations.
2 He will not cry out or raise His voice,
Nor make His voice heard in the street.
3 A bruised reed He will not break,
And a dimly burning wick He will not extinguish;
He will faithfully bring forth justice.
4 He will not be disheartened or crushed,
Until He has established justice in the earth;
And the coastlands will wait expectantly for His law."
5 Thus says God the LORD,
Who created the heavens and stretched them out,
Who spread out the earth and its offspring,
Who gives breath to the people on it,
And spirit to those who walk in it,
6 "I am the LORD,
I have called you in righteousness,
I will also hold you by the hand and watch over you,
And I will appoint you as a covenant to the people,
As a light to the nations,
7 To open blind eyes,
To bring out prisoners from the dungeon,
And those who dwell in darkness from the prison." (Isaiah
42:1-7).

Like Israel of old, this Servant of the Lord is described as the chosen of Yahweh. But whereas Israel has acted unjustly, this servant will bring justice to the nations (42:1). Moreover, he does not accomplish this by force of arms or even by raising His voice. To the contrary, He is so gentle that His coming will not extinguish the faintest flicker of the dimly burning wick.

His ministry is not only to bring justice, but also to open the eyes of the blind and to release those who have been in bondage. He is a liberator and He is also just and righteous.

3.   The Suffering Servant.

13 Behold, My servant will prosper,
He will be high and lifted up, and greatly exalted.

14 Just as many were astonished at you, My people,
So His appearance was marred more than any man,
And His form more than the sons of men.
15 Thus He will sprinkle many nations,
Kings will shut their mouths on account of Him;
For what had not been told them they will see,
And what they had not heard they will understand.
(Isaiah 52:13-15).

From this passage to the end of chapter 53 is set forth in the form of a chiasm. It is a parallel that begins and ends of the same note. The important point of this parallel is see in that which is at the pivotal point.

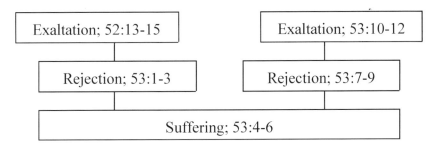

Notice that the aspect of suffering is the central and pivotal point of the passage. But before we read of the suffering of the Servant, we are first guaranteed of the exaltation of the Servant. He will prosper. This is the same message as is found in the book of Revelation. Jesus Wins!

In verse 14 we saw that **many** were astonished. Now in verse 15 we see that **many** nations are sprinkled. The point is that the Messiah not only worked in a surprising manner, but that He also produced some surprising results. His coming would result in the salvation of the nations and even kings would recognize His authority.

1 Who has believed our message?
And to whom has the arm of the LORD been
revealed? (Isaiah 53:1).

Verse 1 is a rhetorical question. After all, this is a message that everyone ought to have believed. But the truth of the matter is that many have not believed the report of the prophet. Why not? It is because of what we read in verse 2:

> *2 For He grew up before Him like a tender shoot,*
> *And like a root out of parched ground;*
> *He has no stately form or majesty*
> *That we should look upon Him,*
> *Nor appearance that we should be attracted to Him.*
> *3 He was despised and forsaken of men,*
> *A man of sorrows, and acquainted with grief;*
> *And like one from whom men hide their face,*
> *He was despised, and we did not esteem Him. (Isaiah*
> *53:2-3).*

Jesus was not the stereotype of a heroic figure. He didn't come across as a conquering king or a majestic ruler. He grew up as a simple carpenter. There was nothing about His appearing that would attract the natural man.

> *4 Surely our griefs He Himself bore,*
> *And our sorrows He carried;*
> *Yet we ourselves esteemed Him stricken,*
> *Smitten of God, and afflicted.*
> *5 But He was pierced through for our transgressions,*
> *He was crushed for our iniquities;*
> *The chastening for our well-being fell upon Him,*
> *And by His scourging we are healed. (Isaiah 53:4-6).*

In these verses we go back and forth between the truth about the work of Jesus versus what people thought about Jesus. It is a contrast between reality versus delusion.

53:4	Reality	Surely our griefs He Himself bore, And our sorrows He carried;
	Delusion	Yet we ourselves esteemed Him stricken, Smitten of God, and afflicted.
53:5	Reality	But He was pierced through for our transgressions, He was crushed for our iniquities; The chastening for our well-being *fell* upon Him, And by His scourging we are healed.

53:6	Delusion	All of us like sheep have gone astray, Each of us has turned to his own way;
	Reality	But the LORD has caused the iniquity of us all To fall on Him.

Unbelieving Israel looked at Jesus on the cross and said, "He got what He deserved." The truth is that He got what WE deserved. The death of Christ was substitutionary in nature. He died in our place.

This was graphically illustrated in the case of Barabbas. This man was a thief and a robber. He had been caught and tried for his crimes and sentenced to death. Seeking to pacify a hostile crowd, Pontius Pilate released Barabbas and crucified Jesus. The one who deserved to die was given life and the One who had done no wrong was sent to the cross. It was a cross that was meant for Barabbas. Verse 6 widens the scope of the cross to show how it extends itself to all.

> ***All*** *of us like sheep have gone astray,*
> ***Each*** *of us has turned to his own way;*
> *But the LORD has caused the iniquity of us **all** to fall*
> *on Him. (Isaiah 53:6).*

This is the same concept that Paul presents in Romans 5:12-18. It is the concept that all were under sin and that all sins were subsequently atoned.

Sheep are not known for their organizational skills. Left to themselves, they will wander and they will keep on wandering. We are like that. Left to ourselves, our tendency is to wander away from God. This is why we need a Savior. In verses 4-8 we see a contrast between our need over against the Servant's divine remedy for that need.

Israel's Need	The Servant's Remedy
Our griefs (53:4).	He Himself bore (53:4).
Our sorrows (53:4).	He carried (53:4).
For our transgressions (53:5).	He was pierced (53:5).

For our iniquities (53:5).	He was crushed (53:4).
For our well-being (53:5).	The chastening... fell upon Him (53:5)
In need of healing (53:5).	By His scourging (53:5).
All of us like sheep have gone astray, Each of us has turned to his own way (53:6).	The LORD has caused the iniquity of us all to fall on Him (53:6).
For the transgression of my people to whom the stroke was due (53:8).	He was cut off out of the land of the living (53:8).

The innocent was punished in place of the guilty. The guilty as permitted to go free.

BORN IN BETHLEHEM

But as for you, Bethlehem Ephrathah,
Too little to be among the clans of Judah,
From you One will go forth for Me to be ruler in Israel.
His goings forth are from long ago,
From the days of eternity. (Micah 5:2).

Bethlehem was the city from which David had come. This was its primary claim to fame, as it was really only a small village. Ephrathah was the place name of the general area, a name that went all the way back to the days of the judges (Ruth 4:11). The use of the term Ephrathah distinguishes this town from another Bethlehem that was located near Mount Carmel in the territory of Zebulun (Joshua 19:15).

Just as David had come from Bethlehem, so also the future ruler of Israel would also come from Bethlehem. He would be the One whose coming had been promised and described from ages past.

Who Is Jesus?

Names and Titles for Christ

When we look at a statistical breakdown of where the various titles for Christ are used in the New Testament, a pattern begins to emerge.

Title	Synoptic Gospels	Gospel of John	Acts	Paul's Epistles
Son of Man	72	13	7	0
Son of God	14	30	2	4
Messiah	0	2	0	0
Christ	37	21	107	243

THE SON OF MAN

This is the Aramaic expression used to describe a man. Ezekiel uses it the most often in this sense. It is also the title that Jesus used the most often of Himself. When used in the New Testament, it is always used of Jesus unless it is a part of a quote from the Old Testament such as in Hebrews 2:6 that uses the Aramaic expression.

1.   The Background for this Title.

> *13 I kept looking in the night visions,*
> *And behold, with the clouds of heaven*

319

One like a Son of Man was coming,
And He came up to the Ancient of Days
And was presented before Him.
14 And to Him was given dominion,
Glory and a kingdom,
That all the peoples, nations, and men of every language
Might serve Him. His dominion is an everlasting dominion
Which will not pass away;
And His kingdom is one
Which will not be destroyed. (Daniel 7:13-14).

This passage takes us to heaven and gives to us a glimpse of the throne of God. It is in this setting that we see one who is said to be like the Son of Man. Daniel sees this "man-like" figure who comes before the Ancient of Days. This is in contrast to the beasts who have been pictured earlier in the chapter.

Four Preceding Beasts	Man-Like Figure
They enjoy temporary dominion.	He is given eternal dominion.
They represent four kingdoms.	A kingdom is given to him.
Each of these kingdoms is destroyed.	His kingdom will never be destroyed.

The "Son of Man" is not a title in this passage, but the description is so powerful that Jesus is able to take it and to use it and to turn it into a title.

2.   Historical Views regarding the Title.

The traditional view concerning this title is that it emphasizes the humanity of Jesus as He identified Himself with mankind. He calls Himself "Son of man" because He has become a man and identifies Himself with men.

In more recent times, Reformed scholars have done a turn-around, seeing the reference to Daniel's vision and therefore emphasizing the deity of Jesus. It is said that the title "Son of man" does not emphasize the "mannishness" of Jesus, but rather that He is the divine one who was "like a son of man."

| Modern Reformed Scholars emphasize only the deity of Christ | | Early Church Fathers emphasized only the humanity of Jesus. |

Which of these views is correct? It seems to me that the actual answer lies in the middle. This title gives a measure of emphasis to both the deity as well as the humanity of Christ.

3.   Why did Jesus give such preference to this particular title? There are several possible reasons.

- This was a designation that had already been used in the Old Testament and therefore contained aspects of His identity that He wished to communicate.
- This designation did not contain the nationalistic or militaristic baggage that might have been attached to other possible titles. It is possible that Jesus intentionally avoided the title "Messiah" for exactly this reason.
- The symbolic aspects of this title allowed Jesus to gradually unfold the various aspects of His person and ministry.

MESSIAH / CHRIST

The terms "Messiah" and "Christ" are each titles that are used of Jesus. They mean the same thing, but in different languages.

Messiah	**Christ**
Hebrew	Greek
Taken from מָשַׁח, "to anoint."	Taken from χριω, "to anoint."

Each title carries the same idea and speaks of "the anointed one." As such, it can refer to any anointed person and is not always a reference to Jesus.

1.   Old Testament Background.

The concept of anointing related to three distinct Old Testament offices. Those holding these offices were initiated into their position through a process of anointing.

- Prophets and Kings: *Jehu the son of Nimshi you shall anoint king over Israel; and Elisha the son of Shaphat of Abel-meholah you shall anoint as prophet in your place. (1 Kings 19:16).*

- Priests: *Then you shall take the anointing oil, and pour it on his head and anoint him. (Exodus 29:7).*

This anointing pictured the Holy Spirit being poured out upon the recipient of the anointing. At the same time, it was understood that these served as pictures of One who would be known as "the Lord's anointed" (Psalm 2:2; Isaiah 42:1-4; 61:1; Daniel 9:26).

2.   Usage by Jesus in the Gospel Accounts.

Jesus rarely used the terms "Messiah" or "Christ" as a self designation. Those times He did so were normally in private discussions and when someone else introduced the term.

a.   Peter's great confession: *He said to them, "But who do you say that I am?" 16 And Simon Peter answered and said, "Thou art the Christ, the Son of the living God." 17 And Jesus answered and said to him, "Blessed are you, Simon Barjona, because flesh and blood did not reveal this to you, but My Father who is in heaven." (Matthew 16:15-17).* In this case, Jesus accepts and agrees with this use of the title, even though He is not the one who introduced it. He points out that the only reason that Peter has come to this conclusion is because it has been revealed from the Father.

b.   In giving instructions to His disciples, Jesus speaks of them as followers of the Christ: *For whoever gives you a cup of water to drink because of your name as followers of Christ, truly I say to you, he shall not lose his reward. (Mark 9:41).*

c.   When the Samaritan woman spoke of the Messiah, Jesus told her, "I who speak to you am He." (John 4:26).

d.   Martha calls Jesus the Christ and He accepts the title from her: *She said to Him, "Yes, Lord; I have believed that You are the Christ, the Son of God, even He who comes into the world." (John 11:27).*

e.   Jesus questions the Pharisees about the Christ: *Now while the Pharisees were gathered together, Jesus asked them a question, 42 saying, "What do you think about the Christ, whose son is He?" They said to Him, "The son of David." (Matthew 22:41-42).* In this case, Jesus is speaking in public, but He does not make any pronouncement that He is the Christ.   Instead He asks the Pharisees what is their understanding of whom the Christ will be.

f.   Jesus uses the title of Himself as He prays to the Father in His high priestly prayer: *And this is eternal life, that they may know Thee, the only true God, and Jesus Christ whom Thou hast sent. (John 17:3).*

There is only one instance in which Jesus publicly proclaims Himself to be Messiah and Christ. It takes place on the night of His betrayal and arrest. As He stands before the high priest, He is asked directly about His ministry.

> *Again the high priest was questioning Him, and saying to Him, "Are You the Christ, the Son of the Blessed One?" 62 And Jesus said, "I am; and you shall see the Son of Man sitting at the right hand of Power, and coming with the clouds of heaven." (Mark 14:61-62).*

It was only now when the high priest asked Jesus point-blank whether or not He was the Christ that He replied in the affirmative. The very fact that the high priest asked this question in such a manner when Jesus had made no previous public proclamation that He was the Christ is itself an evidence of His Messiahship. The question was asked, not because He had made a public claim, but because so many people had seen the prophecies fulfilled before their eyes that the person and work of Jesus served to announce His true identity.

3.   Usage by the Authors of the Gospels: Though they show that Jesus

323

did not publicly pronounce Himself to be Messiah and Christ prior to the trial before the high priest, that does not mean that the authors of the gospel accounts hesitate to make such a pronouncement. Very early in each one of the gospels, we find a statement that Jesus is the Christ.

- *The book of the genealogy of Jesus Christ, the son of David, the son of Abraham. (Matthew 1:1).*
- *The beginning of the gospel of Jesus Christ, the Son of God. (Mark 1:1).*
- *For today in the city of David there has been born for you a Savior, who is Christ the Lord (Luke 2:11).*
- *For the Law was given through Moses; grace and truth were realized through Jesus Christ. (John 1:17).*

After these special introductions of Jesus as the Christ, each of the authors return to a regular using of "Jesus" as they give a gradual unfolding of Jesus as the Christ. They do this deliberately so that the reader will be brought to the same conclusion that Jesus is the Christ.

4.   Usage in the book of Acts: Luke uses the term "Christ" regularly in the book of Acts, often in conjunction with the proper name, "Jesus." Yet he first introduces the title in that book as a clear reference to the promised Messiah when he presents Peter's sermon on the day of Pentecost and explains the prophecy by David of the resurrection of "the Christ" (Acts 2:31).

5.   Usage in the Epistles: This is one of the most popular titles for Jesus in the epistles. The epistle to the Romans alone uses the title 68 times.

THE SON OF GOD

1.   The Old Testament refers to the *Beni-HaElohim* (בְּנֵי־הָאֱלֹהִים), the "sons of God" to refer both to men (Genesis 6:2-4) as well as to angels (Job 1:6; 2:1; 38:7). In this same way, Hosea 1:10 speaks of the Israelites as being "sons of the living God." But at no time is a single individual specifically given the title, "Son of God" in the

unique sense.

On the other hand, the Psalmist speaks of *the decree of the LORD: He said to Me, 'Thou art My Son, Today I have begotten Thee'* (Psalm 2:7). This is a Messianic Psalm in which we see the Lord's anointed (2:2), the Lord's Son (2:7) and the King (2:6).

2.   Usage by Jesus.

Jesus applies the title of "Son of God" to Himself infrequently and upon several special occasions. One of these was at the Feast of Dedication in Jerusalem.

> 30 *"I and the Father are one." 31 The Jews took up stones again to stone Him. 32 Jesus answered them, "I showed you many good works from the Father; for which of them are you stoning Me?"*
>
> 33 *The Jews answered Him, "For a good work we do not stone You, but for blasphemy; and because You, being a man, make Yourself out to be God."*
>
> 34 *Jesus answered them, "Has it not been written in your Law, 'I said, you are gods'? 35 If he called them gods, to whom the word of God came (and the Scripture cannot be broken), 36 do you say of Him, whom the Father sanctified and sent into the world, 'You are blaspheming,' because I said, 'I am the Son of God'?" (John 10:30-36).*

This passage begins with Jesus making what seems to be an extremely strong statement regarding His divinity: *"I and the Father are one."* The strength of this statement is seen in the immediate reaction of the Jews. They *took up stones again to stone Him* (10:31). Why? He asks the same question. *Jesus answered them, "I showed you many good works from the Father; for which of them are you stoning Me?" (John 10:32).*

Jesus was not ignorant. He knew that His words had incited their action. He was well aware of the significance of the statement that He had just made. That is not the question. Rather the question is whether they were truly aware.

They had already seen Him giving sight to a blind man and hearing to a deaf man. They had heard how He fed the hungry and gave forgiveness to sinners. Before it is all over, He will raise a man

325

from the dead. In all of this, He challenges them to find one thing that He has done wrong.

The Jews answered Him, "For a good work we do not stone You, but for blasphemy; and because You, being a man, make Yourself out to be God." (John 10:33). They took the words of Jesus to be blasphemous. They understood that He had claimed to be God. For a mere man to make such a claim would indeed be blasphemous. Notice the reaction of Jesus. He does not retract His statement. He does not say, "Oh, you misunderstood Me. I did not mean to imply such a position for Myself."

Instead, Jesus appeals to Psalm 82:6. It is a Psalm that calls for justice. In the Old Testament there were judges who were placed in positions in which they were to rule over Israel. Their responsibility was to judge the people of Israel. They judged in the place of God who was the Supreme Judge. The idea was that any justice they dispensed was to be God's justice. Any judgments they made were to be God's judgments. Any rebellion against them was considered to be rebellion against God.

Because of this ministry of representation, these judges were called "gods" -- Elohim. They received their office by divine appointment. They were called gods because they ruled and judged in the place of God.

When Jesus quotes this passage, He is making a point from the lesser to the greater. Here is the point. If these judges of Israel were called gods when they were mere human judges, then how much more is it proper that Jesus who came down from heaven be called the Son of God?

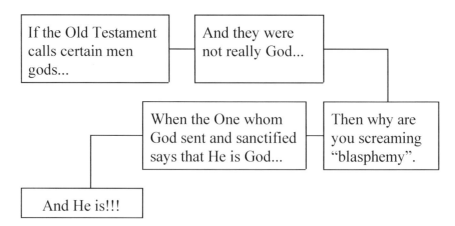

In essence, Jesus says, "If the Old Testament calls certain men gods (and they were not), then why are you screaming "blasphemy" when the one whom God send and sanctified says that He is One with the Father (and He is)? If I didn't do the Father's work, then don't believe. But if I do the Father's work, then you know that I am indeed God."

3.   The Only Begotten Son.

This phrase appears several times in the Gospel of John (1:14; 3:16; 3:18). The Greek phrase is τον υἰὸν τον μονογενη. There is some debate as to how we are to understand the word μονογενής (*monogenes*). The prefix μονο (*mono*) means "only." It is the rest of the word that is the subject of the debate.

- Γενναω (*gennao*) means "to give birth" (only-born son).
- Γινομαι (*ginomai*) means "to be" (only-existing son).

It is interesting to note that this same term -- μονογενής -- is used of Abraham's only son, Isaac in Hebrews 11:17, even though Abraham already another son in Ishmael. It is for this reason that some scholars prefer to view this as the "unique son."

JESUS AS GOD

In only one instance is there a clear cut example of Jesus allowing the title "God" to be used of Himself. That instance is found in John 20:28 where Thomas sees the resurrected Christ and addresses Him as *My Lord and My God*. On the other hand, Jesus says a number of things about Himself that ought only be said about God.

- He says that He is Lord of the Sabbath.
- He claims the power to forgive sins.
- He accepts worship.

Instances in which the New Testament specifically states that Jesus is God are also very rare, though they are not unknown. The following chart lists those passages that specifically refer to Jesus as God.

Text	Greek	Translation
John 1:1	Θεος	The Word was God
John 20:28	Ο Θεος μου	Thomas said, "My Lord and my God."
Romans 9:5	Θεος	...the Christ according to the flesh, who is over all, God blessed forever.
Titus 2:13	Ο μεγας Θεος	Our great God and Savior, Jesus Christ.
Hebrews 1:8	Ο Θεος	But of the Son He says, "Thy throne, O God, is forever and ever."
2 Peter 1:1	τοῦ θεοῦ ἡμῶν καὶ σωτῆρος Ἰησοῦ Χριστου	...the righteousness of God and our savior, Jesus Christ.
1 John 1:18	μονογενὴς θεὸς	...the only begotten God, who is in the bosom of the Father, He has explained Him.

Why are there so few instances in which Jesus is specifically described as God in the New Testament? It is because the term God (Θεος) is normally used of the Father or of God in general while the term Lord (κυριος) is normally used of Jesus. Thus the Bible avoids language that would allow for modalism in favor of that which points us to the doctrine of the trinity.

THE LORD

The Greek word κυριος can be translated as a title of respect ("sir"). It is also used in the Septuagint to translate both יְהוָה (*Yahweh*) and אֲדֹנִי (*Adonai*). The New Testament uses this term of Jesus in both of these senses.

1.   An Honorific.

Matthew 8:2 and 20:33 might be examples of such an honorific. In John 4:11 κυριος is translated "Sir" and is merely a polite address.

2.   Equivalent to God.

This is very obviously the case when Jesus quotes Psalm 110 and asks the Pharisees its meaning in Mark 12:35-37.

	The Lord said...	To my Lord...
Old Testament	Yahweh said...	To my Adonai...
New Testament	The *Kurios* said...	To my *Kurio*...

The writers of the gospels indicate the John the Baptist is the fulfillment of Isaiah's command to *make ready the way of the Lord* (Luke 3:4). He is preparing the way for the coming of Jesus. One of the earliest Christian creeds is the statement that Jesus is Lord (Romans 10:9; 1 Corinthians 12:3; 2 Corinthians 4:5). This is obviously more than a mere honorific. It is a creedal statement of the deity of Christ.

THE WORD

In the beginning was the Word, and the Word was with God, and the Word was God. 2 He was in the beginning with God. 3 All things came into being by Him, and apart from Him nothing came into being that has come into being. (John 1:1-3).

John pens his book with one major theme in mind. He wants to show that Jesus is God. He presents Jesus as both God and also as the Son of God. What does this mean? What does it mean to be the Son of God? He introduces Jesus at the outset by describing Him as the pre-existing Word who created all things.

To the Jews, this term described the Messiah of Israel. The Jews did not necessarily think of the Messiah as being God in the flesh. Rather, they thought of Him as being a descendant of David and a king of Israel who would be filled with the Spirit.

By contrast, the Greeks had a completely different concept of the "son of God. Their mythology contained stories of the Greek gods joining with mortals and producing offspring such as Hercules and Perseus. These

329

were supermen—half god and half man.

While each of these concepts has an element of truth within them, they are by themselves wrong concepts. It is for this reason that John begins his gospel account with a different and distinct title for Jesus. He calls Jesus "the Word." In this way, he will redefine what it means to be the Son of God.

This One known as "the Word" is identified in two different ways. This does not mean that He is two separate persons, but merely that there are two separate aspects to His being.

The Word was God	The Word became Flesh
"In the beginning was the Word, and the Word was with God, and the Word was God." (John 1:1).	*"And the Word became flesh, and dwelt among us, and we beheld His glory, glory as of the only begotten from the Father, full of grace and truth." (John 1:14).*

It is evident from this second passage that "the Word" is a reference to Jesus of Nazareth. He is the One who was not originally flesh, yet in a moment of time became flesh. It is equally evident from the first passage that we are meant to regard the man Jesus as being God.

1.   The Designation of the Word.

John's reference to "the Word" brought with it all sorts of connotations. We can see and understand these as we become familiar with the religious and philosophical uses of this term in that day.

a.   The Greek concept of the Word: Plato had made reference to the Word (Greek: *Logos*) as that supreme principle of logic that allowed man to make sense of and to understand his world. As such, the Logos was seen by the Greeks as an impersonal force.

b.   The Hebrew concept of the Word: In Hebrew, a "word" (דבר) can describe both the verbal designation of an object as well as the moving energy of that object. As such, the word of God in the Old Testament is able to refer to more

330

than merely the teachings and proclamations of deity. It refers to the active power and force of God Himself.

> *By the word of the LORD the heavens were made,*
> *And by the breath of His mouth all their host.*
> *(Psalm 33:6).*

The word of the Lord indicated a personification of the manifested power of God. It is interesting to note that the Aramaic Targums (paraphrases of the Scriptures) often used the Aramaic word *Memra* ("word") in the place of God. For example, the Targums say that Moses led Israel to meet, not with God at Sinai, but with the *Memra* (Word) of God at Sinai.

    c.   New Testament usage: Both the Jewish as well as the Greek readers of John's gospel are introduced to a new concept. The Word is not merely an impersonal force. Neither is the Word a mere manifestation of one of God's attributes. The Word is a person.

    A word is the verbal expression of a thought. By the same token, Jesus is the visible and personal expression and manifestation of God. Yet he is not only a manifestation of God—the dialog presented by Jesus to His Father in the prayer of John 17 is a conversation between two persons. Jesus makes reference to the relationship He enjoyed with the Father from all eternity (John 17:24).

2.   Implications of the Logos.

    The use of this title points to the fact that God has revealed Himself to us in a way we can understand. It is because of that self-revelation that we can know truth about God. He is no longer some faceless unknown Being out in the cosmos. He is personal and He has revealed Himself to us in a way we can understand. We can know God. That is a bold statement, but one that is absolutely true. We can enter into a personal relationship with the Creator of the universe.

3.   The Word in the Beginning: *In the beginning was the Word, and the Word was with God, and the Word was God.* ₂ *He was in the beginning with God. (John 1:1-2).*

This passage echoes with a resounding reverberation from the Old Testament. The words, "In the beginning," take us back to the creation. But there is a difference. In the Old Testament, Genesis begins by placing the emphasis upon God's work of creation. Here the emphasis here is not upon God creating, but rather upon His being.

> | | |
> |---|---|
> | Genesis 1:1 | - In the beginning God created... |
> | John 1:1 | - In the beginning was... |

Here we read that in the beginning, something already WAS. When you go back in time as far as you can possible imagine, before anything else ever exists, God was. And yet, it is not God who is the primary subject of this passage, but One who is known as "the Word."

a.   The Pre-existent Word.

John 1:1 does not say that "in the beginning the Word came into being." Instead, it tells us that at the time of the beginning, the Word already was. The Greek text renders the verb for being as an imperfect active indicative. The imperfect tense is used to indicate continuing action in the past. It pictures action in progress. We could translate the passage to say: *In the beginning already was the Word.* The point is that when you go back to the very beginning of the creation of all things, the Word was already there. This same imperfect tense continues to be used four times in the first two verses of John.

> *In the beginning already was the Word, and the Word already was with God, and the Word already was God. He already was in the beginning with God.*

The Word did not have a beginning. The Word was already in existence at the beginning and everything else that exists came into being as a result of the Word.

b.   The Word with God.

When John says that *the word was with God,* this refers to more than merely a physical proximity. The phrasing describes a plane of equality and intimacy. We could translate it to say: *the word was face to face with God.* John uses a similar construction in 1 John 2:1 when he describes Jesus being our advocate with the Father.

This is the language of fellowship. That is significant. It means there was fellowship and communication taking place between the different members of the Godhead before the creation. This same truth is described elsewhere in the Scriptures.

> *And now, glorify Thou Me together with Thyself, Father, with the glory which I had with Thee before the world was. (John 17:5).*

> *Father, I desire that they also, whom Thou hast given Me, be with Me where I am, in order that they may behold My glory, which Thou hast given Me; for Thou didst love Me before the foundation of the world. (John 17:24).*

> *Blessed be the God and Father of our Lord Jesus Christ, who has blessed us with every spiritual blessing in the heavenly places in Christ, 4 just as He chose us in Him before the foundation of the world, that we should be holy and blameless before Him (Ephesians 1:3-4).*

There was existence before the creation and this existence was personal and not static. There was no boredom. There was active relationship. The Father was active with the Word and with the Holy Spirit. This is what we call the Trinity. It is seen in the next verse.

c.   The Word as God.

The statement, "And the Word was God," is emphatic. Not only was the Word pre-existent in past eternity with God, but He was God. When we recognize the force of the imperfect tense, we understand that the Word continually was God. There was not a time in history when He became God. He has always been God. In the beginning He was already God.

4.   The Incarnation of the Logos.

And the Word became flesh, and dwelt among us, and we beheld His glory, glory as of the only begotten from the Father, full of grace and truth. (John 1:14).

In verse 1, we identified the Word as being the one who was in the beginning with God and who, in the beginning, was God. Now we see the Word becoming flesh. The birth of Jesus stands at the very center of human history. It is the supreme meeting place of the temporal with the eternal. It is the place where God and man came together.

The word "became" is the aorist active indicative of *ginomai* (γινομαι), "to become." This is in contrast to the description of the Word as it existed in the beginning. In becoming flesh, the Word did something He had not previously done. There is a dramatic difference between the verbs of verse 1 and verse 14.

Verse 1	Verse 14
In the beginning was the Word...	The Word became flesh...
Imperfect tense indicates continuing action in the past.	Aorist tense indicates an action that took place in a point in time.
Language of continuing existence	Language of change as the Word became something that He previously was not

Takes us back to the time before the creation of mankind	Tells how men beheld His glory, full of grace and truth

The Word took on flesh and, in doing so, brought about a change that will have eternal repercussions. The One who became God and man stayed that way. The One who was touched by a band of Galilean disciples is today worshiped by angels.

Why did the Word take on flesh? It was so that he could dwell among us. The text reads literally, *"He TABERNACLED among us."* In the same way that people used to have to come to the tabernacle and later to the temple to meet God, it is now through Jesus that we must come to meet God.

In Old Testament times, God met His people at the tabernacle. When Moses completed the construction of the tabernacle, a great cloud moved into it so that the priests were forced for a time to evacuate. This was the manifested presence of God. Later, when Solomon built the temple, the presence of the Lord moved into the temple and, once again, this was seen by the presence of a great cloud.

When the temple was destroyed by Nebuchadnezzar in 586 B.C., it was considered to be a great tragedy to the Jews because there was no place else they could go to experience the presence of God. The temple was eventually rebuilt by Ezra and Zerubbabel, but we never read that the presence of God returned to the temple. Malachi, the last of the Old Testament prophets, promised that a time would come when the Lord would return to His temple.

> *"Behold, I am going to send My messenger, and he will clear the way before Me. And the Lord, whom you seek, will suddenly come to His temple; and the messenger of the covenant, in whom you delight, behold, He is coming," says the LORD of hosts. (Malachi 3:1).*

Four hundred years passed and still the Jews waited. When Jesus came, He was the manifested presence of God. He was the Word who tabernacled among men. The Spirit of the living God rested upon Him. But He was not hidden away in a temple where only a priest could approach Him. He was among the people. He was among those who could behold His glory, *glory as of the only begotten from the Father, full of grace and truth.*

One of my favorite stories in the Old Testament is where Moses goes to the Lord and says, "Lord, I want to see your glory." God says to him, "Moses, you can't do that, because to see me is to die. Here is what I will do. I will have you stand in a cleft of this rock and I will cover you with My hand and I will cause My goodness to pass by and then, after I have passed, I will remove My hand and you will see my afterglow."

The coming of Jesus is the answer to the prayer of Moses: "Show me your glory." The disciples who were on the Mount of Transfiguration saw the glory of Jesus and recognized it for what it was, the glory of the only begotten from the Father. There was a single instance where three of those disciples had a chance to see a glimpse of what Moses saw. For a brief moment in time, God took away the veil and they saw the glorified Christ.

God in Flesh Appearing

Understanding the Incarnation

The center point of history was when the One who was God became flesh and was born as a baby to live among us. We call this the incarnation. Philippians 2 contains perhaps one of the clearest presentations and descriptions of the incarnation of Jesus.

> *5 Have this attitude in yourselves which was also in Christ Jesus, 6 who, although He existed in the form of God, did not regard equality with God a thing to be grasped (Philippians 2:5-6).*

While John 1:1 tells us of the One who existed in the beginning and who was God, now we are given to understand that the mode of that existence was not something less than God. He existed in the form of God.

Jesus had an existence prior to His birth. We cannot say that about ourselves. Until we were conceived in the womb, we had no earlier existence. But Jesus did. He existed in the form of God. He is the One who was in the beginning with God because He was God (John 1:1).

Jesus had every right to continue in the form which He held from all eternity. He had been in the beginning with God and He was God, yet He determined not to continue to grasp and hold to the form of that equality.

> *...6 who, although He existed in the form of God, did not regard equality with God a thing to be grasped, 7 but emptied Himself, taking the form of a bond-servant, and being made in the likeness of men. (Philippians 2:6-7).*

Jesus Christ made an active choice not to remain equal with God. He did not regard His equality with God as a thing to be retained. This choice

337

involved the emptying of Himself. What does this mean? In what sense did Christ "empty" Himself? Several views have been presented.

1.   The Kenotic View.

This term comes from the Greek phrase in verse 7 that says Christ *emptied Himself*. The Greek word for "empty" is κενοω. This is the view that says Christ emptied Himself of His relative attributes (omniscience, omnipotence, omnipresence) while retaining His imminent attributes (love, holiness, truth).

This view has certain accompanying problems. The Scriptures teach that Christ knew all men (John 2:24-25), that He demonstrated His power over nature, demons, and death, and that He was able to see Nathanael from afar (John 1:46). These all reflect a continuation of those relative attributes of God.

Furthermore, if God divested Himself of that which makes Him God, then He ceased to be God when He became incarnate. Since Christ continues to be incarnate, He is no longer God and therefore no longer answers prayers.

2.   The Lutheran View.

The Lutheran Church teaches that the divine attributes of Christ communicated themselves to the human attributes. This is the basis for seeing the real physical presence of Jesus in the Eucharist.

| The Divine attributes of Jesus | ⇨ (Communication) | The Human attributes of Jesus |

The problem with this view is that it does not deal with the limitations that Jesus experienced as a man.

- He increased in wisdom and stature (Luke 2:52).
- There were things He did not know (Matthew 24:36).

God has no such limitations. He cannot be hungry or tired. He cannot grow in knowledge or wisdom. He cannot die upon a cross.

3.   The Reformed View.

The view of the Reformers is that the second member of the Trinity took His human shape from His mother, affected by a supernatural virgin birth. The human nature that was taken was sanctified in its very inception and thus kept from the pollution of sin (Hebrews 9:14).

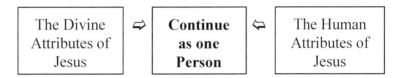

This view is reflected in the language of the Westminster Confession of Faith when it describes the person of Jesus:

> *The Son of God, the second person in the Trinity, being very and eternal God, of one substance and equal with the Father, did, when the fulness of time was come, take upon Him man's nature, with all the essential properties, and common infirmities thereof, yet without sin; being conceived by the power of the Holy Ghost, in the womb of the virgin Mary, of her substance. So that two whole, perfect, and distinct natures, the Godhead and the manhood, were inseparably joined together in one person, without conversion, composition, or confusion. (WCF 8:2).*

How does this help us to understand the "limiting" verses relating to the knowledge and the weakness that Jesus experienced? Buswell suggests that the God-man experienced two levels of consciousness in the way something can trigger your memory so that you can call to mind your third grade teacher whom you had forgotten. In the same way, Jesus was consciously man, but there was another level in which He was, at the same time, fully God.

Thus, in the same passage in which Jesus admits that He does not know the day or the hour of His return (Matthew 24:36), He goes on to place Himself on a level above the angels.

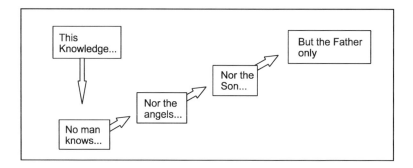

Notice the progression. It goes from man to angels to the Son and then to the Father. The writer to the Hebrews spends the entire first chapter of his epistle pointing out all the ways in which Jesus is better than the angels.

REASONS FOR THE INCARNATION

Why would He do it? Why would One who had eternally existed in the image of God lower Himself to take on human flesh and blood? The Scriptures give us two reasons:

1.   To Communicate God to man: *No man has seen God at any time; the only begotten God, who is in the bosom of the Father, He has explained Him (John 1:18).*

2.   To Taste Death for Every Man: *But we do see Him who has been made for a little while lower than the angels, namely, Jesus, because of the suffering of death crowned with glory and honor, that by the grace of God He might taste death for everyone (Hebrews 2:9).*

FALSE VIEWS OF THE INCARNATION

In coming to terms with the person of Christ, the church wrestled against Greek dualism that said, "Spirit is good and flesh is bad." This led to a number of ideas regarding the incarnation. The church was forced to examine its beliefs regarding the person of Jesus in the setting of these divergent teachings.

Party	Date	Reference	Human Nature	Divine Nature
Docetic	60	1 John 4:1-3	Deny	Affirm
Ebionite	120	Irenaeus	Affirm	Deny
Arian	325	Condemned at Nicea	Affirm	Reduce
Apollinarian	381	Condemned at Constantinople	Reduce	Affirm
Nestorian	431	Condemned by Ephesus	Held that Christ was two persons	
Eutychian	451	Condemned by Chalcedon and Constantinople	Christ had one mixed nature, neither fully human or fully divine	
Orthodox	33	Affirmed throughout	Christ is one person, at the same time fully human and fully divine	

1.   The Docetic Heresy.

One of the sects of Gnosticism was Docetism. The term comes from the Greek word δοκεω (*dokeo*), "to seem." It deals with the issue of appearance versus reality. It stated that Christ's appearance on earth was not real. It maintained that His bodily appearance was only a hallucination. John's first epistle seems to reflect a rebuke against an early form of this teaching.

> *2 By this you know the Spirit of God: every spirit that confesses that Jesus Christ has come in the flesh is from God; 3 and every spirit that does not confess Jesus is not from God; and this is the spirit of the antichrist, of which you have heard that it is coming, and now it is already in the world. (1 John 4:2-3).*

Why is it important to believe that Jesus came in the flesh? There are several reasons.

• He came in the flesh to die for sins. 1 Peter 3:18 says that He was put to death in the flesh. If Jesus did not come in the flesh, then He could not take upon His own body the penalty for our sins. He could not die for us if He were not flesh, because God cannot die.

- He came in the flesh to be a mediator: *For there is one God, and one mediator also between God and men, the man Christ Jesus (1 Timothy 2:5).* If Jesus were not fully man in human flesh, then He is not qualified to be a mediator between God and man.

- He came in the flesh to identify with man: *For we do not have a high priest who cannot sympathize with our weaknesses, but One who has been tempted in all things as we are, yet without sin (Hebrews 4:15).* Because Jesus came in the flesh, we can know that He has gone through the same problems and struggles that we experience. He knows and understands our situation.

2. Ebionism.

The Greek term Εβιοναιοι (*Ebionaioi*) means "poor men." The Ebionites were the theological opposites of the Docetics. They held that Jesus was a

> The Ebionites had a large contingent of Jewish Christians.

man who was born like any other man, but who was adopted into God's family and given the title "Son of God."

The Ebionites also taught that Jewish Christians should continue to keep the Old Testament law—some included the Gentiles in this mandate as well. As such, they were something of a renewal of the Judaizers whom Paul confronted in his Epistle to the Galatians. Irenaeus, in his book *Against Heresies*, noted that the Ebionites recognized only the Gospel of Matthew out of all the New Testament writings. There is today a resurgence of Ebionism in much of the modern Messianic Movement. There is a tendency among some of those in this movement to move away from the deity of Christ and to seek to place people back under the law.

3. Arius.

One of the early controversies raged over the teachings of

Arius who concluded that God could not have become flesh because a good God cannot become bad flesh. He therefore concluded that the Son had been created by the Father.

He said that if Christ were considered to be God, then there would be more than one God and this would be polytheism. In defense of his position, Arius was able to cite Tertullian as authenticating his teaching—Tertullian did teach that Christ became God while Arius never admitted to the divinity of Jesus prior to the incarnation.

Alexander and Athanasius, two of the church fathers, maintained that Christ was one in substance with the Father. The resulting creed that was adopted at the Council of Nicea in A.D. 325 described Christ as "God of very God" (Θεος ἐκ Θεου) and as of the same nature (ὁμοιουσιας - *homoiusias*, from two Greek words meaning "same" and "nature or substance").[4] The creed rejected the teachings of Arius that claimed Jesus was a created being and thus, those teachings were proclaimed to be heretical. The Christology of today's Jehovah's Witnesses reflects the same heresy.

4.   Apollinaris (381 A.D.).

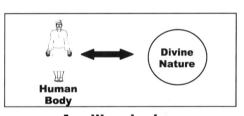

Apollinarianism

Apollinaris was the bishop of Laodicea in Syria (different from the church by the same name mentioned in the book of Revelation). In an effort to uphold the deity of Christ, Apollinaris taught that within the man Jesus dwelled the divine Logos. He believed that all men consisted of body, soul, and spirit. However, in defining the person of Christ, Appolinaris stated that the divine Logos took the part of the human spirit within the person of Jesus. Thus, his view was that, while Jesus was fully God, He was not fully man.

A council was convened at Constantinople in A.D. 381 to deal with this issue. This council affirmed the humanity of Christ, seeing Him as both fully man and fully God.

---

[4] ὁμοιας is the word for "same" while οὐσίας carries the ides of "substance" or "estate."

5.   Nestorius (431 A.D.).

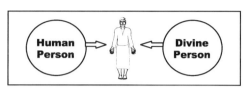

Nestorian

Nestorius was the bishop of Constantinople. While admitting to both the humanity and the deity of Christ, he felt that it was inappropriate to refer to Mary as the *Theotokos* ("God-bearer"). Instead, he suggested that she be called *Christotokos* ("Christ-bearer"). Rather than this being an issue over the status of Mary, the question was really over the identity of Jesus. Nestorius held that the second member of the Godhead was really two persons—one the divine Logos and the other the human Christ.

Nestorius was opposed by Cyril, the bishop of Alexandria. Cyril argued that, if you only refer to Mary as the Christ-bearer while excluding any reference to her as the God-bearer, then you are saying that the One whom she bore was not really God, but that He was only a part of God.

Thus, Cyril contended for the unity of the person of Christ. The council of Ephesus ultimately determined in A.D. 431 that there had been in Christ a union of two natures.

6.   Eutyches.

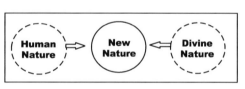

**Eutyches
Monophysitism**

Eutyches was the head of the monastery in Constantinople. Reacting to the ideas of Nestorius, Eutyches stated that Christ was originally made up of two natures, but that these two natures came together in the incarnation to become a single nature. This view was known as monophysitism (from the Greek *monos* (μονος), "one" and *physis* (φυσις), "nature."

A council was held at Chalcedon in A.D. 451 to decide the issue. It faced two extremist views.

•   The Alexandrian School: They tended to be Monophystic, holding to the unity of Christ to the exclusion of His two natures. In answer to this position, the Creed of Chalcedon described the one person of the Son who took into union with His pre-existing divine nature a human nature.

- The Antioch School: They tended to make too much of a distinction between the human and divine natures of Christ. In response to this position, the Creed of Chalcedon described Jesus as "one and the same son, one and the same Christ, Son, Lord, Only-begotten, and one and the same Son and Only-begotten God, Word, the Lord Jesus Christ, who is one person and one subsistence, not parted or divided into two persons, whose natures are without division in the church."

In this way, the creed drew a line of demarcation between a "person" as a self-conscious entity versus a "nature" as a series of attributes. This description of Christ as "one person with two natures" is still used today to explain the incarnation.

The Atonement

What Christ Accomplished

The Bible portrays the cross event as the center point of history. Everything in the Old Testament looks forward to this event and everything in the New Testament looks back to this event. It can be said that nothing in human history is so significant.

THE NATURE OF THE ATONEMENT

When we use the word "atonement" in the theological sense, we are referring to the work that Christ accomplished on the cross.

1.   A Sacrificial Atonement.

From earliest times, the Jew had built an altar for sacrifice. To the altar would be brought a lamb, white and without blemish. The lamb would be laid across the altar and then, as it was held down, the Jewish man would quickly and deftly cut its throat. As the blood poured out upon the altar, the man would place his hand upon the head of the dying lamb, signifying that this lamb was being identified with his sins and that it was dying in his place.

Later, it was the Tabernacle and then the Temple that became the center for sacrifices. It was here that the priests began to minister these sacrifices for the people of Israel. The idea of a lamb being slain was associated with the forgiveness of sins.

When Jesus came on the scene, John the Baptist announced Him as the "Lamb of God who takes away the sin of the world" (John 1:29). The mention of a lamb who was to take away sin was a very

346

familiar concept to the Jew. He had a vivid picture in his mind what this represented. Yet there was something that was unique in the lamb described by John. The uniqueness was in the scope of accomplishment. The death of this lamb would take away the sins of the world.

None of the other animal sacrifices had been able to accomplish this. A lamb could be slain for the sins of a man. A lamb might occasionally be slain for the sins of a family. There were even times when a lamb was sacrifices for the sins of the entire nation. But never had there been a sacrifice for the sins of the world.

> *He was oppressed and He was afflicted,*
> *Yet He did not open His mouth;*
> *Like a lamb that is led to slaughter,*
> *And like a sheep that is silent before its shearers,*
> *So He did not open His mouth. (Isaiah 53:7).*

> *...For Christ our Passover also has been sacrificed (1 Corinthians 5:7b).*

> *...Christ also loved you, and gave Himself up for us, an offering and a sacrifice to God as a fragrant aroma. (Ephesians 5:2b).*

Jesus fulfilled the principle of the sacrifice when He died upon the cross. It was a once and for all sacrifice that never needs to be repeated. This stands in contrast to the Roman Catholic doctrine of the "perpetual sacrifice of Christ." The Council of Trent stated that, since the priesthood of Christ is perpetual, so also the sacrificial offering must also be perpetual. It went on to say that the mass is the true and proper sacrifice—that the mass is the actual sin removing sacrifice of Christ. By contrast, the Bible teaches that our sins are removed by His once for all sacrifice.

> *10 By this will we have been sanctified through the offering of the body of Jesus Christ once for all. 11 And every priest stands daily ministering and offering time after time the same sacrifices, which can never take away sins; 12 but He, having offered one sacrifice for sins for all time, sat down at the right hand of God (Hebrews 10:10-12).*

The writer to the Hebrews could not be more explicit. He notes both that our salvation took place through the once for all offering of Jesus and that this one sacrifice for sins was for all time. The fact that Jesus subsequently sat down at the right hand of God is a sign that the work has been accomplished and never need be repeated.

2.   A Vicarious Atonement.

The principle of vicariousness includes the idea of a legal representative. Jesus served as our representative when He went to the cross in the same way that Adam acted as our representative when he sinned.

> *18 So then as through one transgression there resulted condemnation to all men, even so through one act of righteousness there resulted justification of life to all men. 19 For as through the one man's disobedience the many were made sinners, even so through the obedience of the One the many will be made righteous. (Romans 5:18-19).*

I was not in the Garden of Eden when Adam sinned, yet his sin brought about not only his own fall, but the fall of the entire human race. He acted the part of our legal representative. In the same way, the death of Christ on the cross was as a representative for me. Galatians 2:20 says that I have been crucified with Christ. I had a legal representative on the cross who died in my place.

3.   A Substitutionary Atonement.

The concept of a substitute was an inherent part of a sacrifice. Isaiah spoke of One who would come to take sins upon Himself. Isaiah used the image of a sacrifice to describe this substitution.

> *All of us like sheep have gone astray,*
> *Each of us has turned to his own way;*
> *But the LORD has caused the iniquity of us all*
> *To fall on Him. (Isaiah 53:6).*

Jesus died in our place and instead of us. He was our substitute. He took our place on the cross, dying the death we deserved. Then He calls us to take His place as sons and children of God and co-heirs with Christ.

> *Christ redeemed us from the curse of the Law, having become a curse for us-- for it is written, "Cursed is everyone who hangs on a tree" (Galatians 3:13).*

When we read the Gospel accounts, we learn that the Romans had originally set aside three crosses. There were three thieves who were destined to hand upon those crosses. They had been apprehended, judged, and found to be guilty. They were placed under the sentence of death. But one of them never went to the cross. His name was Barabbas. Instead, another man went to the cross in his place.

Jesus died upon the cross of Barabbas and Barabbas went free. It wasn't that Barabbas did not deserve to be on the cross. It wasn't that he was any better than the other two thieves. He was probably worse. What made the difference? A substitute was provided to die in his place.

The cross to which Jesus was nailed had been set aside for the execution of Barabbas. Barabbas deserved to die. He was a thief and a robber. He was guilty before the law. But Jesus died on his cross instead of Barabbas.

There is a sense in which Jesus died on a cross that had my name on it. He died instead of me. He died in my place and the judgment of God that would have been directed against me was instead directed toward Him.

> *13 And when you were dead in your transgressions and the uncircumcision of your flesh, He made you alive together with Him, having forgiven us all our transgressions, 14 having canceled out the certificate of debt consisting of decrees against us and which was hostile to us; and He has taken it out of the way, having nailed it to the cross. (Colossians 2:13-14).*

It was the custom of that day to post the crimes for which a criminal was being executed on the cross where he hung. This would serve as a warning to other would-be criminals. Do you remember the inscription that was on the cross of Jesus? It read, "Jesus of

Nazareth, King of the Jews." The Jewish leaders didn't like that and they petitioned Pilate to have it changed, but he would not. And so, it remained.

This passage tells us that there was another inscription posted on the cross that day. It was an inscription unseen by human eyes. It was the inscription *consisting of decrees against us and which was hostile to us.* It was the inscription of our sins. Don't miss this! Your sins were nailed to His cross. This indicates that He died for you.

4.   A Penal Atonement.

The penal nature of the atonement is seen in the fact that the death of Jesus was a punishment for sin. It was the payment of a penalty.

> *Christ redeemed us from the curse of the Law, having become a curse for us-- for it is written, "Cursed is everyone who hangs on a tree" (Galatians 3:13).*

Sin brought about a curse on the sinner. Jesus took that curse upon Himself. As He hung upon the cross, He cried out the word, "My God! My God! Why have You forsaken Me?" There was a reason for the cry. It indicated that the Father was turning His back on the Son and bringing judgment against Him.

It is suggested here that there was a moment in history when the First Person of the Trinity was, in a sense, sonless and when the Second Person of the Trinity was Fatherless—when the innocent Son of God was treated as though He were a guilty sinner. He took upon Himself our penalty.

5.   A Propitiatory Atonement.

Propitiation refers to that which satisfies anger; that which appeases. The concept of propitiation is illustrated in the work of the high priest in the temple. This is brought out by the writer of the epistle to the Hebrews when he likens the work of the high priest to that which was accomplished by Jesus.

> *Therefore, He had to be made like His brethren in all things, that He might become a*

*merciful and faithful high priest in things pertaining
to God, to make **propitiation** for the sins of the
people. (Hebrews 2:17).*

When you speak of Jesus being a high priest, that takes you
back to the Temple and to the greatest function of the high priest.
The day of the high priest's ministry took place once a year on Yom
Kippur — the Day of Atonement.

Once a year, on the Day
of Atonement, the high priest of
Israel would enter into the
Holiest of Holies to come before
the presence of God. He would
bring with him a cup of blood
from an animal freshly slain. He
would sprinkle that blood upon
the Mercy Seat. And that blood

The Mercy Seat

would serve as the satisfactory sacrifice for the sins of the nation. A
common prayer among the Jews was that "God be to me a Mercy
Seat." The setting for this ministry is described in Hebrews 9.

> *Now even the first covenant had regulations of
> divine worship and the earthly sanctuary. 2 For there
> was a tabernacle prepared, the outer one, in which
> were the lampstand and the table and the sacred
> bread; this is called the holy place.*
>
> *Behind the second veil there was a tabernacle
> which is called the Holy of Holies, 4 having a golden
> altar of incense and the ark of the covenant covered
> on all sides with gold, in which was a golden jar
> holding the manna, and Aaron's rod which budded,
> and the tables of the covenant; 5 and above it were
> the cherubim of glory overshadowing the mercy seat;
> but of these things we cannot now speak in detail.
> (Hebrews 9:1-5).*

Notice the phrase "mercy seat" in verse 5. That is the Greek
word ἱλαστήριος (*hilasterios*). Neither is this an unusual
translation, for every time you see a reference to the Mercy Seat in
the Old Testament, it is translated in the Septuagint in this same
manner. At the same time, this is also the Greek word that translates

our English term "propitiation" when it is used in Hebrews 2:17. It describes a place of satisfaction.

What was the Mercy Seat? It was the top of the Ark of the Covenant. This was the seat of God. It served as the throne of God within the Temple. It was called a "seat" in that this was considered to be the throne of God. On either side of this "seat" there were statues of angels. Their wings overshadowed the seat and their faces gazed down toward the seat.

The Ark itself was nothing more than a wooden box overlaid with gold. It originally held the broken pieces of the Ten Commandments, a pot of manna, and Aaron's rod. Each of these was symbolic.

- The Pieces: The fact that we have sinned and broken God's law.
- The Manna: God's gracious and nourishing provision.
- Aaron's Rod: God's appointment of a Mediator.

Once a year, on Yom Kippur (the Day of Atonement), the High Priest would enter past the two veils into the Holy of Holies. He would come to the mercy seat. He would sprinkle the blood of goats and calves onto the mercy seat. This would be a propitiation — a satisfactory payment for the sins of the nation — until next year when it all had to be done over again. This is a picture of what Jesus did for us. He is both sacrifice and high priest.

Over the years there had been many high priests. Generation after generation had served this high office. Each year, for over a thousand years, a high priest had entered the Temple to offer sacrifices. But we have something unique. We have something that no Jew ever had. We have the High Priest who passed into heaven itself.

> *But when Christ appeared as a high priest of the good things to come, He entered in through the greater and more perfect tabernacle, not made with hands, that is to say, not of this creation; 12 and not through the blood of goats and calves, but through His own blood, He entered the holy place once for all, having obtained eternal redemption. (Hebrews 9:11-12).*

Jesus did not offer the blood of animals in a temple. He gave

His own blood on the cross. He served as both High Priest and as sacrifice. And then He entered, not a temple, but heaven itself. And He is there today as our High Priest.

- Propitiation presupposes the wrath of God (Romans 1:18; Ephesians 2:3). In the ancient world, when one thought that he had committed some offense against one of the deities, he would go and offer a sacrifice of appeasement. By doing so, he would try to assuage the anger and the wrath of that deity. Thus, propitiation refers to satisfying the wrath of one who has been offended.

  Your sin has offended God. It makes you deserving of the anger and the wrath of God. That is the bad news. The good news is that Jesus was the satisfaction. He satisfied the righteous judgment of God.

  On the wall of the Supreme Court Building in Washington D.C. is the motto: "When the guilty is acquitted, the judge is condemned." If God is to be a just God, then He cannot simply forgive sin. It must be judged. Our sin was judged at the cross.

Means	Death of Christ
Place	The Cross
Result	The Remission of Sins

  Some people have a problem recognizing the truth of God's wrath. That is because they have an inadequate view of both the absolute righteousness of God and the awfulness of sin.

- The price of propitiation was the blood of Christ, although it is appropriated through faith. Romans 3:25 speaks of how God has displayed Jesus Christ *publicly as a propitiation in His blood through faith.* The blood of Christ is the sign of the death of Christ. When we speak of the One who shed His blood, we are speaking of a life that was given.

- Even though the result of propitiation was the appeasement of God's wrath, the initiation of that propitiation was based upon God's love. *In this is love, not that we loved God, but that He loved us and sent His Son to be the propitiation for our sins*

(1 John 4:10). It is not that the Son forced the Father to love us; He already loved us. Neither is it that the Father forced the Son to die for us; He gave Himself for us.

- The propitiation provided by Jesus was sufficient for the whole world. Jesus Christ *is the propitiation for our sins; and not for ours only, but also for those of the whole world* (1 John 2:2). In the Old Testament, the sheep died for the shepherd. In the New Testament, the Shepherd died for the sheep.

Sometimes it is objected that this view of propitiation makes it appear that the Father acts with strict and unrelenting judgment while the Son acts with mercy and love. We must therefore point out that, while propitiation presupposes the wrath of God, it also was brought about through the love of God. This is because love and wrath are not mutually exclusive. John Murray points out that "this love of the Father was at no point more intensely in exercise than when the Son was actively drinking the cup of unrelieved damnation, than when he was enduring as substitute the full toll of the Father's wrath. All of this is implicit in the saying of Romans 8:32, that the Father did not spare his own Son" (1984b:147).

6.   An Expiatory Atonement.

The idea of expiation is closely linked to the concept of propitiation. These can be understood in contrast to one another.

Propitiation	Expiation
To appease or satisfy wrath.	To erase or remove guilt.
Directed toward the anger of God.	Directed toward the quilt of man.
The sacrifice in the Temple appeased the just demands of a righteous God...	...by covering the guilt of the sins committed.

When the High Priest sprinkled the blood upon the Seat of Satisfaction, the blood served as a covering to cover the guilt of the nation. The word "atonement" in the Old Testament is translated from the Hebrew word Kippur—it describes a "covering." The death of Christ covered our sins and removed them as far from us *as the east is from the west* (Psalm 103:12).

7.   A Redemptive Atonement.

Redemption presupposes slavery. The institution of slavery was common throughout the ancient world. Abraham had come out of Ur of the Chaldees owning a small army of slaves. The Israelites had become a nation of slaves in Egypt. Slavery was still enforced during the days of Christ.

Under most legal codes of those days, a slave was merely a piece of property with little or no personal rights. If you killed another man's slave, you might suffer the same punishment as if your had killed his cow.

There were a number of ways in which a man might become a slave. He might be born into slavery. The son of a slave was himself considered to be a slave. Or he might be captured by an invading army and become a prized captive, led away in chains to a foreign country to be sold as a slave. Or he might fall into debt so that he was forced to declare bankruptcy. This involved selling yourself into slavery to pay the debts that were owed.

Picture the situation. An Israelite living in the land of Canaan is hit with economic disaster. Perhaps a famine has come over the land and wiped out his crops. Rather than resort to begging, he can sell himself into slavery, using the proceeds to pay off his debts or care for his starving family. And so, he becomes a slave. How can he regain his freedom? It can only be if the redemption price is paid.

> *Now if the means of a stranger or of a sojourner with you becomes sufficient, and a countryman of your becomes so poor with regard to him as to sell himself to a stranger who is sojourning with you, or to the descendants of a stranger's family, 48 then he shall have redemption right after he has been sold. One of his brothers may redeem him, 49 or his uncle, or his uncle's son, may redeem him, or one of his blood relatives from his family may redeem him or if he prospers, he may redeem himself. (Leviticus 25:47-49).*

If we look very closely, we can find four qualifications which were necessary for a Kinsman Redeemer to accomplish this redemption. It was only when a man possessed these four qualities that he was permitted to perform this task.

- He must be a Kinsman. The passage is very specific that this redeemer must be related to the one whom he is going to buy back out of slavery. There must be some family connection.
- He must be Free Himself. A slave was unable to purchase another slave. The most that a slave might be able to do would be to free himself from slavery. Therefore, a Kinsman Redeemer must himself be free of the debt and of the bondage which had fallen on the one who was to be redeemed.
- He must be Able to Pay the Ransom Price. If he did not have the necessary sum of money which was required to pay the purchase price, then he would not be able to redeem his relative. Good intentions were not enough. He must have the wherewithal to accomplish those intentions.
- He must be Willing to Pay the Price. It was not enough to have a kinsman who was able to accomplish the work of redemption. He must also be willing to make the sacrifice of paying the price. I imagine that there were a number of slaves with rich uncles who just didn't want to spend the money to release their unfortunate relative from slavery.

Each of these qualifications was fulfilled in the person of Jesus. God sent Him into the world's slave market to purchase men from their bondage to sin.

a.   He was a Kinsman.

This is why it was necessary for God to become flesh - to be born and to grow up and to walk this earth as a man. It was because only a man could die for other men to buy them back from the bondage of sin and death.

> *Since then the children share in flesh and blood, He Himself likewise also partook of the same, that through death He might render powerless him who had the power of death, that is, the devil; 15 and might deliver those who through fear of death were subject to slavery all their lives. (Hebrews 2:14-15).*

356

God could not die, for He is eternal life and the source of all life. It was only by being born as a man and taking on human flesh and becoming a man that He could experience death for us.

b.   He was Free Himself.

Jesus was the only man since Adam who has ever been free from sin. From the first sin in the Garden of Eden to this day, all men are under this bondage. Another man could not die for my sins since he would have to pay the penalty for his own sins. Only someone who is free from sin could be a substitute for the sins of another.

> *For we do not have a high priest who cannot sympathize with our weaknesses, but one who has been tempted in all things as we are, yet without sin. (Hebrews 4:15).*

Jesus lived His entire life on earth without committing a single sin. This qualifies Him as the only free man.

c.   He was Able to Pay the Ransom Price.

Even if there had been a man who had been without sin, his death would not have had the infinite merit to pay for the sins of the whole world. At best, the sacrifice of a single finite man could atone for the sins on only a single man. But the death of Jesus was not the death of a mere man. It was also the death of an infinite being. It was the death of God in the flesh. God experienced death. He died in our place. Only the death of such a One could have been sufficient to save the world.

d.   He was Willing to Pay the Ransom Price.

> *Have this attitude in yourselves which was also in Christ Jesus, 6 who, although He existed in the form of God, did not regard equality with God a thing to be grasped, 7 but emptied Himself, taking the form of a bond-servant, and being made in the likeness of*

men.

> *And being found in appearance as a man, He humbled Himself by becoming obedient to the point of death, even death on a cross. (Philippians 2:5-8).*

Jesus learned obedience by coming to do the will of the Father. No man took His life from Him — He willingly gave up His life for us.

The story is told of a little boy who built a toy wooden sailboat, sanding it and then painting it with great care. He loved his little boat and was heartbroken when it was stolen. One day, as he was walking down the street, he happened to see the boat in a craft shot. He went in and bought the boat. Holding it in his hands, he said, "Now you are twice mine." God created us and then He purchased us for the highest possible price. We are twice His.

8.   A Triumphant Atonement.

The world looks at the cross and sees a scene of defeat. They think a good teacher did the best he could and it got him crucified. But the truth is that the cross was a victory. It was a triumph over sin.

On the night of His betrayal and arrest, Jesus said: *Now judgment is upon this world; now the ruler of this world shall be cast out (John 12:31).* The rest of the New Testament confirms the triumphant victory of the cross.

> *...The Son of God appeared for this purpose, that He might destroy the works of the devil. (1 John 3:8b).*

> *But thanks be to God, who always leads us in His triumph in Christ, and manifests through us the sweet aroma of the knowledge of Him in every place. (2 Corinthians 2:14).*

> *When He had disarmed the rulers and authorities, He made a public display of them, having triumphed over them through Him. (Colossians 2:15).*

In the Roman world, when a general had won a great victory,

he was awarded the honor of a Triumph. This was a glorious parade in which he rode in on a horse, leading a host of captives in chains down the streets of the city. The Arch of Titus still stands in Rome today as a testimony of his conquest of Jerusalem in A.D. 70 and of the triumph that was enjoyed by him. This same language is used to describe the victory Jesus won in His death, burial, and resurrection.

> *7 But to each one of us grace was given according to the measure of Christ's gift. 8 Therefore it says, "When He ascended on high, He led captive a host of captives, And He gave gifts to men." (Ephesians 4:7-8).*

This passage has mistakenly been used by some to describe the Lord moving taking believers to heaven. But the language does not describe believers. The phrase "lead captivity captive" was a byword among the Jews that described the conquest of an enemy (Judges 5:12; Psalm 68:18). This is a picture of Jesus leading captives in victory. This joining of the victory of Christ with His giving gifts to men has an Old Testament counterpart.

> *Therefore, I will allot Him a portion with the great,*
> *And He will divide the booty with the strong;*
> *Because He poured out Himself to death,*
> *And was numbered with the transgressors;*
> *Yet He Himself bore the sin of many,*
> *And interceded for the transgressors. (Isaiah 53:12).*

The conquering king would receive the booty from the battle and then would distribute it to his most valiant warriors. The problem is that we have not been very valiant. But the Bible teaches we overcome through our faith. When we believe, we get to participate in the booty of Christ's victory. That booty consists of all the spiritual blessings that we have in Christ Jesus (Ephesians 1:3).

Aspect	Presupposes
Sacrificial Nature	Inadequacy of animal sacrifices
Vicarious Nature	Adam's sin
Substitution Aspect	Man's inability to save himself

Penal Nature	A divine judgment
Propitiation	God's wrath against sin
Expiation	Man's guilt
Redemptive Quality	Man's slavery to sin
Triumphant Nature	The kingdom of evil

QUALITIES OF THE ATONEMENT

1.   The Atoning Work of Christ was Historically Objective.

The atonement is more than mere theory. It really happened in a real place and in real time. If you could have gone back to Jerusalem on the day Jesus died, you could have gotten a splinter in your finger from a real wooden cross. Furthermore, its accomplishment regarding sin and salvation is no less real.

This is in opposition to the Neo-orthodox position that says it does not matter if there is a historical foundation to Christianity as long as it is "real to you." Those sorts of word games fall far short of the Biblical concept of truth.

2.   The Atoning Work of Christ was Final.

The atonement was a "once and for all" event. This was seen in the final cry of Jesus on the cross. John 19:30 tell us that *He said, "It is finished!" And He bowed His head, and gave up His spirit.* What was finished? The work on the cross. The work He came to do. Our salvation.

This is in contrast to the Roman Catholic stance that has a repetition of the Lord's death in the offering of the Eucharist as well as the addition to Christ's work through the faithfulness of the saints and the suffering of purgatory. The truth is that Christ completed His work on the cross and no one need ever add anything to that work.

3.   The Atoning Work of Christ was Unique.

There has not been another Savior. There may be many roads that lead to Rome, but there is only one that leads to God.

> *And there is salvation in no one else; for there is no other name under heaven that has been given among men, by which we must be saved. (Acts 4:12).*

Jesus said that He is the only way of salvation (John 14:6). He is exclusive. Only He is able to atone for sins. That sounds narrow-minded to our Postmodern way of thinking. But truth is always narrow-minded. Truth does not involve a popularity contest. It keeps right on being true even if nobody believes in it.

THE EXTENT OF THE ATONEMENT

There are two commonly held views with regard to salvation. There is the Natural View that says man brings about his own salvation and there is the Supernatural View that says God intercedes on man's behalf to bring about his salvation. John Murray offers the following series of questions (1984a).

How is Man Saved?			
Natural View	**Supernatural View**		
Man saves himself by self effort	Go accomplishes the work of salvation through the death of His Son, Jesus, upon the cross		
	How does God save Man?		
	Sacerdotal View	**Evangelical View**	
	Man is saved through the partaking of the sacraments as the church dispenses salvation	Man is saved through the preaching of the Gospel. The Holy Spirit brings salvation to those who believe.	
		For Whom Did Christ Die?	
		For all men equally.	For the elect.

How is a man saved? The Roman Catholic Church says this salvation is dispensed through the sacraments—the Eucharist, baptism, penance, and confession. By contrast, the Scriptures tell us that the gospel is the power of God unto salvation (Romans 1:16-17). The last question in this chart asks the question of the intended recipients of the atonement. For whom did Christ die? There are two possibilities.

1.　He died for all men equally. If the death of Jesus accomplished the same thing for all men equally, then we are left with two further possibilities:

- All men are saved. There are some who have assumed the Scriptures to be speaking only allegorically when speaking of the last judgment or that hell is only temporary and that all men will ultimately be saved.

- The atonement only made it possible for some men to save themselves; it did not actually save anyone.

2.　He died for the elect. This is not to say that the death of Christ was not sufficient to save all men or even that the offer of salvation is not given to all men. What it does mean is that the atonement was effective in actually accomplishing the salvation of some.

EVIDENCES FOR A PARTICULAR ATONEMENT

It has been popular to speak of a "limited atonement" versus an "unlimited atonement." But this is misleading. The atonement is not limited in its power to save men. It is more appropriate to refer to a "particular atonement" or an atonement that was designed to accomplish the salvation of a particular group of people.

When we speak of a "limited" or "particular" atonement, we do not mean by this that the atonement was not sufficient to save all men, as though Christ would have had to do more upon the cross in order to save more people.

The death of Jesus Christ upon the cross is sufficient to save all men everywhere. And yet, it does not accomplish this. Why? Is it because of some shortcoming in what Christ did upon the cross? There are two possibilities:

First, we could say that the death of Christ in itself does not guarantee the salvation of anyone, it merely makes salvation a possibility for all men (anyone who believes in Christ of his own volition is then saved). The result of such a view can be summed up like this...

> Cross + Man's decision = Salvation

The alternative view would be to say that the death of Christ guaranteed the salvation of those whom God, in accordance with His own plan and purpose, had determined to save. It is on the basis of the cross that God actively draws some to Himself, making them spiritually alive so that they trust in Him as Lord and Savior. This view can be pictured like this...

> Cross + God's inward call (which results in repentance and faith) = Salvation

1.   The Emphasis of Scripture.

A great many logical arguments have been presented for both the "limited" as well as for the "unlimited" views. Many of these are extremely convincing. However, the question is not which might be the most logical, but rather, what does the Bible teach on this issue? The Scriptures go out of their way to particularize who it is for whom Christ died.

- He died for His people (Matthew 1:21).
- He died for His friends (John 15:13).
- He died for His sheep (John 10:11).
- He died for His body - the church (Ephesians 5:23-26).
- He died for the elect (Romans 8:32-34).
- He died for Us (Titus 2:14).

How does this particularization take place? Jesus used the image of a shepherd and His sheep to deal with this question.

I am the good shepherd; the good shepherd lays down His life for the sheep. (John 10:11).

Many people today seem to think that the reason people are or are not sheep is based upon whether they will believe or not believe. They would say, "You are my sheep because you believe," or, "You are not my sheep because you do not believe." But Jesus said it differently. He said...

"But you do not believe, because you are not of My sheep." (John 10:26).

Jesus made the basis of whether or not they believe dependent upon whether or not they had been chosen by God to be His sheep. This is just the opposite of the Arminian teaching.

Arminian	Jesus
"You are not my sheep because you have not believed."	"You do not believe because you are not my sheep."

Another example of this type of language is seen in Ephesians 5:25 where Paul tells husbands to love their wives "just as Christ also loved the church and gave Himself for her." The command loses much of its impact if Christ loved everyone with an equal love and gave Himself equally for all. Is a husband to love all women with an equal love? Not at all! He is to show a special love for his own wife.

2.   Only a Limited Number Actually Hear the Gospel.

Although the Lord commanded His church to preach the gospel to all the nations, it is also true that throughout the past He has *"permitted all the nations to go their own ways"* (Acts 14:16). Indeed, Jesus praised His Father for having hidden the mysteries of the Gospel from certain men.

> *At that time Jesus answered and said, "I praise Thee, O Father, Lord of heaven and earth, that Thou didst hide these things from the wise and intelligent and didst reveal them to babes. 27 Yes, Father, for thus it was well-pleasing in Thy sight." (Matthew 11:26-27).*

Jesus had just denounced Chorazin, Bethsaida and Capernaum for their unbelief. Now He turns to the Father and thanks Him that things are still going according to plan.

Sometimes we get the idea that when people hear the gospel and do not accept it, God's plan has somehow failed. This is not the case. God has hidden His kingdom truths from certain people and He has revealed them to others.

3.   The Intercessory Work of Christ was restricted to the Elect.

On the night before His crucifixion, Jesus prayed to the Father. In that prayer, Jesus is seen interceding on behalf of the elect.

> *"I ask on their behalf; I do NOT ask on behalf of the world, but of those whom Thou hast given Me; for they are Thine." (John 17:9).*

Jesus made it a point to differentiate the elect from the non-elect in His prayers. He specifically says that He does not ask on behalf of the world. It is unlikely that He would refuse to pray for those for whom He was about to die.

4.   The Evidence of Faith.

Faith is one of the evidences that the atonement has been effected. The following Scriptures indicate that faith is initiated by God.

> *And when the Gentiles heard this, they began rejoicing and glorifying the word of the Lord; and as many as had been appointed to eternal life believed. (Acts 13:48).*

> *And a certain woman named Lydia, from the city of Thyatira, a seller of purpose fabrics, a worshipper of God, was listening; and the Lord opened her heart to respond to the things spoken by Paul. (Acts 16:14).*

> *For to you it has been granted for Christ's sake, not only to believe in Him, but also to suffer for His sake. (Philippians 1:29).*

If we have received the gift of faith from the Lord, dare we assume that any of the spiritual gifts which we have received is not obtained as a result of the work of Christ on the cross? If Christ died for each and every person, then the gift of faith would have been given to all.

5.   The Goal of the Atonement.

In his first epistle to the Corinthians, Paul makes the point that men do not come to God on the basis of their intellectual reasonings. It is not the intelligent who are chosen. In fact, it is often just the opposite.

Not the wise, but the foolish.
Not the mighty, but the weak.
Not the noble, but the base and the despised.

I think it very likely that Paul sat back for a moment and thought over the status of the membership of the church at Corinth as he wrote these words. He asks the Corinthians to do the same thing.

> *For consider your calling, brethren, that there were not many wise according to the flesh, not many mighty, not many noble (1 Corinthians 1:26).*

Paul is speaking to believers. He exhorts them to consider their calling. They have been called to Jesus Christ. They are among those whom the Father has drawn. There were very few among the Corinthian believers who were rich or powerful or famous or influential. To be sure, Paul does not say that there were not any wise, or that there were not any mighty, or that there were not any noble. But the majority of the members of the church did not fit into those categories.

Why? Why do most Christians come from the ranks of the foolish and the weak and the base and the despised? Karl Marx suggested that it was because the oppressed classes and the weak turned to religion as a crutch to hold them up and to stabilize them. But this is not a Biblical answer. Paul says the reason Christianity is filled with the foolish and the weak and the base and the despised is because God has chosen those kinds of people to be in His kingdom. Notice the emphasis on God's election. Again and again, Paul repeats that it is God who has chosen.

> 26 *For consider **your calling**, brethren, that there were not many wise according to the flesh, not many mighty, not many noble; 27 but **God has chosen** the foolish things of the world to shame the wise, and*

God has chosen the weak things of the world to shame the things which are strong, 28 and the base things of the world and the despised, God has chosen, the things that are not, that He might nullify the things that are, 29 that no man should boast before God. 30 But by His doing you are in Christ Jesus... (1 Corinthians 1:26-30).

The phrase "God has chosen" is repeated three times in this passage. It emphasizes the fact that our calling and our salvation is God's choice. God has not left these things to blind chance. Rather, He has chosen to follow a special plan as to who should be called.

This brings us to a question. Why hasn't God chosen the wise? Why have the mighty and the noble been left out? The answer is given in verse 29. It is so that *no man should boast before God.* The reason God has chosen the foolish and the weak and the base and the despised is so that no man will be able to boast on his own account.

No man can ever say, "I found God as a result of my great intellect." No man has ever been accepted by God because he was of noble birth. No man has ever performed deeds mighty enough to merit his entrance into God's kingdom. You cannot even boast that you were saved because you had the good sense to choose God and to exercise faith in Him. He chose you.

The result of understanding this teaching is that God is glorified. If a man were saved on the basis of his own decision, then he might boast that he had the good sense to come to Christ and to place his faith in Christ. Instead, we are taught that we have been chosen apart from any merit that is within us *that, just as it is written, "Let him who boasts, boast in the Lord" (1 Corinthians 1:31).* The result of a proper understanding of the particular nature of the atonement will be that God is glorified as the One who has brought about your salvation.

6. The Death of Christ either did away with...

- All the sins of all men. If this is the case, then it is impossible to deny that all men would be saved. If all my sins were settled on the cross, then there is nothing left for me to do to obtain my salvation. It is guaranteed. If all the sins of all men are forgiven, then all men shall be saved and none shall come into condemnation. The problem with this sort of universalism is that it goes directly against the clear teaching of the Scriptures (Daniel 12:2; Matthew 13:41-42); 25:31-46).

- None of the sins of all men. If Christ only made it possible for men to be forgiven but did not actually atone for sins upon the cross, then we are all still in our sins and no one can ever be saved. By contrast, the Bible teaches that *He Himself bore our sins in His body on the cross* (1 Peter 2:24).

- Some of the sins of all men. If Christ only died for some of the sins of all men—for example, if He did not die for the sin of unbelief—then we are still in our sins, for it is impossible for us to atone for any of our own sins.

- All the sins of some men. This is a Biblical position. The death of Christ accomplished the salvation of those whom God has chosen.

PASSAGES THAT APPEAR TO BE UNIVERSAL IN SCOPE

There are certain passages of Scripture that, taken at face value, would seem to teach of a universal atonement. These fall into several categories.

1. General Passages.

It can easily be demonstrated that not every passage that uses the word "all" does so in a universalistic sense. There are times when a general statement is made that obviously has a limited sense.

- Jesus said to His disciples, *"You will be hated by all on account of My name"* (Matthew 10:22). That does not mean there were no exceptions to this general rule.

- Paul said, "All the Jews know my manner of life..." (Acts 26:4). This does not mean that there could not have been certain Jews who had never heard of Paul of Tarsus. It is obviously a general statement.

•   Joel gives a prophecy in Joel 2:28 that God would pour forth His Spirit *"upon all mankind."* Peter quotes this prophecy on the day of Pentecost and states that it is being fulfilled in his day. Does this mean that all men everywhere had the Spirit of God? Or does it only refer to all believers? The answer is obvious. It refers to all believers.

2.   Christ said that He would draw all men: *"And I, if I be lifted up from the earth, will draw all men to Myself." (John 12:32).*

Does this teach a universal drawing of all men to Christ? If it does, then it teaches too much, since Jesus has already used this same term to describe the drawing of certain men earlier in John's gospel where he said, *"No one can come to Me, unless the Father who sent Me draws him; and I will raise him up on the last day" (John 6:44).* He went on in that context to say that those who were drawn by God will be taught of God (6:45) and that they will certainly not be cast out (6:37).

Why then does John 12:32 say that Christ will draw all men to Himself? First of all, we should notice that the emphasis given by John's own commentary on the words of Jesus is not focused upon the universality of Christ's drawing, but upon the kind of death He should die. We see this in the next verse: *But He was saying this to indicate the kind of death by which He was to die (John 12:33).*

And yet, verse 32 does say something about drawing all men. How are we to understand this? It must be seen in the context. Philip and Andrew have just brought some Greeks to Jesus (John 12:20-22). This is the first time this has happened in Jerusalem. Up to this point, the ministry of Jesus has been almost exclusively toward the Jews. When He sent His disciples out, He told them not to go to the Gentiles (Matthew 10:5-6).

Now some Greeks have been brought to Him. This takes place at the end of His earthly ministry. He will soon be lifted up and nailed to a cross. When He is lifted up, He will draw all sorts of men, both Jews and Greeks.

Once Christ has gone to the cross, He will gather into one body both Jews and Gentiles. There will be no distinction between races or genders or social strata. His church will draw all to Himself.

3.   Justification to All Men: *So then as through one transgression there resulted condemnation to all men, even so through one act of righteousness there resulted justification of life to all men. (Romans*

5:18).

Does this mean that each and every man in the universe has been justified? It does not. It anticipates two groups of people and clearly refers to all of God's chosen people. This language is similar to what Paul says elsewhere: *For as in Adam all die, so also in Christ all shall be made alive (1 Corinthians 15:22).*

4.   Salvation to all men: *For the grace of God has appeared, bringing salvation to all men (Titus 2:11).*

The context makes it clear that Paul is speaking, not of every man being saved, but of the fact that the gospel is preached to all men. The previous verses mention all sorts of men as Paul has given instructions to old men, old women, young women, young men, and slaves. The basis for the instructions to each of these groups is that the grace of God has appeared, bringing salvation to each of these groups.

5.   God Desires All Men to be Saved. Paul says this in his first epistle to Timothy. The context is helpful in determining exactly to whom these "all men" refer.

> *1 First of all, then, I urge that entreaties and prayers, petitions and thanksgivings, be made on behalf of all men, 2 for kings and all who are in authority, in order that we may lead a tranquil and quiet life in all godliness and dignity. 3 This is good and acceptable in the sight of God our Savior, 4 who desires all men to be saved and to come to the knowledge of the truth. 5 For there is one God, and one mediator also between God and men, the man Christ Jesus, 6 who gave Himself as a ransom for all, the testimony borne at the proper time. (1 Timothy 2:1-6).*

The question is asked specifically about verse 4: If God really desires all men to be saved and to come to the knowledge of the truth, then why does He not save all men? Why are some predestined to salvation while others are not? Why are some saved while others are not?

The Arminian answers this question by insisting it is all bound up in the free will of man. He maintains that God wants all men to be saved but has decided to do nothing about that desire because He has an even greater desire to allow men to exercise their own free will in choosing or not choosing to be saved.

The problem is twofold. First of all, the passage does not say or even hint that all men are going to be saved, even though it does say that:

- We are to pray for all men.
- God desires all men to be saved.
- Christ gave Himself as a ransom for all.

What does this mean? It means that the love and concern of God is offered to all men. All men are commanded to repent and to believe the gospel. Furthermore, it means that the Lord grieves over man's sinful condition. Jesus wept over the unrepentant city of Jerusalem and God weeps over those who remain in their lost condition. It also means that the death of Christ was of a sufficient nature to atone for all the sins of all men. It means that Christ would not have had to spend an extra five minutes upon the cross in order to save an extra million people. His atoning death was infinite in merit.

Is this a denial of the sovereignty of God or of the particular nature of the atonement? Not at all. The same God who weeps over the lost condition of all men also has moved into history to regenerate the hearts of some and to bring them to Himself.

Paul alludes to this in the very next verse when he says, *And for this I was appointed a preacher and an apostle (I am telling the truth, I am not lying) as a teacher of the Gentiles in faith and truth* (1 Timothy 2:7). Notice that on the one hand, God desires that all men be saved and Jesus serves as the ransom to that effect. On the other hand, it is obvious that, while Paul was appointed as a preacher and apostle, this apostolic appointment has not extended to every person. By the same token, neither is the election to salvation extended to every person. Yet this is not a sign of some weakness on the part of God, but rather it is *in order that God's purpose according to His choice might stand* (Romans 9:11). We can conclude by saying that two things are equally true:

- God takes no pleasure in the final destruction of any.
- God finds pleasure in the salvation of every person who is

saved.

God finds no joy in the death of any sinner. *"Do I have any pleasure in the death of the wicked," declares the Lord God, "rather than that he should turn from his ways and live?"* (Ezekiel 18:23). The question is rhetorical and obviously expects a negative reply. God is not vengeful or vindictive. The Creator does not delight in the destruction of any person he has made, not even his enemies. He calls all men to be saved and to come to the knowledge of the truth and He tells us that there is celebration in heaven over every sinner who repents (Luke 15:7,10). He commands all to come to repentance. This command is universal. Paul said that *God is now declaring to men that all everywhere should repent (Acts 17:30).*

6.   God Desires all to come to Repentance: *The Lord is not slow about His promise, as some count slowness, but is patient toward you, not wishing for any to perish but for all to come to repentance (2 Peter 3:9).*

As we have pointed out, the Lord commands all to come to repentance. At the same time, we should note toward whom God is said to be patient. Peter does not say that God is patient toward all men. He says that God is patient toward you. This is because Peter has just finished describing some men with whom God is not patient. But He is still being patient with you. To whom is Peter addressing his epistle? It is to those who have received a faith of the same kind as ours (2 Peter 1:1). It is to those who have been called and chosen by God (2 Peter 1:10).

If God had not been patient with us, waiting for us to come to repentance, then none of us would be saved today. He has held off His judgment and He continues to hold off that judgment until all have repented. It is because of this that Peter instructs us to *regard the patience of the Lord to be salvation (2 Peter 3:15).*

7.   Christ is the Savior of all Men, but especially Believers: *For it is for this we labor and strive, because we have fixed our hope on the living God, who is the Savior of all men, especially of believers (1 Timothy 4:10).*

This passage is particularly striking because it seems to establish a contrast between two different groupings of people: All men versus believers.

| Christ is the Savior of all men | ⟹ | He especially saves believers |

Two possible interpretations have been presented for this passage. The issue revolves around our understanding of the Greek word μαλιστα (*malista*), translated in this passage as "especially." Two possible meanings have been set forth for this word:

•   Most of all, chiefly, especially.

This is the way it has been translated in the NAS, the NIV, and the King James Version in each of the instances it is used. This is also the way the word has generally been understood.

•   Specifically, that is.

The word μαλιστα is found a total of twelve times in the New Testament. All but four of those instances are by Paul. In most of these instances, the translation could go either way and still make sense.

It must be noted that this is not the normal meaning of the word. In 1979, T.C. Skeat published an article in the Journal of Theological Studies that proposed this alternate meaning of μαλιστα. George Knight takes this reading in his commentary on the Pastoral Epistles. If this were the case in this passage, it would be saying that Jesus is the Savior of all men, specifically and by that to mean that He is the Savior of believers.

The problem with this view is that it cannot be proven that μαλιστα has this alternate meaning anywhere in the Greek language. Furthermore, Paul could easily have used the Greek phrase τουτ᾽ ἔστιν to get across the idea of "specifically" or "that is." This phrase is regularly used throughout the New Testament to convey this idea (Matthew 27:46; Mark 7:2; Acts 1:19; Romans 7:18; 9:8; 10:6-8; Philemon 1:12). Because of this, we are obliged the reject Skeat's rendering and proceed with the normal use of the term.

What is this passage saying? It is saying that there is a sense in which Christ can be said to be the Savior of the world while, in a special sense, He is the Savior only of those who believe.

In what sense can Christ be said to be the Savior of the world? It is in the general sense in which He redeems the world by redeeming a remnant of that world. There is coming a day when "all Israel" will be saved. That does not mean that each and every Jewish person is going to be saved and it does not mean that each and every human being is going to be saved, but redemption will ultimately come to the world as that world is made new. This will be seen in greater detail as we examine the next passage.

8.   Christ is the Propitiation for the Sins of the World: *My little children, I am writing these things to you that you may not sin. And if anyone sins, we have an Advocate with the Father, Jesus Christ the righteous; 2 and He Himself is the propitiation for our sins; and not for ours only, but also for those of the whole world. (1 John 2:1-2).*

Jesus is said to be the propitiation both for our sins (referring to the sins of believers) as well as for the sins of the whole world. As in the previous passage, this text makes it obvious that there are two distinct groups of people in view. Who are they?

a.   The world of believers.

This is the interpretation offered by John Murray. The writer would be saying, "It is not only we disciples who are saved, but all other believers as well." Murray defends this view by pointing out that the author uses the plural pronoun in chapter 1 to refer to himself and the other disciples who had seen and heard and touched the resurrected Christ.

However, of the 185 times that κοσμος (*kosmos* — "world") is used in the New Testament, not once does it offer such an interpretation. John uses the term to describe the world of mankind.

b.   Jewish versus the Gentile world.

This view sees John, as the author of the epistle and a believing Jew, speaking of how Christ is the propitiation of he and his fellow believing Jews as well as the propitiation of believing Gentiles. This interpretation fails to account for how κοσμος can refer only to Gentile believers. Neither is there any indication that John is addressing himself to Jews and not to the church at large.

c.   The Elect versus the non-Elect.

This is the Arminian view. It states that Christ is equally the propitiation for all men, both saved and lost. The problem with this view is that if His propitiatory work is equal in all aspects to all mankind and He is the propitiation both for the lost and for the saved, then how can it be of any benefit to the saved? If Jesus did not satisfy all of the wrath of God toward all sins, then man must do something to save himself and we cannot say that God saves sinners.

d.   The Present Elect versus the Past and Future Elect.

This view would focus upon the perpetuity of the propitiation that Jesus provided—that it extends to all time and is therefore chronologically universal in its extent. This interpretation is problematic in that the context makes no mention of past, present, or future.

e.   The Exclusiveness of Jesus.

This view suggests that the emphasis of the passage is that Jesus is the exclusive means of propitiation for all men — that without Jesus there is no other means of propitiation. Jesus is not merely the Savior of John and his little religious group. He is the Savior of all men who are saved so that there is no other Savior.

The strength of this argument is seen in the fact that Jesus, not the world, has been the subject of the book up to this point and continues to be the subject of the rest of the book.

Each of these passages has described the work of Christ as applying to the world or to all men. If these verses are taken to guarantee salvation and redemption and justification to all men, then we would be forced to conclude a universal salvation. I want to suggest that this is exactly what we are to conclude.

This does not constitute a denial of the clear Biblical teaching of the eternal punishment of the damned. It does constitute a recognition of the Scriptural description of salvation in universal terms. Consider the following.

> 25 *For I do not want you, brethren, to be uninformed of this mystery, lest you be wise in your own estimation, that a partial hardening has happened to Israel until the fulness of the Gentiles has come in; 26 and thus all Israel will be saved; just as it is written, "The Deliverer will come from Zion, He will remove ungodliness from Jacob." (Romans 11:25-26).*

Is all of Israel to be saved? In one sense, we can say, "No." There are many who are descendants of Abraham who will find themselves shut off from the kingdom. On the other hand, we read here that all Israel will be saved. The reason for this is that only those who are saved are identified as being the true Israel.

In the same way, Peter could quote the prophet Joel as he pointed to the Pentecost incident and cited that incident as the fulfillment of Joel's words.

> *"'And it shall be in the last days,' God says, 'That I will pour forth of My Spirit upon all mankind...'" (Acts 2:17a).*

Was the Spirit given to all men — literally, to "all flesh" on the day of Pentecost? Did the emperor of Rome receive the Spirit of God on that day? No. And yet, those believers in Jerusalem became representative of all men. God has formed a new race of mankind—*homo electus*—the redeemed of the earth. This is that of what Jesus was speaking when He said:

> *"It is written in the prophets, 'And they shall ALL be taught of God.' Everyone who has heard and learned from the Father, comes to Me." (John 6:45).*

At the same time that He was teaching that some men do not come to Him because they are not drawn by the Father, He turned to speak of those who do come and He said that they are all taught of God. This promise of a universal blessing goes all the way back to Abraham.

...and in you all the families of the earth shall be blessed (Genesis 12:3b).

Will all the families of the earth become blessed in Abraham? Yes, in a sense, we can say that they will. There will be a new heavens and a new earth and all who are a part of that new heaven and new earth will be blessed in Abraham.

UNIVERSAL ASPECTS OF THE ATONEMENT

We must never think of the atoning work of Christ upon the cross as being insufficient to save all men. Augustine proposed the formula: "Sufficient for all, efficient for the elect." While illustrations can break down, the following might be helpful. Let us suppose that I have a million dollar line of credit and I go to an automobile dealership to purchase a car. I pick one out that costs $20,000. My line of credit has been sufficient for a much greater amount, but it was only efficient for the cost of the car. In the same way, the death of Christ was efficient to bring about the salvation of God's chosen people—to God's redeemed who have been purchased from their sins.

Dr. James Oliver Buswell gives us several points that help us understand this tension between the universal and particular aspects of the atonement.

1.   It is sufficient for all.

Christ would not have had to speak another three hours and forty five minutes on the cross to atone for the rest of the sins of the human race. His death was both qualitatively and quantitatively sufficient for anyone who believes.

I have occasionally been asked how the death of a single individual could possibly atone for the sins of so many. The answer, I believe, is found in the nature of the one who Atones. He is the eternal Son of God. Only such an infinite Being could bring forth such a sufficient atonement.

2.   It is applicable to all.

There is nothing in the events of the death of Christ that intrinsically limit its application to all men. What is limited is the application of the atonement and its effectiveness of drawing some to repentance.

3.   It is offered to all.

The offer of salvation is made to all men. Indeed, God commands all men everywhere to repent (Acts 17:30). The Bible closes with this invitation to all men: *And the Spirit and the bride say, "Come." And let the one who hears say, "Come." And let the one who is thirsty come; let the one who wishes take the water of life without cost. (Revelation 22:17).*

Soteriology
The Doctrine of Salvation

The theological term "Soteriology" is taken from the Greek verb *soter*, meaning "to save." It is the doctrine of salvation. Having already examined the atonement, we want now to examine the application of the benefits of that atonement.

The Atonement was accomplished on the Cross		The benefits of the Atonement are applied at Conversion

THE ORDO SALUTIS

The *ordo salutis* is merely a Latin term that speaks of the order of salvation. It seeks to determine the logical cause and effect progress that brings about salvation. There is not a single passage of Scripture that lays out every act and process of this order of salvation. However, an examination of several key passages will give us insight into such an order of the application of some of those aspects of salvation.

1.   The Beginnings of a Framework.

A basic framework of this cause and effect relationship in the order of salvation is presented by Paul in his epistle to the Romans.

> *29 For whom He foreknew, He also predestined to become conformed to the image of His Son, that He might be the first-born among many brethren; 30 and whom He predestined, these He also called; and whom He called, these He also justified;*

and whom He justified, these He also glorified.
(Romans 8:29-30).

There is a definite progression of the different aspects of salvation that are presented in this passage.

Foreknowledge and predestination speak of God's eternal purposes while the remaining aspects point to His temporal purposes. This order begins with God's eternal purpose—with His foreknowing us. This is not to say that there was a time when God had not decided whether or not to save us. Rather, it means that God's predestination springs out of His foreknowledge. He has determined to know us and to love us and therefore He determined to save us.

By contrast to this eternal purpose that looks back to the time before creation, our calling and our justification look to the time of our conversion when we came to Christ in faith and became Christians. Finally, our glorification looks to the climax of God's purpose when we are completely set apart to Himself.

2.   The Position of Faith in the Ordo Salutis.

Where does faith fit into this framework? It obviously comes after foreknowledge and predestination. It is also obvious that it comes prior to glorification. We can also determine where it comes in relation to justification.

> *...knowing that a man is not justified by the works of*
> *the Law but through faith in Christ Jesus (Galatians*
> *2:16a)*.

This passage demonstrates that faith precedes justification in its logical order. This is not to say that they do not take place simultaneously, but that one takes place as the logical basis of the other. Furthermore, it is obvious from the Scriptures that the reason men believe is because they have first been called.

> *No one can come to Me, unless the Father who sent Me draws him; and I will raise him up on the last day. (John 6:44).*

This means we can further chart these aspects of the ordo salutis out like this:

Calling	⇨	Faith	⇨	Justification

3. Faith and Regeneration.

When we speak of regeneration, we are referring to the new birth that takes place when a person is made spiritually alive and receives a spiritual renewal. Which comes first, faith or regeneration?

The Arminian position is that regeneration comes on the basis of faith. He teaches that man uses his own free will to believe and then he is regenerated as a result of that belief. The Reformed view, by contrast, is that God regenerates a man and then out of his new life comes faith.

Arminian View	**Reformed View**
Regeneration comes as a result of a person believing the Gospel.	Regeneration takes place as a work of God and, as a result of this new life, the person believes the Gospel.

What do the Scriptures say regarding this issue? It says that *whoever believes that Jesus is the Christ is born of God* (1 John 5:1a). At first glance, this passage would seem to support the Arminian view. However, the phrase translated "is born of God" is in the perfect tense in the Greek text. This tense indicates an action that took place in the past and which has continuing results. We would therefore translate it as follows:

> *Whoever believes in the present that Jesus is the Christ has been born of God in the past with the result that they have this life.*

This places regeneration prior to faith and repentance.

Another evidence for this is the fact that the natural man is not able to receive the things of the Spirit of God (1 Corinthians 2:14). A man needs to be spiritually wakened in order to hear and understand the Gospel.

As light cannot restore sight to a blind man, so even the light of the Gospel cannot restore life to one who is unregenerate. It takes the life producing work of the Holy Spirit to bring life where there is no life. That is not to say that the Gospel is unimportant to this process. To the contrary, without the light of the Gospel, there is nothing to see.

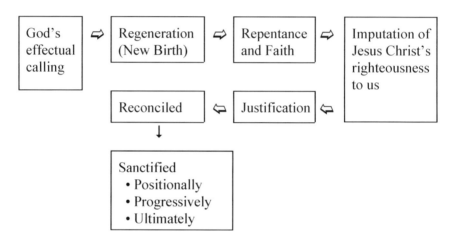

REGENERATION

In his book *Waking the Dead*, John Eldridge reminds us that we are enchanted with stories of transformation.

- Beauty's love turns the beast into a handsome prince.
- Pinocchio becomes a boy.
- The Ugly Duckling becomes a swan.
- Luke Skywalker becomes a Jedi Warrior.
- Strider becomes King Aragorn.
- Neo becomes the One.

These speak to our heart because we long to be more than we can be.

We long to be born again. It has become very popular in certain circles to speak of being "born again." What exactly does this mean?

The new birth is the bringing forth of a new and divinely created life into the soul of the believer. When we speak of "generating" something, we refer to bringing life to that thing. Therefore "regeneration" speaks of the bringing of life to that which had previously been dead.

1.   The Need for the New Birth.

The very fact of regeneration presupposes a spiritual death. I have spent a lot of years in the Fire Rescue profession. And there is one important rule which I learned. You do not bring someone back to life unless they are first dead.

You were born as a son or a daughter of Adam. This was an existence of spiritual death. The only way of escape was to bring new life to that dead existence. God does not save you by cleaning up your old life. Instead He declares you to be legally dead. And then He starts over.

> *Knowing this, that our old self was crucified with Him, that our body of sin might be done away with, that we should no longer be slaves to sin; 7 for he who has died is freed from sin. (Romans 6:6-7).*

There is an identification truth here. When Christ died on the cross, you were legally considered to have died with Him. When He was buried and the tomb was sealed with the stone, you were reckoned to be in the grave with Him. And when He arose from the grave, you were declared to have risen with Him into a new life. This is why Peter says that our new birth is "through the resurrection of Jesus Christ."

> *Blessed be the God and Father of our Lord Jesus Christ, who according to His great mercy has caused us to be born again to a living hope through the resurrection of Jesus Christ from the dead. (1 Peter 1:3).*

The new birth brings about a living hope. That is a quality we need. Everyone needs hope. I was talking recently to a man whose son had been in a coma. It was uncertain whether the boy would live or die. One of the nurses came in and told him, "I don't want to give you any hope." She meant well but, at this point in the process, he needed to hope. The good news is that his hope was not without foundation, for his son soon awakened and was restored to health.

If you have come to faith in Jesus Christ, then you have been born again to a living hope. It is a hope of life that is rooted in the resurrection of Jesus. He rose from the dead and He gives to you a similar resurrection, raising you out of your former manner of living to live your life in a new realm of existence.

2.   The Source of the New Birth.

> 12 *But as many as received Him, to them He gave the right to become children of God, even to those who believe in His name, 13 who were born not of blood, nor of the will of the flesh, nor of the will of man, but of God. (John 1:12-13).*

Notice that all men are not called the children of God. Only those who have come to Christ in faith have the authority to be called children of God. Some people are children of another father. Some people are the children of Satan (John 8:44; 1 John 3:10).

This tells me something about Christianity. It tells me that Christianity is not simply another religion. Christianity involves a relationship. When we tell someone about Jesus, we are offering them entrance into the family of God.

This passage tells us that the source of this new birth is not man's free will. Man cannot will himself to be born again any more than a baby can conceive himself and be born. The source of the new birth is the will of God.

3.   The Cause of the New Birth.

> *In the exercise of His will He brought us forth by the word of truth, so that we might be, as it were, the first fruits among His creatures. (James 1:18).*

The new birth is brought about by the exercise of God's will. That is quite different from the way in which we normally think. We normally speak of believing the gospel and then, as a result of that faith, you enter into new life and are born again. But James tells us that it is an exercise of God's will that brings our new life.

What is true of the spiritual world is illustrated in natural birth. You don't get yourself born by something you do. Your natural birth is due to the actions of your parents. These actions are not initiated by you. It is through the exercise of their will and their actions that you are brought forth.

In the same way, your spiritual birth begins, not with your decision or your faith, but with the will of God. It is the exercise of His will that causes you to experience new life. A result of that new life is faith.

Conception is not outwardly obvious. That is why people take a pregnancy test. The test tells you if there is life. That life will eventually lead to growth and, it time, a birth will take place. What is true in the natural realm is also true in the spiritual realm. The new life imparted by God will eventually lead to faith and to spiritual growth.

4.   The Means of the New Birth.

> *For you have been born again not of seed which is perishable but imperishable, that is, through the living and abiding word of God. (1 Peter 1:23).*

The means by which the new birth is imparted to man is through the instrumentality of the gospel. Although regeneration is the work of God, that work does not take place apart from the gospel. Paul said that the gospel is the power of God for salvation to everyone who believes (Romans 1:16).

5.   The Dynamic of the New Birth.

Jesus taught on the subject of the new birth during a midnight conversation He had with a man named Nicodemus. It must have been an interesting conversation. On the one hand was a Galilean carpenter-turned-rabbi. On the other was a recognized religious leader of the Jewish religion.

> *3 Jesus answered and said to him, "Truly, truly, I say to you, unless one is born again, he cannot see the kingdom of God."*
> *4 Nicodemus said to Him, "How can a man be born when he is old? He cannot enter a second time into his mother's womb and be born, can he?"*

385

5 Jesus answered, "Truly, truly, I say to you, unless one is born of water and the Spirit, he cannot enter into the kingdom of God (John 3:3-5).

When Jesus speaks of the new birth, we should understand that the Greek can be understood in one of two ways. It is an example of a homonym. There is a word here that has two possible meanings. Usually, you can tell a homonym from the context, but in this case, either meaning makes sense. The phrase "born again" can mean one of two things:

- Born again.
- Born from above.

Which meaning is intended here? Is Jesus speaking of being born again or is He speaking of being born from above. I am not certain. Either one is doctrinally accurate. Either one fits the context of this verse.

Born Again	***Born from Above***
The reply of Nicodemus indicates that he assumes Jesus is speaking of a second birth	In verse 31, Jesus speaks of how He who comes from ABOVE is ABOVE all.
Focuses upon the contrast with the physical birth.	Focuses upon the divine origin of our spiritual life.

There is another possibility. It is that this is worded in such a way that we are to understand both being in view. There are times when we speak in such a way as to intentionally give a double meaning to our words.

Jesus continues to explain the contrast between the physical birth of which Nicodemus has spoken and the new birth that is of the Spirit. In effect, He says that each gives birth after its own kind. This is not a new concept to Nicodemus. The first chapter of Genesis repeats again and again how things are created to produce after their own kind.

*And the earth brought forth vegetation, plants yielding seed **after their kind**, and trees bearing fruit, with seed in them, **after their kind**; and God saw that* *it was good. (Genesis 1:12).*

> *And God created the great sea monsters, and every living creature that moves, with which the waters swarmed **after their kind**, and every winged bird after its kind; and God saw that it was good. (Genesis 1:21).*

> *And God made the beasts of the earth **after their kind**, and the cattle **after their kind**, and everything that creeps on the ground **after its kind**; and God saw that it was good. (Genesis 1:25).*

Even when it came time for Adam and Eve to bear children, we read that this same principle continued to be in effect.

> *When Adam had lived one hundred and thirty years, he became the father of a son in his own likeness, according to his image, and named him Seth. (Genesis 5:3).*

Adam and Eve were created in the image of God. They were designed to be like God. That does not mean God has two arms and two legs or that He is merely a glorified man. It does mean that man has been created to be God's representative on planet earth and that he has been invested with a stewardship over the planet. Man has been given to assume the role of rulership over the world. There is a sense in which he stands in the role of being God to the world.

Furthermore, God is described in the Bible as having personality, emotions, intellect and will. The fact that we share in those might reflect other ways and means in which we are also in the image of God. That pattern was distorted when Adam sinned. Sin affected every part of his life. His personality became self-centered. His emotions became subject to sin. His intellect became clouded. His will fell under the bondage of the flesh.

This same distortion of God's image has been passed on to Adam's descendants. Adam's children were not made in the image and likeness of God. They were born in Adam's own image and likeness. They were polluted by the effects of sin in the same way that Adam reflected this polluted image. His descendants gave rise to a fallen race.

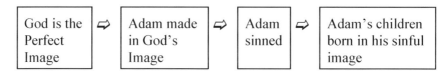

| God is the Perfect Image | ⇨ | Adam made in God's Image | ⇨ | Adam sinned | ⇨ | Adam's children born in his sinful image |

It took the work of a second Adam to restore us to the image and likeness of God. Just as the condemnation had come upon all the world through the sin of a single man, so also through the obedience of a single man has come salvation to all.

> *45 So also it is written, "The first man, Adam, became a living soul." The last Adam became a life-giving spirit. 46 However, the spiritual is not first, but the natural; then the spiritual.*
>
> *47 The first man is from the earth, earthy; the second man is from heaven. 48 As is the earthy, so also are those who are earthy; and as is the heavenly, so also are those who are heavenly. 49 And just as we have borne the image of the earthy, we shall also bear the image of the heavenly. (1 Corinthians 15:45-49).*

The first Adam was given life and became a living soul. The last Adam gave life to the world by laying down His own life. The first Adam sinned by eating of the fruit of the tree. The last Adam obeyed by dying upon the tree. The first Adam brought condemnation and death to all who bore his image and likeness. The last Adam brings justification and life to all who enter into union with Him. It is through Jesus Christ that man is able to return to the place of a true and even better pattern of the image of God.

6.   An Illustration of the New Birth.

> *The wind blows where it wishes and you hear the sound of it, but do not know where it comes from and where it is going; so is everyone who is born of the Spirit." (John 3:8).*

Jesus brings out an illustration of the new birth in John 3:8. He uses the example of the wind. It is not only a fitting example, but it is also a play on words as the term for "wind" and the term for "spirit" are identical in both Greek and Hebrew. Why does Jesus use this play on words? I think it is because He wants to make a comparison. He wants to paint a picture of the work of the Spirit and He does this by picturing the work of the wind.

Try to look at the wind. You cannot see it. You do not know from where it comes. You do not know where it is going. But you believe it is there. Why? Because you see how it affects the physical world around you. You see the leaves swirl. You see sailboats move across a churning sea. You see these evidences of the wind and they convince you that the wind is at work. That is what the new birth is like. You cannot see it. You do not know from where it comes. But you can believe it is there when you see how it affects those who have partaken of it.

I have had the opportunity to pilot both a motorboat as well as a sailboat. Piloting a motorboat is easy. You just start the motor and point the boat in the direction you wish to go and you go there. A sailboat is different. It does not carry its own power. It relies on the wind. When the wind blows, the sailboat goes. If the wind does not blow, the sailboat does not move. The pilot's task is not to generate more wind; it is only to do what is necessary to catch the wind and to be moved by the wind. The spiritual life is like that. We cannot turn it on and off. But we can allow ourselves to be moved by the Spirit when it does blow.

Moses could not produce a burning bush, but when he was confronted by that manifested presence of God, he was able to allow it to change him. How about you? Has the Spirit of God been at work in your life? Are you different today because of the blowing of God's Spirit in your life? If it is not, then don't try to fake it. You will be like the little boy who spreads his sails and then blows to make the sound of wind. Don't settle for cheap sound effects. Spread the sails of your faith and then look for the Lord to move you with His Spirit.

REPENTANCE

A problem has arisen in the recent understanding of repentance. One reason for this problem is that Bible scholars have attempted to adopt a thoroughly Greek idea of repentance instead of finding the foundation for their doctrine in the Old Testament Scriptures. I am not merely arguing over the difference between Covenant Theology versus Dispensationalism, but rather the fact that all of the writers of both the Old and the New Testaments wrote from a Jewish perspective.

1.   Repentance in the Old Testament.

Repentance was a common theme in the Old Testament. There were two basic Hebrew words that were associated with the idea of repentance.

- *Nacham* (נָחַם) is the most common word for repentance. It reflects the idea of sorrow and often includes with it a change of purpose. The origin of the word seems to reflect the idea of "breathing deeply." This word can also be used of the comfort that takes place as a result of repentance. Genesis 5:29 uses this term to speak of how Noah would give "comfort" or "rest" from the toil of the cursed ground.

- *Shuv* (שׁוּב) is a more general word—it is the twelfth most used verb in the entire Old Testament (over 1050 times). It means "to turn" or "return." It conveys the idea that you were going in one direction and you turned so that you headed in the opposite direction. There are over a hundred instances where it carries the idea of repentance (1 Kings 8:47; Ezekiel 14:6; 18:30).

One of the classic references to repentance in the Old Testament is found in the prophet Joel.

> 12 *"Yet even now," declares the LORD, "Return* [שׁוּב] *to Me with all your heart, And with fasting, weeping, and mourning; 13 And rend your heart and not your garments." Now return* [שׁוּב] *to the LORD your God, For He is gracious and compassionate, Slow to anger, abounding in lovingkindness, And relenting* [נָחַם] *of evil. 14 Who knows whether He will not turn* [שׁוּב] *and relent* [נָחַם], *And leave a blessing behind Him, Even a grain offering and a libation For the LORD your God? (Joel 2:12-14).*

It will be observed that both these words are used both of sinners who repent of their sins as well as of God relenting of the calamity He had promised. As it refers to men, the concept of repentance sees man who has run from the presence of God pausing in his headlong flight and returning to the presence of the Lord.

2.   Greek words for Repentance.

There are two primary Greek words used in the New Testament to speak of repentance. They correspond to the two Hebrew terms that we have just seen.

English	Hebrew	Greek
Repent	*Hacham* — נָחַם	*Metanoeo* —Μετανοεω
Turn	*Shuv* —שׁוּב	*Epistrepho* — Επιστρεφω

The Greek word ἐπιστρεφω (*epistrepho*) comes from a compound made up of the joining of the word ἐπι ("upon") and στρεφω ("to turn"). It is used to describe the process of conversion. The Greek word μετανοεω (*metanoeo*) is a compound of two Greek words.

Classical Greek used the word in a general sense of a change of mind, heart, or direction, including times when a person repented of doing something good to turn to a path of evil.

   •   Μετα (*meta*) is the preposition "with" or "after"
   •   Νοεω (*noeo*) is the word for "mind."

This origin has caused some to think that repentance in the New Testament is only a change of mind and nothing more, but that would be an inaccurate use of the language. Compound words are often more that the sum of their roots and μετανοεω as used in the New Testament involves more than a mere change of mind.

Luke twice uses the parallelism, "Repent and turn" (μετανοήσατε καὶ ἐπιστρέψατε - Acts 3:19; 26:20). This parallelism is also found in the Old Testament Septuagint, the Greek translation of the Old Testament (Isaiah 46:8; Jeremiah 4:28; Joel 2:14; 3:9).

Faith and repentance are essentially two sides of the same coin. Repentance focuses upon that from which you turn away; faith focuses upon that to which you turn.

3.   John the Baptist Preaches Repentance.

Now in those days John the Baptist came,

*preaching in the wilderness of Judea, saying, 2
"Repent, for the kingdom of heaven is at hand."
(Matthew 3:1-2).*

John's command to repent was linked to his announcement
that the kingdom of heaven is at hand. We must remember that John
is announcing something that was promised from the Old Testament
and therefore his command to repent is given from an Old Testament
context. The repentance he demands is no mere change of mind, but
demands a resulting change of life. This is made clear in Luke's
account of John's preaching.

> *"Therefore bring forth fruits in keeping with
> repentance..." (Luke 3:8a).*

When questioned as to what form such fruit in keeping with
repentance ought to be, John painted a very vivid picture.

> *11 And he would answer and say to them, "Let
> the man who has two tunics share with him who has
> none; and let him who has food do likewise." 12 And
> some tax-gatherers also came to be baptized, and they
> said to him, "Teacher, what shall we do?" 13 And he
> said to them, "Collect no more than what you have
> been ordered to." 14 And some soldiers were
> questioning him, saying, "And what about us, what
> shall we do?" And he said to them, "Do not take
> money from anyone by force, or accuse anyone
> falsely, and be content with your wages." (Luke 3:11-
> 14).*

John's focus was not merely upon a repentance that remained
theoretical, but upon one which produced a changed life. As such,
his baptism came to be referred to as a "baptism of repentance" (Acts
13:24; 19:4).

4.   Jesus Preaches Repentance.

All three of the Synoptic Gospels characterize the general
preaching of Jesus as one of repentance (Matthew 4:17; Mark 1:15;
Luke 5:32). The gospel of John is distinct in that it does not use the
word "repent." In its place is the word "believe." This underscores

an important point. It is that faith and repentance are two sides of the same coin.

5.   Repentance in the Preaching of the Church.

From the very first sermon at Pentecost, the preaching of the early church was one of repentance.

- Peter called for repentance and baptism, both in public sermons (Acts 2:38; 3:19; 5:31) as well as in private rebukes (Acts 8:22).
- Paul declares repentance to be the program of God for all men of this age (Acts 11:16; 17:30; 20:21). He describes this repentance in terms of turning to God and performing deeds appropriate to repentance (Acts 26:20).
- Repentance is directly related to and brought about through the agency of godly sorrow (2 Corinthians 7:9-10).

6.   Elements of Repentance.

In his Systematic Theology, Louis Berkhof lists three elements of repentance.

- An intellectual element. Repentance involves a change of thinking, a recognition of the guilt of personal sin.
- An emotional element. We have already seen that a proper sorrow for our sins leads to repentance (2 Corinthians 7:9-10). In the same vein, Jesus said, "Blessed are those who mourn, for they shall be comforted" (Matthew 5:4).
- A volitional element. This is a change of purpose and direction as the sinner turns from his sin and directs himself to trust in and follow the Lord (Acts 2:38, Revelation 2:5).

7.   Repentance is Granted by God.

In 2 Timothy 2:25, Paul speaks of those who are in opposition to the truth and say that "perhaps God may grant them repentance leading to the knowledge of the truth." The implication is that repentance is not something the pagan initiates in his own life. It is a work of God within him.

In a similar way, the Psalmist prays, "O God, restore us" (Psalm 80:3). This pleas, found three times in this chapter (verses 7 and 19), uses the Hebrew word *shuv* (שׁוּב), asking God to turn His people to Himself (see also Jeremiah 31:18 and Lamentations 5:21).

      The first church council in Jerusalem alluded to the fact that "God granted to the Gentiles also the full repentance that leads to life" (Acts 11:18).

8.   Repentance and Judgment.

      Most of the references to repentance are seen in a context of coming judgment. In addition to the passages already noted, we should add Revelation 2:5, 10, 21-22; 3:3, 19. Yet Paul points out that the kindness of God leads men to repentance (Romans 2:4).

FAITH

      Repentance tends to focus upon that from which man turns as he departs from the realm of his sin and rebellion. The counterpart to repentance is faith. It pictures man turning toward God and relying upon Him.

Repentance	**Faith**
Focus on the negative.	Focus on the Positive.
Turning away from sin and rebellion.	Turns to God and trusts in Him.

1.   What is Faith?

      Faith is made up of four necessary elements. All of them must be present for it to be that kind of faith that saves.

      •   Cognition.

            The element of cognition means that faith involves a certain amount of knowledge. The Scriptures speak of repentance *leading to the knowledge of the truth* (2 Timothy 2:25). It is popular today for people in our Postmodern culture to say, "It is not important in what you believe, as long as you have faith." It is a foolish statement. You would not think much of a surgeon who said, "It is not important where you cut, as long as you cut." When one makes such a statement, he is really saying there is nothing in which we can believe. Belief is seen merely as an escape to keep from going insane. It is hoping when there is no hope. Real faith is not like that. The apostle John speaks of the evidence of an eye witness testimony to the cross experience of Jesus.

- Convincing.

    This is the element of assent. There are many people who know the facts of the Bible, but who do not necessarily believe that they are true. The first element deals with the enlightenment of the truth. The second element deals with convincing men of that truth. Yet this is not the full scope of faith. Herod Agrippa was convinced of the truthfulness of the prophets without believing in the one whom they foretold (Acts 26:27).

- Confidence.

    Real faith is more than a mere knowledge and a mental assent. James reminds us that the demons have that kind of faith (James 2:19). The Jews who rejected Jesus as their Messiah believed that He really existed and that He was a miracle worker. They even made the effort to come and to see Him. Yet they were not real believers. They only wanted Him to set up a welfare state where they could get free bread and fish. Saving faith is rooted in a person. It is the belief that sees Jesus as the only hope of life and then relies upon Him and submits to Him.

- Commitment.

    When we trust in Christ, we also entrust our entire future to Him, committing ourselves into His hands. This is the issue of Lordship. There are some who would claim that trusting in Jesus without any commitment to Him as Lord of our lives and One to be obeyed is sufficient for salvation. What they are saying is that you can hate Jesus, declare yourself His mortal enemy, yet pray to Him and order Him to save you quite apart from any desire to have your life changed by Him and He will be obligated to do so. Jesus made no such claim. He called men to follow Him without reservation.

> 23 *And He was saying to them all, "If anyone wishes to come after Me, let him deny himself, and take up his cross daily, and follow Me. 24 For whoever wishes to save his life shall lose it, but whoever loses his life for My sake, he is the one who will save it. 25 For what is a man profited if he gains the whole world, and loses or forfeits himself? 26 For whoever is ashamed of Me and My words, of him will the Son of Man be ashamed when He comes in His glory, and the glory of the Father and of the holy angels. (Luke 9:23-26).*

Does this mean we obtain salvation through our own efforts? Not at all. It does mean that the process of salvation changes the life of the believer.

2.   Roman Catholic Versus Reformed Views of Faith.

Roman Catholic View	Reformed View
Faith consists of a mere assent to the doctrines of the church.	Faith involves a commitment to Christ and a reliance upon Him.
Fides Informis—Assent to the doctrines of the church.	Fides Formata—it includes love as a formative principle.
Faith does not require knowledge. One is a believer if he is ready to accept the doctrines of the church, regardless of whether he knows what they are.	Knowledge of certain key propositional truths is an essential part of faith.

3.   From where does Faith come?

We must begin by understanding that our experience is not in itself adequate to tell us from where faith comes. This is because we do not have the total picture. We cannot see our lives and our experiences and our decisions from God's point of view except as we read the Scriptures.

• The condition of unsaved man.

The apostle Paul presents a vivid picture of man as he exists without God. It shows the way in which man naturally uses his free will.

> *10 as it is written, "There is none righteous, not even one;*
> *11 There is none who understands,*
> *There is none who seeks for God;*
> *12 All have turned aside, together they have become useless;*
> *There is none who does good, There is not even one." (Romans 3:10-12).*

The unsaved man has no desire for God. He has turned his back on God and has run away from God. He cannot understand God and he does not want to understand God.

> *But a natural man does not accept the things of the Spirit of God; for they are foolishness to him, and he cannot understand them, because they are spiritually appraised. (1 Corinthians 2:14).*

The unbeliever is described as a "natural man." The phrase in the Greek text is literally, "the soulish man." When the natural man is confronted with the things of the Spirit of God, he does not accept them. He does not believe the gospel. The gospel makes no sense to him. It seems nonsensical. He cannot understand how the death of a man on a cross in a little country in the Middle East could affect the destiny of all men.

It is impossible for the natural man—the unsaved man—to understand the things of God. Just as the physically blind man cannot see the sun, so also the spiritually blind man cannot see the Son.

• The need for an effectual call.

When we speak of an "effectual call," we must distinguish this from a general call. The general call of God is that call for all men to repent. Matthew 22:14 says that "many are called, but few are chosen." An effectual call is a call that necessarily produces an effect. It is an inward call that answers the outward call.

In a context where He was facing the rejection at both the hands of the Jews as well as from some of His own disciples, Jesus spoke of the need for an effectual calling.

> *"No one can come to Me, unless the Father who send Me draws him; and I will raise him up on the last day. 45 It is written in the prophets, 'And they shall all be taught of God.' Everyone who has heard and learned from the Father comes to Me." (John 6:44-45).*

With these words, Jesus is explaining the phenomenon of unbelief. The reason some men do not believe is because it is impossible for any man to believe unless the Lord draws him to Christ. Why is this? Why is it that men will not come to God. on their own initiative? Why will they not come unless God draws them? It is because man's will has ben corrupted by sin. It has been said that the man who chokes on the doctrine of election has not yet swallowed his own total depravity.

As a sinner, man is helpless to even turn to God for help. Water cannot flow uphill. Neither is it possible for the natural man to act contrary to his nature. It is God who must turn man so that he will seek a cure. Therefore, it is only when a man is drawn by God that he will come to Jesus to be saved.

• Explicit statements of faith as a gift.

There are not a lot of passages that explicitly teach

that faith is a gift of God and I'm not sure that any do clearly, but here are some to consider:

> *Lydia... was listening... and the Lord opened her heart to respond to the things spoken by Paul (Acts 16:14).*

> *...as God has allotted to each, a measure of faith (Romans 12:3b).*

> *For to one is given the word of wisdom through the Spirit... to another faith by the same Spirit (1 Corinthians 12:8-9).*

> *For to you it has been granted for Christ's sake, not only to believe in Him, but also to suffer for His sake, (Philippians 1:29).*

> *Simon Peter... to those who **have received** a faith of the same kind as ours, by the righteousness of our God and Savior, Jesus Christ (2 Peter 1:1).*

The words "have received" in this last passage are translated from the Greek λαχοῦσιν (*lachousin*), the aorist participle of λαγχανω (*lagchano*) and carries the idea of receiving an allotted portion (indeed, it usually has the idea that lots were cast in order for the privilege to be granted; Luke 1:9; John 19:24; Acts 1:17). In the same vein, Jesus said...

> *All that the Father gives Me shall come to Me... (John 6:37).*

The reason that there is response to Jesus is because the Father gives those people to Jesus.

> *No one can come to Me, unless the Father who send Me draws him; and I will raise him up on the last day. 45 It is written in the prophets, "And they shall all be taught of God." Everyone who has heard and learned*

from the Father comes to Me. (John 6:44-45).

The reason that men come to Christ (and that is just another way of saying that this is the reason they believe in Him) is because the Father draws those men and teaches them. It is only those who have been given this internal teaching who come (See also verse 64-65 where Jesus uses this to explain why Judas did not believe).

Does this happen apart from the offer of the gospel and faith? By no means! The invitation to come and believe is seen in the same passage and sometimes in the same verse.

• Faith and Salvation: *For by grace you have been saved through faith; and that not of yourselves, it is the gift of God (Ephesians 2:8).*

Salvation comes through faith. Faith is never looked upon as a cause of your salvation. Rather, it is the instrument through which you receive your salvation. Faith is an instrument. In the same way a fork is utilized to bring food to my mouth, so the Lord uses faith to bring salvation.

JUSTIFICATION

And He also told this parable to certain ones who trusted in themselves that they were righteous, and viewed others with contempt:

"Two men went up into the temple to pray, one a Pharisee, and the other a tax-gatherer. 11 The Pharisee stood and was praying thus to himself, 'God, I thank Thee that I am not like other people, swindlers, unjust, adulterers, or even like this tax-gatherer. 12 I fast twice a week; I pay tithes of all that I get.' 13 But the tax-gatherer, standing some distance away, was even unwilling to lift up his eyes to heaven, but was beating his breast, saying, 'God, be merciful to me, the sinner!'" (Luke 18:9-13).

Two men. Both are Jewish. Both are descendants of Abraham. Both have come to the temple to pray. The first is a Pharisee. He is a religious man. He holds to the literal interpretation of the Scriptures. As a member of the sect of the Pharisees, he has dedicated his life to the keeping of the Law of God. He reads the Law daily. He prays several times a day. He gives his tithe to the Temple. He is respectable in the eyes of the religious hierarchy. Everyone agrees that he is a good man.

Standing nearby is the other man. This man is a tax-gatherer. He has gone to the Roman officials and has purchased a franchise from the Roman Empire to collect taxes from the subjugated people on behalf of Rome. He is required to turn over a specified amount of money to the Romans, and anything over this amount he is permitted to keep for himself. Therefore, he makes his profit by deliberately overcharging people on their taxes. He has betrayed his countrymen to become a thief for the Romans. He is a Benedict Arnold. He has sold out to the Romans for money. No one will have anything to do with him. He holds the same social caste as a prostitute.

Each of these men comes to the Temple. Each of them pray. I think that I can even say that each of them was sincere in his prayer. Now I want you to notice what Jesus said about these two men and the results of their prayers...

> *"I tell you, this man went does to his house justified rather than the other; for every one who exalts himself shall be humbled, but he who humbles himself shall be exalted."* *(Luke 18:14).*

Both of these men were sinners when they came into the Temple, although one was much more obvious in his sinning. But one of these men went out of the Temple different than the other. The Tax-collector was justified.

1.   Justification Defined.

What does it mean to be "justified"? The most common definition which I have heard is that it makes me "just-as-if-I'd never sinned." This contains a certain amount of truth, but it is inadequate.

The word "justify" is taken from the Greek root word for "righteous." This gives us a clue as to its meaning. It has to do with righteousness. It describes the act of declaring that a person or thing is righteous.

Now this it important. The act of justification does not make a person righteous. It is merely a declaration that he is righteous. This is seen in the fact that it is used to describe the righteousness of God...

> *And when all the people and the tax-gatherers heard this, they **acknowledged God's justice**, having been baptized with the baptism of John. (Luke 7:29).*

This phrase should literally be translated, "They justified God." This tells us something of the meaning of justification. They were not doing anything to make God more righteous than He already was. They were merely declaring that God was righteous.

This concept of justification was commonly used as a legal term in which a court of law might officially declare that a man was righteous - that he had not broken the law. This is different from being pardoned. A man who had been pardoned might be released, even though he were a guilty criminal worthy of death. However, a man who was justified was being declared innocent of any wrong-doing.

Now we come back to the case of the tax-gatherer in Luke 18:14. This man was a guilty sinner. He was one who had freely admitted his guilt. And yet, he had not merely been pardoned. Jesus said that this man went away justified. This man was declared to be righteous.

Does this mean that he had not really sinned? Does it mean that his sins were not all that bad and that they could be overlooked? Does it mean that the man stopped sinning?

There are crucial questions here that go far beyond this one man. WE have been justified. God has declared us to be righteous. But how can God declare a man to be righteous when that man is really a guilty sinner? The answer can only be found in the imputation of righteousness.

2.   The Imputation of Righteousness.

> *He made Him who knew no sin to be sin on our behalf, that we might become the righteousness of God in Him. (2 Corinthians 5:21).*

In this single verse, Paul pictures two different aspects of the work of Christ on our behalf.

•   The Imputation of our sins upon Christ.

Jesus became sin on our behalf. This does not mean that He actually became a sinner or that He began to sin. He has lived through all eternity without sin and He will always be perfect in His righteous character.

How did He become sin on our behalf? What really happened on the cross? Our sins were put to His account. He was credited with our sins. While He was on the cross, God the Father treated Him as though He were a guilty sinner. Jesus was judged in our place. The wrath of God was poured out on Him. In the midst of this condemnation, He cried out, "My God, my God, why have You forsaken Me?"

The sinless Son of God was judged as though He had committed all of the sins which have ever taken place throughout the entire history of mankind. He was judged in our place. Our sins were imputed or credited to Him. But this is not all.

• The Imputation of Christ's Righteousness Toward Us.

Just as our sins were put to His account while He was on the cross, so in the same way, the righteousness of Christ is put to our account when we believe in Him. We are credited with the righteousness of Christ. We are reckoned to be righteous. On this basis, we are justified — declared to be righteous. And for all eternity, God will treat us as though we were as righteous as Jesus Christ.

Now, this does not mean that I actually become righteous when I believe in Christ. If that were true, then no believer would ever sin and this just is not the case. Rather, I am legally credited with the righteousness of Christ so that I can be legally declared to be righteous.

3.   The Significance of Justification.

What is the significance of this imputation of Christ's righteousness to our account? Is it merely another doctrine to be tucked into our spiritual notebooks and quietly forgotten? Or does it have some practical value on how I can live my life for today?

If I have been declared by God to be righteous, then God is now free to bless me with every spiritual blessing. You see, God can never act in a way that is contrary to His own character. He could never say, "I know that man has sinned and is deserving of eternal condemnation, but I want to be a God of love and so I'm going to ignore man's sinful condition and give him eternal life anyway."

For God to accept sinful man as he is and to fellowship with him in this condition would be for God to accept and to fellowship with SIN. It would make God a sinner. It is for this reason that God formed a plan which would save man and at the same time would satisfy the righteousness of God.

4.   The Necessity of Imputation.

> *But now apart from the Law the righteousness*
> *of God has been manifested. (Romans 3:21a).*

With these words, Paul introduces the doctrine of justification by faith. Rather than being contrary to God's righteous character, the doctrine of justification actually emphasizes the righteousness of God. This principle is seen most vividly when we examine the necessity of an imputation of righteousness.

- God is infinite. He is without beginning or end, both in the realm of time and space as well as in the perfection of His holy character.

- God's righteousness is infinite. Just as all of the other attributes of God are infinite, so also is His righteousness infinite. This means that we cannot think of His grace as overpowering His righteousness. All of His attributes are equally infinity.

- Anything less than God's righteousness is separated from that righteousness by an infinite gulf. This is the very nature of anything that is infinite. It is always infinitely apart from the non-infinite. There can be no such thing as that which is "almost infinite."

- Therefore, the righteousness that God demands must always be an infinite righteousness, since anything less is not true righteousness by His standards. We have a tendency to look at one another in terms of different levels of relative righteousness. To say, "I'm not as bad as he is," doesn't mean that we are righteous in God's eyes. To the contrary, God says that "all our righteous deeds are like a filthy garment" (Isaiah 64:6).

- Sin is contrary to God's righteousness. This is obvious when we consider what sin is. The Westminster Confession defines sin as "any want of conformity unto or transgression of the Law of God." Sin in the Biblical sense can only be defined as that which is in violation of God's ultimate standard - His own righteousness. Paul made this very clear when he pronounced that "all have sinned and fall short of the glory of God" (Romans 3:23).

- Therefore, sin is infinite in demerit. There is an infinite gulf fixed between the righteousness of God and the sinfulness of men. Man's relative righteousness could never bridge that gulf, for even a single sin would be enough to establish it forever (and we have committed a lot more than a single sin). But that is not all. Because sin is infinite in demerit, it demands an infinite punishment against the sinner. This is why I believe that Hell will be eternal. A man could not be sent to Hell and then have his sentence completed after a certain number of years, now to be allowed into the presence of God. A single sin would be enough to condemn one for all time and eternity. It is not until you understand the awfulness of sin and its consequences that you can begin to appreciate the magnificent gift of God.

- The righteousness that God credits to the believer's account is an infinite righteousness.

    We have been credited with the righteousness of Christ. He is infinitely righteous. He has not merely imputed a portion of His righteousness to our account. Rather, the very nature of His character of complete righteousness has been credited to us. We are regarded by God as having the very righteousness of Christ.

    We can sum this concept up in three short sentences: God is righteous. God demands righteousness. God freely provides what He demands.

5.   Objections to the Doctrine of Justification by Faith.

    Several objections have been raised against the Reformed teaching that justification takes place by faith in Christ alone and apart from any works.

- It is argued that it encourages sinful living.

    Paul himself responded to this objection in his epistle to the Romans when he said, *And why not say (as we are slanderously reported and as some affirm that we say), "Let us do evil that good may come "? Their condemnation is just. (Romans 3:8).*
    The fact that Paul perceived such an objection indicates that we are correct in our understanding of the doctrine of justification. Indeed, a correct teaching of justification by faith will necessarily give rise to the question of license to live sinfully.
    Paul meets this objection with the teaching that we have been united with Christ and are therefore obligated to see ourselves as dead to sin (Romans 6:1-4). He says to us, "I have declared you to be righteous; now go and live that righteous life."

- It is argued that justification by faith is contradicted by James.

    The Council of Trent argued that James 2:14-26 contradicts the Reformed doctrine of justification by faith alone when it speaks of the importance of works.

    > *What use is it, my brethren, if a man says he has faith, but he has no works? Can that faith save him? (James 2:14).*

    There are two rhetorical questions presented in this verse. A rhetorical question is one in which the answer is assumed because it is obvious. The first rhetorical question deals with the man who claims to have faith, but has no works in his life that accompany the attested faith. It is not that he is insincere in his faith. He really might believe. But there is nothing in his life to indicate he has truly come to trust in Jesus. There has been no change in his life. He continues to have no works in his life.
    The question is asked, "What use is this kind of faith? The man was once an unbeliever and he lived his life in sin.

He now claims to be a believer and he still lives his life in sin. There has been no change. The answer to the question is obvious. It has produced no effect. Such a faith is of no use at all.

This brings us to the second question. Can this kind of faith save a man? Of what kind of faith are we speaking? It is the kind of faith that produces no change in the life of the believer. The answer is very obvious. This kind of faith cannot save anyone.

When I was a young Christian, I studied under an evangelist who taught that this question could be answered in the affirmative—that this kind of faith could save. [1] However, the Greek text makes it very clear that the question expects a negative answer. The kind of faith that does not manifest itself in works cannot save anyone. This is clarified in the ensuing verses.

> *Even so faith, if it has no work, is dead, being by itself. (James 2:17).*

There is one kind of faith that results in a changed life. It is a supernatural faith. It is a faith that God Himself beings about in the life of the one in whom He does His saving work. It is the faith that comes when God enlightens the heart of a man who has formerly lived in darkness. It is the faith of one who has been born again. This is the only kind of faith that saves.

> *21 Was not Abraham our father justified by works, when he offered up Isaac his son on the altar? 22 You see that faith was working with his works, and as a result of the works, faith was perfected; 23 and the Scripture was fulfilled which says, "And Abraham believed God, and it was reckoned to him as righteousness," and he was called the friend of God. 24 You see that a man is justified by works, and not by faith alone.*

---

[1] Stanford, A. Ray, <u>Handbook of Personal Evangelism</u>, Hollywood, FL: Florida Bible College, Pages 102-103.

(James 2:21-24).

Both Paul and James use the example of Abraham to illustrate faith (Romans 4:1-5). Abraham was the father of the Jewish nation. There is also a sense in which he is the father of the church — we are his children when we believe in the God in whom he believed.

Abraham was justified by faith when he believed the promise of God (Genesis 15:6). He was also justified by works when he offered Isaac upon the altar (Genesis 22). Which of these events took place first? The former took place over twenty years before the latter.

Do you see the difference? Paul deals with justification in the sight of God. James deals with the outward and physical demonstration and outworking of that justification.

Paul	James
Looks at the issue of justification by faith as it impacts our standing before God.	Looks at the issue of justification by works in the sight of men

• It is argued that the final judgment is on the basis of works.

There are a number of Scriptures that point out that the final judgment will be on the basis of works. It is our works that shall be judged (Ecclesiastes 12:13; Matthew 16:27; 25:31-46; John 5:29; Romans 2:5-10; 1 Corinthians 3:13; 4:5; 2 Corinthians 5:10; Galatians 6:7-9; 1 Peter 1:17).

Why are we judged by our works? Because the good works that we do are an evidence of the Holy Spirit working within us (Philippians 2:13). Only the Christian can manifest those kinds of works. And yet, we are not justified by those works in the sight of God, but the works come as a result and as an evidence of that justification.

• It is argued that the need for seeking God's forgiveness is negated.

This is the result of failing to distinguish between the wrath of God against the ungodly versus He fatherly displeasure toward His children who have sinned. Hebrews 12:5-8 speaks of the discipline of sons and this stands in contrast to God's judgment of those who are apart from Him.

Justification deals with the actions of a judge against one who is a rebellious law-breaker. Discipline deals with the actions of a loving father toward his children.

SANCTIFICATION

13 But we should always give thanks to God for you, brethren beloved by the Lord, because God has chosen you from the beginning for salvation through sanctification by the Spirit and faith in the truth. 14 And it was for this He called you through our gospel, that you may gain the glory of our Lord Jesus Christ. (2 Thessalonians 2:13-14).

The word "sanctification" simply means "to make holy." The words "sanctify" and "holy" and "saint" all describe the same thing. While we have these as separate words in our English language, both the Greek and Hebrew all translates this with a single root word.

The greatest picture of holiness is that which is presented by the prophet Isaiah. At the beginning of his ministry, this prophet came face to face with the holiness of God.

In the year of King Uzziah's death, I saw the Lord sitting on a throne, lofty and exalted, with the train of His robe filling the temple. 2 Seraphim stood above Him, each having six wings; with two he covered his face, and with two he covered his feet, and with two he flew. 3 And one called out to another and said, "Holy, Holy, Holy, is the LORD of hosts, The whole earth is full of His glory." (Isaiah 6:1-3).

Isaiah was given a rare vision. It was a vision of heaven itself and of the Lord and His glory and His angels. There was a great deal of things that could have been said to describe the character of God. The angels could have pointed to His great power. Or they could have focused upon His wisdom and His knowledge. They could have praised His grace and His lovingkindness. But instead, they focus upon His holiness.

"Holy, Holy, Holy, is the LORD of hosts!"

The royal announcement of the holiness of God is too much for Isaiah. He cannot help but to contrast the holiness of God with His own lack of holiness. Rather than singing with the angels, he finds himself woefully inadequate to speak of the holiness of God.

> *Then I said, "Woe is me, for I am ruined! Because I am a man of unclean lips, And I live among a people of unclean lips; For my eyes have seen the King, the LORD of hosts." (Isaiah 6:5).*

Coming face to face with the holiness of God will always have this effect. Peter did exactly the same thing when he was first confronted with the reality of the power of Jesus.

You remember the story. Jesus told Peter to let out the fishing nets. Peter had already spent the entire night fishing and had nothing to show for it, but he nevertheless followed the instructions of Jesus. The result was a huge catch of fish. *But when Simon Peter saw that, he fell down at Jesus' feet, saying, "Depart from me, for I am a sinful man, O Lord!" (Luke 5:8).*

1.   Sanctification in the Old Testament.

The Old Testament Hebrew uses the word קָדַשׁ (*kadash*) to refer to the idea of sanctification.

> *Then God blessed the seventh day and* **sanctified** *it, because in it He rested from all His work which God had created and made. (Genesis 2:3).*

> *"And I will meet there with the sons of Israel, and it shall be* **consecrated** *by My glory. 44 And I will* **consecrate** *the tent of meeting and the altar; I will also* **consecrate** *Aaron and his sons to minister as priests to Me." (Exodus 29:43-44).*

> *Now the word of the Lord came to me saying, "Before I formed you in the womb I knew you, and before you were born I* **consecrated** *you; I have appointed you a prophet to the nation." (Jeremiah*

1:4-5).

In each of these cases, the principle of sanctification is seen to refer to something that has been set apart from its normal usage for a special and exclusive purpose.

2.   Sanctification in the New Testament.

There are several terms which are taken from the same Greek root word found in the New Testament: Holy, saint and sanctify.

- Ἅγιος (*hagios*) - "Holy; a sanctified one (saint)."
- Ἁγιαζω (*hagiazo*) - "To Sanctify or make holy."

The root word ἅγιος literally means, "to set apart for a special purpose." Sanctification is the work of God in which He sets a believer apart, washing him from his sin and making him into the character of Christ. The Greeks used ἅγιος to describe that which had been set apart and consecrated to the gods. It was used this way of temples, altars, offerings, and even of people. Ἅγιος could also be used to describe an offering that would be given at a temple. Money that was given would now be set apart for the use of the priesthood of that temple.

When we speak of the holiness of God, we are looking at His transcendence and the fact that He is other than the rest of His creation. This sense of "otherness" is His holiness. But there is also a sense in which we are also set apart from creation. We are a called-out people who have been separated out in order to be a people of God's own possession. In this sense, there is both a negative as well as a positive aspect of sanctification.

Negative aspect of Sanctification	Positive aspect of Sanctification
We have been set apart from the world and from sin and from the dominion of Satan.	We have been set apart to God and to His good works and to righteousness and purity.

Our sanctification can be seen on three different planes: a positional standing, a progressive experience, and a future culmination.

3.   Positional Sanctification.

When Paul gave his defense before Agrippa, he made reference to *those who have been sanctified by faith* (Acts 26:18). Those who have come to faith in Christ are said to have been sanctified. The universality of this position for those who are in Christ is seen in the words of Paul to the Corinthians.

> *Paul, called as an apostle of Jesus Christ by the will of God, and Sosthenes our brother, 2 to the church of God which is at Corinth, to those who have been **sanctified** in Christ Jesus, **saints** by calling, with all who in every place call upon the name of our Lord Jesus Christ, their Lord and ours (1 Corinthians 1:1-2).*

Note that the words "saints" is merely the noun form of the word "sanctified." It points to those who have been "saint-I-fied." When we read through this epistle, we learn some things about the Corinthian believers. They had broken up the church over petty disputes. They had allowed immorality to come into the church. They were hauling each other into court and suing each other. They were dishonoring the Lord's Table. There were even some who were denying the resurrection of the dead. And yet, in spite of all these things, Paul calls them "saints" and says they have been sanctified in Christ Jesus.

Their identity was no longer rooted in their sinful condition. They had been given a new identity. They were now in Christ and that position was the source of their new identity.

There is an important implication to this truth. It means my identity is no longer rooted in my performance. Why is this important? Because my performance will always fall short of what it ought to be. I am a sinner and I am going to go on being a sinner as long as I am in this life. My performance as a Christian will always fall short of what it ought to be. What will this do to my self-esteem? If my focus is on my performance, it will drive me to frustration and then I will end up doing one of two things.

I could give up. If I honestly try to build my life on the basis of my performance, I will quickly come to the place where I am defeated. That might be for the best. God often brings us to the place where we are defeated, because only then can we see that His grace is sufficient (2 Corinthians 12:9).

Or I might try to fake it. There are many Christians who hide behind a mask of pseudo spirituality. The New Testament has a word for this. It is called a *hupokrites*. This described the Greek actor who held a mask in front of his face as he played a part in the theater. It is from this word that we derive our term "hypocrite."

Churches today are full of people who are hiding behind a mask of good works and church attendance, seeking to satisfy their self esteem by impressing other people. The reason for this is that we tend to build our self esteem on the basis of what we think other people think about us. What we need to focus on is what God thinks about us. God sees us with a new identity. He has an image of us that is exactly the same as the image of Jesus Christ.

> 16 *Therefore we do not lose heart, but though our outer man is decaying, yet our inner man is being renewed day by day.* 17 *For momentary, light affliction is producing for us an eternal weight of glory far beyond all comparison,* 18 *while we look not at the things which are seen, but at the things which are not seen; for the things which are seen are temporal, but the things which are not seen are eternal. (2 Corinthians 4:16-18).*

We are called to see ourselves in the way God sees us. God sees beyond the physical. He sees those things that are eternal. How can we see into those eternal areas? We see through the eyes of faith. We see by reading what God says in His word and by believing it.

4.   Progressive Sanctification.

> *For by one offering He has perfected for all time those who are sanctified (Hebrews 10:14).*

The Greek text is quite revealing in this passage. The word "sanctified" appears in the present tense and thus refers to "those who are being sanctified." While it is true that you were completely and totally set apart in an eternal sense when you believed in Christ, there is another sense in which you are experiencing a setting apart of yourself on a day by day basis. This is called growth.

The Shorter Catechism of the Westminster Confession of Faith gives this definition of sanctification.

> *Sanctification is the work of God's free grace, whereby we are renewed in the whole man after the image of God, and are enabled more and more to die unto sin, and live unto righteousness. (Shorter Catechism 35).*

Progressive sanctification can best be understood as we contrast it to God's work in justification and regeneration. Before we look at the differences between sanctification versus justification, we ought first to see the similarities between these two.

- Both come from the grace of God.
- Both are a part of the work of salvation that God provides.
- Both are to be found in all the converted. There is no such thing as a person who has been justified who has not also been sanctified.
- Both begin at the same time.
- Both are necessary to salvation.

Justification	Sanctification
To be declared as righteous.	To be set apart and thereby made holy or consecrated.
Justification is the *reckoning* and *counting* of a man to be righteous on the basis of the imputed righteousness of Christ.	Sanctification is the *making* of a man to be inwardly righteous.
The righteousness of justification is an imputed righteousness received by faith and is not our own.	The righteousness of sanctification is an imparted righteousness brought about in us by the Holy Spirit.
Justification is an absolute	Sanctification in the progressive sense is relative and in part.
Speaks of a work done for you.	Speaks of a work done in you.

You are declared righteous on the basis of the merits of Jesus Christ.	You are set apart for God's special use by the work of the Holy Spirit.

Both justification and sanctification...
- Come to the believer through faith (Galatians 2:16; Acts 26:18).
- Are on the basis of the blood of Christ (Romans 5:9; Hebrews 10:29; 13:12).

Justification	Regeneration	Sanctification
Delivers us from the guilt of sin	Delivers us from the power of sin	Delivers us from the presence of sin
It is done for us	It is done in us	It is done for us and in us
It is a legal declaration	It is a creative act	It is a growing process
It brings about a changed standing	It brings about a change in your very nature	It brings about a change in your life
Happens at the point of salvation		Begins with salvation and progresses
To be declared righteous	To be born again	To be set apart to God

Regeneration is sanctification begun. Sanctification is regeneration unfolding. In both cases, these involve a work of God.

> *For I am confident of this very thing, that He who began a good work in you will perfect it until the day of Christ Jesus. (Philippians 1:6).*

It is God who does the work of sanctification. He began the good work in you and He will continue it until the day of Christ Jesus. At the same time, you are called to *work out your salvation with fear and trembling; 13 for it is God who is at work in you, both to will and to work for His good pleasure (Philippians 2:12-13).* Sanctification is a work of God, but it is also a work in which we share. We labor like the farmer who plants and who plows and who waters, but it is ultimately God who gives the growth.

Another important aspect of this growth is that it takes time. God is building for eternity. He is building a work in you that is meant to last. It has been said that when God wants to grow an oak tree He takes a hundred years, but when He makes a squash, He takes only six months. God is building within you the very person of Jesus Christ. Christ is being formed in you.

My children, with whom I am again in labor
until Christ is formed in you (Galatians 4:19).

Paul speaks to the believers in Galatia and tells them that Christ is being formed in them. This takes time. There is no short cut to maturity. Searching for short cuts will lead you into dead ends and pitfalls as you attempt to use certain experiences and "second blessings" to bring you to maturity. The problem with these is that they lead you to look for the source of your growth within yourself rather than where it should be — in Christ. He is both the source as well as the goal of our sanctification.

14 As a result, we are no longer to be children, tossed here and there by waves, and carried about by every wind of doctrine, by the trickery of men, by craftiness in deceitful scheming; 15 but speaking the truth in love, we are to grow up in all aspects into Him, who is the head, even Christ, (Ephesians 4:14-15).

This is our goal. It is that we will be like Jesus Christ in all aspects. This process will continue until the day that we see Him face to face. This brings us to the destination of our sanctification.

5.   Ultimate Sanctification: *Beloved, now we are children of God, and it has not appeared as yet what we shall be. We know that, when He appears, we shall be like Him, because we shall see Him just as He is. (John 3:2).*

We have a promise for the future. It is that we shall see the Lord. When we see Him, we will be like Him. Moses asked that he might be permitted to see the glory of God, but he was only permitted to see God's "after glow." No man has ever seen the full glory of God, but there is coming a day when we shall see Him just as He is. How will that be possible? It is because we shall be like Him. We are going to be changed. The work of sanctification will have its completion. The process of growth will terminate with an eternal summer of glory. We will be like Christ. His character is today being formed in us and one day it will be completed.

Today we are saints in transition. We are never where we were, but neither are we ever where we want to be. We are a walking contradiction. Yet there is hope for the future. We will be changed. This hope for the future has an obligation for the present. This has an effect on how we live today. It gives us a goal for which to attain. This goal is stated in the following verse.

> *And everyone who has this hope fixed on Him*
> *purifies himself, just as He is pure. (1 John 3:3).*

This is a doctrine of comfort, but it is also designed to motivate us and teach us how we are to live today. It moves us to live a life of purity and holiness.

ETERNALLY SECURE

Security is something needed by everyone. This is most obvious when we look at children. They have not learned to cover their needs. One of their biggest needs is security. Our daughter once asked my wife if she and I would ever divorce. She had seen divorce pictured on television as a regular way of life and many of her friends and peers came from homes that had been broken by divorce. The splitting of a family tears apart a child's security. Everything on which the child has based a life comes crashing down. The result is often fear, hostility, and rebellion.

Children are not alone in their need for security. We all need security. There is job security, marital security, social security, but the most important thing is eternal security. The Bible is very explicit to the matter of eternal security. The reason Jesus came to earth was to provide us with a security that would be eternal.

1.   Our Security is seen in the work of Jesus.

Jesus gives words of assurance to all who follow Him when He says, *"My sheep hear My voice, and I know them, and they follow Me; 28 and I give eternal life to them, and they shall never perish; and no one shall snatch them out of My hand. 29 My Father, who has given them to Me, is greater than all; and no one is able to snatch them out of the Father's hand." (John 10:27-29).* Notice the double assurance that is given. He says that no one shall be able to snatch them out of His hand. But that is not all. He also says that no one shall be able to snatch them out of the Father's hand.

2.   Our Security is seen in the Removal of our Sins: *As far as the east is from the west, so far has He removed our transgressions from us (Psalm 103:12).*

Paul concludes his study of our salvation and then asks the rhetorical question: Can anything ever separate us from the love of Christ? In Romans 8:35-39 he lists all of the possibilities before concluding that nothing shall ever be able to separate us from the love of God.

3.   Our Security is seen in the Sealing Ministry of the Holy Spirit.

> *13 In Him, you also, after listening to the message of truth, the gospel of your salvation-- having also believed, you were sealed in Him with the Holy Spirit of promise, 14 who is given as a pledge of our inheritance, with a view to the redemption of God's own possession, to the praise of His glory. (Ephesians 1:13-14).*

The believer has been sealed by the Holy Spirit. A seal was a device, usually crafted into a signet ring or a cylinder that was engraved with the owner's name or with some identifying sign. A seal could be used to signify several things.

- Ownership: *The Spirit Himself bears witness with our spirit that we are children of God (Romans 8:16).* I have a rubber stamp with my name engraved on it. If you pick out a book from my library and look on it, you will see that it is stamped with my name on the binding. It indicates the book belongs to me. In the same way, when you placed a seal upon something in ancient times, it signified that you were the rightful owner of that property. Under Jewish law, a slave could also be stamped with a seal. A slave who wished to devote the rest of his life to the service of his master would have his ear pierced. This act would seal him as the permanent property of his master (Deuteronomy 15:12-18).

- Protection. Another significance of a seal was protection. When Pilate had the tomb of Jesus sealed with an official Roman seal, it was with the purpose of protecting the contents of the tomb from being disturbed. Anyone caught tampering with that seal would have been stopped by the Roman soldiers posted without.

- Authentication. A third purpose of a seal was authentication and verification. A seal would serve as a signature to authenticate a letter or official document. Rulers frequently wore a signet ring — a ring with an elaborate engraving identifying the wearer. The ruler would spill hot wax onto the document and then press his fist with the sealing ring into it, leaving its mark. This would authenticate the document and make it official.

The Holy Spirit accomplishes all three of these duties on behalf of the believer. He is the sign of ownership, signifying that we belong to God. He is also the sign of protection, indicating that our Heavenly Father will care for us and that nothing takes place in our life that has not first passed through a nail-scarred hand. He is also the mark of authenticity, showing by the fruit He produces in the life of a Christian that He is resident in that life.

What shall we say about the person who comes and makes a profession of faith and who, for a time, exhibits all of the characteristics of a Christian, but who then leaves and who rejects Christ? John describes this sort of person. *"They went out from us, but they were not really of us; for if they had been of us, they would have remained with us; but they went out, in order that it might be shown that they all are not of us"* (1 John 2:19). Notice what John does not say. He does not say that they lost their salvation. Rather he says in essence, "By the very fact that they left, they showed that they were not saved in the first place."

When God saves a person, a process begins that will continue throughout his entire life. Paul says, *"For I am confident of this very thing, that He who began a good work in you will perfect it until the day of Christ Jesus" (Philippians 1:6).* Sanctification is not an option in Christianity. It is for this reason that 1 John can describe a Christian as one who is continually...

- Walking in the light (1:7).
- Confessing his sins (1:9).
- Keeping the commandments (2:3; 4:7).
- Loving his brother (2:10).
- Practicing righteousness (3:10).
- Believing that Jesus is the Christ (5:1).

For this reason, I believe in the eternal security of the believer, but the eternal insecurity of the make-believer as illustrated in the following chart:

Eternal Security	A Biblical Balance	Loss of Salvation
Once a person comes to faith in Jesus Christ, they will be saved no matter whether or not they continue to believe.	It is possible for one to experience a faith for a time that is not saving faith. Such a one often falls away after a time.	A person might come to Christ and be saved and then, because of sin or unbelief, might lose that salvation and be lost.
Reads the parable of the sower and believes that only the first one is lost while the others merely suffer "loss of rewards."	The parable of the sower pictures some who initially experience a measure of spiritual growth, but who ultimately fall away and are not saved.	The parable of the sower tells of some who were initially saved but who lost their salvation because they did not endure.
Once saved, always saved; no matter what.	The perseverance of God's elect is guaranteed by the work of the Holy Spirit.	Salvation is a matter of enduring to the end.

THE PERSEVERANCE OF THE SAINTS

There are four primary views regarding the perseverance of the saints. The first three of these views have this perseverance dependent upon man and his strength. The fourth view presents God as the deciding factor in man's perseverance.

Church	View of Perseverance
Roman Catholic	Perseverance is dependent upon the uncertain obedience of man.
Lutheran	Perseverance is dependent upon man's continued faith.
Arminian	Perseverance is dependent upon the will of men to believe and upon their own continuing good works.
Reformed	Perseverance is dependent upon God.

Perseverance is much more than eternal security. While eternal security states that salvation cannot be lost, the doctrine of perseverance says that the man who is saved will continue to manifest the evidence of that salvation in this life. Berkhof defines it as "that continuous operation of the Holy Spirit in the believer, in which the work of divine grace that is begun in the heart, is continues and brought to completion" (1971:546).

This does not mean that everyone who claims to believe in Jesus Christ is necessarily saved. There are those who might be members of the church and who, for a time, exhibit the earmarks of the redeemed, yet they are not really a part of the family of God.

> *They went out from us, but they were not really of us;*
> *for if they had been of us, they would have remained with us;*
> *but they went out, in order that it might be shown that they all*
> *are not of us. (1 John 2:19).*

When a person who has called himself a Christian falls away, it does not mean he has lost his salvation. It may be an indication that he was never really saved to begin with. Nor do the Scriptures mandate that all such false brethren fall away. Jesus told the parable of the wheat and the tares and how there would be unbelievers and believers together until the Second Coming.

1.   A Confident Expectation: *For I am confident of this very thing, that He who began a good work in you will perfect it until the day of Christ Jesus (Philippians 1:6).*

What is the work that was begun in the lives of the Philippians? In one sense, it was seen in the gifts they had given to Paul for the ministry. But in a larger sense, it was the work of God that was taking place in their lives to bring about those gifts. The Christian life is a work in progress, but it is a work that is headed toward a specific goal. Paul expresses his confidence that the work will be "perfected" — the Greek word ἐπιτελέσει
that the work will be "over-completed."

Notice who is doing the work versus who is the recipient of that work. It is God who is doing the work and the work He is doing is "in you."

2.   A Dependence upon God's Faithfulness: *But the Lord is faithful, and He will strengthen and protect you from the evil one (2 Thessalonians 3:3).*

The perseverance of the saints is dependent upon the faithfulness of the Lord. He is the One who will accomplish your strengthening and protection.

> 7 *...so that you are not lacking in any gift, awaiting eagerly the revelation of our Lord Jesus Christ, 8 who shall also confirm you to the end, blameless in the day of our Lord Jesus Christ. 9 God is faithful, through whom you were called into fellowship with His Son, Jesus Christ our Lord. (1 Corinthians 1:7-9).*

This promise was given to the Corinthian believers. As we read through the epistle to the Corinthians, we can easily note that these people did not look blameless. They appeared to be anything but blameless. But that is because God was not yet finished with them.

When we speak of the perseverance of the saints, there is a sense in which it is a misnomer. It is not really the perseverance of the saints that is described here. What we see in this passage and others like it is the perseverance of the Lord Jesus Christ. The saints do not persevere because they grit their teeth and struggle to successfully overcome every obstacle. They persevere because God is faithful. He has promised that He will bring us to perfection and He can be trusted to accomplish his promises.

A promise is not stronger than the character of the one who makes the promise. If I promise something to you, it might not come to pass because I might fail you. But God never fails. He never falls down on the job. He never changes His mind. If He has promised you something, you can rest on His promise with complete assurance.

None of those who have been saved will ever be lost. You have God's word on that. If you belong to Him, then He will keep you and confirm you to the end.

3.   A Dependence upon God's Power: *Now to Him who is able to keep you from stumbling, and to make you stand in the presence of His glory blameless with great joy (Jude 1:24).*

The doctrine of the perseverance of the saints reflects a faith and a dependence upon the power of God. It is God who is able to keep you from stumbling. It is God who is able to make you stand as blameless in the presence of His glory. The same God who promised to save you also assures that He is able to keep that promise.

Ecclesiology

The Doctrine of the Church

The term "ecclesiology" refers to the study of the church. In developing a philosophy of the church, it will be helpful to first see the church as a whole before examining the particulars.

WHAT IS THE CHURCH?

Our English word "church" is translated from the Greek word ἐκκλησια (*ekklesia*). It is a compound word made up of the joining of two Greek words.

- Εκ (*ek*): "Out of"
- Καλεω (*kaleo*): "To call."

The resulting word describes a called-out assembly. It can refer to a secular assembly, a legal assembly, or to a religious assembly. It is the last usage that we normally see in the New Testament when we hear the word "church." As such, it can refer to four different types of church.

1.   The Local Congregation.

This is the most common use of the word in the New Testament. It refers to the gathering of people into a local congregation. In 1 Corinthians 1:2, Paul addresses his epistle to the church of God which is at Corinth.

2.   The Universal Church.

This speaks of the complete body of Christ, made up of all believers throughout the world and throughout all time. Ephesians

1:22 speaks of the universal church when it describes Jesus being the head of the church (see also Ephesians 5:23-24). In the same way, Ephesians 3:10 speaks of the manifold wisdom of God being given to the church.

3.   A Group of Local Congregations.

The word "church" can be used of a group of local congregations in a particular area that goes beyond a single group of people.

- Acts 9:31 tells us how *the church throughout all Judea and Galilee and Samaria enjoyed peace.* [2] It might be argued that these local congregations were merely the local manifestation of the universal church.
- The Jerusalem Church was of a size that made it obvious that it met as a number of congregations, yet it is described in the Bible as a single church.
- House churches met as a part of the local church (1 Corinthians 16:19; Romans 16:3-5; Colossians 4:15-26; Philemon 1:2).

THE UNIVERSAL CHURCH

There are five major and foundational truths set forth in the Scriptures concerning the universal church that play a vital part in our understanding of how the church functions and operates.

1.   There is only One Church: *There is one body and one Spirit, just as also you were called in one hope of your calling (Ephesians 4:4).*

The fact that there is one church is to be the basis of unity among believers. This becomes immediately obvious if we examine the context of Ephesians 4:4. This unity is so strong that it is to break past any prejudices between Jew or Gentiles, male or female, slave or free. This means there is not to be one church for Jews and another for Gentiles. There is not to be one church for slaves and

[2] This reading is generally preferred to that of the Textus Receptus which reads "churches," making it plural.

another for free men. We are all one in Christ.

This principle has some implications with regard to Dispensationalism—the view that God has two separate and distinct assemblies of people in Israel and the church. By contrast, Paul says that there is only one assembly of God's people. There is only one church. It had an Old Testament manifestation, but it is one church.

2.   Jesus Christ is the Head of the Church: *For the husband is the head of the wife, as Christ also is the head of the church, He Himself being the Savior of the body (Ephesians 5:23); He is also head of the body, the church... (Colossians 1:18).*

The head is the most important part of any body. It is indispensable. Even the heart can be transplanted and replaced, but a body without its head is unthinkable. Just as a human body is controlled and directed by its head, so also the church is to be controlled and directed by its Head, Jesus Christ. He is the leader of the church, its Chief Shepherd (1 Peter 5:4), and its High Priest (Hebrews 9:11).

3.   The Church is Holy: *Do you not know that you are a temple of God, and that the Spirit of God dwells in you? 17 If any man destroys the temple of God, God will destroy him, for the temple of God is holy, and that is what you are. (1 Corinthians 3:16-17).*

Notice that Paul does not say merely that the church will someday become holy. It is holy right now. This quality of holiness indicates that which is set apart from the world and set apart from the sinfulness and impurity of the world and set apart for a special purpose. Though the church is still in the world, it is no longer of the world.

4.   Every Believer is a Priest of God.

In the Old Testament economy, God set apart a group of men who were designated as priests. They were the sons of Aaron from the tribe of Levi. They wore special robes and were given the responsibility of ministering in the temple. They were the only ones who could enter into the temple. They were the only ones authorized to administer the sacrifices. In this way, they served as mediators between God and men.

Jesus Christ did away with this system by becoming our

perfect High Priest, offering up Himself as the perfect sacrifice. He also brought about an assembly in which every member is a priest.

> *...you also, as living stones, are being built up as a spiritual house for a holy priesthood, to offer up spiritual sacrifices acceptable to God through Jesus Christ (1 Peter 2:5).*

> *But you are a chosen race, a royal priesthood, a holy nation, a people for God's own possession, that you may proclaim the excellencies of Him who has called you out of darkness into His marvelous light (1 Peter 2:9).*

Every member of the body of Christ has been set apart and consecrated as a priest of God. This is a special priesthood. It is called a "royal priesthood." The priesthood in the Old Testament economy was never known by this title. This priesthood is unique in that it does not come down through Aaron, but through the King of kings, Jesus Christ.

5.   The Mandate of the church is to Make Disciples.

This mandate was given in the last words of Jesus to His disciples before he departed to heaven. It was a command to make disciples of all men.

> *Go therefore and make disciples of all the nations, baptizing them in the name of the Father and the Son and the Holy Spirit, 20 teaching them to observe all that I commanded you; and lo, I am with you always, even to the end of the age. (Matthew 28:19-20).*

The main verb of this passage and therefore the primary command is to "make disciples." The other verbs are all given in the Greek text as participles and thus describe the steps that are to be used in making disciples.

- Going. The church is to be mission-minded. It is not to have a fortress mentality in which it isolates itself from the world. Instead, it is to be invading the world, going out to accomplish its work of making disciples.

- Baptizing. The reference to baptism is a summarization of the evangelistic and conversion ministry of the church. Baptism is the outward sign of such inner conversion.
- Teaching. It is not enough to make converts. The business of the church is to take those converts and to train them so that they will become disciple makers.

UNIVERSAL PRINCIPLES FOR A LOCAL CHURCH

The five principles we have just examined are very basic and are generally met with agreement by all within the realm of Christian orthodoxy. However, there is considerably less agreement as to how we are to take these principles and put them into practice within the local church.

The point should be made that the Bible never makes a clear distinction between the universal church versus the local church. It is because of this lack of a distinction that I want to suggest the local church is to be seen as a microcosm of the universal church. The qualities that are true of the universal church are to be mirrored in the practices of the local church.

1.   There is Only One Church.

        This principle is to be demonstrated in the face of the differences that exist within the church. It requires us to hold to our unity in the face of our disagreements. The obvious question arises as to the place of denominations within Christianity. I believe the answer is just as obvious — they have come about as a result of sin in the church.

        Does this mean we should take a stance of non-denominationalism? Not necessarily, since the very stance of non-denominationalism has become in itself a denomination of its own. What it does mean is that the Christian church should always be ready to unite and to work with other Christians at whichever level it is able. There will be times when, due to differing doctrinal persuasions, this will not be possible. But the effort should be made to break down the barriers whenever possible.

2.   Jesus Christ is the Head of the Church.

Most local churches are ruled by a head known as the pastor, the preacher, the reverend, or some other exalted title. This is a very old tradition, going all the way back to the apostolic fathers and witnessed as early as the epistles of Ignatius. However, such a tradition is remarkably absent from the pages of the New Testament. Instead of a one-man-rule, we see the pattern of a plurality of elders within the book of Acts and in the epistles.

Not once in the New Testament is any one man besides Jesus Christ held up as the leader of any local church. Even when Paul speaks of those particular elders who rule well and who are considered worthy of double honor (1 Timothy 5:17), he refers to them in the plural.

In a day when too many churches have departed from this Biblical pattern, it is not surprising that people tend to focus their attention on the man in the pulpit rather than on the true Head of the church. The adoption of this principle will have a tremendous effect upon the direction of the church. Most churches derive their vision and their identity from one man — the senior pastor. If he is primarily an evangelist, then the church will have evangelism as its primary emphasis to the exclusion of other aspects of ministry.

However, a plurality of leaders allows for emphasis and vision in different areas of ministry within the church because different leaders will focus their efforts along the separate lines in which they have been gifted. This does not preclude having a single man who serves as the senior pastor, but it allows other leaders to utilize their own gifts within the church.

3.   The Church is Holy.

The holiness of the local church is to be manifested in both doctrinal and practical purity. This brings up the question as to the level of doctrinal purity. At what point is doctrine to cause division within the church? Many artificial lines have been drawn by well-meaning people, but I think they have been generally drawn without regard for an appreciation of the relationship of the universal church to the local church.

The doctrinal purity is to be such that the requirements for entrance into the local church ought to be no more and no less than the requirements for entrance into God's universal church. The requirement is one of true and sincere repentance and faith in the Lord Jesus Christ.

The Scriptures give us very specific guidelines as to the

maintaining of practical purity within the church, both through the positive means of exhorting and encouraging us, as well as through the negative means of discipline and excommunication.

4.   Every Believer is a Priest of God.

The priesthood of the believer ought to be manifested within the local church in a way that is similar to the way in which the Aaronic priesthood was manifested under the Old Testament economy. How was the Aaronic priesthood manifested? The priest was one who performed the service of worship on behalf of the people.

Today's church services are often constituted as a spectator sport in which the participation o the audience/congregation is limited to singing and putting money into the offering plate. The pattern displayed in the New Testament is quite different.

> *What is the outcome then, brethren? When you assemble, each one has a psalm, has a teaching, has a revelation, has a tongue, has an interpretation. Let all things be done for edification. (1 Corinthians 14:26).*

This picture of the meeting of the early church is one of group participation in which every believer served as a priest to every other member of the group. This was not to be done in as disorganized manner, but neither was it so restricted in its regulation that it was only the ministry of a single individual.

> *29 And let two or three prophets speak, and let the others pass judgment. 30 But if a revelation is made to another who is seated, let the first keep silent. 31 For you can all prophesy one by one, so that all may learn and all may be exhorted; 32 and the spirits of prophets are subject to prophets; 33 for God is not a God of confusion but of peace, as in all the churches of the saints. (1 Corinthians 14:29-33).*

The preaching and teaching and exhortation and prayers of the church were never designed to by only the activity of a single man. Paul's language makes it clear that there is to be a plurality among those who preach and prophecy in the meeting of the church. There are several reasons for this.

First of all, it is so that there can be a system of checks and balances within the meeting of the church. This is to guard against a single pastor going off the deep end. The other leaders of the church are to keep him answerable to the word of God.

Secondly, this pluralization of ministry is so that the Spirit can minister to the body through a multiplicity of spiritual gifts. I have yet to meet a single person who possesses in himself all of the spiritual gifts. The tendency within a typical one-man-ministry is to focus only upon those gifts that the one man in the pulpit possesses. By divesting the leadership of the church into a number of different men, the focus of that ministry ceases to be limited.

5.   The Mandate of the Church is to Make Disciples.

The primary duty of the church is not to stop abortion or to elect Republicans into political office or to close down all ungodly establishments by passing Christian legislation. That is not to say that Christians should not be involved in these issues, but it does mean that this should never become the primary focus of the church. The church is to make disciples. The way in which this is to be accomplished has already been laid out for us.

- Going: The work of evangelism is not to take place exclusively or even primarily within the walls of the church or its regular meeting. This is not to say that the gospel cannot be presented within the worship service, but it does mean that our emphasis should be in taking the gospel to those who are outside of the church.
- Baptizing: The church is to have an emphasis on evangelism and in converting people to the cause of Christ.
- Teaching: Once converts have been made, then it is the business of the church to train them up in the faith so they can be involved in this same ministry. Paul gave these instructions about passing on the faith: *And the things which you have heard from me in the presence of many witnesses, these entrust to faithful men, who will be able to teach others also (2 Timothy 2:2).*

THE IMPORTANCE OF A PROPER VIEW OF THE CHURCH

One's view of the church and of prioritizing the various aspects of the church will have a major effect upon how ministry is structured. This is observed in the major Christian denominations.

Roman Catholicism	Sees the Mass as being central to the church. For this reason, there is limited emphasis upon preaching, to the extent that for much of the history of the church the Mass was conducted in a foreign language.
Reformed Tradition	Placed a high priority upon the reading and study of the Scriptures. The sermon was seen as central.
Baptist	Tends to view evangelism as preeminent and this is the basis for the "altar call" and the "pulpit evangelism" that characterizes the service.
Charismatic	Their priority is a "worship experience" that emphasizes group interaction and participation within the service.

A view of the church also has an influence on how the church relates to society. This has had a major impact in the church in history.

Roman Catholicism	Sees the church as properly being over society. All things, including government, are to be subservient to the church
Reformed Tradition	Sees the church as exerting transformation influence upon society as it is salt and light to the earth. This mandates the church's involvement in politics and social issues.
Baptist & Independent Churches	They have often adopted a stance of separation of church and state that sees the church as separated from and having nothing to do with society.

Religious Liberalism	This is the exact opposite of the Reformed Tradition. It attempts to make the church a part of society by transforming the church so that it fits the patterns and morals of society. Thus if society affirms homosexuality, the church will also accept and affirm a homosexual lifestyle.

METAPHORS OF THE CHURCH

The Bible uses a number of word pictures to portray the church. We call these pictures "metaphors." In each of these metaphors, a physical object is used to illustrate some specific aspect of the church.

1.   The Church as a Body.

> *For even as the body is one and yet has many members, and all the members of the body, though they are many, are one body, so also is Christ. 13 For by one Spirit we were all baptized into one body, whether Jews or Greeks, whether slaves or free, and we were all made to drink of one Spirit. (1 Corinthians 12:12-13).*

The point made by Paul in this passage is that the church is much more than an organization. It is an organic living body. Though it is composed of many different parts, it is still a single body. This has several ramifications.

- The principle of unity: There is to be unity within the church. A body that is divided is soon a corpse. If the church is to be healthy and alive, it also needs to be united.
- The principle of diversity: This means there should be diversity within the unity of the body. Just as the body is made up only of arms or only of legs or only of eyes, so the church is not to be made up only of pastors or only of evangelists or only of exhorters.
- The principle of headship: Jesus is the head of the body. Each of these metaphors has a focus upon Jesus as the leader of the church.

2.   The Church is a Vine.

We no longer live in an agricultural economy, so we are not as attuned to such metaphors. This particular symbol is drawn from the Old Testament nation of Israel.

> 8 *Thou didst remove a vine from Egypt;*
> *Thou didst drive out the nations, and didst plant it.*
> 9 *Thou didst clear the ground before it,*
> *And it took deep root and filled the land. (Psalm 80:8-9).*

The nation of Israel was God's vine. He chose Israel out from all of the other nations of the world to be His own nation and His own people. Like a farmer who chooses one vine out of his vineyard upon which he bestows special care, so the Lord brought Israel out of Egypt and planted her in a cultivated field of His own choosing, giving her His law and His ordinances. However, there came a time of harvest. It was a time for God's nation to produce fruit.

> *Let me sing now for my well-beloved A song of my beloved concerning His vineyard. My well-beloved had a vineyard on a fertile hill. 2 And He dug it all around, removed its stones, And planted it with the choicest vine. And He built a tower in the middle of it, And hewed out a wine vat in it; Then He expected it to produce good grapes, But it produced only worthless ones. (Isaiah 5:1-2).*

After all the care and devotion that the Lord gave for His vine, when the time arrived that there should be fruit, the fruit that was produced was not of a kind to be desired. It was fruit, but it was not the right kind of fruit. Isaiah goes on to say in verse 7 that the Lord *looked for justice, but behold, bloodshed; for righteousness, but behold, a cry of distress.*

Jesus takes this same analogy of the vine of the Lord and adds something new and different. He says that He is the vine and that we are only considered to be a part of that vine if we are connected to Him.

> *I am the true vine, and My Father is the vinedresser. 2 Every branch in Me that does not bear*

> *fruit, He takes away; and every branch that bears*
> *fruit, He prunes it, that it may bear more fruit. (John*
> *15:1-2).*

As the vine, Jesus is the source of nourishment to all of the branches that make up its different parts. When Jesus calls Himself the true vine, He seems to be distinguishing Himself from those other false vines that might claim to be vines in their own right.

The principle that is the key ingredient in the fruitfulness of the church is centered in its relationship with the Lord. It is only as the branch is connected to the vine that it is able to bear fruit. Cut a branch from the vine and you also cut it off from the very source of life. Inversely, it is by the fruitfulness of the branch that you can tell whether it is connected to the vine.

3.   The Church is a House.

> *So then you are no longer strangers and*
> *aliens, but you are fellow citizens with the saints, and*
> *are of God's household, 20 having been built upon the*
> *foundation of the apostles and prophets, Christ Jesus*
> *Himself being the corner stone, 21 in whom the whole*
> *building, being fitted together is growing into a holy*
> *temple in the Lord; 22 in whom you also are being*
> *built together into a dwelling of God in the Spirit.*
> *(Ephesians 2:19-22).*

The concept of the house of God goes back to the Old Testament. When Moses led the Israelites into the wilderness, God gave specific instructions for the building of a tabernacle. When it was completed, the presence of God, as manifested by the cloud, came and rested upon the tent of meeting.

Later, when the tabernacle was replaced by Solomon's temple, the same cloud was seen to fill the temple, signifying that God had moved into His house. Likewise, the prophets of the exile spoke of the presence of the Lord departing from His temple. Even when the temple was rebuilt after the Babylonian Captivity, the post-Exilic prophets would do no more than promise that one day the Lord would return to His temple.

When Jesus spoke of the temple of God being destroyed and raised again in three days, He was referring to the temple of His body (John 2:19-21). In Him all of the fulness of the Godhead was pleased to dwell (Colossians 1:19). The New Testament teaches us that the church is the house and the temple of God, both individually as well as collectively.

- Collectively the church is the temple of God: *Do you not know that you are a temple of God, and that the Spirit of God dwells in you? (1 Corinthians 3:16).*
- Individually each member of the church is a temple of God: *Or do you not know that your body is a temple of the Holy Spirit who is in you, whom you have from God, and that you are not your own? (1 Corinthians 6:19).*

We should understand it is not the physical structure in which the meeting of the church is held that is to receive such a high priority as the people who meet within that structure. They are the church. A church that recognizes this principle will not place so much emphasis upon the physical church structure and will center its attention on people.

4.   The Church is a Bride.

The nation of Israel was often described in the Old Testament as the wife of the Lord. The Song of Solomon was not only an ancient love story, it was also seen to be a picture between Yahweh and Israel. Likewise, Hosea's adulterous wife was a type of Israel going after false gods.

The same imagery is seen of the New Testament Church. In Ephesians 5:25-33, as Paul presents an exhortation to husbands and wives, he said that these same truths apply to Christ and to the church. As such, the church is to be chaste, giving her single minded attention to her husband, We are not called to be "once-a-week saints."

5.   The Church is a Kingdom.

God promised to Abraham that He would make him a great nation (Genesis 12:2). When Moses led the Israelites from Egypt, God said they would be "a kingdom of priests and a holy nation" (Exodus 19:6). This same language is used by Peter to refer to the church.

But you are a chosen race, a royal priesthood,

> *a holy nation, a people for God's own possession, that*
> *you may proclaim the excellencies of Him who has*
> *called you out of darkness into His marvelous light (1*
> *Peter 2:9).*

In the nation of Israel, the priesthood came through the line of Aaron while the kingly line descended from the tribe of Judah. During the days of the Old Testament, one could be a priest or one could be a king, but one could not be both. However, in the new kingdom there is a royal priesthood after the order of the very first priest-king, Melchizedek. The fact of the kingship of Christ means that, although we are still in this world, it no longer holds our citizenship. We have now become citizens of another kingdom.

6.   The Church is a Flock.

The Lord in the Old Testament often described Himself as the Shepherd of Israel. Psalm 23 starts off by saying, "The Lord is my shepherd." Throughout Ezekiel 34, the Lord refers to the nation of Israel as His flock.

Jesus takes up this same title for Himself in John 10:1-18, saying in verse 14, *"I am the good shepherd; the good shepherd lays down His life for the sheep."* We are the sheep who belong to the Good Shepherd and, as His flock, we are called to follow our Shepherd with faith and obedience, listening to His voice so that we will recognize Him.

The description of the church as a flock is not particularly complementary. Sheep are not known for their obedience, their nobility, or their bravery. Sheep are known for their helplessness.

7.   The Church is a Family.

Jesus speaks of entrance into spiritual life as being born again. When you are born, you find yourself entering into a family. We have been born again into the family of God and we have been given the privilege of calling ourselves the children of God (John 1:12). We have received an adoption—a placement into God's family as legal children and heirs. With this privilege comes great responsibility. We are to act the part of God's children.

THE ORGANIZATION OF THE CHURCH

When we begin to speak about the organization and the structure of the church, some people will object that we are trying to bring alien forms and trying to impose them upon the body of Christ. "The church is a natural organism," they say. "You should just let it be itself."

The problem with this line of thinking is that even natural organisms have their own organization and structure. We have a God of organization and structure who tells us to *let all things be done properly and in an orderly manner (1 Corinthians 14:40)*. The Lord established the form of government for His church by means of the officers that he gave for the duty of oversight. This is stated in Paul's address to the Ephesian elders:

> *Be on guard for yourselves and for all the flock, among which the Holy Spirit has made you overseers, to shepherd the church of God which He purchased with His own blood. (Acts 20:28).*

Notice who it was that made these men overseers in the church. It was not Paul or any of the other apostles. It was the Holy Spirit. This is the principle of Just Divinum — "Divine Right."

1.   The Principle of Divine Right.

        This principle has been used in the past to say that kings received a divine right from heaven to rule over their nations. I am not so sure that the principle necessarily applies to all forms of human government, but I do think it applies to church government. The Lord Himself ordained leadership within the church and we are called to be respectful of such leadership.

2.   The Regulative Principle.

        This principle states that God regulates His church and the activity that goes on in His church. Practically speaking, it means that God regulates how He is to be worshiped. We are not free to worship God in any way we like. He demands that He be worshiped in the ways in which He has ordered. This is vividly illustrated in Leviticus 10:1 when Nadab and Abihu attempted to worship the Lord using "strange fire," that is, fire that was not according to that which had been prescribed by God. They were struck dead for their transgression.

The church has had some very different ideas concerning the regulative principle. Luther and Calvin each came into the Reformation with a kettle full of traditions in worship. Luther said, "Let's take anything that is condemned by the Scriptures out of the kettle." Calvin said, "Let's dump the kettle and anything that the Bible teaches about worship can go back into it."

Roman Catholic & Lutheran	Reformed Tradition
We are free to worship the Lord in any way that is not forbidden.	We are to worship the Lord only in those ways He has commanded.
That which is not expressly forbidden in the Scriptures is permitted.	That which is not expressly commanded in the Scriptures is forbidden.

The Reformed view of worship has some very practical implications. It means you cannot say, "I know that Jesus taught His disciples to pray to the Father, but I would like to pray to the Virgin Mary." You are not allowed to worship any way you like. You are to worship God in the way He likes. You are to follow the pattern of worship set forth in the Bible.

3.   A Responsible Leadership.

> *Obey your leaders, and submit to them; for they keep watch over your souls, as those who will give an account. Let them do this with joy and not with grief, for this would be unprofitable for you. (Hebrews 13:17).*

It is a very heavy responsibility to be an elder or a deacon in the church. Leaders will have to give an accounting of their people to the Lord. Notice that there is a dynamic overlapping tension between leaders and the people they lead. Leaders are responsible to lead in a way that shows their submission to the Lord and those whom they lead are to follow in a way that shows that same submission. This results in a two-fold responsibility, both to those who lead as well as to those who are to be led:

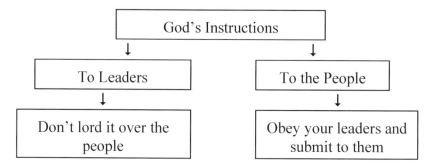

On the one hand, God says to the leaders, "Don't get carried away with your authority." But when those whom they lead are tempted to say, "That's right, they can't tell me what to do," the Lord says to them, "You obey those leaders and submit to them."

4.   The Revelation of God's Plan for Church Organization.

How has Jesus manifested how He wants His church ordered? Did He preach a sermon entitled, "Rules for Church Structure?" No. He has used to specific means:

   •   Explicit teaching.
   •   Apostolic example.

All Christians agree on the first point — that certain passages of the Bible give explicit teachings that ought to be followed. It is this second area, that of apostolic example, that leads to greater uncertainty. Are we to follow the example of the apostles? Are their examples to be normative to us today? I submit that under certain conditions their example is to be considered both normative as well as didactic.

a.   All Scripture is profitable. When Paul says in 2 Timothy 3:16-17 that *all Scripture is inspired by God and is profitable*, he does not say that the applies only to the teachings portions of Scripture.

b.   Historical passages are didactic. The New Testament states in a number of instances that the Bible is written for our instruction. This is often stated in a context that cites historical episodes (1 Corinthians 10:6; 10:11; Romans 4:23-24; 15:4). If an Old Testament historical passage can give us principles of how we ought to live, how much more will a

New Testament historical passage give us normative principles?

c. The representative character of the apostles: *So then you are no longer strangers and aliens, but you are fellow citizens with the saints, and are of God's household, 20 having been built upon the foundation of the apostles and prophets, Christ Jesus Himself being the corner stone (Ephesians 2:19-20).* The apostles were given by Christ to begin His church. That was their function. Because of this design function, their actions should be considered both significant and normative.

- Paul speaks of his teaching in all the churches (1 Corinthians 7:17).
- There was a practice in all of the churches that was to be seen as a pattern to be followed (1 Corinthians 11:16).
- Paul's written instructions were, in effect, the Lord's commandments (1 Corinthians 14:37).
- Paul and Silas gave to the churches decrees that had been established by the Jerusalem council that were to be observed (Acts 16:4).
- Paul writes so that people would know how they are to act within the church of God (1 Timothy 3:14-15).
- Paul calls his readers to join him in following his example, and to observe those who walk according to the pattern they have in him (Philippians 3:17; 4:9).

In 1 Corinthians 11:1, Paul calls the believers in that city to be imitators of himself. He then cites the traditions he delivered to them (11:2). When the gospels make mention of the traditions of men, it is in a negative sense, but the traditions described in the epistles are all to be obeyed.

d. The historical and didactic passages can be seen in parallel to one another. They are not contradictory, but complementary.

Subject	Example	Teaching
Elders	Acts 14:23	Titus 1:5

Authority in the Church	Acts 16:4	1 Thessalonians 5:12-13
Laying on of hands	Acts 6:6; 1 Timothy 4:14; 2 Timothy 1:6	1 Timothy 5:22

This is not to say that every practice ever mentioned in the New Testament must necessarily be followed. We must ask whether the practice was local or universally followed and whether there was a principle to be found behind the practice.

THE MEETING OF THE CHURCH

1.   The Purpose of the Meeting.

In the book of Hebrews, the writer gives several admonitions to Christians. One of these involves a warning against the forsaking of the practice of assembly.

> *Let us hold fast the confession of our hope without wavering, for He who promised is faithful; 24 and let us consider how to stimulate one another to love and good deeds, 25 not forsaking our own assembling together, as is the habit of some, but encouraging one another; and all the more, as you see the day drawing near. (Hebrews 10:23-25).*

All Christians are to hold fast to the faith. The reason we can do this is seen in verse 23. It is because we have been given promises from One who is in the promise-keeping business. He is faithful. We are to hold to the faith and we are to consider how to stimulate one another to love and good deeds. This is only accomplished in a group. It is only accomplished when we assemble together.

I could go off on my own and live the Christian life as a hermit. But I wouldn't. Neither would you. We need each other in order to grow. The further along we get, the more we need each other. We will never be too old or too spiritual to outgrow this need.

2.   The Pattern of the Meeting.

Most of us today are used to a meeting in which a song leader or a worship team gets up and leads everyone in the music of the church. Then the preacher gets up and does all of the talking in the church. In such a service, the role of the people is very limited. Their role is to sit and to listen and to try not to fall asleep. That is not the New Testament pattern for the church. The service in the New Testament church was characterized by corporate involvement.

> *What is the outcome then, brethren? When you assemble, each one has a psalm, has a teaching, has a revelation, has a tongue, has an interpretation. Let all things be done for edification. (1 Corinthians 14:26).*

> *And do not get drunk with wine, for that is dissipation, but be filled with the Spirit, 19 speaking to one another in psalms and hymns and spiritual songs, singing and making melody with your heart to the Lord; 20 always giving thanks for all things in the name of our Lord Jesus Christ to God, even the Father; 21 and be subject to one another in the fear of Christ. (Ephesians 5:18-21).*

> *Let the word of Christ richly dwell within you, with all wisdom teaching and admonishing one another with psalms and hymns and spiritual songs, singing with thankfulness in your hearts to God. (Colossians 3:16).*

Notice who was involved in the meeting of the New Testament church. It was not just the elders or the deacons. It was not just the seminary or Bible college graduates. It was not just the ordained ministers. The meeting of the church was made of the various members of the church who were involved in teaching, in the giving of a revelation, in the speaking and interpreting of a language, in the sharing of a song or a psalm.

The members of the church enjoyed the exercise of their spiritual gifts in the meeting of the church. This was the place where they came to use their spiritual gifts. The result was that the entire body was edified. Paul does not say that he wants the believers to stop doing this. Instead he wants them to regulate it.

443

- They are to speak one at a time.
- They are to take turns speaking.
- Only three representing each gift is to speak.

I personally believe we need a return to this kind of corporate life. I am not saying that it needs to become a disorganized mob. That was the problem Paul dealt with in Corinth. But we have a tendency to go to the other extreme. We tend to be so regulated that we have regulated the use of spiritual gifts right out of the church.

DISCIPLINE IN THE CHURCH

Confrontation is necessary to a healthy relationship. This is seen in marriage. If you are married, then you know that confrontation is sometimes necessary. I did not say that it is pleasant. But it is healthy. It clears the air.

When Paula and I were first married, we really did not know how to engage in constructive confrontation within the realm of our marriage. I would see something that she did that bothered me and I would hold it in and think about it and it would fester and grow, but I would not say anything. Likewise, Paula would get her feelings hurt and would go off and pout and not say anything. By the time the problem came out into the open, what had started out as a minor matter had grown and grown until it was affecting our relationship. Fortunately, we are both a lot older and a lot wiser now. We have learned the value of immediate constructive confrontation in our marriage.

The same is true of the church. We pick up the idea that it is not spiritual to confront other believers when they have offended us. As a result, we hold it in and let it fester and grow until it begins to affect our Christian walk.

1.   A Pattern for Church Discipline.

Jesus Himself gave what is considered to be the classic pattern for conducting discipline within the church.

> 15 *And if your brother sins, go and reprove him in private; if he listens to you, you have won your brother.* 16 *But if he does not listen to you, take one or two more with you, so that by the mouth of two or three witnesses every fact may be confirmed.* 17 *And if*

he refuses to listen to them, tell it to the church; and if he refuses to listen even to the church, let him be to you as a Gentile and a tax-gatherer. 18 Truly I say to you, whatever you shall bind on earth shall be bound in heaven; and whatever you loose on earth shall be loosed in heaven. 19 Again I say to you, that if two of you agree on earth about anything that they may ask, it shall be done for them by My Father who is in heaven. 20 For where two or three have gathered together in My name, there I am in their midst. (Matthew 18:15-20).

There is a progression given here that moves from the small to the large. It begins with a one-on-one situation. It ends before the courts of both heaven and earth.

•   Step One: *If your brother sins, go and reprove him in private (18:15).*

Our problem is that we usually run to a third party from the outset. This is gossip and should not take place. The Bible presents us with a pattern for confrontational Christianity.

Why is church discipline so important? Because it gives glory to Christ because it is obedient to His command. It is also important because it serves to restore the wayward brother and thus preserves the unity of the church.

•   Step Two: *If he does not listen to you, take one or two more with you (18:16).*

In giving this step, Jesus is quoting directly from Deuteronomy 17. It is a passage that stresses the importance of witnesses. Why are the witnesses necessary? So that you can gang up on the guilty party? No. It is so that they can make certain that what is said is understood. They are there to further the process of communication.

There is usually a direct correlation between the intensity of your anger at an insult and your lack of understanding of what was really said. There is also usually a correlation between the intensity of your anger and your ability to accurately express yourself. That is why you need a neutral third party.

- Step Three: *And if he refuses to listen to them, tell it to the church (18:17).*

     This does not necessarily mean all of the dirty laundry and all the gory details must be broadcast to every member of the congregation. I want to suggest that we tell it to the church by taking it to the representatives of the church made up of the elders and overseers. Beyond this, we make the announcement as public as the sin.

- Step Four: *If he refuses to listen to them, tell it to the church; and if he refuses to listen even to the church, let him be to you as a Gentile and a tax-gatherer (18:17).*

     This is the principle of excommunication. The sinner is excluded from the fellowship of the Lord's table. It is important that excommunication does not come merely as the result of sin. If that were the case, then nobody would be left in the church. Excommunication has to do with repentance. It comes when the sinner refuses to hear the words of the church and a call to repentance. It comes as a result of rebellion and a desire to continue in sin.

Rebellion and sin against God are contagious. Remember the story of Joshua and Achan at the battle of Ai? Achan and his family were put to death because of his sin. Why? Because sin does not affect just one person. It spreads like a cancer and can affect an entire church.

At this point, we ought to clarify that we are not speaking of throwing people out of the church for spitting on the sidewalk or for chewing gum on Sunday or for falling asleep during the sermon. This is speaking of serious unrepentant sin. Once a person repents of sin, then the next step is restoration to the church.

Furthermore, in the case of public sin, the church is not required to go all the way back to step one. Paul was not doing wrong in 1 Corinthians 5:1-5 when he told the church at Corinth to move directly to step four and to remove the one who was unrepentant in his public sin.

2.   The Power of Church Discipline.

> 18 *"Truly I say to you, whatever you shall bind on earth shall be bound in heaven; and whatever you loose on earth shall be loosed in heaven. 19 Again I say to you, that if two of you agree on earth about anything that they may ask, it shall be done for them by My Father who is in heaven. 20 For where two or three have gathered together in My name, there I am in their midst." (Matthew 18:18-20).*

This passage has been used out of context to teach a variety of things. However, when we consider the context, we are reminded that it is not speaking primarily of prayer. It is speaking of church discipline. What is it saying? It says that when the church agrees on discipline, there is a heavenly authority that is also in agreement.

What happens in church is not confined to a building. It has ripples that are felt in heaven. When two people exchange wedding vows on earth, there is something taking place in heaven. When elders and deacons are ordained on earth, there are angels in heaven saying, "Amen!" When the church agrees to discipline a sinning brother, there is a corresponding agreement that is to be found in heaven.

- This agreement is based upon the presence of Christ: *For where two or three have gathered together in My name, there I am in their midst (18:20).*

   When the church comes together, there is an additional presence that the ushers do not count. Jesus is there. That is what gives power to the church. The absence of His presence can give death to a church.

   There is a story of an old black man who became a Christian and who tried to attend an all-white church in a segregated community, but the deacons blocked his way at the door and would not let him enter. The man was praying that night and he told the Lord how he had tried to attend the church, but had been prevented. As he was praying, the Lord came to him and said, "Don't worry, My son. I've been trying to get into that church for years and they won't let Me into it, either."

   There is a point to the story. The reason we exercise discipline within the church and remove sin from the church is so that Christ's presence will remain in the church. Either you will have sin present within the church or you will have Christ present in the church but you will not have both.

The same is true of your own life. Either you are enjoying the presence of Jesus Christ in your life or else you are holding to sin in your life, but you do not have both. If you are holding onto your sin, take another look and you will see that Christ has gone and you just hadn't noticed.

- This agreement involves forgiving and retaining sins: *"Truly I say to you, whatever you shall bind on earth shall be bound in heaven; and whatever you loose on earth shall be loosed in heaven.* 19 *Again I say to you, that if two of you agree on earth about anything that they may ask, it shall be done for them by My Father who is in heaven." (Matthew 18:18-19).*

This does not describe a power that exists independently of God to forgive or to secure sins. Only God can forgive sins. This is a picture of God working through the instrumentality of the church.

Eschatology

The Study of Last Things

The Bible has quite a lot to say about the future. Such things are not left in the realm of idle speculation. Instead, God sent a series of prophets and prophecies. Among those messages were certain truths about the future. Indeed, one of the evidences that a prophet was from God was that he would foretell certain events before they took place and their words would be substantiated in subsequent events.

THE MINISTRY OF THE PROPHETS

> *God, after He spoke long ago to the fathers in the prophets in many portions and in many ways... (Hebrews 1:1).*

The prophets served as spokesmen for God. They were the means which the Lord used to communicate His message to His people. This means that the work of the prophets went far beyond the mere predicting of future events. Their message went in three directions:

- They looked back to the past faithfulness of God.
- They looked to the present work of God in the nation and in the world.
- They looked to the future.

This means not everything that was said by the prophets was necessarily for the future. It can be argued that, even when they were foretelling events for the future, that they were doing so for purposes in the present. The preaching of the prophets was always practical. That means

449

their message always had a present application. It was never merely to satisfy curiosity about the future or even to lay out some future time-line. It was always to make you live differently in the present. This brings us to the purpose of prophecy.

THE PURPOSE OF PROPHECY

Prophecy has been described as "history written beforehand." But this is incorrect. If this is the sole purpose of prophecy, then the prophets have done a miserable job. They could have written a much more concise and understandable history.

Biblical prophecy always serves a specific purpose. That purpose may be to rebuke those who are out of the will of God and to warn of the consequences of continuing in sin. Another purpose for Biblical prophecy is to comfort Godly believers. Thus, the same prophecy may be a judgment on one person and an encouragement to another. Our understanding of the specific purpose of the prophecy will be assisted as we learn the historical setting of the passage. This means we must always examine prophetic passages in the context in which they are given, taking into account the reason for the prophecy.

1.   The main purpose of prophecy is to affect the conduct and commitment of those who hear the prophecy. It is to make you live differently in the present. This is seen in Titus 2:12-13 where we are to *live sensibly, righteously and godly in the present age, 13 looking for the blessed hope and the appearing of the glory of our great God and Savior, Christ Jesus.* It is the expectancy of the return of Christ that is to be one of our motivations for godly living.

2.   Another purpose of prophecy is to build faith. It is to establish confidence in the Lord who miraculously foretold events which then came to pass.

> *From now on I am telling you before it comes to pass, so that when it does occur, you may believe that I am He. (John 13:19).*

> *And now I have told you before it comes to pass, that when it comes to pass, you may believe. (John 14:29).*

Obviously, this is related to the previous point, for as one's faith is increased and strengthened, so also his commitment and conduct will be affected.

3.   Another reason is to encourage believers who are in the midst of difficult situation. Prophecy brings hope because it allows us to see just a bit of the bigger picture. If you have ever had opportunity to look at the underside of a Turkish carpet, you know it is not a pretty picture, especially if you are looking at it through a magnifying glass. It is made up of a tangle of woven threads. But if you turn it right-side-up and then stand back so that you can see the entire carpet at a single glance, you will find yourself gazing upon an elegant design. Being able to see a bigger part of the picture is an encouragement when you are going through hard times.

4.   Finally, prophecy is given that you might be ready for the future. We are all going there in one way or another. Future prophecy is given to get us ready for the journey.

SOME CHARACTERISTICS OF BIBLICAL PROPHECY

1.   Biblical Prophecy is Historically Relevant to the Time of the Writing.

   Even though the fulfillment might not take place for over 2000 years, the prophecy is written to a particular group of people living in the prophet's own lifetime. This means we ought not to ignore the context in which the prophecy was given. At the same time, we can realize that a prophecy given for one period may not see the completed fulfillment for a very long time.

2.   Biblical Prophecy sometimes contains Multiple Fulfillments.

   This has also been termed the "Law of Double Reference." It means that the prophecy often contains a fulfillment in the days of the prophet but also carries a reference to an event which is to take place far in the future.

   For example, Isaiah 7:14-16 gives a prophecy to Ahaz, the king of Judah concerning a young maiden who shall give birth to a son. Then, in Isaiah 8:1-4, we see what seems to be the immediate fulfillment as we read of someone named Immanuel. However, Matthew 1:23 reveals that there was ultimately a second fulfillment of this verse that is to be found in the birth of Jesus.

Another example is seen in 2 Samuel 7:12-16 which gives the prophecy of David's son, Solomon. But there is within this prophecy a further reference to a future son of David which is fulfilled in Jesus. This is seen in the words of Hebrews 1:5 which cites the words of 2 Samuel 7:14, echoing the words, *I will be a Father to Him And He shall be a Son to Me* and pointing out that it was indeed fulfilled in Jesus.

3.   Time Gaps are Not Always Indicated.

Prophecy often has its own peculiar time perspective. Certain high points of future history are seen while certain "valleys" are often hidden.

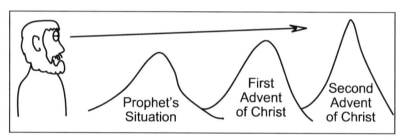

An example of this is seen in Luke 4:16-21 where Jesus reads a passage from the book of Isaiah and states that it had been fulfilled in Him. An examination of Isaiah 61:1-2 will reveal that the remainder of this passage deals with the Day of God's Judgment which presumably shall take place at the Second Coming of the Lord.

4.   Biblical Prophecy is Sometimes Conditional.

A prophecy is sometimes dependent upon the resulting reaction on the part of the hearer. There may be varying levels of conditionality and the conditions might not be specifically stated within the actual prophecy.

This can be seen when Jonah prophesied of the destruction of Nineveh. The prophet stated in no uncertain terms that it was to take place within 40 days (Jonah 3:4). When the people of Nineveh repented, their city was spared. Evidently, this prophecy was conditional on the attitudes of the people of the city.

The use of conditional prophecy is a demonstration of the sovereignty of God. The Lord points this out in Jeremiah 18:7-10 where He gives a vivid parable involving a potter at his wheel. Just as the potter has the right to work on a pot and then change midway, either setting the pot aside or using it for some other purpose, so also God is able to supersede His own prophecies.

5.   Prophetic Fulfillment can be Literal, Figurative, or Spiritual. An example of a literal fulfillment of prophecy is seen in the case of Ezekiel 26:1-14 which gives a very detailed account of the several falls of the city of Tyre. The prophecy took place very literally, the city being actually thrown into the sea. Similarly, we can compare Zechariah 9:9 with Matthew 21:5 where the Messiah rides into Jerusalem on a donkey. However, the context of that prophecy is anything but clear, demonstrating that elements of a prophecy might have a literal fulfillment while other elements of that same prophecy might not be seen to be fulfilled at that time or in the same manner.

On the other hand, there are times when the language of a prophecy is clearly figurative and not meant to be taken literally. For example, in John 2:19 Jesus stands in the Temple in Jerusalem and says, "Destroy this temple and in three days I will raise it up." We read in verse 21 of that same chapter that "He spoke of the temple of His body." Many more examples of this phenomenon can be observed:

- Compare Psalm 118:22 with Acts 4:11 and 1 Peter 2:7 where Jesus is the stone which the builders rejected.
- Compare Isaiah 22:22 with Revelation 3:7 where the key is a representation of the authority of Jesus.
- Compare Zechariah 13:7 with Matthew 26:31 where Jesus is seen to be the shepherd that was smitten.

There are also occasions in which we find a spiritual realization. In these cases, what seemed to be a literal prophecy is later seen to have a spiritual fulfillment. An example of this is Jeremiah 31:31-34 which promises the New Covenant with Judah and Israel. This covenant is said to be fulfilled in Christ (Hebrews 8:12; 10:15-17). Similarly, Isaiah 2:2-3 speaks of the mountain of the house of the Lord being established and raised above the hills. This passage is echoed in Hebrews 12:22 which shows that this is a picture of people turning to Christ in this age. Amos 9:11-12 tells how God will "raise up the fallen booth of David, and wall up its breaches" and "raise up its ruins, and rebuild it as in the days of old." Rather than pointing to the erection of a literal tabernacle, James used this same passage to refer to the Gentiles coming into the New Testament Church (Acts 15:13-18).

THE SECOND COMING OF CHRIST

And after He had said these things, He was lifted up while they were looking on, and a cloud received Him out of their sight. (Acts 1:9).

This was the ascension of Christ. The disciples were with Jesus on the Mount of Olives and suddenly Jesus was lifted up before their eyes. They saw Jesus go up. Then they saw a cloud and then they didn't see Jesus any longer. Some of these disciples had seen this cloud before (Luke 9:28-36).

Transfiguration	Ascension
A cloud	A cloud
Disciples saw two men: Moses & Elijah	Disciples see two men in white clothing: Angels
When it was over, only Jesus and the disciples remained	When it is over only the two men and the disciples remain

What was this cloud? It was likely the Shekinah Cloud, the cloud that hid the presence of God in the days of the Old Testament. It was the same cloud of smoke that Isaiah saw in Isaiah 6:4. It was the same cloud that led the Israelites through the wilderness. It was the cloud that filled the tabernacle and it was the cloud that filled the Temple. It was the cloud that represented and which hid the presence of God.

And as they were gazing intently into the sky while He was going, behold, two men in white clothing stood beside them. 11 They also said, "Men of Galilee, why do you stand looking into the sky? This Jesus, who has been taken up from you into heaven, will come in just the same way as you have watched Him go into heaven." (Acts 1:11).

Who are these two men? They are called "two males" (ἀνδρης δύο).

If they are the same as those described in the parallel account in Luke 24:4, then they are angels. Their words seem almost by way of a rebuke. "Why are you standing here looking? Why aren't you headed back to Jerusalem where He told you to go?"

The message of the two men is that the going of Christ will one day be reversed. He who went up and was hidden by a cloud will one day return in the clouds. As He left, so shall be His return. How did He leave?

- From the Mount of Olives.
- In the clouds.
- In a visible manner.

This is not the only promise of the Second Coming, but this is one of the most striking because it is accompanied by a visual lesson. If you want to know the nature of the Second Coming, then look at the way Jesus departed, for the angels clearly stated that His return will be in "just the same way."

Description	Testimony of Scripture
His Coming Will Be Visible	*Behold, He is coming with the clouds, and every eye will see him (Revelation 1:7).*
His Coming Will Be Audible	*For the Lord Himself will descend from heaven with a shout, with the voice of the archangel and with the trumpet of God... (1 Thessalonians 4:16).*
His Coming Will Open the Graves	*...and the dead in Christ will rise first (1 Thessalonians 4:16).*
His Coming will bring judgment	*For the Son of Man is going to come in the glory of His Father with His angels, and will then repay every man according to his deeds (Matthew 16:27).*
His Coming will involve a gathering of God's people	*And He will send forth His angels with a great trumpet and they will gather together His elect from the four winds, from one end of the sky to the other (Matthew 24:31).* *We who are alive and remain will be caught up together with them in the clouds (1 Thessalonians 4:17).*

To this list, we can also add that His coming will be a surprise. While the Scriptures do say that Jesus is coming like a thief, the Scriptures point out that His "thiefly coming" will be anything but secret or quiet.

> *But the day of the Lord will come like a thief, in which the heavens will pass away with a roar and the elements will be destroyed with intense heat, and the earth and its works will be burned up (2 Peter 3:10).*

This is not a quiet coming. But it is unexpected and hence can be likened to the coming of a thief.

> *For you yourselves know full well that the day of the Lord will come just like a thief in the night. While they are saying, "Peace and safety!" then destruction will come upon them suddenly like birth pangs upon a woman with child; and they shall not escape. (1 Thessalonians 5:2-3).*

Once again this coming is not secret. It comes with all of the force of a woman going into labor. I can tell you from experience as both a father and a grandfather that such things do not take place secretly. The point instead is that it hits unexpectedly and without warning.

> *But be sure of this, that if the head of the house had known at what time of the night the thief was coming, he would have been on the alert and would not have allowed his house to be broken into. 44 For this reason you be ready too; for the Son of Man is coming at an hour when you do not think He will. (Matthew 24:43-44).*

The point is that, because the return of Christ will be without warning, we are to always be ready and in anticipation, living in the light of His return. The teaching of the unexpectedness of His coming is a call to faithful living.

PROPHECY AND DISPENSATIONALISM

Dispensationalism is still a relatively recent phenomenon, having first made its appearance in the early 1800's and being popularized at the beginning of the 20th Century. It is a doctrinal system that seeks to keep Israel and the Church distinct. This system teaches that throughout history God is seen to have two distinct purposes and two distinct people and these distinctions are maintained throughout eternity (or at least throughout the end of a future millennium). Dispensationalists regularly hold to the following distinctives:

Distinction #1: Plan & Purpose of God.

Dispensationalism teaches that God has two separate plans and two separate and distinct peoples through whom He works — Israel and the Church. Lewis Sperry Chaefer described it this way:

> *The Dispensationalist believes that throughout the ages God is pursuing two distinct purposes: one related to the earth with earthly people and earthly objectives involved which is Judaism; while the other is related to heaven with heavenly objectives involved, which is Christianity* (1936:107).

Charles Ryrie cites Fuller's doctoral dissertation when he says that "the basic premise of Dispensationalism is two purposes of God expressed in the formation of two peoples who maintain their distinction throughout eternity" (1982:44-45). By contrast, the Bible teaches that God has one unified people. In the Old Testament that was Israel, but even then not all Israel was Israel, but only those who entered into covenant relationship of faith in God. Those who are not of faith are not His people. And those who are of faith are His people. This is true in every age. This is why Paul can say that *"those who are of faith who are sons of Abraham"* (Galatians 3:7).

Distinction #2: the Law.

Dispensationalism says that the Mosaic Law is done away in Christ. Some Dispensationalists go to the extreme of maintaining that even the teachings of Jesus in the Sermon on the Mount have no relevance for today, being given in a context of the Law. It is true that the Bible sees the Ceremonial Law as being fulfilled in Christ, but the Moral Law as contained in the Ten Commandments are repeated throughout the New Testament, showing that those commands are still in force (though admittedly the nature of the Sabbath is described differently since we have now entered into the rest provided by Christ). Indeed, Jesus Himself said, *"Do not think that I came to abolish the Law or the Prophets; I did not come to abolish, but to fulfill"* (Matthew 5:17). Does His fulfillment of the Law mean that it has passed away? To the contrary, He explains His meaning with a careful and sober warning: *"Whoever then annuls one of the least of these commandments, and so teaches others, shall be called least in the kingdom of heaven; but whoever keeps and teaches them, he shall be called great in the kingdom of heaven"* (Matthew 5:19).

Distinction #3: the Nature of the Church.

Dispensationalism sees the church as a parenthesis, a temporary situation lying between God's two dealings with Israel. The Bible sees the church as the culmination of all God's people, the very body of Christ and the fullness of God. Paul speaks of the message given to him *"to bring to light what is the administration of the mystery which for ages has been hidden in God, who created all things; in order that the manifold wisdom of God might now be made known through the church to the rulers and the authorities in the heavenly places"* (Ephesians 3:9-10). Far from being a parenthesis, the church is the culmination of something begun in Old Testament times. Paul goes on to point out that *"this was in accordance with the eternal purpose which He carried out in Christ Jesus our Lord"* (Ephesians 3:11).

Notice that the Church is described as a part of the eternal purpose and not merely a temporary parenthesis. God didn't just create the Church on the fly as a desperation measure after the Jews blew it. Rather, the eternal purposes of God toward the world as well as toward Israel are fulfilled in the church. She is God's eternal covenant people gathered from every nation, tribe, people and tongue. There is no longer Jew nor Gentile, bond nor free, male versus female. Instead, Jew and Gentile alike are be reconciled *"to God in one body through the cross"* (Ephesians 2:16).

Distinction #4: Church in the Old Testament.

Dispensationalism usually teaches that the church is neither found nor mentioned in the Old Testament. The Bible states that the Old Testament did look forward to a time when Gentiles would enter into the Covenant. The promised Messiah was to be both a *"covenant to the people, and a light to the nations"* (Psalm 42:6). God also said, *"I will call those who were not My people, 'My people'"* (Romans 9:24-25). Paul is specific to tell us that the coming of Gentiles into the church was a confirmation of *"the promises given to the fathers, and for the Gentiles to glorify God for His mercy; as it is written, 'Therefore I will give praise to Thee among the Gentiles, And I will sing to Thy name'"* (Romans 15:8-9). Peter says that *"the prophets who prophesied of the grace that would come to you made careful search and inquiry, seeking to know what person or time the Spirit of Christ within them was indicating as He predicted the sufferings of Christ and the glories to follow. It was revealed to them that they were not serving themselves, but you"* (1 Peter 1:10-12). The Old Testament prophets not only prophesied of those glories that would follow the cross, but also acknowledged that their prophecies were to benefit the future church.

Distinction #5: Old Testament Promises.

Dispensationalism says that all of the promises given in the Old Testament must be fulfilled to a political nation of Israel. Over and over again, the Bible sees these promises being fulfilled to the Church as the "Spiritual Israel" and people of God. The Bible teaches us that *"they are not all Israel who are descended from Israel"* (Romans 9:6). Conversely, we have already seen how the presence of Gentiles in the church was a fulfillment of the Old Testament promise that God would *"call those who were not My people, 'My people'"* (Romans 9:24-25).

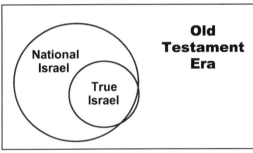

This is illustrated graphically in the following chart. Most Dispensationalists will agree that, in the days of the Old Testament, being a part of the nation of Israel did not automatically mean that one was a part of the true Israel. Being Jewish did not automatically save anyone. Yet at the same time, those who were a part of this true Israel were primarily those who were a part of national Israel. There were few exceptions to this rule.

Likewise, at the birth of the New Testament church on the day of Pentecost, the same situation held true in that the church was composed almost exclusively of those who were a part of national or physical Israel -- those who were physical descendants of Abraham. It has only been in the ensuing years that this has changed so that today there is a great deal of the church that is no longer a part of national Israel.

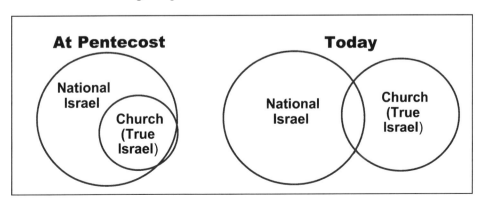

The writer to the Hebrews says that those Old Testament saints *"did not receive what was promised, because God had provided something better for us, so that apart from us they should not be made perfect"* (Hebrews 11:39-40). This is completely antithetical to the Dispensational teaching that says, "Israel gets the promises to Israel and the church gets the promises to the church and never the twain shall meet."

It is significant that when James wanted to demonstrate the legitimacy of the New Testament program of bringing Gentiles into the church, he turned to the Old Testament, saying, *"Simeon has related how God first concerned Himself about taking from among the Gentiles a people for His name. And with this the words of the Prophets agree, just as it is written, 'After these things I will return, and I will rebuild the tabernacle of David which has fallen, and I will rebuild its ruins, And I will restore it, in order that the rest of mankind may seek the Lord, and all the Gentiles who are called by My name'"* (Acts 15:14-17). The passage to which James turned was that of Amos 9:11-12.

Old Testament Prophecy	New Testament Fulfillment
"I will rebuild the Tabernacle of David"	The growth of the church
"...in order that the rest of mankind may see the Lord"	Gentiles to become Christians in the growing church.

James had no problems looking to the events that were going on in the church of his day and seeing them as fulfillments of Old Testament prophecies.

Distinction #6: Two Comings of Christ Versus One.

Dispensationalism teaches that Christ will return to the earth is a secret "Rapture" in which all believers will be removed from the earth. This is later followed by the "Second Coming of Christ" which is a distinct and separate event.

The Bible makes mention of only one future coming of Christ, a coming in which "every eye shall see Him" and "every knee shall bow." Instead of a second and third future coming, the Bible teaches that Christ, *"having been offered once to bear the sins of many, shall appear a second time for salvation without reference to sin, to those who eagerly await Him"* (Hebrews 9:28).

Dispensationalism can best be understood in light of a contrast with what has come to be known as "Covenant Theology."

Dispensationalism	Covenant Theology
Stresses "literal" interpretation of the Bible	Accepts both literal and figurative (spiritual) interpretation of the Bible
"Israel" always means only the literal, physical descendants of Jacob	"Israel" may mean either physical descendants of Jacob, or spiritual Israel, depending on context
"Israel of God" in Galatians 6:16 means physical Israel alone	"Israel of God" in Galatians 6:16 means spiritual Israel, parallel to Gal. 3:29; Rom. 2:28-29; 9:6; Phil. 3:3.
God has 2 peoples with 2 separate destinies: Israel (earthly) and the Church (heavenly).	God has one covenant people. Those in this age have become a part of God's continuing covenant people.
All Old Testament prophecies for "Israel" are only for the physical nation of Israel, not for the Church	Some Old Testament prophecies are for national Israel, others for spiritual Israel
The Church is a parenthesis in God's program for the ages	The Church is the culmination of God's saving purpose for the ages
The main heir to Abraham's covenant was Isaac and literal Israel	The main heir to Abraham's covenant was Christ, the Seed, and spiritual Israel which is "in Christ"
Jesus made an offer of the literal Kingdom to Israel; since Israel rejected it, it is postponed	Jesus made only an offer of the Spiritual Kingdom, which was rejected by literal Israel but has gradually been accepted by spiritual Israel
Teaches that the Millennium is the Kingdom of God. They are always Premillennial, usually Pre-tribulation	The Church is the Kingdom of God. This can be interpreted both within the Premillennial, Post Millennial or Amillennial framework.

The Old Testament animal sacrifices will be restored in the Millennium, as a memorial only	The Old Testament sacrifices were fulfilled and forever abolished in Christ

Though there is some considerable differences among various Dispensationalists, their view of eschatology generally can be outlined as follows:

- In a sudden and unannounced instant, all those who have died will rise from the dead and will be gathered along with all living believers to meet the Lord in the air. At this time, their bodies shall be changed as they receive new glorified bodies (1 Thessalonians 4; I Corinthians 15:51-52).
- All of these believers will then be taken to heaven (John 14:3).
- In heaven there will be a judgment of all the believers who are there (1 Corinthians 3:11-15; 1 Corinthians 5:10-11).
- With all Christians suddenly disappeared from the earth, the world will be plunged into a terribly destructive seven years of tribulation (Daniel 9:27; Revelation 6-18). During this time, Russia will invade Palestine (Ezekiel 38-39) and a world-wide dictator will arise - the Anti-Christ who will mandate that all must receive his mark on the forehead or on the hand (Revelation 13).
- Toward the end of this period, all of the nations of the world will be gathered together to the northern plains of Israel known as Armageddon.
- Jesus will return with His saints and will divide between the just and the unjust in a judgment of "sheep and goats" (Matthew 24-25). The "sheep" will be ushered into His kingdom while the "goats" will be cast into hell. The basis of this judgment will be the treatment that people accorded the Jews since only Christians will befriend the Jews during the tribulation (Matthew 25).
- Jesus will begin a 1000 year reign from His throne in Jerusalem (Revelation 20:4-6).
- At the end of that time, the will be another rebellion against God's rule as Satan is loosed upon the earth. Fire will come from heaven and devour them and a final judgment shall take place in which all heaven and earth is destroyed (Revelation 20:11-15).
- A new heaven and a new earth will be instituted which shall exist forever (Revelation 21-22).

The Dispensationalist typically charts out these events like this:

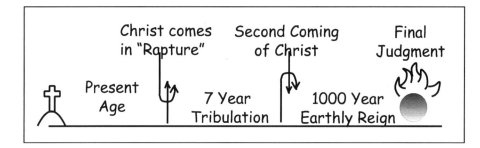

One of the initial problems that the Pretribulationalist runs into is that of terminology. How shall he differentiate between these two future comings of Christ? The verses that he uses to teach of these events simply refer to "His coming." This itself is a clue that the writers of the Bible believed that there was only one future coming of Christ and simply referred to it as "His coming." Therefore, the phrase "rapture of the church" has been coined to describe the initial coming - the "secret" one. There is nothing wrong with coining a theological term is coined; we coin terms all the time. However the absence of any biblical distinctives is troubling to this view.

Have you ever tried to deliberately cross your eyes? The result is that your vision becomes blurred and you begin to see things with a "double vision." If you are looking at a coffee mug, you will instead see two of them. Dispensationalism suffers from this kind of spiritual myopia.

- It sees two future comings of Christ (or in some cases, three).
- It sees multiple judgments in which people shall come before Christ and to be judged.
- It sees multiple days of the Lord.

By contrast, the Scriptures are unified in its descriptions of the return of Christ and are consistent in its depiction of that event. This is seen when we compare those passages taken by the Dispensationalist which is supposed to foretell the "rapture" and compare them with those which clearly speak of Christ's Second Coming.

"Rapture"	Second Coming
For the Lord Himself will descend from heaven... (1 Thessalonians 4:16).	*They will see the Son of man coming... (Matthew 24:30).*

With the trumpet of God...(1 Thessalonians 4:16).	*He will send forth His angels with a great trumpet (Matthew 24:31).*
We who are alive shall be caught up together... (1 Thessalonians 4:16).	*And they will gather together His elect from the four winds... (Matthew 24:31).*
We... shall be caught up together with them in CLOUDS (1 Thessalonians 4:17).	*They will see the Son of Man coming on the CLOUDS of the sky... (Matthew 24:30).*
...if you will not wake up, I will come like a thief (Revelations 3:3).	*The Son of Man is coming at an hour when you do not think He will (Matthew 24:44; see also 1 Thessalonians 5:2-6 and 2 Peter 3:10).*
...the coming of our Lord Jesus WITH all His saints" (1 Thessalonians 3:13).	*...the Lord came WITH many thousands of His holy ones (Jude 14).*

As you look at the way Christ's coming is described in each of these verses, they appear to be speaking of the same thing. That is because they are the same event. There is not a single passage of Scripture that makes a clear distinction between two future separate comings of Christ.

One of the hallmarks of Dispensationalism is to insist that all prophecy must necessarily be interpreted literally. Charles Ryrie points this out when he says:

> "Dispensationalists claim that their principle of hermeneutics is that of literal interpretation. This means interpretation which gives to every word the same meaning it would have in normal usage, whether employed in writing, speaking or thinking" (1974:86).

This insistence on an overly literal interpretation has led to all sorts of outlandish interpretations and speculation. By contrast, when we read New Testament fulfillments of Old Testament prophecies, we find that they were not all interpreted in this manner. For example, Jeremiah 31:15 does not in its context seem to be a literal prophecy of Herod executing the infants of Bethlehem. Yet Matthew 2:17-18 is given as a fulfillment of that passage. Similarly, Isaiah 40:3-5 speak of a time when valleys are lifted up and mountains made low. But Luke 3:4-6 quotes this passage as taking place in the ministry of John the Baptist. The truth is that no one always interprets every part of the Bible literally. We all read in Daniel of certain beasts and understand that they are not literal beasts, but that kings and kingdoms are in view. We all read in the book of Revelation of the Lion of the tribe of Judah and recognize this to be a picture of Jesus.

In the final analysis, prophecy is much easier to interpret after it has been fulfilled and even then there are sometimes difficulties and a lack of agreement among Bible students. This should make us careful against being too dogmatic on how we hold various eschatological views.

TRIBULATION: PAST OR FUTURE?

There are a number of passages in the Bible that speak of the onset of a great tribulation that is to take place prior to the return of Christ. A few of these passages will serve as representative samplings:

> *For thus says the LORD,*
> *"I have heard a sound of terror,*
> *Of dread, and there is no peace.*
> *6 Ask now, and see*
> *If a male can give birth.*
> *Why do I see every man*
> *With his hands on his loins, as a woman in childbirth?*
> *And why have all faces turned pale?*
> *7 Alas! for that day is great,*
> *There is none like it;*
> *And it is the time of Jacob's distress,*
> *But he will be saved from it. (Jeremiah 30:5-7).*

> *Therefore when you see the abomination of desolation which was spoken of through Daniel the prophet, standing in the holy place (let the reader understand), 16 then those who are in Judea must flee to the mountains. 17 Whoever is on the housetop must not go down to get the things out that are in his house. (Matthew 24:15-17).*

> *For then there will be a great tribulation, such as has not occurred since the beginning of the world until now, nor ever will. (Matthew 24:21).*

One of the things that we must do when looking at prophecy is ask ourselves if the prophecy in question has already been fulfilled. In this case, I want to suggest that it has been fulfilled quite literally. And furthermore, it has been fulfilled twice. The first time took place in the year 168 B.C. During that time, an invading king named Antiochus Epiphanes came down from the north and committed great atrocities against the Jews, forbidding them to read the Scriptures or to circumcise their children or to observe the Sabbath day. He even went so far as to have a statue of himself erected inside the Temple with orders that it be worshiped by all on pain of death. This was the "abomination of desolation" which Daniel prophesied of in Daniel 11:31.

However, Jesus told His disciples that it would happen again (Matthew 24:15 cited above; Mark 13:19). Sure enough, in 66 A.D. the Jews in Jerusalem rebelled against the Roman empire. The following war lasted 7 years. In 70 A.D. Jerusalem was taken and the Temple was again trodden underfoot by Gentile soldiers. This time, the Temple was destroyed and a great carnage ensued. However, the last resistance did not fall until the year 73 A.D. when the Romans took Masada, only to find that the last remnant of 930 Jews had committed suicide rather than be taken captive.

Is there still a future time of tribulation? I do not know. But I do know that Jesus said to His disciples that "in the world you have tribulation" (John 16:33 - notice the present tense). Indeed, the history of the church has been a history of tribulation.

ANTICHRIST

The term "antichrist" is found in only four verses in the entire Bible. All four of these instances are in the epistles of John. All four of these speak of antichrist as a present reality.

> *Children, it is the last hour; and just as you heard that antichrist is coming, even now many antichrists have appeared; from this we know that it is the last hour. (1 John 2:18).*

The first and most obvious thing we note from this passage is its references to that which is in the present. It is already said to be, not merely the last day, but the last hour. The suggestion is that John is making in his own day is that he and his readers have already been through the last days, through the last day, and are coming to the final hour.

Secondly, we note that he references a pre-existing teaching. He says that his readers already have knowledge that "antichrist is coming." Was this merely an oral tradition or was it based on previous Scripture? We have no need to assume the former, even though the term "antichrist" has been previously absent from the Scriptures. There have been other descriptive terms that have been used in its place.

- Daniel 7:20-21 described a "little horn" that would rise up and do battle with the saints of God.
- Daniel 11:36 speaks of a king who would magnify himself above every god and who would *speak monstrous things against the God of gods*. While this saw fulfillment in the actions of Antiochus Epiphenes, Jesus referenced the "abomination of desolation spoken by Daniel the prophet" and said that it would take place in the future (Matthew 24:15).
- Paul speaks of how *"that lawless one will be revealed whom the Lord will slay with the breath of His mouth and bring to an end by the appearance of His coming"* (2 Thessalonians 2:8).

Where shall we look for the fulfillment of these prophecies? As we have already noted, some have at least a measure of fulfillment in the past. The events of Daniel 11 have been fulfilled so exactly that most critics of the Bible who reject supernatural revelation and its fulfillments of prophecy are forced to assume that Daniel must have been written after the Maccabean conflicts. On the other hand, Jesus referenced those same writings and looked for a future fulfillment.

Others have noted the manner in which at least some elements of these prophecies find fulfillment in the A.D. 70 fall of Jerusalem in which Titus, the son of Roman emperor Vespasian entered the temple and subsequently burned it to the ground. It is to this end that some have insisted in an early date for the book of Revelation, despite the fact that early church fathers consistently assigned its writing to the reign of Domitian (81-96).

The idea that the antichrist was still to come in the future has an early tradition within the church. Irenaeus, writing from the second century, equates the antichrist with Paul's description in 2 Thessalonians 2 and looks to a future fulfillment of his coming:

> *When the anti-christ shall have devastated all things in this world, he will reign for 3 years and 6 months, and sit in the temple in Jerusalem, and then shall the lord come from the heaven in the clouds, in the glory of the Father, sending this man and those who follow him, into the lake of fire, but bringing for the righteous the times of the kingdom that is the rest the hallowed seventh day and restoring to Abraham the*

promised inheritance in which the kingdom of the lord declared that many coming from the east and from the west should sit down with Abraham, Isaac, and Jacob. (Ante-Nicene Fathers, vol 1, 560)

The Reformers, for their part, identified the Roman Catholic pontiff as the antichrist and the popes seem to have been quite willing the return the favor. There is thus a longstanding tradition of seeking to identify the antichrist with this leader or that personage and none have passed the test of time. It is the better part of discretion to withhold such judgments.

THE MILLENNIAL QUESTION

Does the Bible teach that there will be a future 1000 year millennial kingdom on earth? Instead of beginning with Revelation 20, it is advantageous to go back and see what Jesus and the apostles taught concerning the kingdom.

Jesus warned those who were looking for a future kingdom on earth that *"the kingdom of God is not coming with signs to be observed, nor will they say, 'Look, here it is!' or 'There it is!' For behold, the kingdom of God is in your midst"* (Luke 17:20-21). This is not to say that there can be no future kingdom manifestation, but it does say that the Kingdom has a present reality.

When Jesus describes the end of the age, He tells of the Son of man sending forth His angels and gathering all of the unrighteous out and judging them in *"the furnace of fire"* (Matthew 13:42). He goes on to say that *"the righteous will shine forth as the sun in the kingdom of their Father"* (Matthew 13:43). Similarly, in John 6, Jesus says that all believers will be raised up at the same time — the last day.

> *"And this is the Father's will which has sent me, that of all which he has given me I should lose nothing, but should raise it up again at the last day. 40 And this is the will of him that sent me, that every one which sees the Son, and believes on him, may have everlasting life: and I will raise him up **at the last day**." (John 6:39-40).*

> *"No man can come to me, except the Father which has sent me draw him: and I will raise him up at the last day" (John 6:44).*

"Whoever eats My flesh and drinks My blood has eternal life, and I will raise him up at the last day" (John 6:54).

If all believers are to be raised up on the last day, and Jesus says this is the case, then it stands to reason that there will not be several different resurrections of believers separated by a thousand years. Indeed, if the last day is really the last day, then we might find it difficult to postulate a few more days to follow, let alone a thousand years.

The Apostle Paul does not teach of a future millennium in which people in their natural bodies enter into an earthly kingdom. To the contrary, he says that *"flesh and blood cannot inherit the kingdom of God"* (1 Corinthians 15:50). This statement would seem to preclude any possibility of an earthly flesh and blood millennium which is inherited by people of flesh and blood.

Premillennialism	Pauline Theology
Some people will enter into the kingdom in their natural flesh and blood bodies to inherit the kingdom	*Flesh and blood cannot inherit the kingdom of God*

Paul presents this present age as culminating when *"death is swallowed up in victory"* (1 Corinthians 15:54). This takes place when Christ returns *"at the last trumpet; for the trumpet will sound, and the dead will be raised imperishable, and we shall be changed"* (1 Corinthians 15:52). If Paul is saying that death will be defeated at Christ's return, then we can understand that Christ is reigning now and will continue to reign until death has been defeated.

For He must reign until he has put all His enemies under His feet. The last enemy that will be abolished is death. (1 Corinthians 15:25-26).

If death is defeated at the rapture/second coming and if this is the last enemy to be defeated, then Paul's theology does not allow room for a further enemy to arise a thousand years later. Further evidence of Paul's view of eschatology is seen in his second epistle to the Thessalonians:

For after all it is only just for God to repay with

affliction those who afflict you, 7 and to give relief to you who are afflicted and to us as well when the Lord Jesus shall be revealed from heaven with His mighty angels in flaming fire, 8 dealing out retribution to those who do not know God and to those who do not obey the gospel of our Lord Jesus. 9 And these will pay the penalty of eternal destruction, away from the presence of the Lord and from the glory of His power, 10 when He comes to be glorified in His saints on that day, and to be marveled at among all who have believed-- for our testimony to you was believed. (2 Thessalonians 1:6-10).

This passage promises that the present difficulties of Christians shall be relieved when the Lord is revealed from heaven with His angels, to take vengeance on the ungodly with everlasting destruction, and be glorified in the saints.

Premillennialism teaches that everlasting judgment takes place only at the end of an earthly millennium and judgment leading to the wicked being be punished with everlasting destruction. But the above verse states something totally different. Paul says that it is when Christ returns that the wicked are judged with an eternal judgment.

Premillennialism	Pauline Theology
Unbelievers only given a temporary judgment at the Second Coming; the final and eternal judgment of unbelievers takes place after the millennium.	Unbelievers **will pay the penalty of eternal destruction**, *away from the presence of the Lord and from the glory of His power, 10 when He comes to be glorified in His saints **on that day**.*

Peter warns of a coming judgment which is going to come "as a thief." The Premillennialist would have us believe that this judgment takes place at the end of a 1000 year kingdom.

> *But the day of the Lord will come like a thief, in which the heavens will pass away with a roar and the elements will be destroyed with intense heat, and the earth and its works will be burned up. (2 Peter 3:10).*

Does Peter speak of these events in such a way as to indicate that they will come at least a thousand years in the future? Not at all! Rather, he goes on to say that we are to be looking for two things:

- We are to be *"looking for and hastening the coming of the day of God, on account of which the heavens will be destroyed by burning, and the elements will melt with intense heat"* (2 Peter 3:12).
- We are to be *"looking for new heavens and a new earth, in which righteousness dwells"* (2 Peter 3:13).

The Premillennialist does not look with immediate expectancy for either of these events for he believes that they must be preceded by Christ's return and then a 1000 year period and only then can he look for these events to take place. In contrast, Peter describes the return of Christ as ushering the judgment of God and the resulting new heavens and new earth. We must therefore conclude that there is not a future 1000 year period in Peter's theology.

Does John give new revelation of a future 1000 year millennium in his book of Revelation? Remember that it is only in Revelation 20 that this mention of 1000 years is laid out. Our question is twofold:

- Is John teaching something new that has not been previously revealed?
- Are John's vision ("I saw") in Revelation 20:1 and the verses that follow to be interpreted with a rigid literalism?

The first question will be answered by the second. Revelation is filled with a number of the visions detailing the things seen by John. At the same time, those things he sees are often symbols of greater truths. For example, in chapter 1 John sees a vision of One who had feet like bronze, eyes of fire, a voice like running water, a sword coming from his mouth, and stars in his hand. But this can be understood to be symbolic of Jesus. Similarly, in chapter 5, John sees a lamb standing before the throne of God. This lamb has seven horns and seven eyes and has the appearance of having been slain. John really saw this lamb, but it is only symbolic of Jesus, the real lamb of God. In Revelation 12 where a woman who is clothed with the sun and wears a crown of 12 stars gives birth to a child and then, after he has been caught up to heaven, flees to the wilderness. What shall we make of this vision? To take it with rigid literalism would be to say that the Virgin Mary had an incredible wardrobe and that she spent her later career in the desert running from dragons and avoiding floods. Preposterous? Yes, I think that it is. But that is what happens when you try to interpret prophetic symbols with rigid literalism.

It must be emphasized at this point that the only way to make the Bible teach a literal millennium is to interpret Revelation 20 with this same

471

sort of rigid literalism. If we instead approach it in the same manner that we approach the rest of the book, we might understand something other than a literal, fleshly millennium.

The Premillennial scheme (and for the present I am only dealing with Historic Premillennialism rather than the Dispensational brand) has the following events at the Second Coming of Christ:

> (1) Resurrection.
> (2) Judgment of wicked.
> (3) Judgment of Satan.
> (4) Entrance into 1000 year Kingdom.

As the chart below will demonstrate, the Premillennial scheme has these events taking place both at the beginning and at the end of the Millennium.

Premillennial Scheme	
At the Second Coming of Christ	**At the End of the Millennium**
(1) Resurrection. (2) Judgment of wicked. (3) Judgment of Satan. (4) Entrance into 1000 year Kingdom.	(1) Resurrection. (2) Judgment of wicked. (3) Judgment of Satan. (4) Entrance into the eternal kingdom.

It might be suggested from this that the Premillennial is suffering from "double vision" in that he sees the events of the future happening twice. Perhaps it all will happen twice; after all, we believe that Christ came once and that he will come again. But alternate millennial views give another suggestion as to how we are to understand Revelation 20.

There is a general rule of Biblical interpretation that we are always to interpret the unclear passages by looking to see what the Bible clearly and plainly teaches. It is because of this principle that we should take great care before allowing an interpretation of the symbolism of Revelation to dictate a view that is contradictory of the plain teachings of the rest of the Bible.

- The judgment takes place at the end of this age in which the wicked are burned up and the righteous shine forth: *Therefore just as the tares are gathered up and burned with fire, so shall it be at the end of the age. 41 The Son of Man will send forth His angels, and they will gather out of His kingdom all stumbling blocks, and those who commit lawlessness, 42 and will cast them into the furnace of fire; in that place there shall be weeping and gnashing of teeth. 43 Then the righteous will shine forth as the sun in the kingdom of their Father. (Matthew 13:40-43).*

- The resurrection of all believers is on the last day: *Every one which sees the Son, and believes on him, may have everlasting life: and I will raise him up at the last day (John 6:40).*

- The return of Christ and the resurrection of believers shall take place on the Day of the Lord: *For the Lord Himself will descend from heaven with a shout, with the voice of the archangel, and with the trumpet of God; and the dead in Christ shall rise first. 17 Then we who are alive and remain shall be caught up together with them in the clouds to meet the Lord in the air, and thus we shall always be with the Lord. 18 Therefore comfort one another with these words. 1 Now as to the times and the epochs, brethren, you have no need of anything to be written to you. 2 For you yourselves know full well that the **day of the Lord** will come just **like a thief** in the night. (1 Thessalonians 4:16 - 5:2).*

- The world ends with the Day of the Lord: *But the **day of the Lord** will come **like a thief**, in which the heavens will pass away with a roar and the elements will be destroyed with intense heat, and the earth and its works will be burned up (2 Peter 3:10).*

Therefore, the resurrection and the second coming and the end of the world all occur at the end of this age, which is the day of the Lord, which is His return, which is the last trumpet. Instead of presenting a confusing hodgepodge of differing events and timetables, the Scriptures clearly and consistently present all of these as one and the same event.

The term Amillennial specifically means "no millennium." However that is not entirely accurate as a designation. Those who hold to this position do not deny the words of Revelation 20 - they merely see John's vision as a symbol for the present reality of this age. This is understood when we examine the particulars of the Millennium.

1.   The Binding of Satan.

Jesus spoke of the concept of the binding of Satan in Matthew 12. It was in the context of His having cast out a demon. There were those present who suggested that He was able to do this because He was secretly in league with Satan. But He pointed out that Satan does not work at cross purposes with himself and the fact that he was being bound by Jesus made it evident that they were no allies.

> *"And if I by Beelzebul cast out demons, by whom do your sons cast them out? Consequently they shall be your judges. 28 But if I cast out demons by the Spirit of God, then the kingdom of God has come upon you. 29 Or how can anyone enter the strong man's house and carry off his property, unless he first binds the strong man? And then he will plunder his house." (Matthew 12:27-29).*

The characters of whom Jesus speaks are obvious. When he speaks of binding "the strong man," it is evident that He is speaking of the manner in which He has bound Satan by the casting out of demons. The very fact that Satan was being cast out and the strong man was being bound was in itself evidence that the kingdom of God had come.

Notice the specific manner in which Satan is said to be bound in the Millennium. It is with regard to his ability to deceive the nations.

> *And he laid hold of the dragon, the serpent of old, who is the devil and Satan, and bound him or a thousand years, 3 and threw him into the abyss, and shut it and sealed it over him, SO THAT HE SHOULD NOT DECEIVE THE NATIONS ANY LONGER, until the thousand years were completed; after these things he must be released for a short time. (Revelation 20:2-3).*

Prior to the first advent of Christ, the nations were completely deceived by Satan to the point that very few outside of the confines of the tiny nation of Israel ever heard the truth of the gospel. But with the coming of Christ and the advent of the church, the gospel exploded throughout the world. The very fact that the gospel has gone to the nations and that gospel has been received by people in those nations is a sign of Satan's having been bound.

OLD TESTAMENT PERIOD	CHURCH PERIOD	END TIME PERIOD
SATAN LOOSE	SATAN BOUND	SATAN LOOSE
Nations deceived by satanic rulers	Nations no longer deceived by a satanic ruler	Nations again deceived by Satan and Antichrist
People of God oppressed	Nations of world reached by Gospel	Saints attacked

The Bible says that during the kingdom, *"the earth will be flooded with the knowledge of the glory of the Lord as the waters cover the sea"* (Isaiah 11:9; Habakkuk 2:14). At the same time, Revelation 20 makes it clear that evil is also present in the Millennium as it ends in revolt against the reign of Christ. This brings up a legitimate objection. The objection comes from 2 Corinthians 4:3-4.

> *And even if our gospel is veiled, it is veiled to those who are perishing, in whose case the god of this world has blinded the minds of the unbelieving, that they might not see the light of the gospel of the glory of Christ, who is the image of God. (2 Corinthians 4:3-4).*

Paul says that people and nations have been blinded to the gospel. Does Paul mean that no one believes or that only a very few will necessarily believe because everyone else has been blinded? It would seem to me that this is the case and would continue to be the case were it not for the binding of the god of this world as per Revelation 20. If Satan had not been bound, then we would not see the growth of the gospel in the world today. If Satan had not been bound, then you would not be able to find Christians in every nation of the world. At the same time, Paul indicates that there is still a blinding. In other words, both of these phenomenon are taking place today. There has been a blinding that has taken place since the beginning. Yet despite this ongoing blindness, Satan is being bound with respect to his blinding abilities and therefore the gospel has and continues to be preached in and believed by many of those who are in the nations.

2.   The Thousand Years.

>   *...they came to life and reigned with Christ for*
> *a thousand years. (Revelation 20:4b).*

The Amillennial view is that this reference to a thousand years is symbolic of a long, undesignated period of time. This should not surprise us. When the Psalmist tells us that the Lord owns the cattle on a thousand hills (Psalm 50:10), we do not thereby conclude that the Lord does not own the cattle on hill number 1001. Likewise, when we read that a thousand years with the Lord are as a single day (Psalm 90:4), we do not press this in an overly literal manner.

The number 10 is presented in the Bible as a complete number. There were ten commandments and we read of a beast with ten horns. The kingdom is said to be of a duration of ten cubed: 10x10x10=1000. It is a number of fulness.

3.   A Reigning Priesthood with Christ.

>   *And I saw thrones, and they sat upon them,*
> *and judgment was given to them... and they came to*
> *life and reigned with Christ for a thousand years.*
> *(Revelation 20:4).*

>   *...they will be priests of God and of Christ and*
> *will reign with Him for a thousand years (Revelation*
> *20:6).*

The New Testament makes it clear that today's church is a kingdom of priests. *But you are a chosen race, a royal priesthood, a holy nation, a people for God's own possession, that you may proclaim the excellencies of Him who has called you out of darkness into His marvelous light* (1 Peter 2:9).

John has already set forth this principle in the opening verses of the book of Revelation: *He has made us to be a kingdom, priests to His God and Father; to Him be the glory and the dominion forever and ever* (Revelation 1:6). Notice the tense of the verb. John does not say that God will in the future make us to be such a kingdom. The aorist tense gives no hint that we are to wait for the future for such an action. It is a present reality.

4.   The First Resurrection.

> *And I saw the souls of those who had been beheaded because of the testimony of Jesus and because of the word of God, and those who had not worshiped the beast or his image, and had not received the mark upon their forehead and upon their hand, and they came to life and reigned with Christ for a thousand years.*
>
> *The rest of the dead did not come to life until the thousand years were completed. This is the first resurrection.*
>
> *Blessed and holy is the one who has a part in the first resurrection; over these the second death has no power, but they will be priests of God and of Christ and will reign with Him for a thousand years. (Revelation 20:4-6).*

There are several references here to a "first resurrection." What is the nature of this first resurrection? Remember that the author of this book is the Apostle John. He has already set forth the mention of a first resurrection in his Gospel Account.

> *"Truly, truly, I say to you, an hour is coming and now is, when the dead shall hear the voice of the Son of God; and those who hear shall live." (John 5:25).*

Jesus was not denying the reality of a future physical resurrection - He would mention that in verse 29. But before that resurrection comes, there is a first resurrection - one that is spiritual and that "now is." In the same way, Paul speaks of how there was a time when we were dead in trespasses and sin (Ephesians 2:1), but God made us alive together with Christ and raised us up with Him (Ephesians 2:5-6).

Notice the blessing that John bestows upon those who take part in the first resurrection: *Blessed and holy is the one who has a part in the first resurrection; over these the second death has no power*. Only those who have a part in the first resurrection are exempt from the second death. This is what Jesus told Nicodemus when He said, *"Unless a man is born again, he shall not see the kingdom of God"* (John 3:3).

	First	Second
Resurrection	Resurrection of the Soul to Spiritual Life	Resurrection of the Body at Christ's Second Coming
Death	Spiritual Death	Eternal Death

Here is the promise of Revelation. If you have the first resurrection, you don't have the second death. But if you have the first death, then the only thing awaiting you is the second death and that lasts an eternity.

STRUCTURE OF THE BOOK OF REVELATION

Even a cursory look at the book of Revelation reveals that it is a book with a stylized structure. Everywhere you turn within this book there are groupings of sevens.

- Seven churches
- Seven lamps and seven spirits of God before the throne
- Seven Seals
- Seven peals of thunder
- Seven Trumpets
- Seven Vials
- A seven headed dragon with seven crowns

Too often people have taken the book as though it were a chronological planner for a futuristic prophetic timetable when, instead, it clearly offers a series of pictures that reveal Christ in His workings in heaven and on earth (that is why its official title is "the Revelation of Jesus Christ").

What we have in Revelation are a series of parallel visions, each of which presents a portrait of Christ at work in the world. Sometimes, as is the case of Revelation 12, we are taken all the way back to the birth of Christ. No matter what the beginning, the end is always the same. It is that Christ returns in victory to judge the world and redeem His people. This can be illustrated by comparing the sixth and seventh of the series of seals, trumpets and bowl judgments:

6th & 7th Seal	6th & 7th Trumpet	Seventh Bowl
1. Great earthquake.	1. Great earthquake.	1. Great earthquake.
2. Voices, thunderings, lightnings and an earthquake.	2. Lightnings, voices, thunderings and an earthquake.	2. Voices, thunders, lightnings and a great earthquake.
3. Angel cried with a loud voice	3. Great voices in heaven	3. Great voice from heaven
4. Every mountain and island taken out of their way	----	4. Every island fled away & mountains were not found
----	5. Great hail	5. Great hail
----	6. Temple opened; voices heard	6. Great voice out of the temple
7. Day of his wrath is come.	7. Thy wrath is come.	7. Fierceness of his wrath.

How does this relate to Revelation 20 and the Millennial Question? In Revelation 19 we are treated to a vision of the return of Christ in judgment. Accordingly, the very next section takes us back to still another recapitulation of the workings of Christ in this age. It is thus seen that the context of Revelation 20 can at least allow the Amillennial view of eschatology. On the other hand, if we take Revelation 20 at face value, we will follow in the footsteps of many of the early church fathers in adopting a Premillennial view of prophecy. Whichever view is adopted, it is the belief of this writer that these millennial issues ought not serve as an issue over which we divide the church. It is unfortunate that so many Christians have used disagreements in this area to try to bring division and discord to the body of Christ. That does not mean we cannot discuss or study such subjects, but it does mean that such studies ought to be carried out in such a way that demonstrates the love that we share in Christ.

A SUMMARY OF ESCHATOLOGICAL VIEWS

The following list is not meant to be exhaustive, for there are many variations to be found among the different views of eschatology. However, we can describe several primary categories of such views:

1.   Dispensational Premillennial.

We have already described Dispensational Premillennialism. Though there are occasional differences, it generally holds to a pre-tribulational rapture of the church. It sees an initial and temporary return of Christ in which He suddenly gathers out all believers and takes them to heaven while earth subsequently goes through a seven year period of tribulation.

One of the evidences used in support of this position is the Jewish nature of the tribulation. The passages which are used to teach of the future "great tribulation" always describe a time of judgment when God is dealing specifically with the nation of Israel. As such, it is called "the time of Jacob's distress" in Jeremiah 30:7. Accordingly, it is argued that the Church cannot be present on earth while God is dealing with Israel. Therefore, the Church must first be removed from the earth before this future period of tribulation can begin.

The objection raised under this point is really an objection based upon the theological system of Dispensationalism. As we have previously noted, this is a system which holds that God has two different plans and programs and people through whom He works and that He shall always keep them separate and distinct. It is supposed that He cannot be working with Israel while He is also working with the church.

This objection is removed when we examine the book of Acts. All of the events and the growth of the Church which are recorded in the books of Acts took place while the nation of Israel was still in existence. In fact, certain passages in Acts seem to show that the Kingdom was still being offered to the Jews during the first years of the Church (Acts 3:19-26; 28:20-31). Thus, we have an excellent example of God dealing with the Church and Israel at the same time.

A second line of evidence for the Pretribulational view is the nature of the church. The Church is the Body and the Bride of Jesus Christ (Ephesians 5:23; Colossians 1:18). It is the object of His infinite love and the recipient of every spiritual blessing. The believer finds himself in union with Christ. If the Church is to go into or through such a time of future tribulation, she will be subjected to the wrath and judgments which will characterize that period. Thus, it is argued that the Church cannot go into the tribulation, since she has been delivered from judgment (Romans 8:1; John 5:24).

The problem with this argument is that there have been many instances in history when the Church has gone through terrible persecutions and tribulations. To say that Christ would not permit His Bride to go through this time of trouble is inconsistent with history. At the same time, I would submit that just because the Church goes through tribulation, it does not necessarily follow that the judgments and indignations of such tribulation would be directed at her, any more than the plagues against Egypt meant that God was judging the Israelites in the days or the Exodus.

Another line of evidence used by Pretribulationalists involve the promise to the Thessalonian believers that the will be delivered from the wrath to come. This fact is used by Pretribulationalists to teach that the church must be "raptured away" before that wrath can take place.

> *For they themselves report about us what kind of a reception it. had with you, and how you turned to God from idols to serve a living and true God, and to wait for His Son from heaven, whom He raised from the dead, that is Jesus, who delivers us from the wrath to come. (1 Thessalonians 1:9-10).*

> *For God has not destined us for wrath, but for obtaining salvation through our Lord Jesus Christ. (1 Thessalonians 5:9).*

We need to make several observations from these two passages. First of all, notice that neither of these passages tell us specifically to what this "wrath" refers. Neither make reference to a period of seven years and neither speak of something that must necessarily take place prior to the Second Coming of Christ.

The word "wrath" is translated from the Greek word *orge* (ὀργη) which is found 35 other times in the New Testament. When describing the anger of God, it is often seen as describing the judgment of Hell (Matthew 3:7; Luke 3:7), the wrath which is seen on the unbeliever in general (John 3:36; Romans 1:18), as well as the day of coming judgment which takes place when Christ returns (Revelation 6:16-17; 11:18; 19:15). An unbiased reading of this passage in its context would lead most people to think that this was a reference to the deliverance from the eternal condemnation that shall take place when Christ returns in the judgment of His Second Coming.

Finally we should note that this deliverance does not look to the future but to the present. 1 Thessalonians 1:9 states that Jesus delivers us from the wrath to come. Notice the tense that is utilized. The wrath is in the future (it is to come), but the deliverance is present. The believer is delivered today from God's wrath at the very moment when he places his faith in Jesus Christ.

It is maintained by the Pretribulationalist that Christ is going to come back twice; the first time as He comes *for* His saints and the second time as He returns *with* His saints. But do the Scriptures actually keep such a distinction? Remember that the "Rapture" is to be descriptive of Jesus coming back only *for* His saints. Yet we read the following in a Passage that the Pretribulationalist regards as testifying to this separate "Rapture":

> *For if we believe that Jesus died and rose again, even so God will bring* **with** *Him those who have fallen asleep in Jesus. (1 Thessalonians 4:14).*

By the same token, how can it be denied that a passage that describes the Lord coming and gathering together *His elect from the four winds, from one end of the sky to the other* is a coming *for* those very elected ones? The language of Matthew 24:30-31 is admitted by the Pretribulationalist to describe the Second Coming of Christ and yet obviously pictures Him coming *for* those who are alive and remain upon the earth.

The truth is that the return of Christ involves both a coming for His saints as well as a coming with His saints. Those who have already died in the Lord shall come with Him while those who are alive and remain shall find that Jesus comes for them.

2.   Historical Premillennialism.

This view is similar to the Dispensational scheme as outlined above, but without the separate "rapture." It instead sees the rapture to be the same as the 2nd coming.

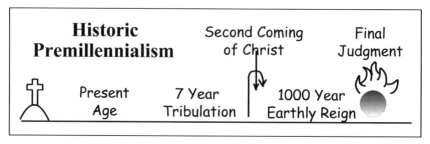

Historical Premillennialism is based upon a literal reading of Revelation 20 and has a long tradition within Christianity going back at least to the second century of the church. Unlike its Dispensational counterpart, it does not hinge upon an acceptance of the more recent tenants of Dispensationalism nor does it mandate a separation between Israel and the church. Tertullian gives the following description of his adherence to this view:

> *We confess that a kingdom has been promised to us on earth, but before heaven and in another state of existence. It will be after the resurrection for a thousand years in the divinely built city of Jerusalem, let down from heaven, which the Apostle also calls, "our mother from above."* (Against Marcion. 3:24:3).

Likewise, Justin Martyr speaks of *"a thousand years in which Jerusalem will be built up, adorned and enlarged, as the prophets Ezekiel and Isaiah and others declare"* (Dialogue with Trypho the Jew).

The problem that this view faces is in understanding the Kingdom to be limited only to a thousand years when 2 Peter 1:11 speaks of the "eternal kingdom." This problem is solved by maintaining that the 1000-year millennium is only the first phase of the eternal kingdom.

3.   Amillennialism.

This view sees the prophecies of tribulation and the kingdom as being fulfilled throughout this present age. Christ returns at the end of this age to usher in the eternal state. It looks at Revelation 20 and sees it as symbolic language for the present continuing kingdom today.

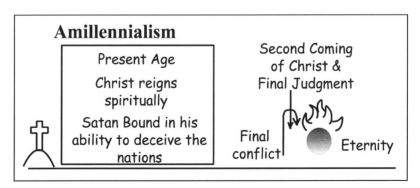

Satan is seen to be bound with reference to his ability to deceive the nations. It is for this reason that the gospel has gone out to all of the nations and there are today believers to be found in every nation.

This view answers the previous dilemma about the kingdom being an everlasting kingdom. Furthermore, it can view a passage like 2 Peter 3:10-12 at face value instead of insisting that this is an event taking place at the close of a 1000 year kingdom in which Jesus has ruled; a description that hardly sounds like "a thief." Finally, it takes literally the words of Jesus when he speaks of the resurrection of the faithful taking place on the "last day" (John 6:39-40, 44, 54).

4.   Postmillennialism.

This view sees the church spreading throughout the world and the Lord eventually establishing His kingdom through the preaching of the gospel. Christ returns at the end of the age to find a church victorious. This is different from Amillennialism in that the former views this entire age as being a manifestation of the kingdom, albeit in mystery form, while Postmillennialism looks forward to such a kingdom eventually being established as the gospel is victorious in converting the nations.

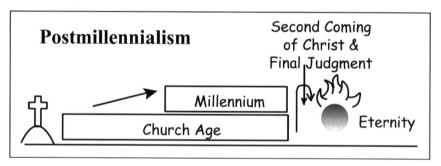

It is in this view of a literal, physical kingdom that Postmillennialism shares a likeness to Premillennialism. They both postulate a literal kingdom upon earth.

Postmillennial thinking underwent a drastic decline after World War One, brought about largely because of a disenchantment with the effects of the church upon society. It might be argued that this same disenchantment brought about the growth and popularity of Dispensational pessimism in the Twentieth Century.

Posmillennialism has seen some slight resurgence in recent years and is sometimes seen hand-in-hand with a fifth view known as

Preterism.

5.   Preterism.
        The word "Preterist" is taken from the Latin word meaning "past." This view denies any future fulfillment of the book of Revelation and sees the events it describes as already having been fulfilled within the first century after Christ. There are several different forms of Preterism. Full Preterism views all of the prophecies of the Bible as having already been fulfilled in their entirety since the fall of Jerusalem in A.D. 70 as pictured below:

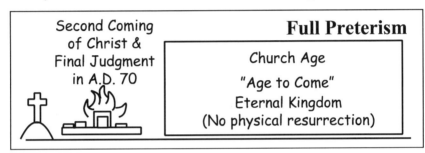

        Full Preterism is a very recent innovation that has no adherents in any of the writings of the early church. Partial Preterism maintains a future return of Christ, but views His "coming in the clouds" as described in Matthew 24:29-31 as having been fulfilled in A.D. 70 with the fall of Jerusalem.[3]
        It is clear from a reading of the apostolic and church fathers that all of them expected a future return of Jesus Christ. It would be strange indeed if the entire church failed to understand the fulfillment of so many of the New Testament prophecies on such a major point. This is especially striking when we remember the promise of Revelation 1:7 that tells us, *He is coming with the clouds, and every eye will see Him, even those who pierced Him; and all the tribes of the earth will mourn over Him.* A Preterist interpretation calls for this to be a reference to the "tribes of the land" of Israel, even though Israel was never described in such a way elsewhere in the Bible. But such an interpretation would demand that the Jews who suffered through the A.D. 70 event would have recognized that their

---

        [3] Technically, the term "partial Preterist" can be taken in a variety of ways, even to refer to those who hold that any prophecies of the Bible have been fulfilled in history. For the purposes of this discussion, I am using the term to describe only those who hold that the A.D. 70 event was a return of Christ as per such promises as are seen in Matthew 24:29-31..

sufferings were a punishment for their treatment of Jesus since the prophecy is not merely that they would mourn, but that they would mourn "over Him." Just as there is no evidence that anyone in the church ever recognized the fall of Jerusalem as the return of Jesus, so also there is a complete absence of evidence that the Jews ever recognized the coming of Jesus in those events.

Fundamental to full Preterism is the idea that there is no future physical resurrection of the dead. But the pattern for our resurrection is that of Jesus. The big idea presented in 1 Corinthians 15 is that Jesus arose from the dead. This was not merely some sort of spiritual resurrection. The point is made throughout this chapter that His resurrection was bodily and physical. Furthermore we are told that His resurrection serves as the paradigm for our own resurrection. *But now Christ has been raised from the dead, the first fruits of those who are asleep* (1 Corinthians 15:20). He is the firstfruits and we are the "later fruits."

When Paul came to Athens, he was mocked by the Greeks for believing in a physical resurrection. Such mockery would not have been forthcoming had he held that the resurrection was only going to be of a spiritual or mystical nature. But he went out of his way to side himself with the Pharisees who believed in a physical resurrection of the dead (Acts 23:6-8).

In denying any future resurrection at the coming of Christ, the Preterist also finds himself out of accord with the words of Paul when he says, "We shall not all sleep, but we shall all be changed" (1 Corinthians 15:51). The reference to sleep is used throughout this epistle as a euphemism for death (11:30; 15:6; 15:18; 15:20). While Paul says of the coming of the Lord that it will be a time when all do not die, the Preterist is left with the rather obvious historic truth that everyone who lived in the first century did indeed die.

When it comes to the resurrection, the Bible teaches that Jesus is our prototype. His resurrection is the forerunner and the pattern for our own resurrection. This point is made in 1 Corinthians 15 where Paul says that if there is no resurrection then even Jesus has not risen.

The resurrection of Jesus was a physical resurrection. He was able to stand before His disciples in His resurrection body and say, *"See My hands and My feet, that it is I Myself; touch Me and see, for a spirit does not have flesh and bones as you see that I have."* (Luke 24:39). 1 John 3:2 says that *when He appears, we shall be like Him, because we shall see Him just as He is.* Therefore we can conclude that our future resurrection will be of a physical and spiritual nature.

Preterists like to point out that Jesus and the disciples stated that the kingdom was near and at hand. What they often ignore is that this same formula was used in the Old Testament in instances where the eventual fulfillment was a long way off. An example of this is seen in Isaiah 13:6 where, speaking of a coming judgment against the city of Babylon, the prophet says, *"Wail, for the day of the LORD is near! It will come as destruction from the Almighty."* Isaiah writes these words in the 8th century B.C. but it is not until 539 B.C. that Babylon fell to the Persians.

The Preterist attempts to make a similar case via the words of Jesus in Matthew 24:34 where Jesus says, *"Truly I say to you, this generation will not pass away until all these things take place."* The Preterist points to this verse as the primary argument for his preterism. On the basis of this passage, he determines that all of the events of Matthew 24 including the return of the Son of Man and the gathing of God's elect all took place in their entirety within the lifetime of the apostles. He views the complete and total fulfillment of all of the prophecies in the A.D. 70 fall of Jerusalem.

Bible scholars have suggested other interpretations, but most of them fall flat. One interpretation is to view the term "generations" as being a reference to the race of Jews. But this is an unnatural use of the term and inconsistent with the way that Matthew uses it elsewhere in his Gospel. Another suggested interpretation is that Jesus is referring to the generation that is alive when the prophecies begin to be fulfilled, as if to say that once the fulfillments begin to take place they will all culminate in their fulfillments within a single generation. Were this the case, we would expect Jesus to say, *THAT generation will not pass away until all these things take place.* He does not. He uses a specific term that implies that it is the present generation that is in view.

Royce Gruenler points out that reading this as an ingressive aorist would have us translate it "from the perspective of initiated action" and therefore render it: "I tell you the truth, this generation will certainly not pass away until all these things *begin* to come to pass" (2003:193). The same sort of language is seen when Jesus says, *"Truly I say to you, there are some of those who are standing here who shall not taste death until they see the Son of Man coming in His kingdom" (Matthew 16:28).*

What shall we say to these things? I believe that the answer to both passages is seen in the fact that a partial and typological fulfillment took place in that day. In the case of the Matthew 16:28 passage, we are given the partial fulfillment in the following verses that describe the Transfiguration of Jesus. In the case of Matthew 24, it is true that the destruction of Jerusalem served as a type and a shadow of the future destruction and judgment that face all men and that this process began to take place within the lifetime of those who were present in that day.

The early church seems to have understood this point, for their treatment of the events of Matthew 24 was to look for a future fulfillment. Such an interpretation should not surprise us. We see this take place regularly in Biblical prophecy.

Prophecy	Initial Fulfillment	Ultimate Fulfillment
And I will bless those who bless you, And the one who curses you I will curse. And in you all the families of the earth shall be blessed. (Genesis 12:3).	Points to Israel as a blessing	Jesus is the ultimate blessing
I see him, but not now; I behold him, but not near; A star shall come forth from Jacob, And a scepter shall rise from Israel, And shall crush through the forehead of Moab, And tear down all the sons of Sheth. 18 And Edom shall be a possession, Seir, its enemies, also shall be a possession, While Israel performs valiantly. 19 One from Jacob shall have dominion, And shall destroy the remnant from the city. (Numbers 24:17-19).	References to Edom and Moab indicate it is fulfilled initially in David	Jesus is the ultimate fulfillment whose coming is announced by a Star
Therefore the Lord Himself will give you a sign: Behold, a virgin will be with child and bear a son, and she will call His name Immanuel (Isaiah 7:14).	Context of the passage points to a child in that day	Jesus is the ultimate fulfillment of the virgin born child.

Another problem facing the Preterist is seen in the promise that was given to the disciples at the ascension of Jesus. The event took place on the Mount of Olives.

> *And after He had said these things, He was lifted up while they were looking on, and a cloud received Him out of their sight. 10 And as they were gazing intently into the sky while He was departing,*

behold, two men in white clothing stood beside them;
11 and they also said, "Men of Galilee, why do you
stand looking into the sky? This Jesus, who has been
taken up from you into heaven, will come in just the
same way as you have watched Him go into heaven."
(Acts 1:9-11).

The promise that was given by the angels is that Jesus would come again in exactly the same way as they had watched Him go into heaven. This had not been a spiritual ascension, but a physical and visible one. It is for this reason that Christians throughout the ages have fully expected a future physical and visible return of Christ.

In Romans 8, Paul teaches that the creation has fallen as a result of sin and that *the creation itself also will be set free from its slavery to corruption into the freedom of the glory of the children of God* (8:21). He goes on in verse 22 to describe how the *whole creation groans and suffers the pains of childbirth together until now* as it looks to its final redemption.

The Preterist foresees no physical redemption of creation. According to his scheme, the world is fallen and will always be fallen. In this way, Preterism embraces the tenants of Gnosticism with its lack of regard for the redemption of the physical world.

Because they believe there is no future Second Coming or final judgment, Preterists believe that sin will continue indefinitely. 1 Corinthians 15:26 tells us that *the last enemy that will be abolished is death*, but the Preterist would have us believe that death will never be abolished and that it will always continue to exist.

There are some eschatological differences that exist between Christians that I consider to be relatively benign and within the realm of Christian orthodoxy. This is not one of them. To the contrary, the teaching of Preterism comes uncomfortably close to the spiritual gangrene that is described by Paul in 2 Timothy 2:18 when he speaks of those *who have gone astray from the truth saying that the resurrection has already taken place, and thus they upset the faith of some*. The teachings of Preterism have not resulted in stronger and more loving Christians. Though I am happy to report that there are some exceptions, this teaching for the most part has been divisive and destructive. I cannot help but to be reminded of the litmus test given to us by Jesus: *You will know them by their fruits. Grapes are not gathered from thorn bushes, nor figs from thistles, are they? 17 Even so, every good tree bears good fruit; but the bad tree bears bad fruit* (Matthew 7:16-17).

	Post Millennial	Amillennial	Historic Premillenial	Dispensational Premillennial
Hermeneutic	Context and genre are important interpretive considerations			Inclination toward literalism
Second Coming	Christ's 2nd coming takes place after the millennium. This coming initiates a general resurrection, the last judgment and eternal state for all people		Christ's 2nd coming takes place before the millennium	Christ comes in a rapture and then again after a 7-year tribulation to establish an earthly kingdom
Timing of the Kingdom	God's kingdom is a present spiritual reality that started with Christ's first advent.		Present spiritual reality to the kingdom, followed by future 1000 year kingdom	An earthly kingdom lasting 1000 years will be established by Christ after His 2nd coming
Nature of the Kingdom	Kingdom is spiritual in nature. It will grow to fill the whole earth	The kingdom is spiritual in nature.	The 2nd coming will establish a literal 1000 year kingdom on earth	The literal 1000 year kingdom on earth will be primarily Jewish in nature
Millennium Description	We are in millennium now. It will slowly grow into a "golden age."	Millennium is today's church age and gospel unbound to reach the world.	Millennium is future. Christ will reign with absolute control.	The millennium is future. The Old Testament Jewish economy will be restored.
Millennium Duration	A prolonged period of time greater than a 1000 year period. The 2nd coming follows the millennium.		Exactly 1000 years. The 2nd coming precedes the millennium	

Satan's Binding and Current Status	At Christ's death and resurrection Satan was bound with respect to his ability to deceive the nations and prevent them from hearing the truth about God.		The future 2nd coming of Christ will cause Satan to be bound 1000 years. He is not bound now, but rules the kingdom of this present world.	
Tribulation	Took place in the destruction of Jerusalem in 70 A.D.	The church is in tribulation in this age.	A future 7 year tribulation will precede the 2nd Coming. The church will go through this tribulation	A future 7 year tribulation will precede the 2nd Coming. The church will escape this tribulation by being "raptured."
Rapture	The Rapture and the 2nd coming take place at the same time.			The Rapture precedes the 2nd Coming by 7 years.

ON HEAVEN AND HELL

Jesus spoke about hell on a number of occasions and using a number of different terms. Occasionally he used the term "Gehenna," which was Hebrew for "Valley of Hinnon," the location of the city garbage pits on the east side of Jerusalem where the refuse was burn. This place of stink and destruction became a vivid picture of God's judgment against the wicked.

- It was described as a place where both soul and body were destroyed: *And do not fear those who kill the body, but are unable to kill the soul; but rather fear Him who is able to destroy both soul and body in **hell** {literally "Gehenna"}. (Matthew 10:28).*

- It was described as a place of unquenchable fire: *And if your eye causes you to stumble, cast it out; it is better for you to enter the kingdom of God with one eye, than having two eyes, to be cast into **hell**, 48 where their worm does not die, and the fire is not quenched. (Mark 9:47-48).*

This place of judgment was described as a place of darkness: *The*

491

sons of the kingdom shall be cast out into the outer darkness; in that place there shall be weeping and gnashing of teeth. (Matthew 8:12). In his second epistle, Peter tells us how *God did not spare angels when they sinned, but cast them into hell and committed them to pits of darkness, reserved for judgment (2 Peter 2:4).* Instead of the word Gehenna, Peter uses the term Tartaros, a term used by the Greeks in their mythology to describe the abode of the dead. One of the most vivid portrayals of hell is in the parable that Jesus told of the Rich Man and Lazarus.

> *And in Hades he lifted up his eyes, being in torment, and saw Abraham far away, and Lazarus in his bosom. 24 And he cried out and said, "Father Abraham, have mercy on me, and send Lazarus, that he may dip the tip of his finger in water and cool off my tongue; for I am in agony in this flame."*
>
> *But Abraham said, "Child, remember that during your life you received your good things, and likewise Lazarus bad things; but now he is being comforted here, and you are in agony. 26 And besides all this, between us and you there is a great chasm fixed, in order that those who wish to come over from here to you may not be able, and that none may cross over from there to us." (Luke 16:23-26).*

Once again we see a description that encompasses burning and suffering. Furthermore, one of the points of the parable is that once such a fate has begun there are no second chances. Today is the day of salvation and there are no guarantees for tomorrow. God has given a call for all men to repent. Such a call mandates a decision on your part. To make no decision is to decide against God.

Universalism teaches that hell is not eternal and that the punishment effected there will only be of a temporary nature. This teaching seems to be borrowed from the Roman Catholic doctrine of Purgatory. But what do the Scriptures say about such a thing? Hell is described as an eternal punishment and, as such, is contrasted with eternal life: *And these will go away into **eternal punishment**, but the righteous into eternal life. (Matthew 25:46).* The Bible speaks on several occasions of the eternal fire of hell: *Then He will also say to those on His left, "Depart from Me, accursed ones, into the **eternal fire** which has been prepared for the devil and his angels"* (Matthew 25:41). *And if your hand or your foot causes you to stumble, cut it off and throw it from you; it is better for you to enter life crippled or lame, than having two hands or two feet, to be cast into the **eternal fire**. 9 And if your eye causes you to stumble, pluck it out, and throw it from you. It is better for* *you to enter life with one eye, than having two eyes, to be cast into the fiery hell.* (Matthew 18:8-9).

There are some who are quick to point out that the word translated "eternal" in each of these instances is the Greek word αἰώνιος (*aionios*) and that it is derived from the Greek term αἰών (*aion*) that can describe merely "an age." The problem is that this same term is also used to describe the eternality of eternal life (John 3:16 and everywhere else in John) as well as the eternality of God Himself (Romans 16:26 speaks of του αἰωνιου θεου -- the everlasting God).

In Matthew 25 this term is used in the same verse to parallel the fate of both the wicked as well as the fate of the righteous. The judgment of the sheep and the goats concludes that *these will go away into eternal punishment, but the righteous into eternal life.* It is inconsistent to maintain that the first of these is uses of "eternal" is different from the second use. Both the wicked and the righteous are said to go into a state that is eternal.

In warning of the seriousness of hell, Jesus described it both in terms of *unquenchable fire* (Mark 9:44) as well as by using a graphic symbolism of a worm that does not die (Mark 9:48). On the other hand, there are some scholars who, while affirming the Bible's teaching of an eternal hell, question the literalness with which we are to hold to such descriptions as a burning fire, an undying worm or darkness. Charles Hodge writes of the fire in hell:

> "There seems to be no more reason for supposing that the fire spoken of in Scripture is to be literal fire, than that the worm that never dies is literally a worm. The devil and his angels who are to suffer the vengeance of eternal fire, and whose doom the finally impenitent are to share, have no material bodies to be acted upon by elemental fire. As there are to be degrees in the glory and blessedness of heaven, as our Lord teaches us in the parable of the ten talents, so there will be differences as to degree in the sufferings of the lost: some will be beaten with few stripes, some with many" (Systematic Theology, Part 4, Chapter 4).

The Hebrew term for heaven is rather vague. שָׁמַיִם (*shamayim*) seem to have been derived from the root שָׁם (*sham*, "there") and simply means "the over there place." Given the context, it can refer to the sky or to the dwelling place of God. Do God's elect go to heaven when they die? There are several elements of the Scriptures that make it clear they do.

1.   Jesus told the parable of Lazarus upon his death being taken by the

angels to "Abraham's bosom" (Luke 16:22). This is pictured as a place where he is comforted (16:25). While it must be pointed out that this is a parable and not a specific declaration of such a place, the very nature of parables is that they are generally true-to-life stories given to teach a spiritual truth. This suggests the description of "Abraham's bosom" out to be taken as being descriptive of the afterlife.

2.   Paul speaks in 2 Corinthians 5:6-9 of being "absent from the body and present with the Lord." There is no idea suggested in this passage that would allow for an intermediate state between these two conditions. To the contrary, Paul specifically says that while we are at home in the body we are necessarily absent from the presence of the Lord.

3.   Paul says in Colossians 1:5 that the believer's hope is laid up "in heaven."

4.   Paul speaks of every family that is both on earth and in heaven (Ephesians 3:15). Such a statement is meaningless if no families are to be found in heaven.

5.   Paul speaks of a man (perhaps himself?) who was caught up to the third heaven (2 Corinthians 12:2-4). In that context, he refers to this "third heaven" also by the term "paradise."

6.   Jesus told this thief who was dying upon the cross next to him, "Today you shall be with Me in Paradise" (Luke 23:43). Some have argued both from the English as well as from the Greek text that Jesus is merely telling the thief "today," not that this is when the described action would take place. However, the way in which this construction normally appears elsewhere in the New Testament regularly supports the idea that Jesus was describing what the man would experience on that same date.

7.   Jesus is currently in heaven and, upon His return, shall bring *with Him* those who have died (1 Thessalonians 4:14).

What shall heaven be like? The final two chapters of the book of Revelation give us glimpses using all sorts of imagery, but we must understand it as such and not attempt to make dogmatic assertions of the nature of the eternal state by an overly literal approach to those passages.

There is a description of the New Jerusalem coming like a bride out of heaven and we are to understand that we are a part of that marriage. We read of the dimensions of the city and take note that it is in the same shape of the Holy of Holies, though measured to the number of twelve thousand stadia on a side. The NAS conveniently converts this number into miles, but it is not the distance that is important but what the numbers represent. The point is that we will enter the place of the presence of God and that it will be big enough for all to come. In the final analysis, we must echo the words of the Apostle Paul as he commented upon the still older words of the prophet:

> *...but just as it is written, "things which eye has not seen and ear has not heard, and which have not entered the heart of man, all that God has prepared for those who love him" (1 Corinthians 2:9).*

BIBLIOGRAPHY

Albright, William F.
1960   *The Archaeology of Palestine.* New York, NY: Penguin

Ausubel, Nathan
1964   *The Book of Jewish Knowledge.* New York, NY: Crown Publishers

Berkhof, Louis
1971   *Systematic Theology.* Carlisle, PA: Banner of Truth

Berkouwer, G. C.
1954   *The Person of Christ.* Grand Rapid, MI: Eerdmans

Brown, Colin (ed.)
1975   *The New International Dictionary of New Testament Theology*; 3
        volumes. Grand Rapid, MI: Zondervan

Buswell, James Oliver
1962   *A Systematic Theology of the Christian Religion.* Grand Rapid, MI:
        Zondervan

Chafer, Lewis Sperry
1936   *Dispensationalism.* Dallas, TX: Dallas Seminary Press

1971   *Systematic Theology.* Dallas, TX: Dallas Seminary Press

Chilton, David
1987   Paradise Restored: A Biblical Theology of Dominion. Fort Worth,
        TX: Dominion Press

Clark, Gordon H.
1978   *Predestination in the Old Testament.* Phillipsburg, NT: Presbyterian
        & Reformed

1979   *Biblical Predestination.* Phillipsburg, NT: Presbyterian & Reformed

Eldridge, John
2006   *Waking the Dead: The Glory of a Heart Fully Alive.* Nashville, TN:
        Thomas Nelson

Engelsma, David J.
2001   *Christ's Spiritual Kingdom: A Reformed Defense of Amillennialism.* Redlands, CA: Reformed Witness

Evans, William
1981   *The Great Doctrines of the Bible.* Chicago, IL: Moody

Geisler, Norman
2002   *Systematic Theology; Volume 1: Introduction & Bible.* Minneapolis, MN: Bethany

Geisler, Norman & William Nix
1968   *A General Introduction to the Bible.* Chicago, IL: Moody

Grudem, Wayne
1994   *Systematic Theology.* Grand Rapids, MI: Zondervan

1999   *Bible Doctrine.* Grand Rapids, MI: Zondervan

Gruenler, Royce Gordon
2003   "Exegetical Insight", *Basics of Biblical Greek*, Editor William Mounce, Grand Rapids, MI: Zondervan

Harris, R. Laird
1971   *Inspiration and Canonicity of the Bible.* Grand Rapids, MI: Zondervan

Harris, R.Laird, G.L. Archer & B.K. Waltke
1980   *Theological Wordbook of the Old Testament.* Chicago, IL: Moody

Hodge, Charles
1999   *Systematic Theology*, Peabody, MA: Hendrickson Publishers

House, H. Wayne
1992   *Charts of Christian Theology & Doctrine.* Grand Rapids, MI: Zondervan

Kennedy, D. James
1994   *Foundations for your Faith*, Grand Rapids, MI: Revell

Lewis, C. S.
1996   *Mere Christianity.* New York, NY: Touchstone

McDowell, Josh
1972   *Evidence that Demands a Verdict.* Campus Crusade for Christ.

Murray, John
1984a *Redemption Accomplished and Applied.*   Grand Rapids, MI: Eerdmans

1984b *Collected Writings of John Murray: Volume 2 - Select Lectures in Systematic Theology.* Carlisle, PA: Banner of Truth

Nash, Ronald H.
1983   *The Concept of God: An Exploration of Contemporary Difficulties with the Attributes of God.* Grand Rapids, MI: Academie Books

Packer, J. I.
1993   *Knowing God.* Downers Grove, IL: Intervarsity

Pentecost, J. Dwight
1973   *Things to Come.* Grand Rapids, MI: Zondervan

Raymond, Robert L.
1998   *A New Systematic Theology Of The Christian Faith.* Nashville, TN: Thomas Nelson

Robertson, Archibald Thomas
1932   *Word Pictures in the New Testament.* New York, NY: Harper

Robertson, O. Palmer
1980   *Christ of the Covenants.* Phillipsburg, NJ: Presbyterian & Reformed

Ryrie, Charles
1974   *Dispensationalism Today.* Chicago, IL: Moody

Sproul, R.C.
1999   *Who is Jesus?* Orlando, FL: Ligonier

Stott, John R. W.
1986   *The Cross of Christ.* Downers Grove, IL: Intervarsity

Tenney, Merrill C., Ed.
1975   *The Zondervan Pictorial Encyclopedia of the Bible, 5 Volumes.* Grand Rapids, MI: Zondervan

Thiessen, Henry Clarence
1949   *Introductory Lectures in Systematic Theology*, Grand Rapids, MI: Eerdmans